CUBAN MEMORY WARS

ENVISIONING CUBA

LOUIS A. PÉREZ JR., EDITOR

Envisioning Cuba publishes outstanding, innovative works in Cuban studies, drawn from diverse subjects and disciplines in the humanities and social sciences, from the colonial period through the post–Cold War era. Featuring innovative scholarship engaged with theoretical approaches and interpretive frameworks informed by social, cultural, and intellectual perspectives, the series highlights the exploration of historical and cultural circumstances and conditions related to the development of Cuban self-definition and national identity.

CUBAN MEMORY WARS

RETROSPECTIVE POLITICS IN REVOLUTION AND EXILE

MICHAEL J. BUSTAMANTE

THE UNIVERSITY OF

NORTH CAROLINA PRESS

Chapel Hill

This book was published with the assistance of the
Anniversary Fund of the University of North Carolina Press.

© 2021 The University of North Carolina Press
All rights reserved
Designed by Richard Hendel
Set in Utopia and Klavika by Tseng Information Systems, Inc.
Manufactured in the United States of America

The University of North Carolina Press has been a
member of the Green Press Initiative since 2003.

Front cover sculpture: Rubén Torres Llorca, *Aún con mi enemigo bajo el mismo techo* (Still with my enemy under the same roof), 1988. Back cover: Cuban flag draped over Llorca, *Aún con mi enemigo bajo el mismo techo*. Both artworks courtesy of the Farber Collection and the artist.

Library of Congress Cataloging-in-Publication Data
Names: Bustamante, Michael J., author.
Title: Cuban memory wars : retrospective politics in revolution and exile / Michael J. Bustamante.
Other titles: Envisioning Cuba.
Description: Chapel Hill : The University of North Carolina Press, 2021. | Series: Envisioning Cuba | Includes bibliographical references and index.
Identifiers: LCCN 2020038676 | ISBN 9781469662022 (cloth) | ISBN 9781469662039 (pbk. ; alk. paper) | ISBN 9781469662046 (ebook)
Subjects: LCSH: Collective memory—Cuba. | Cubans—United States—Attitudes. | National characteristics, Cuban. | Cuban Americans—Ethnic identity. | Cuba—Historiography. | Cuba—History—Revolution, 1959—Public opinion.
Classification: LCC F1773 .B87 2021 | DDC 972.9106/4—dc23
LC record available at https://lccn.loc.gov/2020038676

Contents

Acknowledgments	vii
Introduction. The Cuban Past's Presence/Presents	1
1 Origin Stories of Revolution, Exorcisms of the Past	25
2 Cuban Exiles and the Search for "Total Unity"	63
3 Remembering (through) Girón	96
4 Antinostalgias in an Exile Age of Fracture	128
5 Anniversary Overload? Memory Fatigue at Cuba's Socialist Apex	155
6 Confronting Return	179
Conclusion. Inconsolable Memories	215
Notes	241
Index	291

Figures

I.1. Alfredo Manzo Cedeño, *Cuba's Condensed History Soup*, ca. 2003 / 2
1.1. Cover of *Album de la Revolución Cubana, 1952–1959*, 1959 / 26
1.2. "Now Finally I Know What's Good!," 1959 / 31
1.3. Antonio Rubio, "Waiting Room at a Ministry," 1959 / 50
2.1. The Revolution betrayed? Antonio Rubio, no title, 1964 / 70
2.2. Antonio Rubio, "Enter the Cuba of Yesterday," 1971 / 93
3.1. Eduardo García Delgado's last statement of revolutionary devotion, 1961 / 106
3.2. Scenes from the televised interrogations of Brigade 2506 prisoners, 1961 / 111
5.1. Advertisement for *En silencio ha tenido que ser*, 1979 / 173
6.1. Advertisement for package tours for Cuban exile visitors, 1979 / 200
6.2. Mary Lynn Conejo, with her cousins in Havana, Cuba, 1979 / 208
C.1. José Ángel Toirac, "Eternity," 2019 / 227
C.2. Bruce McCall, "Life in the Cuba of Tomorrow," 2015 / 233
C.3. "The Golden Age Aged Well," "Real Havana Club" ad campaign, 2016 / 236
C.4. "#TenemosMemoria" ("#WeHaveMemory"), 2019 / 238

Acknowledgments

This is a book about memory. But now that I have to thank all who made it possible, I just hope there is no one I forget. I am grateful first and foremost to my advisors and mentors at Yale University: Gilbert Joseph, Lillian Guerra, Matthew Jacobson, and Albert Laguna. Each helped steer this project's first iteration to completion. Gil Joseph pushed me to follow my instincts even when I felt daunted. I owe so much to his guidance, example, and generosity of spirit, beginning in my undergraduate days. Both Matthew Jacobson and Albert Laguna believed in the importance of this work and offered invaluable suggestions for revisions.

Lillian Guerra (now at the University of Florida) deserves special recognition. In 2005, on the basis of an essay I left in her office the fall of my junior year, she invited me to spend a summer in Havana to conduct research for my undergraduate history thesis. Those formative ten weeks led me to academia more than ten years and many more trips to Cuba later. Her devotion to her students is unmatched, and she has given me the confidence to come into my own as a historian and writer. *Gracias miles*, Lily. Your unflagging support has meant the world.

I am also indebted to Stuart Schwartz for his guidance and support over my academic career. To fellow graduate students at Yale in Latin American history—especially Erika Helgen, Marian Schlotterbeck, Christine Mathias, and honorary cohort member Antonio Córdoba—thank you for your camaraderie. To Jennifer Lambe, my closest colleague, critical reader, collaborator, and instructor in all things *timba*, your counsel, partnership, and example have enriched my development as a scholar. I am lucky to call you a friend.

I am extremely fortunate that Cubanists or *cubanólogo/as* in and out of the United States are a close-knit group. I am also grateful that the field includes many Cubans and Cuban Americans who have paved the way. Over the years, I have benefited from the encouragement, intellectual inspiration, and kindness of senior colleagues Alejandro de la Fuente, Ada Ferrer, Rafael Rojas, Manuel Barcia, and María Cristina Garcia in my home discipline of history, as well as Carmelo Mesa-Lago, Katrin Hansing, Ana Dopico, José Quiroga, Lillian Manzor, Iraida López, Emilio Cueto, Lisandro Pérez, and Silvia Pedraza in adjacent fields. Julia Sweig has been a model of what it means to be both a scholar of Cuba and a public voice. Cuban studies traces its roots to the founding of area studies programs during the Cold War. But the field's early commitment to forging scholarly bridges with the island and close connection to (and research on) the Cuban diaspora exceeded the limitations of that framework. I am proud to be part of this tradition and community, and to have gotten to know some of its founders and brightest new stars. The latter include Devyn Spence Benson, Michelle Chase, Rachel Hynson, Ariel Lambe, Christina Abreu, Armando Chaguaceda, John Gutiérrez, Julio Capó Jr., and Daniel Rodríguez. During research trips, workshops at NYU (thanks Ada!), and social occasions in between, Elizabeth Schwall, Jesse Horst, Rainer Schultz, María Antonia Cabrera Arus, Romy Sánchez, Kelly Urban, and Raquel Otheguy became a second graduate school cohort beyond my own institution's walls. Coming shortly behind were/are Lexi Baldacci, Billy Kelly, Cary García Yero, Daniel Fernández, Emily Snyder, and Lauren Krebs. At conferences, and in reading drafts of each other's work, I have learned and continue to learn from you all.

Admittedly, the *cubanólogo* label is not one that applies comfortably to Cuban scholars in Cuba, or to Cubans who have equal knowledge of their country's past simply because they lived it. Happily, though, the lines dividing inside from outside the island have become more porous (whatever the political ups and downs between Washington, Miami, and Havana), and I could not have completed this book without the generosity, friendship, and assistance of Cuban colleagues. I am grateful to Casa de las Américas, particularly its program in Latino studies, for supporting the research in 2013 and 2015 that became the basis for this book. Both Antonio Aja and Ana Niria Albó showed enthusiasm for my work from the moment they invited me to present at their program's first international conference in 2011. I hasten to add, however, that the arguments, interpretations, and any errors that follow in these pages are entirely my own responsibility. The staffs at the José Martí National Library (former director Eduardo Torres Cuevas and Juan Carlos Fernández, especially) and the Biblioteca Casa de las Américas fielded my requests to dig out rare periodicals with a spirit of openness. As happens in the life of a country riven by diaspora, some of my closest friends and collaborators on the island are now abroad, while others remain or have carved out transnational lives with feet on multiple shores. So wherever they may be, to Lenier González Mederos (*y familia*), Danny González Lucena, Jorge Macle, Reinaldo Funes, Ricardo Quiza Moreno, Mabel Suárez, Marial Iglesias, Julio César Guanche, María del Pilar Díaz Castañón, Victor Fowler, Luciano Castillo, Roberto Veiga, Carlos Velazco Fernández, Elizabeth Mirabal, Elaine Díaz, Carlos Alzugaray, and Rafael Hernández, thank you for offering advice on leads, lending your ears for conversation, and accepting me as *un cubano más*, even when my own identity crises made me think I did not deserve it. To my real and adopted families in Cuba—the extended Morán and Velasco clans in Santiago (Teresita, Quique, and Delia especially) and Samuel Weinstein Trujillo (QEPD) and Alberto Medina in Centro Habana—your love and hospitality mean more than you know.

A number of organizations and institutions in the United States made the writing of this book possible. The Roberto Goizueta Foundation sponsored preprospectus and dissertation fellowships at the University of Miami's Cuban Heritage Collection. To the CHC's staff past and present—particularly María Estornio, Gladys Gómez-Rossié, Lesbia Orta de Varona, Elizabeth Cerejido, Martin Tsang, and Amanda Moreno—thank you for offering a welcoming environment and for helping me track down sources and contacts. At Yale, fellowships from the MacMillan Center for International and Area Studies and the program in International Security Studies made lengthy research stays in Cuba possible in 2013. A dissertation fellowship from the Mrs. Giles Whiting Foundation provided the opportunity to spend a year writing between 2014 and 2015.

Since arriving at Florida International University in 2016, I have been privileged to join a group of colleagues whose commitment to our students motivates me every day. In the Department of History, I am especially appreciative of Bianca Premo for her mentorship, as well as Ken Lipartito, Rebecca Friedman, and the late Aurora Morcillo. Department chair Victor Uribe has been a constant support and facilitated a semester of course releases that allowed me to undertake the bulk of revisions from dissertation to book. Under the leadership of Jorge Duany, Frank Mora, and John Stack, respectively, the Cuban Research Institute, the Kimberly Green Latin American and Caribbean Center, and the Steven J. Green School of International and Public Affairs have provided intellectual community and research funding. I have learned much from conversations with Guillermo Grenier about contemporary Cuban diaspora politics. Graduate students John Ermer, Maite Morales, Richard Denis, and Rozzmery Palenzuela have each read and provided helpful feedback on portions of this work.

Louis A. Pérez Jr. is a trailblazer in the field of Cuban history whose prolific scholarship continues to set the standard for depth and erudition. I am beyond grateful to Lou for his early interest in bringing this manuscript to the Envisioning Cuba series at the University of North Carolina Press. Having read so many books in the series, to work with Lou and editor Elaine Maisner has been a dream come true. As part of that process, I am deeply appreciative of the comments and suggestions from María de los Ángeles Torres (another pathbreaker in the field I greatly admire) and a second anonymous reader. This feedback improved the manuscript immeasurably. Also at UNC Press, Andrew Winters, Jay Mazzocchi, and Catherine Hodorowicz guided me through the editorial process.

A few last expressions of professional and personal appreciation. Carlos Velazco Fernández provided research assistance at a late stage in the writing. Elizabeth Schwall and Ada Ferrer both gave me feedback on chapters as I approached my submission deadline. Alex Correa was a constant cheerleader and hype man. Alexander Stephens, Terrence Phillips, Rachel Weiss, María Antonia Cabrera Arus, Ernesto Menéndez Conde, Carmen Sesin, Howard Farber, and Victoria Bona all helped locate, identify, scan, and/or format illustrations. To all of those in and out of Cuba who agreed to be interviewed for this book—particularly for chapter 6—*gracias por su confianza*. Claire Boobbyer proofread the entire manuscript. I have presented portions of this book at too many conferences to list here. But to everyone who engaged my work, including Robin Derby, James Green, Seth Fein, Esther Allen, and Ariana Hernández Reguant, I have not forgotten. Portions of chapter 4 appeared as "Anti-communist Anti-imperialism? Agrupación Abdala and the Changing Contours of Cuban Exile Politics, 1968-1986," *Journal of American Ethnic History* 35, no. 1 (Fall 2015): 71-99. Thank you to the University of Illinois Press. A condensed version of chapter 5 appeared in *The Revolution from Within: Cuba, 1959-1980*, a volume of essays I coedited with Jennifer Lambe, which was published by Duke University Press in 2019.

Finally, I owe my immediate and extended family undying gratitude in ways that are impossible to distill. To my paternal grandparents, Isabel Rosa (QEPD) and Juan Manuel Bustamante, thank you for unknowingly sowing the seeds of my interest in Cuba's contested past from a young age. Your sacrifice as immigrants will always inspire. To my parents, Beth and Jorge Bustamante, you have always been and remain my biggest champions. To my wife and life partner, Heather Torretta, your unwavering belief in me from Jupiter to New Haven, South Bend, Washington, Baltimore, New Haven again, Miami, Havana, and Miami again leaves me with two words: *te quiero*. That Daniel joined us as this book was taking final shape is the best memory of all.

CUBAN MEMORY WARS

INTRODUCTION
The Cuban Past's Presence/Presents

There are two widely familiar versions of the Cuban story. According to the first, on January 1, 1959, a ragtag band of rebels swept down from the Sierra Maestra, delivering Cuba from the clutches of short-term dictatorship and longer neocolonial submission to the United States. In this view, the "triumph" of the Cuban Revolution marked the definitive end of one period of the island's history—nearly six decades of "pseudo-republican" scandal following the island's "mortgaged" independence in 1902—and the beginning of true liberty under the banner of revolutionary change. The second version of the saga accepts its rival's chronological pivot point, but it inverts the order of praise. In the alternate tale, the Cuban Revolution represented not a fulfillment of nationalist dreams but an unmitigated tragedy. For many of those who left the island in the 1960s, Cuba's turn to socialism made the prerevolutionary period look like paradise lost, transforming their homeland into an island in chains.

In Havana, Miami, and the many coordinates of Cuba's far-flung diaspora around the globe, these dueling master narratives are still routinely on display. More than sixty years after Fidel Castro's rise to power, and more than four since his death, diametrically opposed accounts of Cuba's past continue to square off in competing public spaces, museums, and now even social media campaigns. But dig beneath either iteration of the tale and less streamlined or comfortable narratives of Cuba's history emerge. In reality, Cubans' arguments about their past, and the ways they have related to it since 1959, have never been so straightforward or stable. It may be tempting to reduce Cubans' battles over their history to a metaphorical standoff between one set of voices shouting from Revolution Square in Havana and another positioned atop Miami's literal and figurative Freedom Tower.[1] But if popular visions of the Cuban Revolution's legacies today seem polarized, that polarization conceals more nuanced viewpoints, and it is the result of political processes that were and continue to be anything but neat.

Figure I.1. Alfredo Manzo Cedeño, *Cuba's Condensed History Soup*, ca. 2003. Courtesy of Ada Araluce and the artist's family.

Cuban Memory Wars: Retrospective Politics in Revolution and Exile tells the history of Cubans' mobilizations of, reckonings with, and debates over their past during the Cuban Revolution's crucial first twenty years in power. Inspired by the prominent place that competing understandings of the island's history occupy in Cuban political culture to this day, this book elucidates the longer trajectory of such disagreements, revealing that Cubans' "competing selective remembrances" have neither been static nor strictly cyclical over time.[2] In bridging the Florida Straits, this book tells a transnational story. At the same time, it relays a thoroughly national tale. "The past is a foreign country," the writer L. P. Hartley famously noted.[3] But for Cubans, the past *was* the country in many ways, as prominent struggles over history and memory within, between, and beyond the synecdochical cities of Havana and Miami fueled enduring contests over the Cuban nation itself.

Cuban Memory Wars reveals that the trajectory of Cuban retrospective conflict after 1959 was not only uneven but also central to the course of Cuban history in its own right. From the first months of Fidel Castro's rise to power, history and memory emerged as prominent battlegrounds on which revolutionary officials, cultural producers, and diverse political actors endeavored to invest Cuban citizens in specific understandings of the Revolution's origins and purpose as a national quest. Disagreements, however, over precisely how and why the Revolution came to be, and which factions should shape its future, sparked competitions for historical prerogative that did not easily go away. Drawing upon rare press, untapped correspondence, visual media, and to a lesser extent oral history, this book tracks such tensions as they developed in Cuba, evolved following Cuba's conversion into a hot spot of the Cold War, and trailed those Cubans decamping to the United States. As Cubans disenchanted with the revolutionary government went into exile, and as those who stayed navigated the promises and perils of a socialist regime, they regularly reflected upon what had happened, why, and how to further propel or, for some, reverse history's course.

This book is not the first to note the salience of the past to Cubans' political presents. Historian Lillian Guerra has excavated "how the grand narrative [of the emergent Cuban revolutionary state] ... gave mass participation [in the revolutionary process] meaning" during the 1960s.[4] Critic Rafael Rojas, in turn, has explored the shifting inclusions and exclusions in Cuban intellectual, literary, and historical canons before and after 1959.[5] Historian Louis A. Pérez Jr. has offered incisive reflections on the "meanings and purpose" ascribed to the past across Cuban history, including in the revolutionary period.[6] And scholars like Nicola Miller, Kate

Quinn, and Pablo Alonso González have analyzed the ways Cuban culture workers (e.g., scholars, heritage professionals) collaborated in, or complicated, the construction of a veritable "official history" of Cuba's revolution over time.[7]

Neither is this the first book to relay the histories of Cuban revolution and exile in parallel. María de los Ángeles Torres did just that in her study *In the Land of Mirrors: Cuban Exile Politics in the United States*.[8] Notwithstanding its focus on the exile community, that book compelled us in its title, and in its text, to understand expatriate and island affairs relationally. Her work was complemented by testimonial anthologies in the 1990s and beyond that brought diverse accounts of life under the Revolution and in the émigré community together as part of a shared history.[9] More recently, scholars like Anita Casavantes Bradford, Devyn Spence Benson, Jennifer L. Lambe, and Iraida H. López have followed diverse cultural, social, and political processes affecting Cubans in both Havana and Miami, particularly in the 1960s.[10]

Building on these precedents, *Cuban Memory Wars* tracks polemics over the past among Cubans in the revolutionary era and in the exile community more in real time and more closely on the ground than previous studies. It draws on newly available archival evidence and cultural materials to illuminate the textures of Cubans' mobilizations of, and conflicts over, their history in greater detail than available sources previously allowed. Whereas most histories of the Cuban Revolution and the Cuban exile community continue to focus on the 1960s, this book gives equal attention to the Revolution's second decade. Between 1959 and 1979, I argue, the past helped Cubans orient themselves amid, but also critically evaluate, extraordinary junctures of crisis and change. Tracking the interplay between these processes of reflection across the Florida Straits pushes Cuban history beyond the dualistic visions we associate with either side, exposing the contradictions of both.

But where do we find evidence of retrospective narration and contemplation if, by their nature, such processes are abstract rather than material? Scholars often have looked to the literal and figurative inscription of dominant versions of a given society's understanding of its past in physical spaces. I, too, am interested in competing rituals of Cuban public memorialization, the contents and functions of museums, as well as discourses of commemoration that shaped popular celebrations of national heroes and events. Yet this book is more focused on mundane stages where divergent appreciations of the Cuban past were routinely on display: the speeches of political leaders, dueling editorials in the revolutionary or exile press, organizational records and broadsides, and cultural products like television, cartoons, song, and film. Looking beyond the features of monuments, I analyze the ways historical knowledge, reflection, and argument infused the everyday. Not all of these sources can be treated equally, especially in terms of their ability to frame a shared historical language for Cubans themselves. Nonetheless, by bringing to bear a diversity of materials, one can appreciate the breadth of actors involved, as well as the multiple ways the specter of the Cuban past—as inspiration, trauma, keenly felt epic or, at a certain point, repetitive official script—pervaded so many aspects of post-1959 Cuban and Cuban diasporic life.

Such a wide view of the politics of the past allows us to see that, in truth, Cubans have never been divided into just two camps. History certainly constituted an appendage of Cuban revolutionary power and a resource for oppositional and exile forces determined to overthrow it. But it never served as a straightforward political tool. Rebels-turned-leaders proved masterful at creating a compelling narrative of the Revolution's emergence and foundational legitimacy. Nevertheless, Cuban officials periodically found themselves tinkering with this origin story in ways that reflected the ongoing challenges, choices, and popular anxieties they faced. Conversely, in attempting to create a unified counternarrative to that of the revolutionary state, early exile activists attempted to bury legacies that might divide them, but they still often failed to unify due to persistent retrospective dissension within their ranks. For many Cubans, mismatches between utopian promises and on-the-ground achievements also served to periodically reopen retrospective wounds. The past provided a source of motivation and apprehension, while at other times supplying a reserve of referents to question the truisms of consolidated exile dogma or the just-so stories of the revolutionary state. And as is true for all nations and cultures, for Cubans memory also proved selective. Contending processes of remembering and history-telling on both sides of the Florida Straits necessarily involved parallel—and sometimes overlapping—forms of forgetting.

Unfinished Histories

The omnipresence of history in a revolutionary context presents us with a paradox. Namely, why would history matter so much if the Cuban Revolution, as a project devoted to bringing about a utopian future, was so invested in leaving the past behind? The answer goes beyond the power of short-term contrast. On the one hand, the image of a shameful "before" under the authoritarian rule of Fulgencio Batista reinforced the premise and promise of a revolutionary "after," especially as that "after" assumed increasingly radical form. On the other hand, as I describe below, the victory of revolutionary forces in 1959 also channeled longer-held nationalist dreams. At the start of 1959, most Cubans understood the Revolution as not just the response to a recent political crisis but also as Cuba's best chance to leave behind longer cycles of "desire and disenchantment" in the island's history.[11]

In many ways, Cuba's history resembled a saga of unfinished business dating to the nineteenth century, a running series of "what ifs." In 1868, a first concerted effort to achieve independence from Spain prompted ten years of brutal war and ended in stalemate. A final major independence effort beginning in 1895, under the leadership of national heroes like Antonio Maceo and José Martí, ended in considerable frustration, too. Not only did Maceo and Martí die in battle, but in 1898, after the explosion of the USS *Maine* in Havana harbor (where it had been sent to cast a watchful eye over U.S. interests in Cuba's colonial economy), the U.S. government intervened militarily in Cuba's independence war after years of unsuccessfully trying to buy the island from Spain outright. Cuba became independent in 1902 after four years of U.S. military occupation. Yet, as a condition of that independence, the island's Constitutional Assembly was forced to adopt the Platt Amendment (1902–34), a provision that allowed the United States to intervene in, and exercise political and financial oversight over, Cuban affairs.[12]

Cubans still welcomed the inauguration of a republic with pomp and circumstance. The nation's incipient political system, however, soon became bogged down in political standoffs and intermittent violence. U.S. troops reoccupied the island between 1906 and 1909. With them came more U.S. businesses and corporate sugar interests than had already taken advantage of cheap land prices at the end of the devastating independence war. By the 1920s, political actors young and old clamored for a return to the independence movement's original principles, and many demanded an end to the island's economic and political dependence on the North. Still, a new president, Gerardo Machado, perpetrated a new treachery when he illegally extended his term in office. Violent opposition to his increasingly dictatorial rule would lead to the first revolution of Cuba's postindependence period, beginning in 1930.[13]

That revolution was also thwarted, however. Machado was forced from office in August 1933. A rising of junior military officers in September, including a young sergeant named Fulgencio Batista, put a radical coalition in power that called for the unilateral abrogation of the Platt Amendment and other nationalist reforms. Yet when the young Batista got word that the United States saw him as the only acceptable candidate to restore political stability, he overthrew the so-called Government of 100 Days and established a populist but strongman's regime over which he ruled, directly and behind the scenes, for six years. Curiously, after first repressing the labor movement that had helped drive Machado out of power, Batista established a popular-front alliance with Cuba's still young communist party, which, since its founding in the 1920s, had become influential in labor's ranks.[14]

By 1940, a more enduring democratic spring seemed in the offing. Batista convened a new constitutional convention that rewrote the island's Magna Carta along robustly social democratic lines. Batista was then legitimately elected to a four-year term in office. Ramón Grau San Martín, a veteran of the 1933 "Government of 100 Days," followed him into the presidency at the head of the Partido Auténtico (Authentic Party) in 1944, and Batista retired to Florida's Daytona Beach. Once again, though, hope turned to cynicism as successive Auténtico administrations (under Grau San Martín, from 1944 to 1948, and Carlos Prío Socarrás, from 1948 to 1952) proved corrupt, leaving the political promise and many social commitments of the Constitution of 1940 unfulfilled. In the early 1950s, a splinter group, the Partido Ortodoxo (Orthodox Party), emerged to "sweep out" the abuses of its former allies. (The party's emblem was a broom.) Nonetheless, just as its leader, Senator Eduardo Chibás, seemed poised to usher in a new era of reform, in 1951, he accidentally took his own life in a radio stunt gone wrong. Notably, it was in Chibás's nationalist, but avowedly anticommunist ranks that a young Fidel Castro got his political start.[15]

After Chibás's death, the elections of 1952 (in which Castro was running for Congress) were thrown into doubt. Fulgencio Batista had stepped back into Cuban political life a few years before when he returned to Cuba to take up a seat in the Senate. Now he mounted a new campaign for the presidency. But even with Chibás eliminated from the competition, Batista trailed in the polls. Rather than face defeat, the man derisively nicknamed *el indio* ("the Indian," because of his mixed racial heritage) or, more self-assuredly, *el hombre* ("the man") launched a bloodless coup on March 10, 1952. So ingrained was the language of "revolution" in Cuban political tradition—and in Latin American tradition more broadly—that he called his evidently undemocratic action a "revolution" for "progress and democracy, liberty and justice," pledging to "save" Cuba anew.[16]

The second Batista regime was anything but revolutionary. Cuba's historic strongman did not abandon his populist taste for social programs, educational campaigns, or public works from the late 1930s.[17] But the Constitution of 1940 was in tatters, and Batista responded to protests with repression. Washington recognized him as head of state, while his government became in some respects the Latin American prototype for an anticommunist authoritarian ally in line with U.S. prerogatives in the Cold War. Famously, Batista in the 1950s extended a friendly hand to U.S. interests. He also strengthened Havana's reputation as a modern city catering to decadence-seeking North American tourists. But while national economic and social indicators put Cuba at or near the top of its Latin American peers, prices for the island's all-important sugar exports trended downward across the decade, already chronic seasonal unemployment in the sugar sector ballooned, and even the island's substantial middle class found itself bristling under declining per capita incomes and the rising cost of living. For too many, the U.S. consumer ideal advertised incessantly in the Cuban media remained out of reach. Meanwhile, what many would later consider the "golden age" of Havana's urban nightlife, mass culture, and music scene only made contrasts with life in the still impoverished countryside harder to justify.[18]

Such, then, were the deep stakes of change when Fidel Castro and scores of other activists began their struggle against Batista in the 1950s. Cuba may have been one of the more developed Latin American countries at the time in the aggregate—a point that Batista apologists would later harp upon from abroad. Nonetheless, diverse political movements that began to coalesce against his rule spoke about not just restoring democratic order but also addressing entrenched inequalities at home and historical asymmetries in Cuba's political and commercial relations with nations abroad—namely, the United States. When Castro launched his first attempt at rebellion by attacking the Moncada Barracks in Santiago de Cuba on July 26, 1953, he and his followers drew inspiration from both the proximate insult of the 1952 coup as well as the sense that Batista's reign epitomized the longer-term political and economic ills plaguing Cuban society since 1898. The Moncada attack failed disastrously, and survivors would spend twenty months in jail before making their way to Mexico as exiles. But after landing on Cuban shores in late 1956 aboard the yacht *Granma*, Castro and insurgents of the renamed Movimiento 26 de Julio (26th of July Movement) renewed their fight. An affiliated urban underground movement awaited their arrival, while a number of separate insurgent organizations were already active, similarly convinced that the island's historical destiny was incomplete.[19]

When Castro's *barbudos* (bearded ones) emerged victorious at the head of an uneasy coalition of revolutionary forces in 1959, therefore, they assumed more than political power; they effected an "appropriation of history." "Central to the claim of [the Revolution's] historical authenticity," Louis A. Pérez Jr. has argued, "was the proposition" and sincerely believed conviction "of the triumphant revolution as culmination of a process whose antecedents reached deep into the nineteenth century."[20] "Because in Cuba there has only been one Revolution," Fidel Castro would later claim, portraying his own movement as the extension of a continuous "100 years of struggle" since the launch of Cuba's independence movement a century before.[21] Historians rightly question this frame as overly teleological, as the events leading to 1959 were not preordained. Yet at the popular level, the notion that the Revolution in power represented the "fulfillment of past political dreams deferred," and not only the response to the coup of 1952, proved deeply compelling.[22]

The problem was that evaluations of the Revolution after that point would not only be informed by discussions about the injustices, economic conditions, and violence (especially at the hands of the Batista regime) that predated it. Nor did they revolve simply around how to commemorate the heroes of the anti-Batista movement or understand that struggle's course—complex and contentious arguments in their own right, given the number of factions and organizations involved. What happened *after* the Revolution took power also became grist for the retrospective mill. Events subsequent to the "triumph" of 1959, as well as the Revolution's broader political, economic, and social results, either provided evidence that "the process" was fulfilling its historic mandate or falling short—or worse, betraying its "true" goals. Just what these original goals were would prove to be another much debated point amid the radicalization of the Revolution toward socialism between 1959 and 1961. Officials and citizens occasionally worried, too, about the shadows of pre-1959 life that persisted in the Revolution's wake. Such evaluations led to outright opposition in some cases, while driving others, including one-time revolutionaries, into exile. And even those who did not break with the direction of the Revolution explicitly occasionally found ways to indirectly challenge whether the present had lived up to 1959's messianic hopes.

The omnipresence of the past in the exile community is perhaps easier to explain, though it was no less consequential. Naturally, those who became disenchanted with the Revolution's results—no matter their feelings about it originally—felt a need to articulate a shared understanding of where things had gone wrong. Rather than bring an end to Cuba's cycles of "desire and disenchantment," many exiles felt Fidel Castro had perpetrated them anew. While Cuba's new leadership positioned the Revolution as one past's negation, others who fled the island tended to idealize the lives they left behind and the homeland to which they hoped to return. The political identity of the exile community found an anchor in common memories of displacement that felt indirectly and directly forced. Exiles also understood themselves as victims of the revolutionary state, whether through property and business confiscations, surveillance and ostracism due to their opposition to the new government, or instances of state violence against those who attempted to actively resist the Castro regime, especially as of 1960. All together, such experiences fostered a wider sense that the Revolution was Cuba's latest and most devastating national calamity. If a movement to overthrow Castro was to gain strength, the task required preserving the "true" history of the Revolution's destructive legacy.[23]

The difficulty, though, was that Cuban exiles after 1959 also brought complex political baggage with them to the United States. While they shared a common enemy and often similar class backgrounds (especially initially), they also found reason to fiercely debate which political factions among them were most complicit in the nation's predicament. No less than revolutionaries, exiles hoping to combat the revolutionary regime needed to define a vision for the island's future. But they struggled to cement its terms because of differing understandings of what had led to Fidel Castro's victory in the first place. More conservative voices adopted the premise that the Revolution had always been an unnecessary communist conspiracy. Many others struggled to square their opposition to Castro with their memories of the political, economic, and social conditions that had driven them to support a more moderate version of the Revolution initially. From this perspective, the theoretically unifying logic of nostalgia for a "lost Cuba" was not as unifying as it seemed. Taken to their uncritical extreme, longings for a fallen Eden not only concealed ongoing retrospective quarrels about what prerevolutionary Cuba had really been like; they also contradicted the notion that exiles stood for any kind of future at all.

A further complicating factor in understanding the past's centrality in Cuban political life after 1959 — and especially beyond the 1960s — is its relationship to the question of generation. Generation, of course, is an elusive concept to define, with borders that are always in some sense artificial and thus difficult to locate. Yet it is an important construct given the strong association in Cuban history between political change and youth.[24] (For example, Fidel Castro and his followers were later dubbed "the Generation of the Centenary" for having launched their attack at Moncada during the hundredth anniversary year of the birth of national founding father José Martí.) The Cuban Revolution, philosopher Jean-Paul Sartre noted after a highly public visit to the island in 1960, could alternately seem an inspiration and a "scandal" because it "brought children to power."[25] But it was one thing for young adults and their parents who had lived through the pre-1959 period to latch onto countervailing narratives of the Revolution's redemptive results or original sins, and quite another to sustain these commitments beyond the high points of mass mobilization and conflict in the 1960s. A later generation of Cubans (and Cuban Americans) born just before or after the Revolution would only have faint memories of the immediately pre- and post-1959 eras before they came of age. Innocence could have made such individuals prime candidates to embrace the narratives handed down to them. But by the 1970s, some showed signs of openly questioning inherited historical truths, particularly in the exile community.

The final, and perhaps most important, wrinkle in this story is that Cubans' battles over their past on and off the island between 1959 and 1979 did not transpire in isolation. These were deeply relational struggles and debates. How could it be otherwise when today's exiles were often yesterday's revolutionaries, at least nominally? If shadows of "the Republic" (itself a fraught memory frame) at times reared their head under the Revolution, the history of the Revolution was also everywhere in Miami. This is not to say the barrier of what some have called the Cold War "sugar curtain" dividing Cuba from its expatriate community in the United States was not real. But the "sugar curtain" was also made permeable through ongoing migration, letters, and radio waves, meaning that retrospective understandings of the nation's trajectory took shape in transnational political and cultural space.[26]

In the end, the Cuban memory wars became one of the defining fronts of the Cuban conflict itself. As the revolutionary state consolidated its power and real (i.e., armed) challenges to its authority on the ground dissipated across the 1960s, the battle over the past—to preserve, extend, or contend with its legacies, or to buck its course—became one of the major active fronts of dispute that remained. Yet more than the desire to win an argument fueled these passions. It was the periodic overlap between retrospective paradigms, as well as fissures within hegemonic camps, that imbued Cubans' contending invocations of history and memory with an ongoing sense of urgency. Unlike in other cases of civil conflict, warring Cuban sides continued to share significant national idols, symbols, and reference points. All of this made for processes of remembering and forgetting that were not only sharply contested but also deeply intertwined.

Contributions and (Memory) Interventions

In chronicling Cuba's memory wars after 1959, this book approaches the history of the Cuban Revolution in a way that may be new to some readers. Audiences outside of Cuba (and sometimes on the island as well) tend to understand the Cuban Revolution as strictly a series of epic confrontations: first against dictator Fulgencio Batista and then against the political and economic power of the United States. Popular portrayals of Cuban history, therefore, tend to reduce the Revolution in power to a series of flashpoints in a quickly accelerating feud with the North: the nationalization of major U.S. businesses on the island in 1960, the 1961 Bay of Pigs invasion, the 1962 Cuban Missile Crisis, and all manner of covert operations (many involving Cuban exiles) to unseat the Castro regime. These and other events were undoubtedly critical markers for Cubans too. How to remember (or forget) them, and how they fit into or challenged long patterns in Cuba's relations with the United States, all became important subjects of historical memory battles in the Revolution's wake. Indeed, the Cuban government's success at fending off U.S. efforts to topple it became a central element of the Revolution's story of itself. Such a U.S.-centric view of Cuba's past, however, ironically reinscribes patterns of external economic and political dependence that Cuba's 1959 revolution initially sought to reverse.[27] By contrast, this book highlights what to many Cubans has been obvious all along: the island's most enduring and intimately felt conflicts—in this case, debates over the Revolution's historical origins and results—were fought among Cubans first.

The history recounted in the following pages also blurs the divide between "Cuban" and "Cuban exile" (or "Cuban American") histories in new ways. Some scholars have crossed this metaphorical and disciplinary bridge previously, as noted above. But in popular accounts of the early revolutionary years and resulting exodus, a reductive, fratricidal metaphor still often prevails: that of a nation "severed" in two parts—communist revolutionaries in Havana, uniformly condemning the pre-1959 "pseudo-republic," pitted against freedom-loving, capitalist exiles in Miami, who idolize the prerevolutionary Cuba that the Revolution forced them to leave.[28] In reality, disputes over the past within each camp were much more complex. Cubans for and against Fidel Castro, on and off the island, occupied overlapping and, as I have indicated, interactive political fields. Exiles constructed their own fractious visions of the island's past in implicit opposition to, but with considerable awareness of, the metanarratives of the revolutionary state. Likewise, self-defined revolutionaries, for all of their outward self-assuredness, occasionally found themselves rebutting, or seeking to bury, exile and other oppositional memory claims.

An older concept from Cuban intellectual tradition can help us appreciate this pattern of tension and exchange. In 1940, Cuban anthropologist Fernando Ortiz proposed a well-known metaphor to describe his island nation. Cuba's past and present, he argued, could be understood through the "counterpoint" between its two staple crops: tobacco, symbolizing the autochthonous and the democratic, and sugar, representing the foreign and the exploitative. The relevance of Ortiz's *Cuban Counterpoint* here, however, is that he considered both sides to be not so much opposites but windows into a single, if unruly, synthesis.[29] A musical understanding of "counterpoint" is thus also apposite; in composition, counterpoint refers to lines of notes that move separately but work together harmonically, even when occasionally dissonant in tone. Given the long shadow of Ortiz over Cuban letters, claiming to have identified a "new" Cuban counterpoint may be the most predictable tool in a historian of Cuba's kit. My ambition here is not to replace Ortiz's classic with a fresh post-1959 allegory of revolution and its exile discontents. But the history of the Cuban memory wars since 1959 does follow a contrapuntal storyline. There is a "memory of the Revolution" that partisans of the project and its detractors at home and abroad contest, just as there is a "memory of exile" that is narrated, identified with, and fought over, as we will see throughout this book. Yet there is an intimate relationship between the two. The latter is the former's result, and Cubans' arguments about their past fed and bounced off one another, all claiming to speak for—and thus in effect constituting—the memory and history of the nation as a whole.

More than just tracking this interplay, though, this book also unavoidably *intervenes* in Cuba's memory wars in its own right. That is, in historicizing the course of Cubans' debates over and reckonings with their past across the Revolution's first two decades, I recover significant junctures, processes, and textures from the Cuban memory wars that were erased from official, quasi-official, or otherwise canonical iterations of Cuban historical memory subsequently. Such an interventionist role may be uncommon for an academic study. But even when written in accordance with exacting standards, historical scholarship always does implicit forms of memory work, holding the power to mold our understandings of the past anew.[30] This is all the more the case for a study that has competing visions of national memory as its focus and whose author—a Cuban American—has a personal connection to the histories relayed.

I do not dare predict that this book will enter into feedback loops with contemporary manifestations of the cultural and political processes it describes. But I can be transparent about the fact that I do harbor hopes of reshaping the contours of present-day Cuban retrospective debate. Put simply, this study undermines the two most polarized narratives of Cuban history with which this introduction began by telling the history of the construction and deconstruction of those narratives in the first place. In the process, more layered and today often forgotten ways of understanding and relating to the Cuban past resurface to be newly picked apart and mined for insights. In exposing them, this book reveals that Cubans have been rewriting their history all along. And it offers the possibility of an alternate narrative of that history—one in which Cubans' battles over the past since 1959, and not just their divergent experiences of it, become part of historical memory themselves.

History, Memory, and Other Slippery Concepts

What terms and tools can help us understand the evolving contours of the Cuban memory wars? How can we conceptualize or differentiate between the various actors involved? It may seem, for example, that I have treated "history" and "memory" as more or less interchangeable ideas to this point. "Memory politics," "historical memory," and, again, "memory wars" are other phrases that have made appearances and will continue to pop up.

It is thus worth pausing on several slippery theoretical concepts whose meanings may be unclear. In fact, my terminological flexibility is by design. While terms like "history" and "memory" can have discrete meanings, there is no neat consensus on the specificities of their usage. I thus follow other scholars' lead in questioning strict definitional divides. Instead, I ground this study in a more active concept, "retrospective politics," because it encompasses the wider range of processes I intend to analyze.[31]

Let us begin by exploring the differences, or overlap, between "history" and "memory" with a specific eye to the Cuban case. Sixteen years ago, cultural critic José Quiroga proposed that the politics of the past might prove a ripe subject for analysis in histories of the Cuban Revolution and its resulting diaspora. In "direct and discrete ways," he wrote in 2005,

> the [Cuban revolutionary] state sustained itself by interpellating its population *both* in the past and in the present. The state was not simply using coercive mechanisms, but commanding a symbolic language that registered with the people, always addressed in the plural. This tactic demands an approach that focuses on the representation of *memory* and culture, and on the broad effects ideologies and policies have had on all forms of expression within the collective lives of Cubans who live not only on the island, but also outside of its territorial boundaries.[32]

Importantly, Quiroga did not see Cubans' understandings of the Revolution's origins and the island's past more broadly as developing in isolation. In his view, the Revolution's leaders invited citizens to believe that they were protagonists in a shared, deeply rooted quest. The emotional registers through which Cubans embraced or rejected this premise thus suggest that something more than academic "history" was at stake. Even without their own singular charismatic leader, the same intense relationship traveled with exiles across the Florida Straits. After 1959, Cubans argued intensely about the island's past as a means to understand their predicament in the present. But they also fought over the meaning of experiences they had lived and political trajectories of which they felt deeply a part. Thinking, therefore, about these battles as conflicts over "memory" allows "a more perceptive vision" of the lived experience of revolution and exile than focusing on abstract polemics over "history" alone.[33] "We cannot *forget* the blood that was shed in Cuba," clamored the 26th of July Movement's official anthem.[34] "Beautiful Cuba, I will always *remember* you," grieved one of the unofficial hymns of exile popularized in Miami.[35] (The emphasis in both cases is mine.)

But if more than "history" was up for grabs, "memory" may seem inadequate on its own, or at least require qualification. After all, in its origins, that term refers to how individuals, not groups, process and recall their lived experiences. There is a deep well of research (including in the field of neurology) that explores memory's capacities and limits on those terms.[36] That said, there has long been acknowledgment that our individual recollections of personal and larger societal events are shaped by social contexts.[37] As members of social collectives of varying kinds, we derive a sense of identity from the conviction of having a shared past with others. Communities, cultures, and nations frequently "provide us the stimulus or opportunity to recall; they also shape the ways in which we do so, and often provide the materials."[38] Mass media, political speeches, schools, and other forms of associational activity similarly frame individuals' understandings of their own lives and their relationship to national or other imagined communities. Put another way, what historian Steve J. Stern has called "emblematic frameworks" of history telling in the public sphere can strongly influence how an individual "imparts broad interpretative meaning" to his or her "loose" memories of everyday experience.[39] Yet there is disagreement on whether any such thing as "collective memory" exists. Some insist that the most we can speak of are "collected" reflections and understandings of the past among individuals—shaped, perhaps, by common factors and tending to converge in particular settings or among particular social groups, but not a truly shared consciousness as the term "collective memory" implies.[40]

It is better, then, to think of history and memory not as oppositions, or of memory as somehow easily demarcated into individual, "collective," or "collected" forms. Any sharp distinction tends to fizzle upon close examination anyway. It can be tempting, for example, to fetishize private memory as an authentic, counterhegemonic force, eyewitness evidence that public narratives of history—especially those propagated by a dominant regime or state—would prefer to ignore.[41] Yet individual memory can also be perilously biased and flawed, while history at its academic best at least aspires to document a more comprehensive truth.[42] At the same time, historians themselves are often influenced by, if not beholden to, the emblematic memory narratives to which their societies, social groups, or governments subscribe. This was certainly the case in revolutionary Cuba in the 1960s. As Cuban scholar Manuel Moreno Fraginals argued in an influential essay at the time, many historians on the island saw their craft as a "weapon" of potent ideological reach in service of a revolution in which most believed.[43] The same could be said of Cuban historians in exile committed to defending the prerevolutionary "Republic" against libel from revolutionary acolytes.[44]

In these ways, arguments about the reliability of "history" versus "memory" as repositories or categories of knowledge—in Cuba or elsewhere—quickly become straw men when we begin to view both as interrelated players in a retrospective field. If "memory" is both individual and influenced by social contexts, "history" hardly only manifests as an academic product. It is also written and referenced by political organizations and states, and those actors sometimes appropriate individual testimonies to make their point. By foregrounding a broader notion of "retrospective politics," then, this study is less concerned with what *the* collective memory or history of this or that Cuban group was or was not than with the evolving, diverse claims on memory and history made in the nation's, "the Revolution's," or the exile community's (*el exilio*'s) name.[45]

And yet, the idea of "retrospective politics" also allows us to conceptualize our object of study as more than the active contests between competing narratives, or the manifestations of each in public life. I am equally interested in plumbing the changing contours of Cubans' relationship to their past over time. For that reason, this book looks at not just the shifting inclusions and omissions in opposed accounts of the Cuban past by revolutionary and exile leaders. It likewise explores the place those narratives occupied in the zeitgeist of evolving presents. What role did history and memory play in revolutionary and exile political cultures in the 1960s and 1970s? Did the past serve as motivation or at times resemble a trap? How did the Cuban state and leading exile voices shape not only how Cuban history writ large was told but also how the experiences of revolution and exile were understood? And did Cubans on both sides of the Florida Straits internalize these frameworks or contest their terms?

Methodological Challenges and Topical Limits

There are important challenges to undertaking this kind of study—some general, some specific to the Cuban context. For one thing, "emblematic frameworks" of history telling and remembrance are themselves not timeless. Nor do authority figures always deploy them with purely manipulative aims. Political leaders of varying stripes might selectively wield historical evidence at particular moments to serve predetermined goals. But previously established arguments do not always foreclose the terms of debate. This was particularly true for Cubans in the early 1960s, as multiple revolutionary and exile organizations attempted to shape unified historical imaginaries from heterogeneous foundations, rather than simply defend prebaked narratives. Subsequent policy failures and generational tensions occasionally compelled narrative adjustments or revived dilemmas long thought put to bed. In this way, retrospective politics for Cubans proceeded less along a predictable path than in a dynamic relationship to the present.

Another difficulty relates to the relationship between public narrative and private sentiment, a theme referenced above. If claims in the name of national or other collective forms of historical memory resemble the telling of a story, that story succeeds to the degree influential "storytellers"—governments, society leaders, mass media products—are able "to draw in, indeed implicate, the listeners"—average citizens—in the repetition of the tale.[46] But if that is true, scholars of retrospective politics should seek out evidence of not just politicians' shifting retrospective visions but also, where possible, public narratives' popular acceptance or refusal. This is somewhat easier for the Cuban exile context, where a rich expatriate press, organizational records, and private correspondence have all been well preserved. On the island, however, the centralized nature of the revolutionary state after 1960 has left few unmediated archival trails of grassroots perceptions.[47]

Oral history, one might think, could provide a work-around. Yet there are noteworthy complications to collecting oral testimonies in Cuba. These include the ways political conditions on the island continue to inhibit some individuals' responses—especially in front of a foreign, let alone Cuban American interviewer. Scholars wishing to be transparent must also receive permission from relevant Cuban authorities to carry out interview work. More to the point, when the goal of a study is to unearth the shape of retrospective politics fifty or sixty years ago, interviews conducted in the present are as likely to reveal the nested effects of the Cuban memory wars since.[48] For these reasons, this book mostly uses oral testimony as a complement to other forms of historical evidence, and never as the central object of study.

For the island in particular, any examination of retrospective politics must also contend, as I have already recognized, with the role and influence of the Cuban revolutionary state. Whether in the speeches of Fidel Castro, the contents of municipal museums, or the scripts of documentary films made with public financing, prevailing ways of narrating and understanding Cuban history were buttressed by the imprimatur of an expansive and expanding array of government institutions and imprints, especially after 1960, when the nationalization of virtually all private associations, businesses, and press outlets intensified. Still, the fact that a socialist state became omnipresent in Cuban life should not mean that we treat it as a monolith. We must be careful not to take the construction of an "official" historical canon and language as necessarily the work of a personified, all-knowing puppeteer. The Cuban state was not fully formed at the Revolution's start, and, as we will see, some of the private citizens who anticipated key tenants of "official" memory discourse in 1959 would themselves soon depart in protest for Miami. A more complex understanding of the workings of retrospective politics in Cuba, therefore, must leave space for considering the uneven process of revolutionary state formation. Plus, not all Cubans accepted increasingly "official" memory scripts, or they may have understood them on their own terms. Similarly, we must be open to exploring how those working within and through state institutions—especially in publishing, the arts, and the media—may have fashioned their own interpretations of the historical record that subtly challenged canonical accounts. Archival opacity (or closed doors) may not always allow a full reconstruction of the bureaucratic chains of command by which state actors institutionalized portraits of the Revolution's origins and results, let alone grassroots perceptions of these scripts. Yet in the press (again, state-run after 1960), in cultural production, and in the words of political leaders, we can trace the evolving shape of historical narrations and some revealing clashes over their form.

An inverse word of caution is in order with regard to the exile community. For if the expanding apparatus of the Cuban state after 1960 helped to construct, propagate, and enforce dominant historical memory narratives that would bolster that state's legitimacy—albeit in ways that were messy and not always predictable—in exile the opposite was true: there was no central political authority, no similar set of mechanisms for institutionalizing a singular counternarrative of Cuba's and the expatriate community's history. Yet Cuban exiles did have resources to construct hegemonic memory cultures of their own. Political organizations and media outlets—at times with U.S. government backing—articulated powerful retrospective frameworks for understanding where the Revolution had gone wrong that are equally worthy of being pulled apart and critiqued. Given the drive on the island to place all history telling in the service of the Revolution's national epic, it is tempting to see the Cuban past becoming "confiscated by official discourse," as one critic recently put it.[49] In this vision, the exile community—or the Cuban diaspora broadly—acts as the repository of uncomfortable, dissident, censored, and self-censored memories of events and individuals that revolutionary political culture has repressed. But while there is undeniable truth to this framing, in exile too—as in all contexts, to repeat a point made above—the cult of remembering was accompanied by cults of forgetting. If the Cuban state engaged in retrospective distortions, it also mobilized facets of Cuban history that exiles tended to downplay or ignore. While acknowledging the distinct and often problematic power of the Cuban state to shape an official memory repertoire, we must take shifting patterns of remembering and forgetting in the exile community no less seriously.

Given the potential capaciousness of this kind of inquiry, it is only fair that I also acknowledge, or restate, several topical limitations to this study. Most obviously, this book is bounded chronologically. I track Cuban retrospective politics over the Revolution's and postrevolutionary exile community's first two decades, not their entire history. That is not because the Cuban memory wars came to an end after this point. Far from it. But as I make clear in the chapter descriptions below, 1979 serves as a compelling bookend, bringing the two sides of the story together and marking the end of a first phase of retrospective division and angst. Insofar as the 1970s saw the Cuban revolutionary state undergo a process of institutional consolidation and restructuring, some historians have equated the 1970s with the end of "the Revolution" itself or, at the very least, its most dramatic period of political and social change.[50] In that sense, too, the end of the 1970s represents a convenient, if imperfect, moment to conclude this inquiry.

Similarly, I cannot hope to cover all subjects and events around which Cuban retrospective politics turned. Some—like perennial battles among Cubans over the image and legacy of Argentina-born revolutionary leader Ernesto "Che" Guevara—I deliberately exclude because they have been covered elsewhere.[51] In other cases, controversial episodes during the twenty years under examination did not become fodder for public memory battles in their own right until the 1980s or 1990s.[52] I do, though, reference such events in the course of tracking how they informed or intersected with broader arguments about the Cuban national epic in prior decades. And, as appropriate, I note when they left particularly large, but for the time being publicly buried, retrospective wounds.

The relationship between national memory frameworks and not just grassroots, but specifically subaltern experiences and identities in Cuban society is another topic beyond the scope of this book. In addition to not always capturing individual Cubans' internalization (or rejection) of national memory discourses as richly as I might like, I do not engage the specific challenges female, Afro-diasporic, and queer Cubans—on the island or in the diaspora—faced in making their own stories heard and count, whether as part of the national story or on their own terms. Nor does this book track the ways individual Cubans' memories of particular national events or experiences may have been gendered or raced. There is excellent and growing scholarship on women's, Afro-Cuban, and LGBTQ life under the Revolution.[53] Scholars have also shown how the revolutionary project celebrated and appropriated (while exiles tended to disregard) Cuba's black history in alternately inspirational and problematic ways.[54] However, given the predominant orientation of this book around contests over the *national* story, and the color- and gender-blind terms in which those arguments tended to be framed in Havana and Miami, the absences mentioned above are sadly reflective of who was and was not afforded a prominent place in those debates, not to mention the archives they left behind.[55]

Finally, it is worth briefly considering some of the comparative challenges of examining Cuban retrospective politics vis-à-vis battles over memory and history in other societies. It is striking that as much writing as has been devoted to the problem of memory in twentieth-century Latin America during and after the Cold War, the Cuban case remains largely ignored. This may have something to do with the ideological cast of the Cuban conflict, or the particularly politicized role of migration in the story. But it may reflect more the fact that, unlike for cases in Central America or the Southern Cone, battles over the Cuban past do not pivot around the end of a civil war, sudden secret state archival disclosure, let alone a final point of transition where the chief political regime in question leaves power behind. So much of the literature on the Southern Cone, for example, has responded to and documented those societies' efforts to come to terms with or bury the violence of authoritarianism in the aftermath of military rule.[56] For Cuba, however, save from the original transfer of power after Batista's fall, the orientation to a point of transition does not compute, both for the twenty years under examination in this study and beyond. "The Revolution" is still in power, after all, in some form. Nor do legacies of political violence and imprisonment figure so centrally as the major axis of contention, although for Cubans too, of course, they constituted an important front of retrospective contention and debate.[57]

Unlike citizens in other Latin American contexts, Cubans have benefited from no institutional effort to come to terms, however imperfect. Though contending narratives of the Cuban past have undergone fresh inclusions and omissions over the years, Cuba has had no truth commission to adjudicate responsibility for injustice (before or after 1959) or attempt to establish a purportedly agreed-upon set of facts. To historicize retrospective politics in the Cuban case—even just focusing on the first twenty years of the Revolution—is therefore to dive into an unfinished and partial story, like all stories of memory politics, but in particularly obvious ways. That does not mean that telling it is fruitless, however. As emphasized above, this book recuperates historical arguments and memory struggles that have largely been forgotten in Cuba's seemingly "Manichaean ideological field" today.[58] And in doing so, again, maybe this material can aid processes of collective meditation and reflection in the present, or that have not yet taken shape.

Chapter Organization

In six roughly chronological chapters, *Cuban Memory Wars* offers a transnational history of Cuban retrospection in the crosshairs of revolution, migration, and profound societal change. Chapter 1 dissects totalizing explanations of the Revolution's historical roots that anchored both political authorities' early claims to power in 1959 and 1960, as well as the views of diverse civil society actors before the consolidation of the revolutionary state. Yet, even as speeches, movie scripts, and comic books invested citizens in an irresistible morality tale, disagreements over what direction the Revolution should take dredged up inconvenient pre-1959 political legacies as well as accusations that revolutionary "fakes" were filling its ranks. Only as conflict with the United States ramped up did the historical framework of Cuban anti-imperialism serve to overshadow these internal retrospective fault lines.

Chapter 2 tells the inverse story: that of Castro opponents—many of them former "revolutionaries"—who, as more and more Cubans went into exile and made the choice to ally with Washington, failed to forge a lasting united front. Constant recriminations over where they had gone wrong and who among the exiles was to blame for Castro's rise bred political infighting and paralysis. By the end of the 1960s, therefore, nostalgia only offered a partial salve. The memory of exile for many, like that of the nation in their view, was one of failure and tragedy, not yet immigrant triumph over odds.

Chapter 3 homes in on the Bay of Pigs invasion as a central episode in revolutionary myth. But more than tracking how the event was commemorated on the island, or how it became the most important chapter in Cuba's saga of resistance to the United States, it considers the ways the invasion served as a seminal and repeated point of reference across the 1960s for wider arguments about the Revolution's direction and results. The memory of Girón served to motivate continued revolutionary commitment, but it also became a prism through which to analyze whether the Revolution had lived up to its promise amid subsequent political and economic difficulties. Televised interrogations of exile soldiers held prisoner after the invasion were just one early stage of these debates. Important alternate readings of the invasion's, and by proxy the Revolution's, legacy would also appear in the second half of the 1960s on stage and screen.

Chapter 4 returns to the exile community to tackle a new front of retrospective politics in the Revolution's second decade: generational struggle. Rising to prominence after 1971, the anti-Castro student organization Agrupación Abdala sought to revive anti-imperialist understandings of Cuban history in exile, all while positioning itself as the enemy of the radicalized, pro-Havana contributors to *Areíto* magazine. Despite their rivalry, however, both groups repudiated their parents' complacent longings for their home country, and at the same time, they fought against the temptation among others in their age cohort to adopt a U.S. ethnic identity and leave the history of the island behind.

In chronological parallel, chapter 5 describes how revolutionary mobilization and improvisation in the 1960s gave way to a stable, but more mundane socialist modernity on the island in the 1970s. Against this backdrop of socialist "institutionalization," the Cuban state's grand narratives of the Revolution's emergence and results reached a high point of simplicity. Yet honoring the high points of the previous decade also appeared to acquire greater urgency for a political project striving to maintain legitimacy among young people who had not been protagonists of early revolutionary change. Nostalgia, this chapter shows, was not only the purview of exiles; it could also appear in "revolutionary" forms.

Finally, chapter 6 brings us full circle by exploring a pivotal juncture of memory encounter across the Florida Straits in 1979. That year, 100,000 exiles were allowed to return to the island as visitors for the first time. Divergent explanations for what happened to Cubans over the preceding twenty years thus collided in unprecedented ways. As veritable apparitions from the past, returning exiles disrupted the distortions to which revolutionary discourse had subjected them previously. The gifts and money they brought their relatives also exposed a mismatch between chronicles of the Revolution's historic achievements and the persistence of material wants. But exiles likewise encountered uncomfortable ghosts, as well as evidence that history on the island had continued without them. Far from bringing about lasting reconciliation, as some hoped, the results were often unsettling, proof that the memory scars of revolution and exile remained deep.

Ultimately, this book is not primarily a study of the commemoration of individual events, or the memories of particular subgroups of the Cuban population. Rather, it explores contests over the national epic in political and cultural motion during the Revolution's first two decades. Again, the manifestations of this struggle that I cover are necessarily selective—like memory itself. Yet the themes and actors addressed here allow me to capture predominant terms of argument, as well as their political and cultural stakes. And they prove that the Cuban memory wars have never been a strictly polarized affair. They have always involved a more nested, multivalent set of anxieties and debates.

Final Words

As already noted, Cubans' battles over their past did not come to an end when this book does. When 125,000 Cubans fled the island via the Mariel boatlift of 1980, cycles of mass migration and narrative fracture began anew. In the conclusion, therefore, I survey Cuban retrospective politics since 1979, highlighting continued fronts of mobilization and argument that were extensions of those covered in this book, as well as others in relation to episodes mentioned in passing or newer turning points. In particular, I describe how Cuba's post-Soviet crisis after 1991 forced many Cubans to reevaluate their past political commitments and the Revolution's legacies. At the same time, historic deliverance evaded exile opponents, as the Cuban government found a way to reorient its foundational myths, outlasting all predictions of the Revolution's demise. The incomplete, in many ways nonexistent internal transition since, colored by the reestablishment and now refreezing of diplomatic relations between Cuba and the United States, has also reconfigured the Cuban retrospective landscape in ways that at least warrant tentative critique.

What is true today, though, has been so since 1959. For Cubans, the past has constituted an inescapable presence in public life, at times wielding the power to inspire, at others weighing the present down like a curse. Yet as frequently as political leaders have attempted to fix the meaning of ongoing developments in contending visions of a national epic or tragedy, citizens have also fashioned their own interpretations that challenge established wisdoms. The indirect and direct relationship between revolutionary and expatriate arguments over the Cuban past demands a unified consideration of both. Cubans' ongoing reckonings with their history's successes and failures after 1959 matter enormously, not just as windows into the Cuban experience but as important vectors of Cuban history in the making.

A Note on Terminology

In the Cuban memory wars, terms are not innocent bystanders. They convey and endorse retrospective understandings. What for some was the "triumph" of 1959 for others was the beginning of a great deception. For loyalists of the Cuban government to this day, "the Revolution" is an ongoing, not terminal process, and much more than a descriptor for the anti-Batista insurrection of the 1950s. For its harshest critics, "the Revolution" was ultimately never a revolution at all, just a descent into dictatorship.

In this book, I do my best to avoid reifying the meaning of this weighty label. When I use "the Revolution" (capitalized), I largely do so to echo the ways that historical actors did. That is, I aim to capture how Cuban officials and citizens tended to abstract and, yes, even personify the concept over time. ("The Revolution" not only has a history; it *acts* in the present.) That said, I also deconstruct the embedded meanings of the term and reveal the political contests that its use submerged. That includes highlighting the ways some Cuban exiles held on to their own alternative understandings of revolutionary (lower case) politics, especially early on.

A similar dilemma surrounds the name of the Cuban leader that inevitably looms large over this history. For his adherents, Fidel Castro was and remains "Fidel," a label of caring. For his enemies, he became "Castro" when referenced by name at all. One's choice of name, therefore, tends to tip the hat as to one's Cuban memory camp. I opt in this book for an admittedly promiscuous use of both, while also using the full name Fidel Castro as often as I can. Here, though, my usage reflects not how each was used in real time by historical actors (which proved too awkward as a matter of writing) but instead an effort to avoid repetition and the impression of a preference.

1

Origin Stories of Revolution, Exorcisms of the Past

Many Cubans know it. Thousands of visitors to the island have seen it too. Sold daily in Havana curio markets in countless imitation copies, the 1959 *Album de la Revolución Cubana* (*Album of the Cuban Revolution*) offers the perfect souvenir of radical kitsch. As comic-book supermen, Fidel Castro and militants of his 26th of July Movement appear fit for child's play, members of a toy army dressed in toy fatigues. For the tourist, the drawings reinforce an image of Cuban history as an improbable epic that is simultaneously quaint. The storyline seems inspiring but almost make-believe.

Yet, despite its status as a common traveler's collectible today, the original *Album de la Revolución Cubana* is a remarkable historical document.[1] Partnering with a private sweets company in mid-1959 (the Compañía Industrial Empacadora de Dulces), writers at the Havana-based Revista Cinegráfico S.A. (or the Cinematic Graphics Review Corporation) crafted a slim publication of thirty-plus pages with 268 blank spaces. Those spaces, in turn, were meant to be filled by cartoon cards depicting episodes of revolutionary resistance, which could only be aquired by purchasing cans of Felices brand jams. So popular were these *postalitas* as collectors' items that *Zig-zag*, the island's leading humor newspaper, dedicated a two-page cartoon spread to poking fun at the obsession.[2] History sold well in the heady days of 1959, even as Cubans threw themselves headlong into the promise of a bold new future. Emblazoned on the album's interior title page, the slogan "Consume Cuban Products" advertised a brief, and today largely forgotten, juncture when private capital, middle-class consumers, and the incipient revolutionary government worked as a team.[3]

But if the storyboard squares hint at how quickly insurgent legend seeped into island society's every pore, the particular fable they told reveals much about the changing shape of Cubans' interpretations of their past over time. On the one hand, the album manifested the power of a revolutionary movement whose guerrilla leaders and student allies had

25

Figure 1.1. Cover of *Album de la Revolución Cubana, 1952–1959* (Havana: Revista Cinegráfico, S.A., 1959). Casanas Family Collection, Special Collections and University Archives, Florida International University Libraries, Miami, FL. Image reproduction courtesy of University of Florida Digital Collections and Digital Library of the Caribbean, George A. Smathers Libraries, University of Florida, Gainesville, FL.

quickly become subjects of popular mythology. On the other, while the adventure-tale quality of Fidel Castro's quest lay at the heart of this story of national self, the album also contained numerous features that would sit uncomfortably with dominant renditions of the Revolution's emergence in years to come. Secondary and later overlooked anti-Batista movements received legitimizing coverage in its pages. Cuba's traditional communist party—soon among the primary factions competing for revolutionary political power—was nowhere to be found. Most striking of all was the mixture of faces in the book's concluding pantheon of heroes. As early as a few months after the album's publication, several of the men pictured would begin falling afoul of the Revolution as it radicalized, finding themselves imprisoned or making their way to exile to conspire. One of the earliest, most familiar representations of the Revolution's insurgent history, therefore, quickly became politically incorrect. Excised from official narratives thereafter, a handful of individuals in the book's pages would see their contributions to Batista's defeat discounted or denied.

The *Album de la Revolución Cubana* provides a useful entry point, if not metaphor, for this chapter's central concerns. Scholars have long emphasized the extraordinary sense of historic messianism that attended Fidel Castro's rise to power. For most Cubans, *this* revolution—Fidel's revolution—represented the awaited moral realization not just of the anti-Batista struggle, but of the nation's long-frustrated dreams.[4] Still, if the Cuban Revolution came to power with its story already partially written, competing claims over revolutionary bona fides, and for the historical legitimacy to speak in the Revolution's name, were still taking shape. While Cuba's previously unsatisfied national aspirations finally seemed on the threshold of fulfillment, the anti-Batista front had been a moving target comprised of multiple, often-fractious organizations.[5] Disparate groups embraced common hopes for national dignity and reform, but personality politics, past strategic rivalries, and ideological fractures within and between factions had the potential to drive them apart.

A close look, then, at rare press and other sources from the Revolution's first eighteen months offers a contradictory, and until now underhistoricized, picture of memory mobilization alongside simmering retrospective quarrels. This chapter also reveals the ways the Cuban memory wars did not simply proceed along a predetermined, polarized path, but instead involved multiple political actors engaged in active, complex wars of position. Vast swaths of Cuban society became determined to purge the human and institutional ills of their nation's past. Yet political scores also remained unsettled, and the depth of the economic problems in Cuba's history requiring transformation, not to mention the best way to address them, remained a source of disagreement. Contending visions of the Revolution's future thus quickly turned on not just differing understandings of the project's social and political roots but also on various individuals' and groups' assertions of what they had or had not done in its service. As the rubber hit the road, arguments about the Revolution's direction were intimately related to confrontations over legacies, compromises, and decisions made before its "triumph." These battles persisted alongside unprecedented expressions of nationalist exuberance and faith.

Fidel Castro watched these disputes from a privileged position. As the unquestioned leader of revolutionary forces (even before having formally occupied a government post), his support or disapproval could take contending actors in and out of the political cold. At the same time, for most of 1959 Castro sought to appear above the fray, constructing an ostensibly nonsectarian narrative of Cuban history as deferred deliverance, one that naturally privileged his own movement's leadership and encouraged Cubans to get on board or get out of the way. This does not mean, however, that his was the only relevant voice. This chapter thus decenters Fidel Castro's words and appearances, covered so well by other historians, to foreground political actors and press outlets more commonly overlooked. By late 1959 and 1960, however, Castro's insistence that anticommunism itself represented the historical blight that the Revolution most needed to exorcise would tilt the partisan memory balance in clear, influential ways.

Looking back, another dynamic stands out from these early counterpoints of retrospective argument and agitation—one that further complicates the work of interpreting their meaning. Namely, in the course of staking out their credentials, actors in and out of the new government said and wrote things that later they would find more convenient to forget. Whether Fidel Castro's vague pledges to convene elections, or more moderate anti-Batista voices' defense of early revolutionary tribunals (subsequently remembered by many as the first sign of the Revolution's antidemocratic impulses), the domestic press overflowed with declarations that had the potential to embarrass once the ideological die were cast. The exercise in this chapter, then—like in this book as a whole—becomes double: to track the multiple origin stories and claims to historical standing that competed for credibility during the Revolution's tumultuous first eighteen months or so, while also recovering some of the positions, players, and assertions that a more polarized climate beginning in 1960 would conspire to erase.

As Cuba's domestic memory battles increasingly collided with the international politics of the Cold War, mounting bilateral tensions with Washington deflected Cubans' retrospective fissures away from internal matters toward the longer legacies of U.S.-Cuban affairs. Rivalries for historical position along factional lines from the Revolution's first stage took a back seat to an anti-imperialist dream. Thereafter, privileged narrators in the media and the emerging state would recast what had been a deeply conflicted process of political and economic transformation into a groundswell in favor of unitary change. In this new, radicalized scenario, which led to the declaration of the Revolution's "socialist" character, ideological labels or a nuanced understanding of Cuba's recent history mattered less than patriotic belief.

"Ahora sí . . .": Historical Communion and Rupture

"This time, the Revolution is for real." So proclaimed Fidel Castro upon his triumphal entrance into the city of Santiago de Cuba on January 1, 1959. Euphoria had already gripped the island's streets as news spread the night before that Fulgencio Batista had fled. As the undisputed "maximum leader" of the Revolution's words made clear, much more was at stake than a mere political turnover. "It will not be like in [the war of 18]95," Castro declared,

> when the Americans came and made themselves the owners of this place (Applause).... It will not be like in [19]33, when just as people began to believe that a revolution was being made, Mr. Batista came along and betrayed the revolution, taking over power and installing a dictatorship for eleven years. It will not be like in [19]44, the year in which the crowds got fired up, believing that finally the people were coming to power, when really those who came to power were thieves. Neither thieves, nor traitors, nor interventionists! This time, the Revolution is for real.[6]

No matter how often these lines have been quoted, the clarity and reach of the Revolution's foundational myth continue to be extraordinary. As we saw in the introduction, Cuban politics had been haunted for decades by what felt to many like an "unfinished history."[7] Now, Cubans across the moderate-to-left side of the political spectrum—including some who later became Fidel Castro's enemies—understood the movement's victory as the consummation of a longer quest. "The [national] emancipation struggle," wrote Mario Llerena, former chairman of the 26th of July Movement's New York chapter and future anti-Castro exile, "can be conceived as a continuous process, moving toward one goal, as much as it seems to present itself in different chapters or eras."[8] "The Cuban Revolution," agreed editors at the progressive but anticommunist *Prensa Libre*, "is one, only one, [and it] began at the dawn of the last century and it grew and perfected itself and took shape and authority and victory over the course of space and time, until arriving at our days." These statements reflect the wide berth of the anti-Batista coalition at the start of 1959. Still, it is remarkable just how much the early prorevolutionary rhetoric of many who eventually found themselves in Fidel Castro's crosshairs prefigured and echoed the words of the *comandante* (or commander, one of Castro's many titles).[9]

After half a century of political turmoil, most Cubans were more eager than ever to end cycles of repeated disappointment to which they previously felt condemned. With respect to the politics of historical memory, however, such expectations presented the emergent political leadership with a thorny challenge. On the one hand, new officials needed to position their government as the continuation and outgrowth of nationalist struggles that had come before it. On the other, spokespeople for the nation's new political project also had to differentiate their course, making clear that past mistakes would not be repeated. The first months of the Cuban Revolution in power thus bore witness to ubiquitous displays of historical communion and exorcism—ceremonies headline-grabbing and mundane, all to "render the revolution as vindication of the past and the past as validation of the revolution," as the historian Louis A. Pérez Jr. has written evocatively.[10]

Perhaps more skepticism was warranted. Morality, or the pursuit of moral redemption—not Marxism—had long functioned as the dominant idiom of Cuban political life. It was in this spirit that many believed the time had finally come to break with what sociologist Nelson P. Valdés later called the "identical," tragic "script" of disillusionment—regardless of ideology—that had tended to repeat itself in island affairs to that point.[11] Yet what historian María del Pilar Díaz Castañón has labeled the *ahora sí* or "now, finally" impulse in Cuban political psychology—the idea, or hope, that Cuba's moment had arrived once and for all—already had an "ancient" and clearly discouraging track record in the island's history.[12] After failing in his first attempt to start an anti-Batista insurrection at the Moncada Barracks of Santiago de Cuba in 1953, Fidel Castro confidently declared, "La historia me absolverá" ("History will absolve me") at his subsequent trial.[13] But, as writer Virgilio Piñera wondered "in silence" just two weeks after the rebel victory six years later, "This time now, will it be like other times past?"[14] Cuba's "myth of subjunctive possibility" cried out to finally come to fruition, but reality could once again disappoint.[15]

For most of 1959, those holding such doubts were few and far between. Popular mobilizations and rallies across the island, starting with Fidel Castro's seven-day "Caravan of Liberty" from Santiago to Havana, coalesced a sense of national optimism as never before. Photographs of the spontaneous celebrations greeting his and other rebels' arrivals in town after town—taken by unofficial and soon quasi-official photographers of the Revolution alike—quickly spread across the pages of the press, becoming iconic parts of an emergent collective visual memory of the Revolution in their own right.[16] "When a people learns and knows," wrote a Dr. Pascual B. Marcos Vegueri that September, echoing the sentiments of the majority, "all that the Cuban people have learned and know ... conscious of and justly enthralled with its destiny ... that people rejects with intelligence, energy, and courage, any pretension of regressing to its iniquitous, miserable, and despicable past."[17] The uniqueness of *this* moment in Cuba's history for most seemed beyond dispute.

Nothing united the Cuban people as resolutely in the early days of 1959 as the sweeping, public exposure of the ousted Batista regime's misdeeds.

Figure 1.2. "Now Finally I Know What's Good!," cover of *Zig-zag*, January 17, 1959. Artist unknown; possibly Antonio Prohías.

After years of on-and-off censorship, Cuba's national press exploded with gruesome exposés of police repression, aerial bombardments of peasant villages, and illicit enrichment by pro-Batista lackeys. *Bohemia*, Cuba's most important weekly magazine, became the standard-bearer, disseminating detailed reconstructions of the course of the insurrection and anti-Batista resistance. Each of the publication's three January "liberty editions" sold out, even though the magazine had printed 1 million copies. At the same time, editor Miguel Ángel Quevedo popularized the soon canonized claim that 20,000 Cubans had perished at the hands of Batista's soldiers and henchmen. Looking back, many historians now believe that the figure was exaggerated. (Lower estimates put the total closer to 3,000 to 4,000.)[18] Regardless, in 1959 the evidence marshaled in its defense "discredited all memories of normalcy under Batista's rule as false and self-deceiving."[19]

Parallel to exposés in the national press, the Ejército Rebelde (Rebel Army) held televised trials of Batista regime criminals in the first days of January. The proceedings immediately raised eyebrows in the United States, and among some Cubans, due to deficiencies in due process. But as historian Michelle Chase has argued, the trials and subsequent executions solidified revolutionary political authority for most Cubans, positioning the new government as exercising a legitimate monopoly of force while also building a consensus view of what had transpired under the Batista regime. So confident were revolutionary authorities in their actions that instead of seeking to hide these events from posterity, they invited members of the U.S. press to cover the trials in what was dubbed "Operation Truth." At the same time, testimonies broadcast during the trials helped frame and revise historical knowledge of the Batista period itself.

In contrast to the ousted government's pretensions of having been a promoter of stability and development, the trials allowed relatives of the secret police's victims to confront incarcerated repressors—at least those who had not escaped to Miami—with powerful accounts of repression. Infused with a sense of moral outrage, such exchanges helped expose recent events that prior censorship, or simple convenience, might otherwise have conspired to cover up.[20] "Never in a modern country," argued Sergio Carbó from *Prensa Libre*, "—[though] perhaps only in the pogroms of Poland during the Nazi invasion, or in martyred Hungary, during that mass extermination ordered by Khrushchev from Moscow—has there ever been murder in such a gigantic proportion, has there been so much torture, has human dignity been violated so much as during the dreadful years of the March [i.e., Batista] regime."[21] Even through the Cold War-inflected, anti-Moscow lens of Cuba's centrists—and we will see that

Carbó fit squarely in this camp—the trials of Batista henchmen were historically justified, and in arguably hyperbolic terms.

In a related vein, honoring the victims, especially those gunned down in iconic moments of insurgent resistance, became important to identifying a standardized roster of martyrs from what had been a fractious anti-Batista fight. On February 9, Rebel Army leader Fidel Castro (he would not assume the title of prime minister for another week) joined interim president Manuel Urrutia Lleó in presiding over a retrospective burial in Havana of the victims of the fabled *Granma* yacht landing. After arriving from Mexico by boat on Cuba's southeastern coast on December 2, 1956, the 26th of July Movement had lost several dozen men in an initial series of skirmishes en route to starting a guerrilla war. Their corpses now stood on public view at Havana's Capitol building for all citizens to visit and mourn.[22] Four weeks later, officials and Catholic religious authorities organized even larger public rallies both in Havana and the city of Matanzas to honor martyrs of the Directorio Revolucionario (Revolutionary Directorate). Led by student leader José Antonio Echeverría, born in nearby Cárdenas, the Revolutionary Directorate was without a doubt the second-most important and powerful anti-Batista organization after Castro's 26th of July Movement. Here, however, the memory politics were more complex. Famously, Echeverría and twenty-four comrades died during a failed March 13, 1957, raid on Havana's Presidential Palace and a nearby radio station—a brazen attempt to assassinate Batista in his office and then broadcast the news live on air. Yet leaders of Echeverría's urban-based organization and Fidel Castro's 26th of July Movement were hardly on the same page at the time. Both organizations had signed a commitment to collaborate in 1956, but they remained autonomous competitors wary of one another. Now, honoring the second anniversary of the palace attack two months after Batista's ouster, Fidel and his brother Raúl Castro—a leading figure in the 26th of July Movement in his own right and already on his way to becoming the government's minister in charge of defense—put aside their prior view that the Revolutionary Directorate's assault had represented a premature attempted coup by a rival group.[23]

Spectacles of historic righteousness and unity also employed wide-angle allegories. In mid-1959, members of the 26th of July Movement linked to its official newspaper *Revolución* began organizing a mass rally to be held on July 26, the anniversary of Fidel Castro's 1953 attack on the Moncada Barracks. Although Castro's first effort to take power from Batista had dramatically failed, with the attackers imprisoned, they later went into exile in Mexico, where they shaped the eventually successful strategy of the 26th of July Movement. In honor, then, of both the event and the subsequent movement to which it gave birth, planners invited 500,000 rural farmers to the capital and launched a citywide campaign to convince members of the middle and upper classes to take them into their homes. Coming on the heels of the revolutionary government's May announcement of its first agrarian reform law—a massive program to redistribute land from large landowners to smaller famers in private title—the event and its epic imagery suggested that the Revolution was bringing the backward countryside out of its underdeveloped past toward a modern future. Poor farmers were filmed enjoying urban creature comforts for the first time. In the culminating act of national communion, visiting peasants joined more than 1 million citizens in Havana's massive, aesthetically "fascist" (according to early revolutionary critics) Civic Plaza, a Batista-era creation, propelling its informal and later official transformation into Revolution Square.[24] Straw hats given to the visitors and a photogenic delegation of 2,000 arriving from the province of Las Villas on horseback, led by 26th of July Movement commander Camilo Cienfuegos, evoked the appearance of Cuba's nineteenth-century independence army.[25]

Similar references to Cuba's longer history of political struggle were constant in early revolutionary political life, with the new government's leaders positioning themselves as the inheritors of multiple generations of nationalist tradition and memory. On December 7, 1959, to cite one of many examples, Raúl Castro presided over a public ceremony honoring the death of Cuban independence hero Antonio Maceo in 1896. "In the revolutionary laws that we have approved," the younger Castro declared, "beats Antonio Maceo's heart."[26] Four days later, the press reported plans for Fidel Castro to inter the remains of anti-imperialist activist Antonio Guiteras, founder of the radical, anti-Batista organization Joven Cuba (Young Cuba) in the 1930s, in a ceremonial obelisk. After stealing his bones for protection from their original resting place twenty-two years before, a former Guiteras supporter now entrusted revolutionary officials to honor the memory of the activist slain by the forces of Fulgencio Batista's first regime in 1935.[27] In June 1960, surviving veterans of the 1930s-era Directorio Estudiantil Universitario (University Student Directorate)—one of the organizations that had propelled Guiteras to a brief position of influence in the radical 1933 "Government of 100 Days"—performed a similar act of historical communion by honoring Fidel with a formal luncheon. Handed the flag that had once covered the coffin of Rafael Trejo, a student martyr of the anti-Machado struggle two decades prior, Fidel struck a note of humility: "The generations have united." In truth, an earlier, failed cohort had passed the torch.[28]

How to incorporate not only previous legacies of struggle but also old commemorative markers was not always so clear. Take May 20, for instance, the date in 1902 when the U.S. military occupation of Cuba following the "Spanish-American" War finally ended and the island emerged as a republic on its own, albeit under the shadow of U.S. power and oversight, following the terms of the Platt Amendment. In 1959, and even into 1960, Cubans still widely marked the date as the island's independence day, as they had previously, and the holiday would officially remain on the books until 1963.²⁹ Yet the sense that the Revolution was intended to not only overthrow Batista but also to accomplish what all prior governments had not—meaning in part establishing a truly equitable relationship with the United States—colored celebrations with a more ambiguous meaning. This alternative reading of May 20 as a day of ambiguity, if not infamy, was long a hallmark of the Cuban Left. But now, that idea worked its way into the mainstream. If in 1959 *Bohemia* magazine compared the jubilation that had greeted the Revolution on May 1 with celebrations that had greeted Cuban independence fifty-eight years before (in spite of the geopolitical context at the time), by the following year the same publication was emphasizing the "disillusion and bitterness" that purportedly marked celebrations on the original date.³⁰ "On this May 20," the magazine concluded by 1960, "Cuba is truly free," unlike the way it used to be.³¹

This construction of Cuban history as teleology, and of the Revolution's victory as that teleology's climax—indeed, as a new Cuban independence entirely—was found not only in government speeches, the shifting meanings of national holidays, or the political lives of dead bodies (to borrow anthropologist Katherine Verdery's phrase).³² It was everywhere in popular and capitalist business culture too. In the audiovisual realm, Cuba would soon become known for its state film institute, the Instituto Cubano del Arte e Industria Cinematográficos (Cuban Institute for Cinematographic Art and Industry, ICAIC), founded in March 1959 to promote a national, and presumably nationalist, film industry. But long before that government body completed its first documentaries on major revolutionary events, let alone took over nearly all filmmaking and distribution on the island, private newsreel companies took the lead in scripting Fidel Castro's guerrilla insurgency as an adventure story or docudrama that was worthy of remembering.³³ Nor did the first fictional film to deal with the history of the Revolution receive direct sponsorship from the new government. It was instead the work of a Cuban crew that had previously worked for a U.S. subsidiary, RKO of Cuba, which had recently been appointed a government *interventor* (or comptroller) when its North American directors left the country. That *interventor* proceeded to found a private Cuban cooperative under the same name in the original company's place. By the time ICAIC released its first feature films in late 1960 — including *Historias de la Revolución* (*Histories of the Revolution*), a melodramatic three-part epic set during the anti-Batista insurrection — Cooperativa RKO de Cuba's *La vida comienza ahora* (*Life Begins Now*), filmed during 1959, had already linked the ultimate consecration of its protagonists' romance to the larger hope ushered in by revolutionary victory. "Never has the culmination of a great love coincided so much with the liberation of a people," one campy advertisement professed.[34] Meanwhile, in print media, private initiatives like the *Album de la Revolución Cubana* took the lead in narrating the revolutionary victory as recent Cuban history. Che Guevara's *Pasajes de la guerra revolucionaria* (*Reminiscences of the Revolutionary War*), the dominant and most widely read and reprinted testimonial account of the Sierra Maestra insurrection in later years, would not be published in book form until 1964.[35]

Of course, reliving or narrating the revolutionary epic was one thing. Present actions were another. Nothing solidified early confidence that the nation had reached a historical crossroads like the rapid pace of revolutionary reforms, reported frenetically in the press and summarized as often as nightly by Fidel Castro during lengthy appearances on television.[36] Within months of taking power, revolutionary authorities had lowered city rents, declared an end to racially segregated beaches and other private spaces, and begun confiscating the "ill-gotten goods" of Batista-era businessmen, landowners, and bureaucrats allegedly on the take. When officials announced their widely anticipated, though still conceptually capitalist, agrarian reform law in May 1959, U.S. businesses and landowners complained to the State Department about intrusions on their interests. But Cuban citizens were thrilled to see images on TV and in the press of small farmers and peasants who began receiving formal title to small plots of previously fallow and/or commercially owned land. As a result, many — from the maids of a former Cuban president to domestic sugar growers — donated to a *Bohemia* magazine campaign to raise funds for the cause, if in the latter case only to try to sway the results of the reform in their favor.[37] Equally impressive, officials at the newly created Instituto Nacional de Ahorro y Viviendas (National Savings and Housing Institute) began channeling the resources of the former national lottery, infamous for its corruption, into programs of slum clearance and public housing.[38]

Officials were so busy building such policy "monuments" to the future that it is little wonder they at first created relatively few actual monuments to the revolutionary dead. (Those would mostly come after 1960 — though in 1959 some commemorative plaques dedicated to martyrs went up at the sites where they had been killed.)[39] But what common citizens and the government did do right away was rebaptize memory sites of Batista-era and wider pre-1959 infamy into symbols of the past left behind. Famously, activists in Havana toppled statues to some of Cuba's earliest presidents on Presidents Avenue in the Vedado district in early 1959. In a more systematic way, later that year authorities began transforming Batista's military and police facilities one-by-one into schools, echoing, ironically, what U.S. occupation authorities had done to Spanish military barracks between 1898 and 1902.[40] From Camp Columbia in Havana, the military headquarters of the ousted leader's 1952 coup, to the infamous 5th Station, a torture chamber for Batista's secret police, the conversion of former *calabozos* (dungeons) into *ciudades escolares* ("school cities") presaged broader efforts to resignify inherited public space.[41] Never ones to miss the opportunity to draw a historic parallel, officials at the revolutionary-era Ministry of Education in 1960 scheduled the inauguration of the most important new complex at Santiago de Cuba's Moncada Barracks—the site of Fidel Castro's ill-fated armed assault on July 26, 1953—on January 28, José Martí's birthday.[42] "In July as in January ...," the advertisement read, invoking the immediately recognizable and now seemingly fated second line of the independence hero's most famous poem, "Cultivo una rosa blanca" ("I have a white rose to tend"). "As a promise of our destiny, the Moncada Barracks were attacked," the text continued. "In fulfillment of that ideal, they now become a school."[43]

Insurgent Baggage

Yet, despite the impression of unified purpose these and countless other displays conveyed, within and without Fidel Castro's closest circles memory conflicts already brewed. Differences in policy direction and economic diagnosis were one source of tension. But such disagreements were also closely linked to arguments over recent history. All concurred that the Revolution aimed to wipe away a national past of opprobrium, but not all agreed on how deep that opprobrium reached or who had earned the historical authority to shape the appropriate response. Thus, across 1959 and into 1960, hope that the "past will not return," to quote one prorevolutionary journalist, was belied by just how intensely contending forces dredged up historical ghosts.[44]

A certain amount of jockeying for bona fides was to be expected, particularly among sectors of the Cuban public that had opposed the Batista regime but remained outside of the triumphant 26th of July Movement. Until the final months of the insurrection, Fidel Castro's organization had remained remarkably nimble, slowly winning a public relations and guerrilla war while comprised of 200 to 300 rural insurgents, a core of 3,000 to 6,000 hardcore underground urban rebels, and a wider "civic resistance" network drawn primarily from the professional, middle, and student classes. By late 1959, the Rebel Army swelled, but only to perhaps 3,000.[45] Euphoric crowds greeting the rebels' triumphant march to Havana in January 1959 demonstrated that Fidel Castro had emerged as the Revolution's unquestionable commander in chief. Yet, on an island of 6 *million*, the 26th of July Movement's explicit support among a traditionally well-organized urban and rural labor movement had proved relatively weak, even as casual opposition to Batista had become mainstream.[46]

As a result, secondary armed anti-Batista groups, scattered throughout the country, emerged from the fog of war itching to show they had skin in the game. Older political movements, parties, and organizations with roots before Batista's 1952 coup also tried to stake their claims on the revolutionary future to be. The degree to which the 26th of July Movement's own Rebel Army had taken on thousands of bandwagon followers in the final weeks of Batista's regime signaled that the contest for political and historical positions was not complete. Meanwhile, some members of the 26th of July Movement itself watched as early accounts of the Revolution's rise to power (like that found in the 1959 *Album de la Revolución Cubana*) privileged the role of guerrilla fighters over the clandestine, radical, but generally anticommunist urban underground without whose support and supply lines the guerrillas would not have survived.[47]

The stage was set, therefore, for intense and multifaceted retrospective arguments, as much as all invested hope in the Revolution's promise to turn Cuba's historical tides. And one major venue for these arguments was the Cuban press, made up of a highly developed, diverse range of national papers (some printed twice a day) as well as regional equivalents and widely circulated national magazines (like the previously mentioned *Bohemia*). From the dawn of 1959, virtually every press outlet published across the island—some throwing off the mantle of off-and-on censorship from the Batista years, others new publications serving as official voices of no-longer-clandestine revolutionary movements—seemed to speak for a particular point of view, economic program, organization, or faction thereof. Editorial positions reflected detailed disputes over who did what for the Revolution, when, and why, as well as the nature or degree of the island's economic and social injustices that needed remedying. All publications came out in favor of Fidel Castro's new government. But each proffered varyingly well-argued visions of his insurrection's "true" intent, or of the historical precedents, memories, and grievances that mattered most to defining the new project's political and economic shape. "We too fought for the Revolution!" seemed to be everyone's unofficial motto, as a range of actors moved to assert their legitimacy in a new political landscape.

The little-known paper *La Calle* represents an interesting, if unfamiliar case considering its origins as a vehicle for leftovers from the Partido Ortodoxo in the mid-1950s. As glossed in the introduction, the Partido Ortodoxo emerged in 1947 as a splinter faction of the then-ruling Partido Auténtico, decrying the latter's descent into machine politics and corruption. Led by firebrand senator Eduardo Chibás until his untimely death in 1951, *la ortodoxia* promoted intense nationalism, economic and political independence from the U.S. sphere, but also anticommunism based on a populist vision of shared progress between state planners, domestic capital, and labor. In no small way, the party's platform and direct, media-savvy style of public engagement influenced the early messaging of the 26th of July Movement. Recall that Fidel Castro was a member and had launched a candidacy for Congress in 1952 from within the party's ranks.[48] After Batista's coup, however, Castro went his own way and the Ortodoxos entered a period of disarray. Started in 1953 by party cofounder Luis Orlando Rodríguez in a bid to continue the Ortodoxo legacy, *La Calle* offered strident denunciations of Batista's regime on the shoals of the political chaos resulting from his return to power. In 1955, the front page featured articles written by Fidel Castro himself, fresh off of his release from jail after the Moncada Barracks attack two years earlier.[49] Soon thereafter, Batista's political police raided the paper's offices and shut it down.

Like other censored media, then, *La Calle* reopened in July 1959 claiming adherence to Fidel Castro's leadership and seeking to revive its and, indirectly, the Ortodoxos's political fortunes. Since the paper's closure, Luis Orlando Rodríguez had joined the 26th of July Movement, finishing the anti-Batista struggle with the rank of *comandante* as codirector of the guerrillas' underground radio station Radio Rebelde. In this he was like another Ortodoxo notable—Raúl Chibás, Eduardo's brother—who had also become deeply involved in 26th of July affairs, cosigning a major manifesto with Castro in 1957 and mobilizing resources on the movement's behalf.[50] Still, as neither the official organ of a revived Partido Ortodoxo, nor the representative of one of the other major anti-Batista armed groups, the new *La Calle* rested its primary claim to credentials on constantly referencing its connections to Fidel Castro's early days. "Fidel Castro wrote his articles at our offices!," proclaimed the paper's first post-1959 cover, accompanied by a large photograph of the then beardless Castro working at a typewriter.[51] The repeated insistence to have been a privileged witness to Castro's beginnings suggests that editors were struggling to craft an identity for the publication in step with revolutionary times.

The struggle for historical legitimacy extended to the paper's ideological platform. In August 1959, editors ran long paeans to Ortodoxo leader

Eduardo Chibás on the anniversary of his death, arguing that "he did not want a Soviet socialism but ... a transplant of the New Deal that Roosevelt applied in the United States."[52] A photograph showing Fidel Castro among others guarding Chibás's funeral casket suggested that the Revolution's leader must have felt the same. Castro had frequently invoked Chibás at various points in his own insurgent struggle, even visiting his grave shortly after Batista's flight, in yet another gesture of generational harmony. Yet although the victorious Rebel Army honored Chibás's memory that same month with a parade down a prominent avenue in Havana, by the following year the salience of Chibás's example and his "Rooseveltian" economic vision began to fade as the revolution radicalized.[53]

The better circulated national daily *Prensa Libre*, progressive in orientation but ideologically moderate, similarly asserted its right to a voice in 1959 based on a purported record of Batista opposition. Founded in 1941 by the journalist and former anti-Machado activist Sergio Carbó, the paper had since distinguished itself for its liberal anticommunism in line with centrist hemispheric political alignments and reformist economic programs in the early Cold War. After Batista's 1952 coup, *Prensa Libre* was also among the few publications to stay open without receiving government subsidies, which normally came with unstated pressure to report "responsibly" on national affairs. As a result, from day one of 1959, Carbó and company insisted that they not only had earned a reputation for independence but also had done their part for the cause. In the same breath as praising Fidel Castro's insurgent leadership, editors claimed that the paper had "repudiated and combatted" the fallen Batista regime "from its beginnings, facing all of the dangers and accepting all types of persecutions."[54] Frequent reprints of articles from the 1950s, when the paper's columnists had dared to test the censors' limits, attempted to demonstrate their lack of complicity in the ousted government's crimes.[55]

For young people in insurgent organizations who had put their necks more directly on the line, such armchair postures of support appeared presumptuous if not downright cynical. Carbó may have played a role in the anti-Machado struggle of his youth, they acknowledged. But by 1959 he was also a man of the liberal establishment. His paper's quick insistence in February that the "radical" revolution did not require an "ideological or class transformation" also revealed a conservative streak that, to some, dangerously overlooked the depth of dysfunction in Cuba's pre-1959 political and social order.[56] As surviving members of the influential Revolutionary Directorate argued in disbelief in March 1959, "[As] the new generation consolidated with the eloquence of its acts its hierarchy in the historic process, there were those who ... repeated with hope ... [the idea that] the Cuban insurrection was only pursuing ... the conquest of simple liberty and the restoration of the Constitution."[57] Carbó did not respond to this rebuke, or its implicit insistence on the Revolution's deep social, not only political, roots.

All the same, even members of the Revolutionary Directorate, an anti-Batista group with unimpeachable revolutionary credentials, faced difficulties asserting their historical authority in the new order where Castro and his 26th of July Movement were king. Having distinguished itself for its commitment to direct action and targeted political violence against high-ranking officials of Batista's regime, José Antonio Echeverría's organization had earned a place among the vanguard pushing for radical reform. Back in 1955, Echeverría had called for a "profound transformation of [Cuba's] political, social, and economic reality" to "solve the problem of the unemployed, the landless peasants, the exploited workers, and the youth."[58] Nonetheless, after the failure of their assassination plot against Batista in 1957 and the deaths of so many members, the organization lost considerable momentum. Remaining members founded their own small guerrilla front in the central Escambray Mountains in 1958, but in December of that year, Fidel Castro warned Che Guevara against sharing the 26th of July Movement's authority too easily with the organization as his guerrilla column marched west, calling them "a little group whose intentions and ambitions we know all too well, and that in the future will be the cause of problems and difficulties."[59] Then, in early January 1959, the Revolutionary Directorate's leaders accepted Fidel Castro's supreme authority by famously acceding to his public demand that they turn over their arms.[60] The organization's own newspaper *Combate* thus emerged in the early days of 1959 with something of a weak hand. Reading the paper during its first months, one senses a concerted attempt by an insurgent group relatively underrepresented in early high-level government posts to assert its continued relevance by invoking the memory of its martyrs. The paper's promoters also claimed to be the most qualified descendants of the student movements historically at the center of Cuba's struggles for political and social change.[61]

Without newspapers or widely known political and economic programs of their own, other anti-Batista organizations awaited even more marginal fates. The II Frente del Escambray (Second Front of the Escambray) had begun as a splinter group from the Revolutionary Directorate's Escambray-based insurgency in 1958, becoming well known enough to receive significant praise during the Revolution's initial months. In February 1959, the normally humor-focused *Actualidad Criolla* featured a long profile of Second Front founder Eloy Gutiérrez Menoyo, the son of proudly republican Spanish parents, with one brother who had died fighting Francisco Franco years before and another who had perished in the Revolutionary Directorate's failed attack on the Presidential Palace in 1957.[62] Likewise, the widely popular *Album de la Revolución Cubana* gave Menoyo a spot of distinction within its pantheon of revolutionary idols. In August 1959, several of the group's leaders—including U.S. citizen William Morgan—played leading roles as government double agents, infiltrating and foiling a plot by Batista regime elements to take back power.[63] But despite a brief turn as political stars in front of the cameras after the operation was a success, Second Front members had neither the numbers, history, nor media vehicle to stake a central claim to emerging revolutionary mythology. Excluded from representation in the first revolutionary cabinet and significant government positions, the organization soon found itself grasping for political straws.

And yet, among organizations claiming adherence to the new revolutionary project, Cuba's historic communist party—the Partido Socialista Popular (Popular Socialist Party, PSP), so named since 1944—arguably faced the greatest image problem of all. Knee-jerk anticommunism among a portion of the Cuban public was part of the issue. But the party's difficulties had as much to do with reputation and historical memory as any form of abstract skittishness about its militants' ideological leanings. Not just moderates, but veterans of the 26th of July Movement's Havana-based urban underground and affiliated journalists strongly objected to the historic party's claim to revolutionary legitimacy, despite Cuban communists' long history of and achievements in labor militancy, both in urban and rural settings. The conflict would set the stage for the most consequential retrospective dispute of the Revolution's first months.

PSP leaders confronted two major obstacles: one more deeply historical, the other of recent vintage. As noted in the introduction, an earlier iteration of Cuba's communist party had established a pact with Fulgencio Batista during the strongman's initial, more populist stretch in power during the late 1930s and early 1940s. Following Machado's fall in 1933, Batista's "Sergeants' Revolt" had first helped put in power the radical "Government of 100 Days." When the military man of humble origins thereafter usurped political authority for himself with tacit encouragement from the U.S. government, communist-affiliated labor unions, especially in the sugar sector, suffered some of the repression that followed. Yet in a stroke of realpolitik combined with popular-front pragmatism, the communists and Batista began forging an alliance of mutual convenience in 1938, one that persisted after Batista was formally elected to office under a new constitution drafted in 1940. Thereafter, two members of the communist party hierarchy—Juan Marinello and Carlos Rafael Rodríguez, who both later occupied positions of prominence in the revolutionary government after 1959—served as ministers without portfolio in Batista's cabinet. Batista gained progressive credibility and an important connection to labor support in his attempt to pivot to the antifascist center. The Cuban communist leadership, meanwhile, saw itself as acting in accordance with the popular-front policies of the Seventh Congress of the Comintern, the Soviet-backed organization of communist and other revolutionary political parties from around the world.[64] Whatever the political logic of this partnership at the time, members of noncommunist anti-Batista sectors in the 1950s remembered PSP members as having made a deal with the devil. Over the long haul, they alleged, Cuba's communists had facilitated Batista's longevity by giving him their support at a critical time.

The PSP had also committed more recent infractions as far as important, particularly Havana-based, sectors of the 26th of July Movement were concerned. Namely, its leaders had been too slow to embrace the strategy of armed resistance to Batista after his 1952 coup. To be sure, the Batista of the 1950s and the Cold War proved not to be the Batista of the popular front. Whereas in the late 1930s he had legalized the communist party's existence for the first time since its founding in 1925, in July 1953 Cuba's strongman used the pretext of Fidel Castro's attack on the Moncada Barracks to force the party underground. (He alleged, falsely, that the attack was communist-inspired.) Still, among other anti-Batista factions, some felt—fairly or unfairly—that Batista-era authorities continued to treat PSP members with kid gloves.[65] Even more damning, the PSP condemned the Moncada action of 1953 as "putschist" and "bourgeois" in a communiqué published in New York's *Daily Worker*, the newspaper of the U.S. Communist Party.[66] After that point, the PSP's official position on guerrilla warfare wobbled between brief acceptance and renewed rejection. Certain members and future collaborators of the 26th of July Movement—most famously, Raúl Castro, Oswaldo Dorticós, and Che Guevara—did have ties to the PSP, Marxist ideology, or even Soviet interlocutors going back to the early 1950s. Some have argued that PSP members and even Soviet agents cultivated and maintained these relationships with the goal of influencing the 26th of July Movement all along.[67] Yet, although the party agreed to lend support to the 26th of July Movement's eventually failed plan for a nationwide general strike in April 1958, not until the summer of that year (just five months before Batista fell) did PSP leader Carlos Rafael Rodríguez join Castro in the Sierra Maestra to secure a permanent, formal alliance.[68] Regardless of whatever else was happening behind the scenes, this was the knowledge many 26th of July Movement and other anti-Batista affiliates reacted to at the start of the Castro era.

For these reasons, notable, if not all, members of the 26th of July Movement and other revolutionary groups saw the PSP as little better than an old guard political organization wed for too long to vague calls for mass struggle, or even a peaceful electoral outcome to Batista's tyranny. Given their history, others simply doubted—perhaps to an unfair degree—the sincerity of the PSP's anti-Batista rhetoric and claims. It is true that, at the working level, urban 26th of July Movement and PSP rank and file, especially in Cuba's eastern Oriente province, did forge links even when their organization's leaderships balked.[69] Yet for members of the 26th of July Movement's national urban directorate in particular, the communists as a whole, and especially their leaders, appeared to be latecomers, hangers-on not deserving of a central voice in shaping what the Revolution in power was to become.

Legitimacy Disputes and Historical Pretenders

With these kinds of historical clouds clouding the otherwise clear post-Batista skies, the Cuban press exploded in 1959 and 1960 into factional debates about historical responsibility, guilt, the depth of the prerevolutionary period's problems, and who or what was best to address them. All the while, popular euphoria, and Fidel Castro's ever-present voice in the public square, continued to suggest that the country had reached a moment of historic transcendence. As dyed-in-the-wool communists and anticommunists traded shots, accusing each other of being revolutionary phonies, noncommunist veterans of the 26th of July Movement and Echeverría's Revolutionary Directorate also attempted to fend off perceived centrist usurpers of the Revolution's "true" leadership and more ambitious economic goals. "Be careful, fellow citizens," wrote Sergio Carbó as early as January 11, 1959, "not to throw it all to waste with petty group quarrels. Victory has cost too much blood to see the marvelous harmony of the new Cuba destroyed by the lust of factions or the overflowing of arrogance."[70] How prescient those words would become, with Carbó himself as guilty as most.

For all of the reasons already outlined, the PSP—having reopened its own newspaper in the early days of 1959—became the target of earliest attack. Writing in *Bohemia* magazine in February 1959, Catholic intellectual Andrés Valdespino insisted that the communists' theories were irrelevant to the democratic revolution that Fidel Castro himself initially described as being "as green as the palms" (i.e., not "red").[71] "It is true that in Cuba we have to abolish the unproductive large estates, end the abuses of exploitative capitalism, guarantee the farmer decent living conditions, suppress the unfair privileges granted to foreign and domestic monopolies," wrote Valdespino, "but for all of that ... the Revolution does not need communism."⁷² Yet if this argument was more ideological than historical, the PSP's Carlos Rafael Rodríguez responded by arrogating to his party a considerable amount of retrospective credit for how far Cuba had come toward even liberal ideological goals. Describing the PSP's objectives as *not* the transformation of the Revolution into a socialist project but the protection of the "democratic," "liberatory" political process at hand, Rodríguez insisted that the founding of the Partido Comunista de Cuba (Communist Party of Cuba) in 1925—the modern PSP's origin point— "introduced the true struggle for the economic defense of the proletariat" into Cuban political life. "Without arrogance," he continued, "we communists can claim the merit of having opened the path for all of those ideas that now, under the impulse of the Revolution headed by Fidel Castro and his comrades, have already stopped scaring [the public], even though until just yesterday there were few who dared to support them outside of our ranks."⁷³

Writing in *Prensa Libre*, columnist Humberto Medrano could not have disagreed more. Just a few weeks prior to Rodríguez's column, PSP leader Severo Aguirre had headed the Cuban delegation to the Twenty-First Congress of the Communist Party of the Soviet Union in Moscow. There, Medrano alleged, Aguirre gave a speech claiming that Cuba's "Popular Socialist Party was really the group that took up the fight to unify all revolutionary forces." "Those who still have use of their memory," replied Medrano sarcastically, "thought they remembered the communists supporting Batista's candidacy in 1940, and that of his preferred [successor] candidate in 1944." He continued, "How wrong they were—right Severo?— those Cubans in exile [from Batista in the 1950s] who carried through North American streets signs reading 'Under Batista Cuba Is the Hungary of the America.'" This curious reference to the 1956 anti-Soviet uprising in Budapest, common among some expatriate anti-Batista activists in the 1950s, equated the struggle against the Cuban strongman with a struggle against a *communist* regime. The parallels were obviously imperfect and inaccurate given Batista's support from Washington. But the deployment of the comparison suggests that suspicions of a secret, historically rooted cabal between Batista and the PSP persisted long after the former's crackdown on communist "subversion" began internally in 1953.⁷⁴

Packing an even bigger punch were criticisms emanating from the gravitational center of the Revolution's incipient coalition. With a name like *Revolución*, the official organ of the 26th of July Movement could easily be mistaken for the voice of the revolutionary government itself. It was thus noteworthy when, starting in the spring of 1959, the columns of urban underground veteran Euclides Vázquez Candela began taking the PSP to task in a particularly direct way. In response to allegations from the right that the communist party was unduly influencing *his* movement's trajectory, the noted 26th of July Movement member contended that the communists, in fact, had only sent its militants to the battlefront "at the end of the war, upon seeing the growth and even inevitable triumph of our insurrection."[75] Then, in September, Vázquez Candela took to television and again the pages of *Revolución* to emphasize repeatedly that the PSP (or its predecessor in name) had once collaborated with Batista in power, while the 26th of July Movement had not.[76] Importantly, such accusations came on the heels of contested union elections in which 26th of July Movement and PSP labor leaders were active rivals for control. The debate thus had more than rhetorical consequences. What began as a legacy dispute between two organizations had started to ricochet across incipient institutions of revolutionary political and economic life.[77]

The PSP countered aggressively by defending its record, both over the long term and during the anti-Batista fight. Rebutting suggestions that the party had been on the margins of the recent struggle, editors at *Noticias de Hoy*, the revived PSP daily, published recurring features detailing the names, faces, and stories of its own martyrs of Batista-era repression.[78] Faced with allegations that the PSP had hopped late onto the insurrectionary bandwagon, party heads insisted they had acted in good faith. "Now is not the time to revive sterile debates about strategy and revolutionary tactics," Carlos Rafael Rodríguez wrote evasively. "But even if [we] had not become incorporated in this or that time frame to the civil war being fought in the Sierra, the Popular Socialist Party could not be considered 'absent' from the larger struggle of the Cuban people against the tyranny." Noting that the party did order some of its men to quietly join Fidel Castro's Rebel Army in February 1958, he also listed PSP accomplishments in denouncing Batista's dictatorship and organizing sporadic labor resistance.[79] Besides, Rodríguez claimed, whether early or late to the fight, all rebels shed equal tears for the deaths of comrades regardless of ideological pedigree.[80] Less influential groups like the Second Front of the Escambray, later sidelined, might have liked to cash in on a similar spirit of magnanimity.[81]

PSP leaders also took on their prior affiliation with Batista in the late 1930s and early 1940s. "It is true," wrote noted communist intellectual Juan Marinello in January 1960, "that I was Minister without Portfolio for a time under the constitutional presidency of Batista. I was [minister] when Batista was the head-of-state elected by vote ... and when—in the political picture of the moment—his positions were in a progressive direction." He continued, "If one does not forget that this tendency came together in the

Constitution of 1940—a democratic instrument of much positive influence— ... one will realize that, upon occupying the referenced position by the decision of my party, I fulfilled a duty of the revolutionary citizen."[82] But *Noticias de Hoy* also argued that if anyone had responsibility for *pushing* the communists into Batista's camp at the time, it was the group that would eventually become the corrupt Auténticos. Their early anticommunism, editors contended, had disrupted the unity of a prior "Popular Revolutionary Bloc."[83] *Prensa Libre*'s Sergio Carbó, they further accused, was hardly one to talk: in a brief period of authority in 1933 under an ephemeral government known as the "Pentarchy," *he* had promoted Batista from the rank of sergeant to colonel, thus abetting his political rise.[84] After Batista's 1952 coup, the PSP alleged, the newspaperman had even defended the positive potential of the action at first, comparing this newest "revolution" to the initially hopeful "Sergeants' Revolt" following Machado's fall. To prove the point, *Noticias de Hoy* reprinted on its cover a *Prensa Libre* piece from 1952 in which Carbó seemed to welcome Batista back to the presidency.[85]

Consistently, then, PSP members not only fought accusations of hypocrisy with their own similar charges; they also defended their activities in the 1930s and 1940s as having born progressive fruit—namely, the Constitution of 1940 and its social guarantees.[86] All the same, for a party simultaneously, and even in the same newspaper issue, fending off calls in more conservative media for immediate elections by pointing out the prior constitutional order's limitations, one might have expected such positions to paint them into a historical memory corner.[87] If the PSP avoided this fate, it was because Cuba's communists were not the lone organization or media outlet whose past contradictions came under fire. *Diario de la Marina*, for example, the island's oldest and most conservative newspaper, began urging new revolutionary authorities to return the island to a path of electoral normalcy from the first days of 1959. Yet as a publication dating to the nineteenth century that had once defended Spanish colonialism, and whose owners had accepted subsidies from Batista, the paper's talk of "democracy" and the Constitution of 1940 seemed like the pot calling the kettle black.[88]

Retrospective fireworks only continued, touching diverse targets. In October 1959, the Revolutionary Directorate's *Combate* tartly reminded *La Calle*'s founder, Luis Orlando Rodríguez, that he at first had denounced Fidel Castro's Moncada attack as fruitless before welcoming him to publish in his pages.[89] A month later, *Revolución* editorialized against Sergio Carbó's "eternal blackmail" and exaggerated claims of revolutionary credentials based on his minor role in Gerardo Machado's ouster two decades before.⁹⁰ In Carbó's defense, *Prensa Libre* published an endorsement from the Frente Cívico de Mujeres Martianas (José Martí Women's Civic Front), one of the principal all-female anti-Batista protest groups of the 1950s. The paper also printed a letter of support from Fidel Castro's older brother Ramón. (Carbó, Ramón relayed, had once paid to get Raúl Castro out of jail.)⁹¹ Nonetheless, *Revolución* countered by alleging that Carbó had taken luxurious vacations in Mexico as fellow Cubans shed their blood, while *Noticias de Hoy* went on to accuse Carbó of having links to a jailed Batista official.⁹² When a moderate ally of *Prensa Libre*, José Ignacio Rasco, attempted to found a center-left Partido Demócrata Cristiano (Christian Democrat Party) in early 1960, the PSP went on the attack. "Where were you in 1953, 54, 55?," Carlos Rafael Rodríguez asked. "What did you do in 1958?; why didn't you found your group at the moment it was necessary to coalesce forces to combat the tyranny?"⁹³ Coming from a political party that many felt had not been at the vanguard of the armed anti-Batista struggle either during many of those years, this accusation was rather cold.

On top of feuds between revolutionary factions, there was occasional agitation that those complicit with the Batista regime itself had succeeded in insinuating themselves into revolutionary ranks. In mid-1959, for example, the PSP launched a campaign to expose surviving union organizers who had once been accomplices of Batista's sham political parties or his loyal labor boss Eusebio Mujal.⁹⁴ In November, a prominent judge, Elio Álvarez López, took to the pages of the press to refute allegations of having received kickbacks and a sinecure from the Batista government after two new officials at the Ministry of the Interior had levied such charges against him.⁹⁵ For others, retribution for past deeds had not gone far enough. In January 1960, Conrado Rodríguez, a labor organizer and member of the by that point marginal Second Front of the Escambray, appeared on television accusing José Santiesteban, a deputy to Che Guevara at the National Bank (where Guevara had recently taken over as director), of being a known Batista collaborator and union crony who stole millions in pesos from a sugar workers retirement fund. Guevara protested, demanding that Rodríguez produce proof.⁹⁶

In the end, no one—except perhaps for Fidel Castro himself, for the moment—appeared safe from dissections of past statements and positions. So constant did these backward-looking potshots become that they themselves provided material for news, covered by the only strictly nonpartisan national paper, *Información*, in a column called "the Opinion of Colleagues."⁹⁷ "The true revolution," Ulises Carbó (Sergio's son) alleged, "the one forged as a tangible reality by those who fought and sacrificed themselves for it, has found in its way a pitiful conga line of last-minute simulators.... Tightrope walkers of deception and deceit, they announce in full voice their weak participation in the heroic process, pretending to show inexistent karats, and tricking the public with their shouting."[98] But if the anti-Batista center accused Cuba's communists of "infiltrating" themselves into a Revolution to which they did not belong, noncommunist radicals also lambasted bourgeois elements on the sidelines for their chameleon-like opportunism and more conservative economic vision. The long-running satire newspaper *Zig-zag*, no fan of the communists or Batista, predicted this latter point with a two-page cartoon titled "Waiting Room at the Ministry" in January 1959 (figure 1.3). It showed dozens of balding men in suits loitering outside a new government minister's office, frantically preparing to angle for new jobs by searching for emblems of revolutionary affiliation. "Where has my beard fallen?," cries one. "I risked my tail everyday listening to [communiqués from] the Sierra on my shortwave radio!," shouts another. In the corner, one freebooter sells armbands with the insignia of various revolutionary movements, the better to feign radical credentials.[99] Historical pretenders, the cartoonist believed, were everywhere Cubans looked.

Anticommunism as Historical Ghost

So where was Fidel Castro in this multisided fray? Throughout early and mid-1959, he largely chose not to get involved. Privately, a process of reconciliation between the leadership of the 26th of July Movement and the PSP was underway—if perhaps as a strategic hedge. In April 1959, Raúl Castro secretly sent longtime PSP leader Lázaro Peña to Moscow to sound out the USSR on the possibility of lending limited military aid.[100] Still, in public, rather than mediating directly in factional retrospective quarrels, Fidel appeared to calculate that he was most often better off not wading into the memory muck, so long as the ultimate leadership of his 26th of July Movement was clear. Major speeches through most of 1959 were full of references to the reactionary power of monopolies, domestic oligarchies, and powerful interests at home and abroad (namely, in the United States). Together, he alleged, such forces would conspire against the Revolution's chances of addressing rural poverty, domestic industrial development, or other consensus goals. Castro did not, however, generally mention the PSP, the Havana-wing of his own 26th of July Movement, or other feuding revolutionary groups.

All the same, Cuba's new leader did periodically abet memory quarrels between them indirectly. For one thing, Castro at times sent mixed signals as to the depth of the economic and political problems in recent Cuban

Figure 1.3. Antonio Rubio, "Waiting Room at a Ministry," *Zig-zag*, January 31, 1959, 12–13.

history that the Revolution purported to confront. On the one hand, highlighting the historical plight of the rural poor had been a hallmark of the 26th of July Movement's programmatic statements ever since Castro's famous "History Will Absolve Me" speech at his trial for the Moncada attack in 1953. Scarcely an appearance went by in 1959 where the Revolution's leader did not describe the thousands of landless peasants previously condemned to unemployment and malnutrition during the sugar harvest "dead time" and that the agrarian reform would rescue from injustice. On the other hand, in a speech at Princeton University after a high-profile goodwill visit to Washington in April 1959, Castro struck a strangely more moderate tone when describing Cuba's economic situation overall in the 1950s. "Our revolution established two or three new things in the world," he told his audience: "First, that a revolution is possible when there is a relatively good economic situation, when the people are not desperate, [there are] some unemployed, some who are hungry, [but] the same things as in other conditions, as in other places."[101] If that was true, maybe those in the anti-Batista coalition questioning the degree to which a radical transformation of *all* aspects of Cuban economic and social life was warranted, and thus claiming historical legitimacy for more centrist political currents, had a point.

Castro also commented occasionally on flare-ups over how the Revolution was handling the fate of former Batista-government affiliates and civil servants. Initially, the Revolution's leader hailed officials' relative equanimity in "limit[ing] ourselves to executing the war criminals and embezzlers" when in principle "he who congratulated Batista is guilty, he who grovelingly worked their tail off for Batista is guilty, he who praised Batista is guilty."[102] "In what place in the world," he noted proudly in April 1959, "upon concluding such a [revolutionary] victory that cost so much blood have more than 50 percent of employees in the public administration under the tyranny been allowed to keep their jobs?"[103] Yet just as some alleged that too many hidden *batistiano* holdovers were still walking the streets, others believed the new government had gone too far in alleging complicity and cleaning house in branches of government like the judiciary.[104] On this score, then, Castro's initial instincts proved right: it was better to not intervene too directly in such scandals. Average Cubans likely cared less about the internal problems of revolutionary administration than broader historical allegories and messaging that channeled the Revolution's transcendent hopes.

Still, if revolutionary government leaders were to get on with the work of building the Revolution's future, something had to give. Allowed to continue, the memory wars of the first months of 1959 between political factions might endlessly rage. Unless they were careful, *Prensa Libre*'s Humberto Medrano had warned perceptively back in February 1959, Cubans would repeat the acrimony that had frustrated the hope following Machado's fall in 1933.[105] Thus, as the memory conflicts described above continued apace—with figures like Medrano hardly heeding his own call—a new drive for unity began to crystallize as 1959 moved into 1960. Crucially, this shift involved not shutting the door on retrospective recriminations completely but slowly supplanting competing claims to revolutionary legitimacy *between* factions with a quest to exorcise a purportedly more ubiquitous Cuban historical ghost. The most dangerous hidden holdover of the prerevolutionary past, leading officials of the revolutionary government began to argue, was not a Batista acolyte donning insurgent clothes or this or that revolutionary pretender but anticommunism itself. Importantly, this evolution was facilitated by the excessively broad terms in which some doubters levied accusations of "communist infiltration" at the government, as well as Cuba's intensifying place in the geopolitics of the Cold War.

The hazard of a generic, overzealous anticommunism was not a new problem to revolutionary authorities and sympathizers. "In the name of anticommunism," declared PSP member Ursinio Rojas on a television talk show in February 1959, responding to the rhetoric of early U.S. and pro-Batista detractors, "hundreds and thousands of the best combatants of the working class were murdered" over Cuba's history.[106] The numbers might have been exaggerated, but the basic claim was right, and many noncommunists agreed. Batista himself had sought to delegitimize any opposition to his government as the work of an international Red conspiracy. Internationally, examples like the 1954 U.S.-backed coup d'état against the elected leftist government of Jacobo Árbenz in Guatemala were also front of mind. Thus, Cubans found it crude when Fidel Castro was repeatedly asked whether he was a communist in forums like *Meet the Press* during his April 1959 goodwill visit to the United States.[107] "What do you call being 'in league with the communists,'" Castro replied to one U.S. journalist during the trip, "if it is not persecuting anyone for their political ideas, not killing because they think differently than I, not throwing people in jail who defend other ideologies?"[108]

It was in this pluralistic spirit that revolutionary government leaders treated the headline-grabbing early defection of chief of the Fuerza Aérea Revolucionaria (Revolutionary Air Force), Pedro Díaz Lanz, in June 1959. Arriving in Miami on a sailboat, the rogue pilot who had become famous for running guns to Fidel Castro's rebels in the Sierra Maestra received a warm welcome from Batista allies and in early July denounced Castro's vaguely "communist" intentions on the U.S. Senate floor. At a time when cross-class support for the Revolution was still at its peak, his actions struck most island observers as treason. To play into this Cold War accusation so early, many Cubans felt, would only revive ideological hysterias that tended to put a brake on change.[109] The timing of his denunciation was also suspicious, coming precisely as U.S. landowners were beginning to be affected by the first nationalizations of their property under Cuba's recently announced agrarian reform. The otherwise moderate anticommunist Sergio Carbó argued that Díaz Lanz's defection had all the markings of a *Soviet* disinformation campaign because it provoked U.S. animosity toward what he still saw as a revolution genuinely committed to democracy.[110]

In the late summer and fall of 1959 further defections helped what we might call Cuban "anti-anticommunism" coalesce into a full-fledged discourse, with clear implications for the kinds of criticisms that were to become off limits, as well as for how Cubans were to understand the past the Revolution was leaving behind. This began when President Manuel Urrutia—a judge by training, who had famously defended the rights of 26th of July Movement activists charged with "antigovernment activities" in a 1957 court case—raised concerns of communist political influence in the government. The same month as Díaz Lanz's appearance in the U.S. Senate, Urrutia publicly accused "the communists" of creating a "second front" against the real Revolution that Cubans needed. Fidel Castro expressed frustration with Urrutia's work as president and dramatically resigned as prime minister. In a lengthy appearance on television to explain his decision, he charged Urrutia with holding up key revolutionary laws, keeping his own salary as high as Batista's had been, and even balking on a measure that would have transferred ongoing revolutionary tribunals from military to civil jurisdiction. (Castro thus once again positioned himself as a moderate on questions of historical retribution.) Fidel also accused Urrutia of not denouncing Díaz Lanz vigorously enough and hatching a similar plan to defect using the "blackmail of communism" as his excuse.[111]

Faced with popular pressure, Urrutia stepped down. When spontaneous demonstrations erupted demanding Fidel's return, Castro masterfully complied during the July 26 gathering in Havana's Civic Plaza of 1 million citizens, including the 500,000 farmers invited to the capital for the occasion, thus turning the rally into a reaffirmation of his legitimacy.[112] As for the veracity of Urrutia's accusation, Castro was clear: the choice between an abstract communism and democracy was false, a historic mentality that the Revolution was determined to erase. "We want to free man from fear, we want to free man from political dogmas.... Without dictatorships of any kind, or terror of any kind, because the [false] problem that they have placed before us is choosing between capital that kills man from hunger and communism that resolves economic problems but suppresses liberties.... We are advancing toward the realization of a Revolution with democratic means, and we understand that if we achieve it, it will go down as a classic revolution all around the world."[113]

The subsequent and better-known resignation of Rebel Army *comandante* Huber Matos three months later further revealed the new state of play. Far from a politician in a suit, Matos was known among landowners in Camagüey province (where he was Rebel Army chief) as a zealous enforcer of the revolutionary government's agrarian reform. In a private letter to Fidel Castro, however, he protested the granting of officer commissions in the Rebel Army to what he felt were undeserving PSP militants. Unlike Urrutia, his decision to step aside was grounded in insurgent memory claims. But though angry at the prominence of those who had only "appeared on the scene on January 1," he kept his resignation private to not be an obstacle to unity or exacerbate the "struggle between groups."[114] Regardless, Castro publicly accused Matos of participating in a vast counterrevolutionary plot, and Matos would go on to spend twenty years in jail.[115] "Let us respond once and for all to the slanderers and the Revolution's detractors so that they finally speak clearly," lambasted Castro in a speech shortly after Matos's arrest. "Their accusations that we are communists exclusively reflect the fact that they do not have the bravery to say that they are against revolutionary laws; and so because they have nothing to say about the revolutionary government ... they grab on to the cooked-up pretext of fear and the ghost that they have been planting for fifty years."[116] Castro overlooked the specificity of Matos's objections to the PSP's past record and credentials, instead falsely alleging that he had labeled the Revolution "communist" as a whole.

Together, such incidents suggested that any criticism of Cuba's communists was no longer an appropriate memory grievance but rather the latest evidence of a historical bias that Cubans needed to leave behind. In these ways, Fidel Castro began to tacitly intervene in prior memory disputes in a way he had initially avoided. When critics denounced the Revolution's leftward direction, the Revolution's leaders now characterized their actions as related less to particular grievances against the PSP's legitimacy than tired Cold War fears. In some cases, they were right, and good faith actors could harbor legitimate worries about providing a pretext for U.S. provocation. In the process, though, *any* criticisms of the PSP's historic bona fides became equated with an anachronistic and now "counterrevolutionary" anticommunism more generally. Put another way, by implicitly denying the relevance of specific factional grievances, and by characterizing anticommunism as the most dangerous historical phantom facing Cuban society, Fidel Castro started to gradually tilt the factional balance within the anti-Batista ranks. He did so, moreover, while still skirting the substance of most other, and particularly PSP opponents,' specific memory claims.

The key was that enough noncommunists, too—including those with misgivings about the PSP's lackluster role in the insurrection—continued to warn against the risks of an antiquated Cuban McCarthyism that would only serve to scuttle the country's much needed deliverance from a past of inequality and injustice. For many in the Cuban public, Matos's accusations, like Díaz Lanz's and Urrutia's before, were suspect given the stated noncommunist ideological goals of the revolutionary government at the time. Writing after the Urrutia and Matos affairs, José Pardo Llada, a nationally famous radio host who had been a key player in the Partido Ortodoxo, deemed anticommunism a "suspicious political weapon," one that in a domestic context only repeated the biases of the Revolution's external enemies. "What do the AP, the UP, *Time, Life, Newsweek*, and all of that defaming scum in the North American press say?," he asked. "That the revolutionary government is communist.... But the accusation ... is not new. What did Batista and the high command of his army say when Fidel Castro fought in Sierra Maestra? That the rebels were all communists."[117] In this way, he suggested, imputations by even well-meaning critics of the PSP's historical credentials were akin to older, illegitimate, and, importantly, Washingtonian political smears.

Not surprisingly, PSP members were happy to concur. As some argued in occasional moments of self-serving democratic clarity, had not a revolution been fought in part to allow all political groups the right to speak?[118] In the face of what they saw as another instance in a long history of red-baiting, PSP members continued to insist on their commitment as coalition partners to a political project that was fundamentally moral, not ideological, and certainly not overtly socialist in nature at the time. Just before Matos's arrest, the party had even agreed to a provisional political program in which it called for the holding of elections to a unicameral legislature, the legalization of "revolutionary" political parties, and the protection of civil guarantees like freedom of speech.[119] "The Revolution triumphed," asserted PSP intellectual Mirta Aguirre several months before, "because in the Sierra Maestra and the Civic Resistance no one asked anyone what they thought, as long as they were willing to risk their lives for the freedom of Cuba. And now, as foreign imperialists and reactionary native magnates want to stop the program of this revolution in its tracks ... there are those who want anticommunist persecution to sprout and flourish again *in plain, splendid Batista-era form.*"[120]

It did not help matters that serious tensions between Cuba and the United States had indeed begun to mount. Miami had already become home to counterrevolutionary plotters linked to the Batista regime. By the fall of 1959, Cuban authorities and anti-Batista moderates alike had begun to wonder aloud why U.S. officials continued allowing them to walk free.[121] More dramatically, Huber Matos's arrest in October coincided with a flyover of Havana undertaken by previous defector Pedro Díaz Lanz. With Lanz accused of firing shots and killing a number of Cubans on the ground, the incident ramped up suspicions of U.S. complicity in counterrevolutionary plots. When Cuba's government welcomed Anastas Mikoyan, first vice chairman of the Soviet Union's Council on Ministers, to Havana four months later and signed a massive trade deal—in the name of diversifying Cuba's commerce, officials said, not ideological affinity—Washington howled.[122]

To criticize "communism," therefore, was to flirt with permitting the past to return—both internally, and with regard to Cuba's historically dependent relationship on the North. By 1960, not just the PSP but Fidel Castro himself had emerged as a chief proponent of this view. In light of the government's and even the PSP's commitment to a heterodox ideology on paper, anticommunism could be little more than the chief battle cry of forces that "only wanted a Revolution of postcards, to photograph themselves and appear in albums."[123] "It is not communism to eliminate semifeudal landholdings through a radical agrarian reform," *Noticias de Hoy* insisted; "it is not communism to defend national sovereignty, trying to eliminate the foreign monopoly of one country [the United States] on our international commerce."[124] Those making such ridiculous claims, one cartoon satirized, must have been too busy reading issues of *Salaciones* (or "absurdities") *de Reader's Indigest*, a sly reference to the translated publication *Selecciones de Reader's Digest*, which circulated on the island as a transmitter of U.S. popular culture and Cold War norms.[125] Once again, the specificity of previous anti-PSP grievances was lost. Columnists like Euclides Vázquez Candela and Sergio Carbó had argued that the PSP had not earned a right to play a central role in the revolutionary government, not necessarily that it had no right to a voice.

In this context, it is no surprise that newspapers like *Prensa Libre* increasingly found themselves on the defensive, or that, by 1960, anti-PSP cross talk in *Revolución* quieted to a murmur. That conservative papers like *Diario de la Marina* fell into disrepute was even more predictable. But now, both the Revolution's leadership and loyal writers in PSP and 26th of July Movement publications accused avowedly anti-Batista but anti-communist outlets of tacitly colluding in efforts to bring about the Revolution's demise. *Revolución*, in particular—once a vehicle for critiques of the PSP—changed its editorial position and went on the anti-anticommunist attack. Angry citizens, meanwhile, began holding symbolic burnings of newspapers deemed to be channels of antirevolutionary bias. Beginning in January 1960, workers at private newspapers started forcibly inserting denunciatory "corrections" at the end of articles with allegedly prejudiced takes on Cuban affairs reprinted from U.S. wire agencies. Then, in late spring, worker militias in outlets like *Prensa Libre* and *Diario de la Marina* rose up to kick out their editorial boards. Accounts vary as to whether these decisions were really autonomous or encouraged by the new government. Either way, crowds of citizens eagerly participated in mock funerals, dumping coffins with the offending papers' "corpses" into the sea.[126]

The public sphere in Cuba—for retrospective and other kinds of disputes—would never be the same. Still, even as many press outlets barreled toward an endgame of nationalization and state control, memory continued to provide a powerful rubric by which editors and their detractors litigated the downfall. In early 1960, *Diario de la Marina* began publishing a column simply called "The Words of Fidel." The obvious purpose was to remind audiences of prior statements by the Revolution's leader—expressing support for the free press, for instance—to which he no longer appeared to adhere.[127] Critics cried historical hypocrisy. If the "anticommunist" papers cared so much about the "free press," they argued, why had *Diario de la Marina* waged no protest when *Noticias de Hoy* or other leftist publications were shut down by Batista in the 1950s?[128] For its part, *Prensa Libre* made a last attempt to assert its anti-Batista credentials and call out what it perceived as the two-facedness of its rivals. Not only was *Revolución* now "getting along swimmingly" with communists that had once supported Batista, editors argued, but the public burial of *Diario de la Marina* served as a reminder of how easily "humanity execrates its entire memory."[129] No matter. *Prensa Libre* soon suffered a similar fate. Like Batista himself, the paper was now deemed part of a broader "antipatriotic past" that the advancing Revolution was determined to erase.[130]

Conclusion:
From "Anti-anticommunism" to Anti-imperialist March

The Cuban Revolution ushered in an unprecedented wave of optimism and confidence in Cuban society. "Now, finally," many thought, the time had come to definitively right the nation's historic wrongs. Yet while the initial enthusiasm of the revolutionary victory inspired ongoing spectacles of historical communion and faith, it also provided a platform for diverse political actors to hash out contending views of just what the Revolution was about. Debates over who had done the bulk or at least sufficient quotas of the work to make it happen in the first place also threatened to pull the wide anti-Batista coalition apart.

By late 1959 and early 1960, multisided memory feuds, especially regarding the role of Cuba's communist party, had been replaced by a more uniform discourse where anticommunism itself was deemed a holdover from the past most damaging to prospects for change. In contrast to his general evasion of partisan memory quarrels in the Revolution's first months, Fidel Castro's tacit intervention in this transition, while still avoiding the substance of anti-PSP critiques, was key. What followed was an escalating "war of words" that culminated with the closure or nationalization of press vehicles that had previously served as chief forums for retrospective debate.[131] Thereafter, state leaders would popularize increasingly uniform characterizations of the pre-1959 past, both that portion thought to count as inspiration, as well as the legacies of a "pseudo-republic" better left behind.[132] As reflected in a growing array of cultural production, too, what appeared to matter most was not the memory of past insurgent alliances or conflicts but the epochal break between the corrupt prerevolutionary "before" and the revolutionary "after."[133]

Yet if the result of this shift, as we have seen, was that the revolutionary leadership took implicit sides with the PSP, treating all forms of anticommunism as counterrevolutionary bias rather than the result of legitimate disputes, it behooves us to ask why. Members of the 26th of July Movement had plenty of reasons to question the PSP's historic credentials, and some did so. So why did Fidel Castro and the high revolutionary leadership ultimately move to incorporate them into the fold? Was this the fulfillment of a long-held "communist conspiracy" and planned power grab, as many Castro opponents would later allege? Was it the only path to unity? Or was it a strategic choice?

Here we run head first into one of the longest-standing, unsolved disputes in the Cuban memory wars ever since. We also return to the international dimensions of the equation. Surely, Cuban "anti-anticommunism" after 1959 was inseparable from the context of worsening relations with the United States. That discourse only made sense if one could argue convincingly that anticommunist rhetoric abetted conspiracies and biases abroad. Some scholars did later argue that U.S. hostility *pushed* the Revolution into an alliance with the PSP and the Soviet Union.[134] We now know, for example, that the Eisenhower administration approved "fomenting a coherent opposition" to the revolutionary government months before the PSP's incorporation into and Soviet ties with the Cuban revolutionary government were complete.[135] But given evidence of a quiet accommodation between the PSP and some 26th of July Movement leaders dating to the end of 1958, not to mention discreet revolutionary government overtures to the Soviet Union in 1959, the "push theory" for why Cuba "went communist" remains too simple as a memory narrative on its own.[136] Nor, as we will see in chapter 2, did it ever become a predominant interpretation of Cubans who fled to the United States.

Regardless, for Cubans at the time unaware of such behind the scenes developments, rising tensions in U.S.-Cuban relations between 1959 and 1960 reshaped incipient understandings of the Revolution's purpose in permanent ways. Over the remainder of 1960, conflicts over domestic history became subsumed within Cuba's mounting public standoff with the United States. Those tensions increasingly took on the tenor of well-worn polemics of the Cold War. But they also bore the weight of a much longer history of U.S. interventionism in Cuban affairs dating to the early twentieth century. When the French freighter *La Coubre*, carrying Belgian arms, mysteriously exploded in Havana's harbor in March 1960—precisely in the middle of the "anti-anticommunist" campaign against portions of the press—comparisons with the explosion of the USS *Maine* in 1898 were obvious. Was Washington again looking for a pretext to meddle? The war of historical symbols was on, now predominantly in a mode that focused on U.S.-Cuban relations and anti-imperialist legacies.[137]

In this context of escalating tensions, revolutionary unity no longer signified a willingness to work across the anti-Batista coalition's originally broad party and factional lines to achieve shared goals for Cuba's future. To raise demands for democratic process or immediate elections, or to express doubts about the PSP's historical credentials, was to make common cause with the island's historic external foe. By early 1960, some more moderate members of the anti-Batista coalition had started to do just that, forming anti-Castro underground groups that sought out or accepted covert U.S. support.[138] Ironically, then, for a nation intent on throwing off a past of domestic political corruption and economic dependence on the North, clarifying the purpose of the Revolution's historic mission hinged precisely on the eventual preeminence of its Washington foil.

"The camps are clear," said one May 1960 editorial in *Noticias de Hoy*, "You are with the Revolution or against it. There are no other alternatives."[139] "It is now," *Combate* warned the same month, "when those lacking in faith and sufficient mentality to understand the justice of certain transformations let themselves be surprised by imperialism."[140] Because of their unwillingness to come to term with the true international stakes, "many of those who cooperated in the defeat of the Tyranny are the counterrevolutionaries of today."[141] Here was an acknowledgment that the boundaries of what counted as "revolutionary" had changed. But as it became increasingly apparent that the United States was backing an emerging anti-Castro opposition, it is easy to understand why many nationalist Cubans thought their leaders had a point.

No wonder that when the biggest clash yet occurred between Cuba and the United States in the summer and fall of 1960—a snowballing bilateral tit for tat resulting in the takeover of all U.S. companies and the first moves toward imposing U.S. trade sanctions—wide swaths of the Cuba populace marveled at their historic nationalist accomplishments. After the public participated in ceremonial burials of nationalized U.S. corporations, repudiating years of foreign "domination," Cuba's umbrella union, the Confederación de Trabajadores de Cuba (Cuban Workers Federation), invited all Cubans to recite an "oath to the Revolution and the nation" in front of Havana's capitol building. "In light of the criminal aggressions that the Yankee imperialists have promoted against Cuba and against our Revolution," it declared, "we pledge to [defend] with our effort and our sacrifice, with our blood and with our lives, the Revolution that makes the nation ours, that makes the land ours, that makes freedom ours, that gives us the right to decide our destiny and fight for progress, welfare derived from one's own work, happiness, and peace."[142] Once an active domestic battleground for determining the optimal path for the nation's future and the internal historical credentials to deliver it, the Revolution had morphed into a national saga that political leaders now framed primarily as the rejection of a past and ongoing present of U.S. intromission.[143] Given that the Eisenhower administration had moved to put a full "Plan of Covert Action against Cuba" in motion in March 1960, they were at least in part right.

By the time Fidel Castro gathered 1 million citizens in September 1960 to sign and vote by acclamation for the "First Declaration of Havana"— an elegant statement in favor of Cuban national sovereignty—no one was openly debating who fought for and against Batista, and to what end or degree. The original counterpoints of historical memory between revolutionary factions had become passé, at least for the time being. Numerous faces that had once emblazoned the *Album de la Revolución Cubana* as heroes worthy of being remembered had gone underground, been imprisoned, or fled abroad, their names never again to be openly praised. Meanwhile, when the Revolution's rise to and evolution in power became the subject of retrospective narration, popular culture increasingly focused on heroic battles and nonfactional comings to consciousness, as in a slew of ICAIC's early film releases as of 1960.[144] Slowly but surely, the revolutionary government's national educational authorities—prior, even, to nationalizing all private schools—were moving to replace older assigned textbooks and other pieces of the public educational curriculum with new texts that taught anti-imperialist versions of Cuba's history.[145]

Yet when Castro *did* proclaim the Revolution openly "socialist" in April 1961, he and a number of revolutionary factions still might have had some explaining to do. After all, enough citizens might have remembered countless statements in speeches and in the press—even from the PSP, and even into late 1960—that had disputed that socialism was the Cuban government's goal. "What is our aim?," the Revolutionary Directorate's paper *Combate* asked in December 1959. "A society," they responded, quoting Fidel, "where all have the right to freedom, whether they are in the majority or the minority. Not the domination of a minority over a majority, nor the terror of a majority over a minority. Democracy in the real sense, not dictatorship or oligarchy; democracy in a real sense on the basis of social justice."[146] "Those who think we're going to nationalize industries are crazy," advertised one Fidel quote turned into a headline in January 1959.[147] "I will combat communism with social improvements," went another refrain.[148]

Perhaps for most Cubans, as historian Lillian Guerra has argued, "Fidel's sudden reversal on socialism seemed like an insignificant afterthought" as they "stood in awe of their own [anti-imperialist] achievements."[149] Simultaneously, crucibles of mobilization like the Milicias Nacionales Revolucionarias (National Revolutionary Militias), created in 1959, the Comités de Defensa de la Revolución (Committees for the Defense of the Revolution), established in 1960, or the Campaña Nacional de Alfabetización (National Literacy Campaign), conducted in 1961, rendered the early memory of revolutionary experience for many as a saga of collective empowerment, participation, and defense.[150] But in the emerging political landscape of the Cuban exile community—a site of its own strategic memory elisions, as we will see—recriminations over Fidel Castro's allegedly broken promises would occupy a privileged place. Retrospective disputes from the island would also find their echo in analogous factional memory wars brewing across the Florida Straits.

2

Cuban Exiles and the Search for "Total Unity"

They came by boat and plane, some escaping arrest as members of emergent anti-Castro opposition groups, most driven by the broader upheavals of revolutionary change. As the Cuban Revolution radicalized over the course of 1960, what began as a trickle of out-migration from within Batista-linked political circles and the island's economic elite turned into a professional and middle-class flood. By October 1962, 248,070 Cubans would move to South Florida and other points in the United States. More than just immigrants, they constituted a self-identified exile community famous for its anticommunist antipathy, especially in Miami. Many had once been among the Revolution's sympathizers. Now they fled the government's rising centralization of political and economic control, the consequences of Cuba's intensifying standoff with the North, or the alleged usurpation of the Revolution's "true" goals.

Thereafter, Miami became a locus of anti-Castro ideas, plotting, and Cold War dollars, just as revolutionary officials predicted. Within that world, some of the characters from the once diverse anti-Batista coalition and press we met in chapter 1 would play starring roles. The city became "mnemonic real estate" too, a place where everything from business names to record collections would honor an idealized island to which most exiles hoped to return.[1] And against the revolutionary government's own canon of martyrs and heroes, exile activists would position themselves as the guardians of the memory of those executed without due process, imprisoned for conspiring against the new Cuban government, or simply written out of increasingly streamlined stories on the island of how the Revolution had emerged.

Yet the relationship of Cuban exiles to their past would never be limited to a nostalgic gaze, let alone a fixed set of retrospective indictments. As much as exiles returned again and again to Fidel Castro's past pledges to convene elections, more uncomfortable questions also lingered. Just how and why had the nation befallen such a tragedy? And who was responsible for creating the conditions that led to their predicament in the first place? Fidel Castro was the obvious first target of most responses. But underneath the surface of cohesive anti-Castro feeling lay deep insecurities associated with the apportioning of blame.

Let us consider an unconventional source, a satirical poem published in the pages of the comedic newspaper *Zig-zag Libre*, to introduce some of this complexity. As we saw in chapter 1, the original *Zig-zag* in Cuba at first supported the revolutionary government. Along with other outlets of the independent press, however, it began to receive criticism from revolutionary officials (and was even the target of an early boycott) when some contributors began questioning, or poking fun at, the direction of the revolutionary regime. (*Zig-zag* appears to have closed entirely at the end of 1960, well after many of its core original contributors felt pressured to head abroad.)[2] It is ironic, then, to see the paper reborn in Miami and publishing a sharp criticism of former revolutionary supporters turned devout anti-Castroites. After all, this "hypocrisy" in many ways defined the trajectory of key members of the original *Zig-zag* team.

The Meeting (at the Door of the Refugee Center)
by Cundo [pseudonym]

I warned you in advance and you didn't want to believe,
and yesterday I saw you at the Refugee Center
bad-mouthing Fidel ...

What surprises life offers!
One has to live to see!

When Cuba was dressed
for the 26th of July
with red and black signs
saying: "Thank you, Fidel!"
And although already on the execution walls
Cain was shooting Abel
and behind every scapular
hid a Lucifer,
you wouldn't take anyone
speaking badly about him to you:
you were like a bride,
on the opening night of her honeymoon ...!

Who could have told you then
that so soon I'd see you here

at the door of the Refugee Center ...
and bad-mouthing Fidel?!³

The settling of retrospective scores enacted by Cundo's verse echoes a powerful leitmotif of exile politics in the 1960s. For Cubans came to Miami, and other points in the United States, with not only anticommunist convictions but also the historical baggage of past political lives. Much as ghosts of pre-1959 political disputes lurked amid early revolutionary transformations on the island, so did they haunt expatriates as they debated their nation's fate in community newspapers, drafted platforms for political organizations, or gossiped about the latest news while waiting on line, as in the poem, to receive U.S. resettlement aid. If some faulted repentant revolutionary acolytes for backing the aspirations of a would-be despot, others blamed former Batista supporters in their midst for providing the true pretext for Castro's rise.

Arguments about historical responsibility do not feature prominently, or at all, in most accounts of the Cuban exodus to the United States after 1959. Nor are they part of the story Cuban exiles from the early 1960s typically tell about themselves. Today, dominant public articulations of the community's collective history concentrate on images and episodes taken as emblematic of a common saga of refugee trauma: the experience of passing through *la pecera* (the fishbowl), the soundproof waiting room at Havana's airport; the travails of the 14,000 unaccompanied children sent to the United States with the help of the Catholic Church as part of Operation Pedro Pan between 1960 and 1962; and the ritual of registering for financial support at the U.S. government–sponsored Cuban Refugee Center.⁴ At the same time, an equally important anchor of community lore revolves around an immigrant success story, one understood as having been made possible by U.S. benevolence and hard work. Within this frame, Cuban exile nationalism is defined not by a baseline suspicion of the imperial hegemon but rather by gratitude for anticommunist partnership and a willingness to receive refugees from the island with open arms.

This chapter, by contrast, pays less attention to the cultural construction of such touchstones—an important part of the later history of Cuban exile memory politics. Instead, it traces the evolution of arguments that preceded the former's conversion into icons and tropes. We must properly historicize post-1959 Cuban expatriates' search for an *exilio unido*, or a united exile community. And when we do, it becomes clear that early exiles in the 1960s argued and agonized about what had happened to them, and who was at fault, as much as they succeeded in forging a narrative of a shared experience.

Recovering debates over the past among early exiles also helps nuance salient narratives of exile history vis-à-vis the United States. As alluded to in chapter 1, by 1960 some opponents of the Revolution's direction on the island had begun receiving covert support from Washington in their efforts to build an effective anti-Castro movement. Those relationships deepened in Miami, where the Central Intelligence Agency (CIA) would establish its largest base outside of Langley, Virginia, funneling millions of dollars into the anti-Castro cause in the early 1960s. Thus, whereas many Cubans settling in South Florida (and beyond) would later celebrate U.S. generosity, from the beginning the Cuban government would paint Cuban expatriate history as a nefarious tale of collaboration between right-wing Cuban revanchists and the U.S. national security state, as we will see in later chapters. A more rigorous history of Cuban exile retrospective politics from within the community, however, shines light on a different dynamic: the ways community members meditated in real time on the history of U.S.-Cuban relations while struggling to reconcile fickle Washington patronage with a nationalist memory consensus long *opposed* to U.S. intervention in Cuban affairs. If the U.S.-Cuba conflict became an anchor of the Revolution's historic sense of purpose by 1960, overshadowing or displacing internal memory disputes, many exiles on the U.S. payroll found themselves deepening and then resenting the clutches of that trap long before they were willing to look back with appreciation for U.S. charity.

To tell the story of these arguments and anxieties is not to ignore the substantial political, cultural, and memory solidarities that did form among Cuban exiles in the 1960s. But it is to critically interrogate *contemporary* memory narratives, in Miami especially, that portray the exile community as always having been linked by uniform beliefs. In this respect, this chapter, much like chapter 1, recovers positions and disagreements about the Cuban past that later frameworks of remembrance—in this case, in the Cuban diaspora—tended to obscure. Yes, the exile community became the place where memories of revolutionary leaders' original noncommunist assurances were kept alive as weapons of retrospective denunciation. But it was also a site of forgetting as former political enemies sought to reconcile, or skirt over the fact that they once believed some kind of revolution was necessary. In the course of these arguments, appeals to the abstract "historical" record and invocations of the memory of recent history's living participants necessarily blurred as multiple voices staked out retrospective claims.

By the mid-1960s, the results of the community's tightrope walk between ongoing division and appeals to unity had proven deeply unsatisfactory. Fidel Castro remained in power, and the United States, many in Miami believed, appeared to be abandoning the Cuban cause. New attempts to fashion coalitions occasionally made headway, as did more uncritical forms of nostalgic longing. But the memory of exile for many of those who left the island in the immediate wake of the Revolution resembled not an uplifting tale of resilience but a chronicle of discord, deception, and defeat.

Cuba Betrayed? When? By Whom?

Fulgencio Batista's airborne escape from Havana on New Year's Eve 1958 has long been infamous. Denied entry to Mexico, or return to the Daytona Beach, Florida, estate where he had enjoyed a previous respite from Cuban politics in the 1940s, the maligned Cuban leader made his way to the Dominican Republic before retiring to relative anonymity in Portugal and Spain.[5] Yet if Batista remained officially unwelcome by the very U.S. government that had abetted his political career, hundreds of Batista officials and supporters would make their way to South Florida in the wake of the revolutionary victory in January 1959. The specter of former Batista police officials in the exile shadows thus raises a logical starting point for unraveling the memory wars of the post-1959 Cuban expatriate community. What became of the erstwhile members and sympathizers of Batista's government, and what claims to political or historical legitimacy could they muster from abroad?

Not many, one would think. For the better part of two years, the revolutionary government in Havana had wide cross-class support, not only from the middle and professional sectors of Cuban society but also from the country's national industrial groups. So widespread had overt and casual opposition to the Batista government become by late 1958 that regime loyalists found themselves politically cornered. Nonetheless, once Cuban revolutionary authorities began their steady move to the left, oft-repeated *batistiano* denunciations of the Castro movement as communist-infiltrated and inspired, as early as 1953, could suddenly appear clairvoyant. It is no surprise, then, that some former Batista supporters would attempt to claim the historical high ground in debates over exile political legitimacy. Fidel Castro himself publicly joked in late 1960 about scenes in which formerly anti-Batista, now antirevolutionary moderates would concede in Miami that the strongman had been right all along. This, ironically, was still before Castro had openly embraced socialism himself.[6]

Even prior to this point, several press outlets emerged in the budding Cuban exile community to either directly or indirectly validate memories of Batista's rule. The most prominent was *Patria*, a bombastic Miami periodical founded in 1959 and rumored to be financed by Batista himself.[7] *Patria* not only pioneered the robust defense of the former Cuban head of state's legacy but also repeatedly defended Cuba's record of economic achievements before 1959, depicting the island as anything but an underdeveloped nation in need of reorganization or reform.[8] Pointing to high rates of TV and car ownership, literacy, and university education per capita relative to other Latin American countries in the 1950s, editors marshaled the presumed objectivity of internationally validated national statistics to discredit both moderate anti-Batista factions' demands for reform *and* more radical sectors' visions of revolutionary change.[9] Left out of such neat numerical pictures, however, were the wide disparities between urban and rural areas of the country, not to mention the calls for deep political, not only economic or social, transformation also animating Batista's opponents. Nor did such figures capture the more ambitious horizon of expectations for many Cubans long accustomed to comparing their country not with the rest of Latin America but with the United States.[10]

Complementing *Patria*'s editorial line were the exculpatory writings of Batista himself.[11] Beginning with 1960's *Respuesta*—translated in English as *Cuba Betrayed*—the discredited leader embarked on a campaign to not only document his version of pre- and post-1959 events but also refute the scale of violence (20,000 deaths) that revolutionary forces attributed to his regime. *Piedras y leyes* (*Stones and Laws*), published in 1961, offered a nearly 500-page compendium of his multiple administrations' laws, records, and purported economic achievements dating back to the late 1930s, replete with statistical tables and figures. In retrospect, these texts do help lift the veil on the Batista era slightly. As noted in the introduction, Batista the 1950s authoritarian continued to invest resources in educational initiatives and other populist projects as he had in the post-Machado period.[12] But for the ousted leader to insist that constitutional normalcy had reigned after his coup in 1952 was insulting to most current and future exiles' intelligence. For that reason alone there is little indication that Batista's memoirs made major waves in the Cuban exile community in the early 1960s. Nor is it clear how widely they circulated, having been published by a Mexican press and with Washington blocking Batista from traveling to the United States to promote his work.[13]

The truth was that, for most Cubans arriving in the United States in the early 1960s, memories of Batista's rule remained too fresh to be whitewashed, celebrated, or buried entirely. Not all exiles from the upper, middle, and professional classes had been equal opponents of his regime. But most had welcomed the entry of Fidel Castro to Havana as a promising sign of some form of change. Many knew first- or secondhand of cases of repression by Batista's army and secret police. By 1960 and 1961, as we saw in chapter 1, some of those arriving in Miami came from the anti-Batista movement's leadership and included well-placed figures in the early revolutionary government. In this light, the overtly pro-Batista memory framework of outlets like *Patria* was bound to not be the only discourse available for popular consumption. Even for some who might have claimed to dislike Fidel Castro from the start, they could just as easily fault Cuba's historic strongman for creating the opportunity for Castro's meteoric political ascent.

As a result, far more common than unconcealed defenses of the Batista government in the early exile scene were images such as a cartoon in a July 1964 special issue of *Zig-zag Libre* (figure 2.1). On the left of the two-page spread, a joyful Cuban public celebrates the 26th of July 1959 against the backdrop of Havana's famous Morro fortress, still confident in Fidel Castro's commitments to democratic governance, civil guarantees, and nationalist reform. Yet by 1964, the date corresponding to a replicated scene on the right, Cuba's leaders have callously disregarded the Revolution's "true" ideals, swapping the slogan "Viva Cuba libre" ("Long Live Free Cuba") for "Viva el comunismo" ("Long Live Communism").[14] This is but one representation of an anti-Batista narrative of betrayal — a "betrayal" of the supposedly "real" revolution that *batistianos* bitterly and repeatedly insisted was false, insofar as it only vindicated their long-held suspicions that the Revolution had been rotten all along.[15] The idea of a *necessary* revolution sold out to communism, though, claimed pride of place among the early storylines grounding articulations of exile identity and memory.

It is easy to understand why this message resonated. For one thing, early expressions of the idea had originated on the island itself. Before the nationalization of the press in 1960, columns like "The Words of Fidel" in *Diario de la Marina* had lobbed Fidel Castro's quotes back at him as a way to suggest he had broken his word. Moderate revolutionary government officials couched their early defections in similar terms. Other disenchanted revolutionaries who started leaving the country found ways to leave parting shots in even more public ways. Take the case of Miguel Ángel Quevedo, who as editor of the influential *Bohemia* magazine had done as much as anyone else in the Cuban press during 1959 to publicize and document the Batista regime's crimes. For that reason, when Quevedo resigned in July 1960 and sought asylum in the Venezuelan embassy, both the decision and the text of the resignation letter he arranged to be

Figure 2.1. The Revolution betrayed? Antonio Rubio, no title, *Zig-zag Libre*, special supplement, July 1964, n.p.

published in one of the few independent press outlets remaining on the island carried particular symbolism and meaning:

> In constant demand of substantial reforms for our Republic, *Bohemia* combatted the governments that to a greater or lesser degree showed themselves incapable of satisfying those aspirations. And when on January 1, 1959, a revolution arrived in power that represented for our people the great hope of definitive liberation, *Bohemia* put itself at that revolution's side. Just as it had been in the tragic but heroic days of the insurrectional phase, serving the noble cause of those young people who reenacted with unparalleled heroism, in the mountains and in the civic resistance, the achievements of our elders, generously offering their lives. For all of these reasons, from the first moments *Bohemia* stood with the Revolutionary Government. It is not embarrassed by this stance. Nor does it regret it. And it remained at its side as long as it believed in the sincerity of its leaders and in the honesty of its purposes.

So great was the faith that an entire people had placed in that revolution that it was not easy to admit that it had deceived them.... But with profound pain *Bohemia* recognizes that there is nothing left to sustain that remote hope. The Revolution has been betrayed.[16]

Feelings of deception thus traveled with Cubans from the island to the United States. For those who, like Quevedo, identified with Cuba's long quest for historic deliverance, memories of the hopes and nationalist spirit of 1959, and even much of 1960, were not so easily wiped away. Fidel Castro's perceived failure to follow through on promises to convene elections, and especially his formal embrace of socialism in 1961 despite previous protestations to the contrary, would provide clear retrospective anchors for accusations of "betrayal" from anti-Batista resistance veterans and early revolutionary government officials alike. But disenchantment with even the overtly socialist project would not come to all future exiles at the same time. The malleable idea of a necessary revolution "betrayed," then, could allow Cubans of diverse political beliefs and economic stations to register their disappointment with the Revolution's results without disclaiming all progressive commitments. Memoir after published memoir, essay after essay, would project this message to audiences in Cuba, the United States, and Latin America in the years to come.[17] It was also the main narrative plank of a new version of *Bohemia*, *Bohemia Libre*, that Quevedo recreated from New York City.

That said, the discursive life of the betrayal thesis was by no means straightforward. For one thing, it competed in popular lore against *batistianos*' insistence that the 1950s had been the most prosperous time in Cuba's history. But there was also the more cynical notion of the *revolución del callo*, literally the "revolution of the callus." Under this interpretation of recent events, Cubans only turned against the Revolution when it stepped on their toes, nationalized their businesses, or otherwise affected their livelihoods directly.[18] Exiles' nationalistic commitments and ideological principles notwithstanding, perhaps the wisecracking defenders of this theory had a point.

Second, those espousing the betrayal narrative at times harbored historical visions that contradicted its terms. It seems curious, for example, that the cartoon embodiment (in figure 2.1) of the betrayal idea described above should appear in the same publication, *Zig-zag Libre*, that printed Cundo's sarcastic poem about the Cuban Refugee Center. Or perhaps it is the other way around. If Cundo's verse echoes the "I told you so" mantra of Batista supporters, the depiction of Fidel's disloyalty to a noble cause seems much closer to the experience of the once prorevolutionary contributors to the original *Zig-zag* who had grown suspicious of the Revolution and been ostracized when they began satirizing the emerging state.

Most crucially, the emergence and evolution of the betrayal narrative was troubled because it did not take place in a geopolitical vacuum. Exiles' efforts to bring coherence to a vision of the recent past that could drive an oppositional political project in the present would become deeply intertwined with their budding ties to the United States. Not only was the United States the host country where most departing Cuba sought sanctuary; as early as the fall of 1959, as alluded to in chapter 1, Washington had begun to secretly position itself as the principal patron of anti-Castro groups. It was thus significant that U.S. presidential administrations formally adopted the "Revolution betrayed" as the organizing mantra for covert (and often overt) plans to unseat the Castro government. Moderate former revolutionaries benefited from this convergence of interests, though they were also left to worry about the attendant compromises, risks, asymmetries, and frustrations such an "alliance" might entail.

Again, it is easy to understand why the premise of the "Revolution betrayed" was attractive, in this case to U.S. policymakers. As the revolutionary government in Havana ramped up its criticism of U.S. imperial pretensions in late 1959 and into 1960, the Eisenhower administration lacked credibility because it had continued to openly support the Batista government into 1958. In that sense, the notion of a fundamentally liberal and, even better, "middle-class" revolution "betrayed to communism" conveniently allowed the United States to skirt its questionable record of support for Batista and position itself as an ally of "responsible" Cuban political change. Backing early exiles who had opposed Batista was the perfect political choice. That goal undergird the first plans to foster an anti-Castro opposition approved in the fall of 1959, and it was a major premise of the covert action plan against the Cuban government that Eisenhower approved in March 1960. Infamously, the central feature of the latter became an exile-led military assault on Cuba's southern coast, which would transpire just over a year later at the Bay of Pigs.

Not all policy choices, especially in Congress, were consistent with the betrayal narrative. In May 1960, for example, the U.S. Senate put noted Batista military officials before the court of U.S. public opinion at a subcommittee hearing on the "Communist Threat to the United States through the Caribbean," despite the blood on their hands.[19] At the time, however, the CIA was already busy exfiltrating future exile leaders with connections to the broad *anti-Batista* front.[20] Quevedo's *Bohemia Libre* also received the agency's secret support.[21] For the executive branch, anticommunist but anti-Batista groups and individuals in the emerging exile community attracted the most significant financial and political backing.²² And when John F. Kennedy took office in January 1961, inheriting the Bay of Pigs plan, his team was in some sense even more eager and better positioned to embrace moderate anti-Batista voices in exile as a way to distance itself from the Eisenhower administration's record of supporting Batista in the 1950s.

Still, there was no simple betrayal narrative that all in Washington and Miami could agree upon. In an influential March 1961 piece in the centrist *New Leader*, U.S. academic Theodore Draper gave the betrayal theory academic legs.²³ His position closely anticipated the view of an influential white paper by Kennedy aide Arthur Schlesinger Jr. that provided the betrayal narrative with the official White House imprimatur on the eve of the Bay of Pigs.²⁴ Nevertheless, a noted group of former Batista government officials immediately published a long letter rejecting the premises of the State Department's white paper in several newspapers, including the *New York Herald Tribune*. The U.S. government, they argued, had bought into the false premise that any kind of revolution was needed in Cuba to begin with, let alone one with a social component.²⁵

The more prominent hurdle was that, even from within the anti-Batista exile camp, the memory narrative of the "Revolution betrayed" could take on multiple forms. Was the "true Revolution" intended to simply restore the electoral status quo prior to Batista's coup in 1952? Or was it committed to fulfilling, even surpassing the spirit of the Constitution of 1940, stained by the corrupt Auténtico administrations of Ramón Grau San Martín (1944–48) and Carlos Prío Socarrás (1948–52)? What about challenging U.S. interests in the Cuban economy? Or defending Cuba's national sovereignty? How would the "true Revolution" address the fate of Cuba's peasantry and urban poor? Exiles' responses to these questions not only mirrored their varying positions along the progressive to moderate spectrum of Cuban politics prior to 1959; they also revived arguments that had taken place in the press on the island between 1959 and 1960.

The major difference, of course, was that debates on such issues now butted up against the need to make instrumental choices in the vortex of the Cold War. And for those exiles even nominally shaped by a nationalist tradition constitutively suspicious of U.S. involvement in Cuban affairs, accepting U.S. aid required biting their tongues. Would anti-Castro partisans who thought the "true" but "betrayed" Revolution should encompass some challenges to U.S. interests dial back their preferences in the interest of managing relationships with their backers in Washington? When push came to shove, many arrivals to Miami were also sure that the United States simply would not "permit" a communist government to remain in power so close to home. In that sense, even among professed exile nationalists, the memory of and a certain fatalism regarding Cuba's historic dependence on the United States retained a powerful allure.

All told, variably colored characterizations of the Cuban Revolution's "betrayal" in the statements of former revolutionary sympathizers and officials turned anti-Castro opponents had strong implications for not only differing visions of the pre-Castro past but also competing platforms for a post-Castro tomorrow.[26] As we will see, failure to reconcile these visions against the backdrop of offers of U.S. patronage helps to explain the retrospective discord that plagued Cuban exile politics from the start. As Batista partisans continued to insist that the only "betrayal" had been the communist deception Fidel Castro had planned all along, other early exiles held on to their own views of what the "true Revolution" had really been about. This complicated the work of trying to forge a shared political identity on retrospective common ground.

Mirando a Miró (Looking at Miró)

The political activities and trajectory of exile leader José Miró Cardona provide an unparalleled look into the genesis and shifting terms of the betrayal narrative in early Cuban exile politics. As one of the more important political figures and spokespersons for the community in the 1960s, Miró Cardona was closely listened to and observed. He was also a major beneficiary of U.S.-government covert support in the lead-up to the Bay of Pigs invasion in April 1961. That said, his political evolution before and after the invasion failed invites us to consider the relationship between private and public registers of retrospective debate. Put another way, his shifting take on the specters of the recent Cuban past in speeches and published editorials grew out of a dialogue with less visible forums in which friends, enemies, and other letter writers challenged his views.

A criminal lawyer and former president of the Havana Bar Association, José Miró Cardona was well known prior to 1959 for having served as the defense attorney during the trial of Ramón Barquín, the leader of a failed coup attempt against Batista from within his own armed forces in 1956. As head of the later Civic Revolutionary Front—a fundraising and urban political arm of the 26th of July Movement—in July 1958 Miró Cardona helped broker the Pact of Caracas, an agreement notionally unifying all anti-Batista groups (including the 26th of July Movement, though not the PSP) behind a commitment to support a provisional government upon Batista's fall. In January 1959, Miró Cardona was named the first prime minister of that new government. He occupied the position for some six weeks before ceding the job to Fidel Castro. By 1960, however, after a brief stint as Cuba's ambassador in Spain, he had grown wary of the Revolution's left turn. In July, Miró Cardona sought asylum in the Argentine embassy in Havana, and that fall he made his way to the United States.[27]

Not all in Miami welcomed the prominent attorney as an ally of their anti-Castro efforts. Miró Cardona had been prime minister when the controversial revolutionary tribunals of early 1959 were rapidly trying and executing alleged Batista regime criminals.[28] Despite the mass support the trials received in Cuba at the time, footage and photographs of those events had survived thanks to the presence of the international press during "Operation Truth." The images then circulated in exile as memory tokens of revolutionary excesses and misdeeds.[29] Nonetheless, Miró Cardona quickly became the leader, in many ways the figurehead, of a U.S.-dollar-driven attempt to link a number of emerging anti-Castro groups operating on the island and in Miami into a united front. That front would go on to serve as the political leadership—in theory more than reality, as it turned out—of the 1,500 exiles eventually trained by the CIA to invade Cuba at the Bay of Pigs under the "Plan of Covert Action against the Castro Regime" approved by President Dwight Eisenhower in March 1960. As such, Miró Cardona become the best-known political proponent of the betrayal thesis in the exile community, and he was tasked with quietly squaring liberal, and nationalist, ideological commitments with secret U.S. support.

Miró Cardona's first pronouncements from Miami provide insight into his and others' initial thinking on the nature of the "true" Revolution that needed to be saved. Faced with accusations that he had facilitated Castro's rise, Miró Cardona wrote the following in a letter to the editor of the now expatriate version of *Diario de la Marina* being published in Miami: "The Revolution that triumphed on January 1, 1959, was necessary and inevitable. The long series of frustrations that the Republic had suffered since its beginnings unquestionably demanded a profound change in established political modes of governing the country. This continued series of frustrations, attributable to all governments, found its culmination in the regime installed on the March 10, 1952 [the date of Batista's coup], the product of a junior-level mob from the barracks."[30] The Revolution was not only indispensable, Miró Cardona argued; the Revolution came to power with a broad mandate, one not limited to correcting the abuses of the Batista years alone. Miró Cardona even implied that the Batista regime should be understood as the direct outgrowth of the corrupt Auténtico administrations preceding it. His rhetoric fell short of endorsing full-blown *social* revolution. Yet elsewhere in his letter, Miró Cardona spoke plainly about the misery plaguing rural areas of the country and the great "happiness" with which much of Havana's middle and upper classes welcomed early revolutionary reforms benefiting the poor in 1959.

Other member organizations of the coalition Miró Cardona led expressed similar left-leaning or at least progressive views in favor of economic as well as political change. For one thing, the alliance purposefully called itself the Frente Revolucionario Democrático (Democratic Revolutionary Front, FRD) and, later, the Consejo Revolucionario Cubano (Cuban Revolutionary Council, CRC), hoping to reclaim the memory of "revolution" as a goal exiles could still rally behind. More concretely, manifestoes of affiliated organizations spoke of fulfilling the spirit of Fidel Castro's first agrarian reform law of 1959 as well as breaking up (or at least limiting) foreign- and Cuban-owned latifundios, albeit with compensation and a commitment to preserving private property rights.[31] FRD/CRC members also at times celebrated plainly leftist figures in Cuban history who already had been incorporated into the revolutionary government's own pantheon of heroes. For example, the labor wing of the exiled Agrupación Montecristi (Montecristi Group), a fairly well-known, if ultimately minor, anti-Batista group from the 1950s, at one point commemorated the deaths of Antonio Guiteras and Sandalio Junco, both labor organizers, anti-imperialists, and anticapitalist activists from the 1930s.[32] (Junco was even a Trotskyist.) Such references surely did not match the image of liberal moderation U.S. patrons of the FRD/CRC had in mind.

In other respects, however, the FRD/CRC version of the betrayal thesis struggled to cohere on Cuban terms. Conservative, pro-Batista sectors of the exile community continued to condemn Miró Cardona for his role in the revolutionary government's crucial early months.[33] The adhesion to the CRC of Manuel Ray's Movimiento Revolucionario del Pueblo (Revolutionary Movement of the People, MRP) — covertly founded on the island in late 1960 — only made things worse. Ray had served the revolutionary government as minister of public works through November 1959, not to mention directed action and sabotage operations for the 26th of July Movement in Havana in the late 1950s. He thus faced accusations of espousing "fidelismo sin Fidel."[34] Yet from within the CRC/FRD coalition, Ray's MRP and the Movimiento de Recuperación Revolucionaria (Movement of Revolution Recuperation, MRR) led by Manuel Artime, a former minor official of the revolutionary government's Instituto Nacional de Reforma Agraria (National Institute for Agrarian Reform, INRA), also found themselves at odds with more establishment political actors. The founder of the Agrupación Montecristi, Justo Carrillo, for instance, got his political start in the student movements against Gerardo Machado in the late 1920s. But he had gone on to prominent roles in the pre-Batista Partido Auténtico machine. He, too, was a member of the political establishment roundly criticized by some anti-Batista reformists and radical nationalists as having failed the Cuban people going back to the 1940s.[35]

Retrospective anxieties likewise colored the FRD/CRC's position on the historic U.S. role in Cuba. Front leaders positioned themselves as inheritors of Cuba's nationalist tradition, criticizing the early twentieth-century record of U.S. interventionism in Cuban affairs. Yet lingering on references to the Platt Amendment or anti-imperialist currents in Cuban political thought ultimately proved unfeasible, strategically and practically, for a group depending on U.S. government financing. Programmatic documents that questioned U.S. intervention in Cuba pre-1934 thus generally went on to argue that the Franklin Roosevelt administration's Good Neighbor Policy definitively reshaped the U.S. posture in the region—a debatable proposition, to put it mildly.[36] The United States had also continued to play a controversial role in Cuban affairs well after Batista's 1952 coup. At the very least, leading proponents of the "Revolution betrayed" thesis in the CRC might have remained firm in their critique of the United States for having propped up the Batista regime until virtually the end. Perhaps mindful of Washington's purse strings, they did no such thing.

And so it was that the baseline unifying potential of the betrayal thesis as a memory framework for exile politics was compromised by Cold War political pragmatism and enduring intergroup disputes. The very authenticity of the thesis as an expression of many exiles' views might seem questionable when we consider that it was also U.S. policy at the time to explicitly create an opposition that would espouse such beliefs. "We are not, nor could we be, counterrevolutionaries," Miró Cardona and other leaders of the CRC wrote in a published manifesto in the *New York Times* a week before the Bay of Pigs invasion, refuting blanket Cuban government characterizations of its opponents. "We were revolutionists who fought against the previous regime, which had impoverished the whole country for the benefit of a minority lusting for gold and power."[37] That may have been true. But it was precisely to the kinds of right-wing dictatorships *opposed* by mainstream Cuban revolutionaries in the 1950s—Luis Anastasio Somoza's Nicaragua and Guatemala under Miguel Ydígoras Fuentes—that the CIA and the dependent CRC had already turned to host secret training camps that made the impending invasion possible in the first place. The makeup of the invasion force—the so-called Brigade 2506—also failed to line up neatly with the "betrayal" narrative, as it included not only disaffected former members of groups that had welcomed the Revolution, but also Batista-era military men and even children of high-level Batista-era officials. Tensions emerged among the recruits while in training, defined by some veterans as a division between "former rebels" and "batistianos," and by another as a sense of mutual suspicion between "student" and "military" types.[38]

Despite months of preparation, the Bay of Pigs invasion was roundly defeated within seventy-two hours, constituting a major embarrassment for the still young Kennedy administration, and for Miró Cardona, who was forced to await news of the operation under guard, revealing his marginal leadership of the real plan. The idea had been for the Brigade 2506 to hold a beachhead and link up with domestic anti-Castro opposition forces, at which point Miró Cardona and other CRC leaders would have been flown in to take up the mantle of a government in arms and request open (rather than covert) U.S. recognition and support. But regardless of later debates about the plan's execution, at base, the idea that 1,500 men would be met as liberators and initiate the toppling of a government still backed by the better part of a population of 6 million remained an inherently faulty premise.[39] Ignoring this reality, postmortem debates about the plan's failure immediately broke down along the lines of established exile memory camps. Manuel Ray promptly resigned from the CRC, publicly citing not only his distrust of the CIA, but his conviction that Batista-era soldiers should not have been included in the Brigade 2506 in the first place.[40] Batista's last vice president, Rafael Guas Inclán (whose son had fought in the invasion), used a fiery editorial in Miami newspaper *Diario las Américas* to argue that only career military men from the pre-1959 era were suited to carry out the mission.[41] The potshots and blame game would continue for years and eventually home in on the role of the United States, but in the short term defeat at the Bay of Pigs had once again cast the realities of memory conflict within the exile community itself into stark relief.

Thereafter, CRC leaders continued to hold fast to the "Revolution betrayed" platform officially as they tried to regroup and figure out what was next. But perhaps in recognition of the dangers of factionalism continuing unimpeded, Miró Cardona showed signs during the second half of 1961 of slowly opening to the need for more uncritical kinds of exile unity. It was only two months after the invasion, for example, that a powerful plea for reconciliation among the exile community's warring factions landed on Miró Cardona's desk. In June 1961, Carlos J. Bringuier, CRC representative in New Orleans, marshaled perceptive images of a Frankenstein monster and Dracula to describe the fractious, artificially cobbled-together nature of the exile body politic. To end the political feuds, he urged Miró Cardona to construct a broader, more inclusive anti-Castro front:

I hope that you are able to unify [*aunar y aglutinar*] all Cubans in exile. But this unification [*aglutinación*] must revolve around the future. We cannot continue thinking about the ominous past, which in reality was ominous, not only in the lapse of time up until December 31, 1958, but also up until yesterday, because yesterday is also past and it is also ominous. In this Frankenstein, Dr. Miró, we've all got a bit of Dracula [*En este Frankenstein . . . todos tenemos de Dracula*]. . . . I repeat, Dr. Miró, I think that we should move toward unity, not as Batista supporters with or against Batista, supporters of Prío, or as supporters of Fidel sans Fidel [*Fidelistas sin Fidel*], but rather as a total unity of Cubans. And if we are incapable of giving up our own egoisms and personal ambitions . . . then we have to conclude that we overwhelmingly deserve what we are suffering.[42]

For Miró Cardona, this must have been a tough message to swallow. In an undated draft statement likely from mid-1961, he rejected let-bygones-be-bygones politics, responding indirectly to Bringuier's call. The Cuban Revolutionary Council, he wrote, "as representative of the Cuban people and especially those revolutionary sectors that combated the previous tyranny, reiterates with all emphasis that it cannot establish direct or indirect ties with that ominous past, for ethical and historical reasons."[43] Nonetheless, while deflecting a completely indiscriminating brand of unity, Miró Cardona's words also stood in contrast to his previously cited declaration from 1960. Here the scope of the "ominous past" was at best vague, at worst strictly limited to the years of the "previous tyranny," not the pre-1959 period as a whole.

By the fall of 1961, Miró Cardona's thoughts along these lines had solidified. "None of us," he argued in a public speech, "wants to return to a past that should not return and will not return. But we do not make exclusions; let anyone with a clean heart, anyone who wants to join the great work for the freedom of Cuba, come with us. Because political errors are judged belatedly by history, whereas crimes and looting [of public coffers?] will be judged sooner or later in the courts of justice.[44] Once again, Miró Cardona's rhetoric refuted the idea—omnipresent in Cuban government discourse at the time—that the Revolution's opponents wanted nothing more than to return to Cuba's dark past. But he now opened the door even more widely to an alliance with former *batistiano* political enemies. Miró Cardona comforted himself with the suggestion that crimes of political allegiance could be overcome. Yet whereas Carlos Bringuier issued his call for unity by soberly imparting guilt for the nation's ills to *all* governments and *all* citizens—even hinting that much of that guilt fell on the shoulders of exiles themselves—in the passage above Miró Cardona appeared more flippant. Batista's gravest crime, after all, was never "looting" but the assassination and torture of scores of revolutionary activists in Cuba's prisons and streets.

Not all members of the CRC fold or the wider exile community were as willing to abandon revolutionary principles in the name of anticommunist unity. Agrupación Montecristi remained firm in its anti-Batista stance, refusing in March 1962 "to let ourselves be brainwashed by the spokesmen of the intense campaign unleashed in Miami, which aims to convince the exile community that, because—according to them—Fidel is worse than Batista, there is no other remedy but to search out that fugitive of the first of January so that he can assume leadership of the Cuban War.... In reality, they are cut from the same cloth, and the people know that presenting them with this macabre and surreal choice is totally unjust."[45] Similarly, one Julio Rey Calvert, leader of the ephemeral organization LES Mambi in Miami, sent Miró Cardona several bulletins pointedly denouncing any alliance with those Cubans who, in his view, found themselves in exile more out of self-interest than true conviction: "those hardly scrupulous persons when it comes to the basic attributes of duty, [those who] having been born in our homeland, but having shown very few sentiments of love and solidarity toward it, have now become enemies of the cruel regime in Cuba by virtue of a forced destiny. We say forced [destiny], because if they had been accepted without prejudice by the current regime in Cuba, not only would they not have opposed it, but they would have almost certainly collaborated with it, silencing or applauding all of its iniquities."[46]

Curiously, Miró Cardona eventually began harboring more suspicion toward those joining the exile community brandishing past credentials from the political *left* rather than from the right. Writing to Miró Cardona in December 1961 from an immigration internment cell at an air force base just north of Miami in the town of Opa-Locka, Manolo Iglesias, a former affiliate of the 26th of July Movement and radio announcer, angrily demanded to know why no exile organization had come to his defense. Yes, he had been an early supporter of Castro. But like so many others, Iglesias claimed to have rejected the Revolution's devolution into a communist regime. Exile organizations were missing a tremendous opportunity, he complained: "If I was a spokesperson for Castro, and one of the most heard in all of Cuba, and if I came here to fight him, doesn't any revolutionary organization have sufficient vision to realize the tremendous damage that I could do speaking against the man?" Rather than see Iglesias as another victim of the "Revolution betrayed," and a useful symbol or tool, Miró Cardona ignored his plea.[47]

Thus, Miró Cardona's apparent pivot to the center of Miami exile politics in search of common memory ground risked antagonizing other émigrés who clung to their own nationalistic recollections of what the "true" Revolution was supposed to mean. Flavio Luis López, another self-identified former militant of the 26th of July Movement urban underground, lodged one such objection in a letter to Miró Cardona from Spain in August 1962. After fleeing Cuba in December 1961 to Madrid, he established contact with CRC representatives in the Spanish capital who offered to help him secure an entry visa to the United States in exchange for a thorough debriefing. Nine months after providing his testimony, no help had arrived. An angry López therefore became convinced that U.S. politicians were stonewalling him due to an early position as head of an oil workers' union—the same oil workers who took part in the nationalization of the properties of U.S. company Standard Oil in Cuba in the summer of 1960: "Our struggles have amounted to nothing," he wrote. "In front of all of us rises—gigantic, rock-hard, impassive—the great Standard Oil, whose interests [in Cuba] were nationalized with my participation. All of this seems to be an indicator of what will become of our nation's future. Revenge or justice? It seems that one can have killed, robbed the nation, trafficked in drugs ... like Masferrer, Ríos Chaviano, Ventura, Carratalá [noted Batista-regime "enforcers" and military officials], and hundreds more who have found refuge in the United States. But one cannot touch, even 'with the petal of a rose,' foreign interests in Cuba."[48] In this admittedly conspiratorial, though not entirely unfounded reading, dependence on the United States, that most formative ingredient in Cuban historical tradition and memory, was now repeating itself in exile as a curse.

Miró Cardona ultimately resigned from the CRC in the spring of 1963, several months after surviving members of the Bay of Pigs invasion force were released from Cuban prisons in late December 1962 and returned to U.S. shores as part of a negotiated exchange facilitated by the Kennedy administration. His resignation letter cited Washington's indecision and reported breach of commitments to fund a second invasion led by exile "allies." But rather than prompting a return to nationalist roots, his retirement from politics and subsequent move to Puerto Rico further solidified Miró Cardona's transition to the retrospective right of center. "Cuba did not require a social revolution," he proclaimed at a December 1963 speech at the Universidad Interamericana de Puerto Rico in San Germán, noticeably shifting his characterization of Cuba's recent history from previous writings. "The great transformations desired by the Cuban people had already taken place, slowly but surely, over the course of twenty-five years, a quarter of a century that corresponds with the period immediately following the defeat of the dictatorial regime of President Machado in 1933 and extends until 1958. At that time, Castro assumed power and detained Cuba's progressive path, consecrated in law and guaranteed by the Constitution of 1940, [though] later violated by Batista."[49] Three years since leaving the island, Miró Cardona still criticized Batista for breaking constitutional procedure. Yet now the strongman's rule formed part of an idealized trajectory of progress interrupted by communism—hardly reason to justify the "necessary" and not exclusively political revolution in which Miró Cardona and so many other exiles had once believed.

Attempted Reconciliations and Exile Anti-Americanism

Miró Cardona's political evolution was not just a programmatic or political decision, it turns out; it was also shaped by personal ties. For several years, Miró Cardona maintained a correspondence with Rafael Guas Inclán, Batista's last vice president. An exchange from May 1961 testifies to the continued political enmity between the two men in the aftermath of the Bay of Pigs.[50] Yet both would find common ground over their shared experience as fathers of two imprisoned soldiers from the Brigade 2506, forging a friendship in the months and years to come.[51] Slowly, other former enemies in exile would seek to do the same.

That said, the coming to terms with elements of *batistianismo* and the creeping nostalgia in Miró Cardona's and other exiles' views also may have responded indirectly to events on the island. While the exile community found itself bogged down in retrospective recriminations in the wake of the Brigade 2506's defeat, Fidel Castro and the Cuban leadership used the momentum of victory to fuse what remained of once fractious revolutionary organizations into the basis for a one-party state. In late 1961, surviving movements of the anti-Batista struggle—the 26th of July Movement, the Revolutionary Directorate, and the PSP—officially joined forces to create the so-called Organizaciones Revolucionarias Integradas (Revolutionary Integrated Organizations, ORI). In 1962, the ORI became the Partido Unido de la Revolución Socialista de Cuba (United Party of the Cuban Socialist Revolution), the predecessor of the unified Partido Comunista de Cuba (Cuban Communist Party, PCC) consecrated as the superior guiding force of the Revolution in 1965. This was not a perfectly smooth merger, as we will see in chapter 3. But in theory, the "true" forces of anti-Batista opposition, and even several of their once disputatious newspapers, had merged.[52] In this context, once jealous defenders of the anti-Batista legacy in exile may have concluded that the time had come to abandon the purity of their prior convictions so as to answer the Revolution's united front with their own.

Simultaneously, the eventual slowing of the exodus from the island provided a window of opportunity for unifying exile worldviews. For many Cubans on the island still on the fence about whether to stay or leave, the defeat of the Bay of Pigs invasion was the last straw. Consequently, the second half of 1961 and much of 1962 saw increasing numbers of middle-class Cubans seek passage out of the county at whatever cost, convinced that hope for a quick, U.S.-backed overthrow of the revolutionary government was lost.[53] Nonetheless, even as family already in Miami received them with open arms, such "recent" arrivals also faced questions in the press—much as Miró Cardona and others like him had in 1960—as to whether they had been complicit with the Revolution initially and why it had taken so long for them to get out. (Cundo's poem cited at the beginning of this chapter provides a good example of these feelings.) Thus, when the Cuban Missile Crisis in October 1962 ended direct flights to the United States, the pausing of the exodus was tragic for those with relatives still left behind, but it also provided a breather allowing more conservative elements of the exile community to give their own retrospective recriminations a break. From both sides of the pro- and anti-Batista divide, the chance to outline the terms of a genuine reconciliation of exile views was perhaps finally taking shape.

In fact, consistent with Miró Cardona's own thinking, the mid-1960s saw less a merger of historical schools of thought than the "Revolution betrayed" mantra lose influence under the weight of more conservative paradigms. One indication was the emergence of a civic organization called Cruzada Educativa Cubana (Cuban Educational Crusade, CEC), founded in 1962. Ostensibly, the CEC was devoted to nonpartisan tasks like keeping the flame of Cuban patriotism alive among exile children through radio broadcasts, booklets, and educational programs.[54] The group also began planning for the "decommunization" of the Cuban educational system after the revolutionary government nationalized private and parochial schools in May 1961.[55] Yet CEC's programming would also stand out in another way: it slyly naturalized forms of pro-Batista historical thinking. Given the roster of the organization's founders, this was not a surprise. Founder María Gómez Carbonell, the first woman elected to Cuba's Congress, had served as a senator during Batista's lone period of constitutional rule from 1940 to 1944 and later as a minister without portfolio in his cabinet in the 1950s. Vicente Cauce, another of the organization's leaders, had been Batista's last minister of education and was another follower of the strongman across his political career. CEC initiatives thus fostered a depiction of Cuban history before 1959 as a story of continuity and progress, insisting upon Cuba's substantial economic achievements prior to the Revolution. But unlike more overtly pro-Batista outlets, the CEC spoke more amorphously of a "republican" era interrupted, undermined, or destroyed by the internationally driven and domestically abetted forces of communism.[56] The organization sublimated the conflicts over the character of the Batista era itself under the facade of a shared "Republic," a "free Cuba" all exiles had lost.

In this way, supporters of Fulgencio Batista in Miami did indicate a certain willingness to forge shared memory platforms around which all exiles could unite. Just as Miró Cardona had come to accept the premise of letting some pro-Batista elements into the fold, some of the latter recognized that there was little use harboring perennial vindictiveness toward those who had cheered on Fidel's rise. Still, CEC expressed this view in ways that whitewashed rather than acknowledged Batista's record. And as farfetched as the notion of a shared political culture before 1959 may have seemed to Miró Cardona and other enduring critics of Batista's coup, the analytical shorthand simplistically dividing Cuba's "republican" from its "revolutionary" eras began to catch on, proving as, if not more, influential than the betrayal thesis over time. As one college student wrote for a CEC-sponsored essay contest, "The history of Cuba reveals a process of development in which the island was prospering and growing richer. Communism abruptly interrupted this process without any precedents to suggest the coming Cuban disaster."[57] Needless to say, this periodization mirrored, in the inverse, the Cuban government's increasing reliance on a master narrative that cast Cuba's pre-1959 years as a shameful period to be overcome—that of a "pseudo-republic"—save for the efforts of predecessors who had paved the way for revolutionary victory.

At the same time, the "Revolution betrayed" idea also found ways to coexist or even fuse with more bullish appraisals of Cuba's pre-1959 past to which, in theory, it should have been opposed. A good example is the 1963 documentary *Cuba: Satélite 13* (*Cuba: 13th Satellite*), directed by Manuel de la Pedrosa and produced by Eduardo Palmer, with the title referencing Cuba's purported conversion into the Soviet Union's newest pawn (and first outside of Eastern Europe).[58] The film begins with a nostalgic description of Cuba in the 1950s that could have been lifted from Batista's memoirs. "Before falling under the hammer and sickle, this was the Cuba before January 1, 1959, ... a country that was passing through the most thriving moment of its economic history, with cities like Havana experiencing an increasing rhythm of expansion." What follows are four-plus minutes of additional praise, with statistics celebrating Cuba's highly productive prerevolutionary lands, high per capita rates of TV ownership, and even average daily calorie intake. "The constant opening of new industries permitted us to consider that Cuba [before the Revolution] was on the path to its elevation [as a nation]." By this measure, there seems to be no need for a revolution at all.

But then *Cuba: Satélite 13* pivots to narrative hallmarks of the betrayal thesis. The narrator enumerates Fidel Castro's broken pledges to return Cuba to a path of electoral normalcy after the Batista period. Taped clips of Castro denying that he is communist in 1959 confirm the charges. Though the voice-over narration implies that Fidel's promises were always disingenuous, it does not impugn those who collaborated with or defected from the Revolution in its first months. In this way, trademarks of pro- and anti-Batista thought in exile become awkwardly conjoined. This is all the more remarkable as much of the footage in *Cuba: Satélite 13* was lifted from another film de la Pedrosa and Palmer made on the island in 1959, *Gesta inmortal* (*Immortal Feat*), which *celebrated* the road to Batista's fall and the social, not just political, Revolution that threw him out.[59] That is, not only was *Cuba: Satélite 13* a palimpsest because it blended two exile narratives that would seem to be at odds; in *Cuba: Satélite 13* de la Pedrosa and Palmer also literally wrote over how they had once celebrated the arrival of the Revolution themselves.[60]

As time passed, therefore, one could point to evidence of at least partial memory fusions and burials of prior legacy battles within the exile world. Resulting truces remained weak, but they did seem to be gaining ground. Still, we cannot understand this incomplete drift toward greater unity without considering another factor that made it possible: many exiles' growing frustration with the U.S. government. This last element is crucial to understanding the development of Cuban exile retrospective politics, especially in the mid-1960s. For while many in the "Revolution betrayed" camp had been consumed in 1960 and 1961 by arguments against Batista followers, a second accusation of betrayal levied at the United States increasingly blurred into the first. Ironically, just as an anti-imperialist reading of Cuba's history became the anchor of the Revolution's story of self, a streak of anti-Washington sentiment in Miami also helped solidify some exiles' sense of a shared fate.

Of course, U.S. efforts to dethrone Castro had not ceased. In late 1961, the Kennedy administration launched Operation Mongoose, a comprehensive covert plan of action overseen by Attorney General Robert Kennedy. Plots ranged from induced crop failures to assassination attempts, all designed to spark a popular revolt against the Castro government in conjunction with Washington's "Economic Denial Program," the sanctions regime and trade embargo first put in place in the fall of 1960. Run out of Miami, Mongoose involved Cuban exiles of diverse backgrounds, including those who believed the "real" Revolution had been betrayed. Yet Miró Cardona and others, still at the CRC at the time, were right to note a change in strategy. As the CIA began favoring individual exile raids and psywar schemes, a number of actors waiting for a "second invasion" felt increasingly left in the dark.[61]

The Cuban Missile Crisis of October 1962 planted even stronger seeds of doubt toward U.S. intentions, becoming another shared point of retrospective grievance. In one of his secret messages to the Soviet premier, Nikita Khrushchev, during those fateful thirteen days, President Kennedy suggested that a prompt Soviet withdrawal of missiles from Cuba would be met with a U.S. pledge not to invade the island. When news of this tentative commitment broke, the exile press howled with criticisms of the so-called Kennedy-Khrushchev Pact. In reality, no concrete "pact" was signed, and a number of the principal actors involved in Miró Cardona's original coalition would continue to be paid by the CIA. Nonetheless, in March 1963, Kennedy publicly pledged to stem exile raids on Cuban targets, at least those launched from U.S. shores. Groups not directly subordinate to the agency—"freelance" militants funded under Operation Mongoose yet given operational independence—increasingly found themselves surveilled and impeded from carrying out maritime raids.[62]

Then, in mid- and late 1964, the disastrous failure of several freelance commando attacks on the island from outside U.S. territory led to a sharper shift in Washington's approach. In June, a planned raid by the so-called Junta Revolucionaria Cubana (Cuban Revolutionary Junta), a new organization created by Manuel Ray, ended in a debacle when Ray was found adrift by British authorities near the Bahamas. Several months later, Manuel Artime's original MRR, still active and receiving CIA support, accidentally downed a Spanish merchant vessel off the Cuban coast before beating a hasty retreat back to bases in Central America. Finally, former Castro ally turned anti-Castro militant Eloy Gutiérrez Menoyo— the previous leader of the Second Front of the Escambray in Cuba, who had made his way to Miami in 1960—received a thirty-year Cuban jail sentence after a failed incursion onto island soil. Soon thereafter, CIA financial support to these and other similar ex-revolutionaries began drying up.[63] With White House attention increasingly focused on Vietnam, U.S. pressure on exile militants engendered strident, and perhaps delusional, calls that Washington give them "freedom to fight."[64]

In these ways, the U.S. "alliance" that exile fighters and politicians had initially embraced at the risk of compromising their nationalist credentials seemed to be falling apart. Articulations of exile identity, in turn, began coalescing around new targets of retrospective anger. Washington's fickleness provided a fresh point of focus for exiles to vent their frustrations, regardless of which Cuban political camp they belonged to or their vision of who was culpable in Cuba for Castro's rise. Invocations of the Revolution's lost promises became less prominent. Instead, Washington's "abandonment" provided fertile ground for both questioning the terms of partnership going forward and concluding that Washington had been an unreliable sponsor all along.

Yet even retrospective indictments of Washington's broken promises did not proceed in a straightforward way. It has long been an article of faith, for example, that Cuban exiles blame the Bay of Pigs defeat on President Kennedy's last-minute decision to call off a final set of clandestine air strikes prior to the invasion. Bombings of several airports were meant to neutralize Cuba's air force, thus providing the exile invaders cover for an unimpeded amphibious landing. When Kennedy called off the last such strikes for fear of revealing U.S. involvement, members of the Brigade 2506 were left exposed from above. But not until the mid-1960s, in the aftermath of Washington's decrease of support for exile militancy, did this simplistic argument gain significant traction in public. (Even with greater air cover, the invasion still would have failed.) In 1964, the Bay of Pigs Veterans Association, founded after the Brigade 2506 survivors returned to Miami in December 1962, published a note praising Kennedy on what would have been his forty-seventh birthday.[65] Influential texts like Haynes Johnson's *The Bay of Pigs: The Leaders' Story of Brigade 2506* (1964), based on interviews with the Brigade 2506's military chiefs, placed most blame on the CIA's faulty planning.[66] According to invasion veteran Alfredo Durán, the theory of Kennedy's "betrayal" only began to catch on when the Republican Party of Florida worked to convert the idea into an electoral talking point.[67]

By 1968, U.S.-born Cuban lawyer Mario Lazo's retrospective denunciation *Dagger in the Heart: American Policy Failures in Cuba* gave the argument wider form. The book not only blamed Kennedy for the Bay of Pigs but also lambasted previous U.S. policymakers for fecklessly ignoring Castro's nefarious intentions all along.[68] In this way, creeping narratives of U.S. betrayal could also approximate the views of the pro-Batista camp. The United States should have listened, Lazo implied, when some Cubans had warned about Castro's alleged communist inclinations back in the 1950s. But the broader point remains: whether blaming the long-term blindness of Eisenhower's team or Kennedy's air coverage debacle, a new element in exile memory discourse added a complementary culprit to the list of those responsible for their nation's calamity: the United States.

Members of the exile community thus began flirting with the paradoxical characteristics of what historian Phuong Nguyen has called in another context a conditional "refugee nationalism."[69] Many Cuban exiles could and did express gratitude to their host country for opening its doors to them as expatriates. Yet many also resented the whims of U.S. foreign policy strategists who pledged anticommunist commitment but failed, from their perspective, to give them the real tools to succeed. Nevertheless, exile political leaders never devised a successful counterargument to those—especially in Cuba—who construed their links to the U.S. government within the same broader Cuban historical tradition of U.S.-dependent politics that even many versions of the "true," noncommunist Revolution were supposed to have reversed. Some seemed to have forgotten their original skittishness about walking the fine line between their nationalism and the choice of accepting U.S. support. Mainstream voices increasingly argued that the United States had not done enough, not that it was a mistake to have counted on Washington's help in the first place.[70]

Historical Stiff Necks

Despite the potential of shared animus toward Washington to constitute a new basis for a retrospective consensus, lasting unity across the exile community's pre-1959 political divides would remain elusive. The mid-1960s are dotted with dozens of projects that intended to bury past grievances once and for all among feuding early exile groups. But they continued to founder along old factional lines, even as many exiles now shared a goal of advancing the anti-Castro cause with or without Washington's support. In March 1964, for example, well-known historian and former Batista-era official Emeterio Santovenia joined internationally recognized Cuban cardiologist Augustín Castellanos in calling on a who's who of Cuban politicians and activists from the past to put "aside personal or sectarian beliefs."[71] Their proposal for a "Cuban Democratic Coordinating Junta"—like literally dozens of similar bodies proposed over the decade—did not bear fruit.

There are too many other examples to mention. Most successful perhaps was the unity front Representación Cubana en el Exilio (Cuban Representation in Exile, RECE), proposed and funded by José "Pepín" Bosch, the exiled chairman of influential Cuban company Bacardí Rum, in late 1963. (Bacardí, incidentally, had once been among Fidel Castro's financial supporters, only to see its assets nationalized in 1960.) But RECE, too, became less active by the late 1960s, after the Federal Bureau of Investigation (FBI) infiltrated its ranks and curtailed the unsuccessful armed raids it funded by affiliated commando groups.[72] The more exiles tried, the more they seemed to fall into old habits. In 1966, for instance, *Patria*, the typically pro-Batista newspaper, challenged former president Carlos Prío Socarrás, Carlos Márquez-Sterling (head of Cuba's constitutional assembly in 1940 and a founder of the Partido Ortodoxo), and Fulgencio Batista to join forces at the head of a grand exile alliance.[73] When Prío rejected the idea, *Patria*'s director Armando García Sifredo called out the former president for contributing $50,000 to the 26th of July Movement in 1956 as well as failing to break openly with the Castro government until early 1961.[74] Back and forth went the slinging of more memory mud.

Minor and major feuds seemed too deep to be forgotten. Among the longest lasting was that between *Patria* and the exiled veterans of the pre-1959 *Bohemia* magazine. *Bohemia Libre*, as noted above, was an early mouthpiece for the theory of the Revolution betrayed. But *Patria* had long pilloried its editor Miguel Ángel Quevedo for his prior work in Cuba, where *Bohemia*'s coverage of Batista's misdeeds—notwithstanding off and on censorship—was accused of helping to usher in the takeover of the revolutionary regime.[75] Did Quevedo take these and similar accusations to heart? Had he become wracked by self-doubt? Some presumed so: after a failed attempt in 1965, he succeeded in ending his own life in Caracas, Venezuela, in 1969.

The real motive of Quevedo's suicide, however, remains unknown. There is a suicide note attributed to Quevedo that circulates widely today (mostly online). Addressed to *Patria*'s chief editor, Ernesto Montaner, the purported letter appears to give pro-Batista voices several things they long wanted to hear: for starters, a confession that the fabled 20,000 dead attributed to the Batista regime in early 1959 had been a lie that *Bohemia* "invented" along the way. In one portion of the text, Quevedo also appears to identify Cuba's communist tragedy as the natural conclusion of a progressive political tradition that was bound to lead to demagoguery. The United States even comes in for denunciation for ceding to demands that it stop supporting Batista with arms. (This is ironic, given that revolutionaries of all stripes had been unanimous in their criticism of U.S. support for Batista in the 1950s.) Still, if the degree of Quevedo's pivot to pro-Batista thinking in parts of the letter seems surprising, that is because the letter is likely false. Former colleagues of Quevedo deny its veracity. Some even allege that Montaner wrote it himself in a ploy to sully *Bohemia*'s memory.[76]

Even so, the apocryphal text also remains a powerful testament to someone's characterization of recent Cuban history as a wider national tragedy in which all Cubans share responsibility. The "Quevedo" who authored the letter does not only blame himself; he blames all. "I know that after I'm dead mountains of accusations will fall on my tomb," one paragraph reads, "That they will want to present me as 'the only one guilty' for Cuba's disgrace. And I do not deny my errors or my guilt. What I do deny is that I was the 'only one guilty.' We were all guilty to a greater or lesser degree of responsibility."[77] As much as exiles argued with each other or harbored a sense of frustration with the United States, exile retrospective politics were also haunted by suspicions of *collective* culpability. Even former Batista officials would make similar confessions eventually.[78]

Together, this kind of evidence disrupts a more comfortable version of the exile story, one where shared memories of a uniformly "free" country "lost" to communism became the anchors of self-confident, if heartrending historical belief. Despite bonds forged through common longings and shared traumas as immigrants, plenty of exile observers not only fretted about their own roles in the nation's perceived disaster but also lamented the fact that the memory fabric of their community remained internally torn. "I have not known and do not know a plan for liberating our nation that could be classified as serious, logical, realistic, and achievable," wrote former 26th of July Movement gunrunner and later anti-Castro collaborator Ricardo Lorie to José Miró Cardona in 1970, on the heels of yet another failed unity plan to take down the Castro government. Hope was lost, he insisted, because "those who say that Batista was right and that the blame lies with the ex-Fidelistas and those ex-Fidelistas who say and separate and use adjectives to indicate whether or not someone is acceptable based on the portion of guilt that corresponds to them" remained at each other's throats.[79] For some, the act and long-term consequences of leaving Cuba itself represented a source of misgiving. Just consider the possible psychological effect of reading the following characterization of exile as an abdication of historical responsibility in a letter from a "dear friend" still on the island in 1963: "Here, my friend, there are few 'desperate ones' left who are capable of adding to the ranks of the [anti-Castro] martyrs. And the fact that there are [no more martyrs] is something that can be blamed on Yankee 'refugee' policy. In the struggle against Batista, the 'desperate ones' had only one path: go to the mountains [and join the rebels]. In the struggle against Castro, the preferred path is emigrating, where with more or less work one can resolve the basic problems of subsistence."[80]

Ten years after Fidel Castro marched into Havana, Cuban exiles from the first wave of exodus between 1959 and 1962 remained mired in the quotidian memory battles enacted by Cundo's sardonic poem with which this chapter began. Some were also left to wonder whether their departures had served as an "escape valve," playing into the Revolution's hands. The "chronology of departure," exiled Christian Democrat politician José

Ignacio Rasco observed in 1969, remained "a ready source [una cantera, literally a quarry] of divisions," as conservative voices in the community still commonly accused those who came to the United States after 1960 of greater complicity in the enthroning of a tropical communist tyranny.[81] From semiretirement, Miró Cardona expressed deep disappointment at exiles' seeming inability to overcome retrospective divides. "Cuba pains me," he wrote. "It pains me greatly. But [Cuba] will not escape from its current bind as long as our compatriots continue their sterile rivalries, looking back to the past, which because it is past is irreversible."[82] More than irreversible, argued Rasco, history had become useless, a debilitating specter leading to the "petrifaction" of national symbols and the replication of outdated schemes: "El pasado sin pasar" ("The past has not passed").[83]

All told, the exile body politic suffered from debilitating *asincronía*, a sense of being "out of time," Rasco felt. Put another way, he added, the community remained plagued by a terminal case of "tortícolis histórica" (historical stiff neck)—a tendency to look back repeatedly at what was and had been rather than projecting an effective vision of what could be.[84] Yet the exile world was also internally disturbed, divided into distinct cohorts whose views remained grounded in the separate social words and political traditions from whence individual émigrés came. If the "maniac" Fidel, as depicted by one exile cartoonist, had turned Cuba into something it was never supposed to be, the exile community had served as a breeding ground for its own inhabitants' retrospective neuroses.[85] "Exile is a madhouse," noted Armando García Sifredo tersely in *Patria*, "Our brains have gone on vacation."[86] Insanity, agreed José Miró Cardona in a 1964 letter to confidant Adolfo Rivero, described the collective memory of the early exile experience perfectly:

> In Rome, in 1938, I was studying Penal Law, and one of the subjects that we had to study was "Criminal Psychiatry." ... [One day, the Professor] brought us to the cell of some of the most dangerous and criminally insane.... When we opened the cell, the guard on duty, a nurse really, was stretched out on a bench, sleeping like a baby and snoring. Yes, SNORING.... Shocked, I asked[:] "How is possible that this guard can sleep peacefully surrounded by more than forty crazy patients?" The professor looked at me, smiled, and said: "They're crazy. Do you really think it's possible for so many crazy people to come to an agreement? If one of them decides to attack the guard, certainly others will defend him and he'll wake up." In effect, Riverito, only crazy people are incapable of agreement. The moral of the story I leave to you."[87]

Conclusion: Beyond Nostalgia, Memories of Defeat

The Cuban Revolution grounded its historic legitimacy in a claim to realizing the nation's long unfulfilled promise. Cubans leaving the island in the early 1960s framed the island's turn to socialism and radical anti-imperialism as destiny denied. Particularly influential was the interpretation that cast the original anti-Batista movement as necessary but "betrayed," drawing on formulations pioneered in the contentious political environment between 1959 and 1960 back home. Yet this view competed in exile circles with more bullish interpretations of Batista's 1950s, or those that took Fidel Castro's allegedly broken promises as proof that suspicions of his revolution had been justified all along.

The counterpoints of exile memory politics were thus multiple, never quite allowing for the creation of a perfectly united front. They involved Miami's own version of a post-1959 blame game, but they also reflected expatriate attempts to reconcile U.S. tutelage with a historic cannon of nationalist agency. Casting such battles as petty squabbling or purely the stuff of personal rivalries does a disservice to both the history of Cubans in the United States and the seriousness of competing memory formations they brought with them. Ignoring these facets of the exile memory wars risks putting on a retrospective set of rose-colored glasses, ones through which the story of exile becomes simply an epic of shared struggle rather than the terrain of conflict and disappointment that many politically active exiles recognized it to be.

This is not to deny that nostalgia could serve as a powerful binder of community sentiment. By the mid-1960s, local memory industries catering to such predilections were functioning in full force in Cuban enclaves in Miami. Expatriates were busy resurrecting the institutions, brands, restaurants, and even schools they lost after the socialist nationalizations of private businesses and institutions began in earnest in 1960 and 1961. Panart Records—itself a recreation of a no-longer existent company in Cuba—was several pressings in to its *Así cantaba Cuba libre* (*So Sang Free Cuba*), a two-volume compilation that became a staple in countless exile homes.[88] *Añorada Cuba* (*Longed-for Cuba*), an annual Miami revue celebrating the island's past through music and dance, debuted to grand fanfare in 1964. Little Havana was quickly becoming a living memorial to the "Cuba of yesteryear." Together, such communal spaces and cultural texts provided clear contrasts to increasingly ubiquitous depictions on the island of the pre-1959 era as a uniformly dark age.[89]

Likewise, as we saw, increasingly common invocations of a precommunist "free Cuba" among exile organizations and in the expatriate media

Figure 2.2. Nostalgia as unifying force? Ironically, the creator of this cartoon is the same cartoonist who created Figure 2.1, which represents the betrayal narrative. Could exiles believe some version of revolution in Cuba was necessary at the same time that they lamented a paradise lost? Antonio Rubio, "Enter the Cuba of Yesterday," cover of *Zig-zag Libre*, May 20, 1971.

perpetuated a conspicuous and influential retrospective elision. In contrast to those who clung to the belief that some kind of political and social change was necessary in Cuba in the 1950s, the straightforward notion of a lost "Republic" naturalized what had always been Batista supporters' preferred avoidance of their government's lack of democratic credentials, emphasizing a total break. Together with exiles' growing anger at U.S. "abandonment," such discourses created a new anchor for unity, at least ostensibly. Cuba's fate was a shared tragedy, many argued, the story of a "paradise" that both communist machinations and U.S. indecision had managed to "turn into hell."[90]

But the unifying premises of nostalgia and exile anti-Americanism were perhaps less cures for the exile community's factional memory wounds than their complements. As critic Ricardo L. Ortiz has noted, "Nostalgia, as a form of mourning, is necessarily ambivalent, a psychic labor haunted by the guilt one bears for that loss, the sneaking suspicion of complicity and culpability in the loss that weighs the mourner down."[91] In this way, exiles' increasingly prominent longings for the country they left behind— whether the simplistic "restorative" variety that lamented a lost Eden or the more inwardly "reflective" brand that Ortiz limns[92]—can be seen as the necessary extension of contending attributions of historical responsibility that lay at the heart of the community's retrospective disputes. Bearing in mind that the term "nostalgia" itself was coined in the seventeenth century to describe a psychic illness, it might be best understood not as a replacement for the early factionalism of the exile memory wars but as a corresponding symptom of a wider memory malaise.[93] After all, by the mid- and late 1960s, competing individual trajectories of participation in events leading to and after the revolutionary takeover of 1959 were *still* popping up as sources of debate. And as we also saw, hallmarks of Batista-era boosterism and the idea that some kind of revolution against his rule was necessary could at times oddly fuse.

Remembering in exile was thus often the result of "re-membering," a stitching together of preexisting and sometimes inconsistent narrative parts. Vis-à-vis events in Cuba, however, such maneuverings came at a cost. As José Ignacio Rasco suggested at a symposium in 1969, if shared forms of longing provided *some* connective glue for a collective sense of exiles' history, that vision only underscored just how distant the moral universe of the diaspora had become from everyday life in a homeland transformed. With the passage of time, he argued, the mere ninety miles separating exiles from the island was growing into an insurmountable void. "Neither the man on the inside is capable of understanding the exile, nor the latter capable of comprehending the former."[94] Indeed, memory feuds from within the exile world had little relevance for those who embraced the Revolution's turn to socialism. Nor did more uncritical attachments to the past, to the extent they existed, provide a map of a real future that island citizens could embrace.

Ultimately, neither nostalgia nor the presumed universal applicability of the term "exile"—with its ingrained claims for fundamentally common experiences of forced uprooting for political reasons—proved capable of healing the community's memory wounds. Early Cuban exiles in Miami in the 1960s held themselves to the impossible standard of unity, confronting as the years passed a distinct sense of disappointment as that harmony failed to materialize. Regardless of a later record of achievement in their adopted home, some would never get over having lost the battle for Cuba itself. More than idle banter, such testimonies of tragedy and embarrassment remind us that what community supporters today celebrate as a pro-American success story began in many ways as a tale of collective division and regret.

3

Remembering (through) Girón

As Cuban exiles stewed in the remorse born of disappointment, one event persistently haunted Miami's retrospective imagination: the Bay of Pigs. If political contradictions and faulty assumptions doomed the plot from the start, the invasion also served as an inescapable reference point for expatriate lore. In retrospect, it was the one juncture when a unified community might have consolidated, if only Washington had not been so stingy, anticommunist activists concluded. Or if only the fractious historical legacies exiles brought to Miami had not again exploded into public view following the Brigade 2506's defeat.[1]

On the island, the inverse was true. The Bay of Pigs provided a new reminder that revolutionary unity could be a matter of life and death. Faced with a foreign-backed amphibious landing, heterodox, centrist, or constructive critiques of the Revolution's leftward evolution became even more difficult in the "with us/against us" climate that the military incursion sowed. Not for nothing did Che Guevara secretly thank White House emissary Richard N. Goodwin "very much for the invasion" in a now infamous conversation on the sidelines of a regional summit in Uruguay several months later. Girón, Guevara argued, represented both a military and a "political victory" that "consolidated" support for Cuba's radicalizing transformations at the grassroots.[2]

The truth was not quite so neat, or permanent, as we will see. Nonetheless, it was not surprising that Fidel Castro chose the eve of the attack—April 16, 1961, to be precise—to finally describe the Revolution as "socialist" in a public speech. Pending U.S. aggression gave revolutionary authorities the needed impetus, or cover, to match stated ideological affiliation to events on the ground. Simultaneously, the invasion cast Cuba's historic battle for sovereignty against U.S. machinations into such clear relief that many Cubans no doubt ignored the reversal of previous assertions that the Revolution did not fit a prescribed political mold. In subsequent years, the Bay of Pigs—or, in island parlance, simply "Girón," the main beach where the battle took place—would be celebrated repeatedly in public as the turning point when Cubans assumed the full promise and implications of their anti-imperialist ideals. In April 1961, Fidel Castro later argued, the island had faced the clearest choice yet between not just "treason or loyalty to principles, capitalism or socialism," but "past and future."[3]

For these reasons, it is worth exploring initial attempts to identify and characterize the invasion's significance in Cuba, as well as the commemorative practices and discourses that took shape in its wake. Over the 1960s, Girón represented more than legend, legacy, or fable; it generated an ever-expanding corpus of books, films, television broadcasts, memoirs, and countless other artifacts of material and visual reach. It provided the most dramatic example of a wider pattern of U.S.-backed aggression against the Cuban revolutionary government across the 1960s that became central to the Revolution's own memory canon and historical identity. Still, even as victory confirmed Cuba's status as "free territory of the Americas," disquieting ambiguities could trouble the meaning and memory of success. Older historical ghosts from the early factional wars of 1959 and 1960 had a funny way of popping up. In a series of televised interrogations in the days immediately following the exiles' defeat, for instance, imprisoned members of the invading Brigade 2506 advanced their own vexing arguments about where the Revolution had gone wrong. And by the mid- to late 1960s, some Cubans would turn to the memory of the invasion to subtly question whether the Revolution had lived up to the luminous potential that victory at Girón had originally enshrined.

In this sense, this chapter is not just, or even centrally, about how the invasion itself was memorialized in monuments, published paeans to deceased soldiers, or speeches. Rather, it traces the lesser-known story of the event's role as a recurring touchstone for reflecting on the Revolution's wider historic purpose and, for some Cubans by the late 1960s, its diminished hopes. The Bay of Pigs offered a lasting, if not untroubled allegory of revolutionary righteousness and anti-imperialist resistance. It could provide inspiration when in the mid-1960s the utopia that Cuban revolutionaries initially hoped to achieve seemed at times not closer but further away. But it was also a prism through which Cubans could reflect on the Revolution's costs. It is in this last respect that we once again see how the Cuban memory wars involved dynamic processes of reflection and contestation, as well as points of implicit and explicit contact between insular and exilic memory frameworks.

To start the story here, however, would be to skip a crucial prelude. Far before 1,500 exile soldiers ever hit the beach, the Bay of Pigs and the neighboring Ciénaga de Zapata (or Zapata Swamp) had become a geographic symbol pregnant with historical significance. Before the Revolution's rise to power, the Ciénaga was an impoverished backwater where the island's economic inequalities and rural injustices were at their worst. From the early days of 1959, therefore, the area emerged as a prominent site of the Revolution's programmatic and narrative attention. Not just the battle at the Bay of Pigs but the history of the region surrounding it would provide one of the more durable metaphors for elucidating the stakes of the Revolution in the first place, a topographical monument to the oppressive past that Cuban socialism aimed to overcome.

Before the Invasion:
The Ciénaga de Zapata as National Synecdoche

On November 9, 1955, at the University of Havana's Enrique José Varona Amphitheater, aspiring twenty-nine-year-old director Julio García Espinosa screened his short film *El Mégano* for the first time. Shot semiclandestinely with a group of friends in a tiny community of the same name, the piece represented a small attempt to expose the horrific conditions faced by impoverished charcoal makers in the Ciénaga de Zapata. The quickly confiscated drama marked the debut of a socially conscious cohort of filmmakers linked to the PSP, all of whom would be among the founders of Cuba's film institute, ICAIC, in 1959.[4] But, as important, it inaugurated a tradition of turning to the physical place of the swamps as an influential emblem of the national injustice the coming revolution pledged to sweep away.

Located roughly a hundred miles southeast of Havana, the Ciénaga de Zapata was far removed from the hustle and bustle of Cuba's capital. Although the sugar industry in Matanzas province had encroached on its borders long ago, the Zapata swamp still contained one of the largest, most isolated wetlands systems in the Caribbean, seemingly abandoned by history and the "development" that pro-Batista voices in exile would celebrate as the legacy of his rule. To the extent that there was any economic activity in the region prior to 1959, *cenagueros* (Ciénaga residents) had traditionally worked for logging interests. As deforestation set in, however, the only option for inhabitants not tied to neighboring sugar plantations was to join the ranks of the *carboneros*, miserably paid laborers who dug up felled wood buried in the muck, turned it into charcoal (*carbón*) in handmade ovens, and sold it for a pittance to intermediaries for sale in urban centers. As census data collected by the Batista government in 1953 confirms, the region was among the poorest in the country, with rates of infant mortality (65 per 1,000) almost double the national average and illiteracy reaching close to 50 percent.[5]

To be sure, the Ciénaga de Zapata was not the first or even the most significant area of the island to have its particular tribulations turned into national synecdoche by the incipient revolutionary government. That honor went to the Sierra Maestra, where Fidel Castro's guerrilla rebels had established a state in miniature over the course of their insurgency in the late 1950s.[6] After the Batista government fled, the Sierra Maestra remained a preeminent site of political and policy spectacle—a showcase where, for example, the government held July 26th celebrations in 1960 and first assayed policy transformations to come nationwide.[7] Even so, given that the anti-Batista struggle had barely passed through the Ciénaga de Zapata itself, it is surprising how quickly the area emerged as a second major arena of mass-mediated revolutionary exorcism and reform. Fidel Castro quickly took a personal interest in the region, visiting as early as March 16, 1959.[8] He had a knowledgeable guide in Antonio Núñez Jiménez, a noted geologist and member of the PSP who had finished the anti-Batista struggle as a captain in the 26th of July Movement's Rebel Army.

In May 1959, Núñez Jiménez was named head of the powerful Instituto Nacional de Reforma Agraria (National Institute of Agrarian Reform, INRA), the entity charged with implementing Cuba's massive land confiscation and redistribution program. Yet before Fidel Castro established this body or signed Cuba's monumental agrarian reform into law, ambitions to bring physical change to the swamp already had begun to take shape. A plan for the rehabilitation of the Ciénaga de Zapata was in place shortly after Fidel first visited, and in April, the well-regarded national newspaper *El Crisol* reported that Cuba's revolutionary armed forces—a more formalized iteration of the victorious Rebel Army—had begun initial work toward reforestation.[9] Whether Fidel or other government leaders had seen *El Mégano* by this point is unclear. But in *Bohemia* Núñez Jiménez hailed the swamp as a "treasure of nature" waiting to be transformed.[10] First and foremost, this meant converting the Ciénaga de Zapata's natural bounty and pristine beaches into a tourist attraction. Soon, national authorities, geologists, and agricultural planners were also collaborating with a Dutch company to begin sketching a more ambitious and, in retrospect, environmentally catastrophic plan to reclaim close to 500,000 acres of the swampland (or 15,000 *caballerías*, the traditional land measurement used in Cuba at the time) for the growing of rice.[11] "Nature is also *latifundista*," Castro declared during one of his visits in early 1959, equating the swamp with the abusive large landowners that the Revolution would soon begin wiping from Cuba's historical and property map.[12]

Quite literally, revolutionary authorities hoped to erase the geographical constraints of the region's past. The rice initiative also sought to address a national Achilles' heel: a long history of import dependence for a key staple of almost every Cuban meal.[13] Progress, though, appeared in smaller signs at first. In November 1959, *Noticias de Hoy* reported the arrival in Havana of a caravan of eighteen trucks from the Ciénaga de Zapata filled with 400 sacks of charcoal to be sold "for the first time" directly to distributors and shopkeepers in the capital, thus securing the *carboneros* a fair wage. Twenty "People's Stores" were established to provide residents of the swamp's environs with goods that were more local and affordable. Soon, work on new hotel and tourist facilities began, with the aim of making them the pride of Cuba's new Instituto Nacional de la Industria Turística (National Institute of the Tourist Industry). Meanwhile, the construction of highways and canals in the area under government direction provided community members with much needed work. In time, INRA promised, new jobs and homes would accommodate 15,000 or 20,000 families. When plans to convert the swamplands into rice acreage were finished, the area's integration into the national economy would be complete.[14]

It was thus fitting that Fidel Castro opted to spend the revolutionary era's first Christmas Eve, or *Nochebuena*, with *carboneros* in the small settlement of Soplillar, just a stone's throw from the beaches where Cuban exile invaders would land in a year and a half. As Fidel noted in a November 27 speech, spoiled inhabitants of the Cuban capital might profitably visit the area to rid themselves of the urban "gossip" and "intrigue" obscuring the Revolution's transformative rural work.[15] Covered with particular drama in a six-page spread in the eponymously titled magazine of INRA, the *comandante*'s photogenic feast with Ciénaga de Zapata residents supplied a captivating montage where images and words highlighted the leader's instinctive rapport with the island's common citizens. Just shy of one year since coming to power, Fidel also figuratively retraced in this journey his march west at the end of the anti-Batista war. "To be frank, when you all were fighting in the mountains," said one *carbonero* to Fidel, "I didn't believe that his Revolution would be so pure. There were so many disappointments in the past." Now, the *comandante* had come to the swamp not only to connect with some of the Revolution's most deserving beneficiaries but also to demonstrate that his government was delivering on its promises.[16]

From that point, the public relations and mnemonic utility of the Ciénaga de Zapata only grew. Fidel's rustic *Nochebuena* with the *carboneros* went down in revolutionary lore.[17] But in addition to providing domestic audiences a fitting window into the countryside under renovation, Cuba's largest swamp also became a desirable pit stop for distinguished emissaries. In October 1959, Fidel brought noted North American author Waldo Frank to survey the region after the revolutionary government hired him to pen an English-language portrait of Cuba's incipient revolution.[18] When Soviet emissary Anastas Mikoyan touched down in Havana in February 1960, part of his itinerary included a night at the Ciénaga de Zapata's Treasure Lake, a tourist site under development.[19] Perhaps most famous was the visit of Jean-Paul Sartre and Simone de Beauvoir some weeks later. As Sartre later wrote, Fidel had come to treat the swamp as his own personal "El Dorado," acquiring a spartan rural retreat. After showing the French existentialist and a pair of unexpected U.S. visitors around what amounted to little more than a barracks and some bunks, Fidel commented on the value of his performance. "I carried on some excellent propaganda," he joked.[20]

Throughout 1960, attention to the ambitious public works and tourist development initiatives in the Ciénaga de Zapata remained steady.[21] According to INRA, by January 1961, new facilities and capital investments at Playa Girón included "two motels with 180 rooms, 152 furnished beach cabanas, an aqueduct, a small airport, a beach clubhouse for tourists, a large pool, public dining halls, medical centers, hospitals, highways, schools, and a long seaside promenade."[22] The Revolution deployed other social facets of its modernizing project to the area too: formal inscription of residents in a civil registry, as well as mass marriage ceremonies as part of "Operación Familia," a plan to stabilize family structures in underserved communities and in many ways a sign of bourgeois moral impulses persisting in revolutionary times.[23] If *El Mégano* first brought the plight of the *carboneros* to the attention of an underground public in 1955, filmmakers at ICAIC soon revisited the subject for a national audience in the 1960 documentary *Tierra olvidada (Forgotten Land)*.[24] Contrary to the title, this film depicted a swamp that was no longer overlooked but finally beginning to thrive.

And so, by the beginning of 1961, as Cuban exiles and the CIA were finalizing preparations to rescue the island from the Revolution's "betrayal," the stage was set for a confrontation of not just military but symbolic might. Overlooking the retrospective significance the region had acquired in revolutionary discourse, exiles would wade into a physical and figurative quagmire. Perhaps they should have known better, as one of the political leaders of the invasion—former Minister of Public Works Manuel Ray—had been involved in the Ciénaga de Zapata rehabilitation efforts in their first months.[25] Cuba's largest swamp, Fidel Castro would later note, had been "the place on our island that could be considered the most forgotten of all, the most abandoned, the poorest, where today a change has occurred that has transformed the area completely.... [And] it was this place precisely ... that the imperialists chose to attack our country."[26] Worse for the exiles' claims to a moral vision, 200 young members of incipient literacy brigades—a preview of a wider and more famous 1961 literacy campaign that the Cuban government would launch that spring and summer—were already at work in the area teaching local peasants to read.[27] In these ways, the lessons of the invasion quickly connected to a wider national saga of right and wrong, a past that was dark and a future that the Revolution had made bright. Once the exile attack began, the Ciénaga de Zapata as regional memory parable fused with newly prominent anti-imperialist narratives of the Revolution's purpose to convert victory into the nation's ideological point of no return.

Honoring Victory, Celebrating Heroes

On April 12, 1961, Soviet cosmonaut Yuri Gagarin became the first man to orbit the earth. Four days later, on the eve of the Bay of Pigs invasion, Fidel Castro officially declared the Cuban Revolution socialist, drawing an explicit contrast between "the joy, spirit, and hope" of the Soviet space flight and the "repugnance" of looming U.S. and Cuban exile military aggression.[28] Subsequent victory against the CIA-sponsored Brigade 2506 confirmed what the faithful had known all along—that Cuba's revolution, like the Soviet space program, was on the right side of history: the future. Accordingly, when Gagarin visited the island later that year for 26th of July anniversary festivities, Cuban officials awarded him the newly consecrated "Order of Playa Girón." The gesture symbolically linked defeat of imperialist forces to perhaps the ultimate spectacle at the time of scientific and, in this case, socialist achievement.[29]

Due to complications in Gagarin's schedule, a planned visit the next day to meet some of the invasion's most direct victims in the Ciénaga de Zapata never transpired.[30] Yet even the potential convergence of these two symbols of revolutionary aspirations—humble swamp residents and death-defying cosmonaut—suggested something profound about the place the Bay of Pigs would occupy in revolutionary memory. Victory in battle redeemed the hardly extravagant hopes for material improvement among the nation's impoverished. Triumph, however, also accelerated aspirations of another order: industrial development, scientific achievement, and modernizing, now socialist progress.[31] Victims of injustice in the past, in other words, could seek solace in bold visions of the future. The Revolution in power promised to protect both.

This way of remembering Girón as a crucible of nationalist resistance and utopian possibility began taking shape, paradoxically, prior to the invasion itself, during a moment of collective grief. On April 16, thousands of Cubans crowded the streets of central Havana to accompany the funeral march of several Cuban soldiers killed the previous day. CIA-supplied planes dressed up to appear like defectors from Castro's own military had bombed two Cuban airfields in advance of the amphibious exile landing. Aware that further aggression was on its way, revolutionary militiamen gathered at the entrance to Havana's Christopher Columbus Cemetery, perhaps recalling other tragedies in Cuba's recent past attributed to the forces of counterrevolution and deceit. Only a year had passed since the explosion of *La Coubre* in Havana harbor, eerily reprising the destruction of the USS *Maine* on the eve of U.S. military occupation in 1898. Days before, a mysterious fire attributed to Washington-backed anti-Castro conspirators had burned the Havana department store El Encanto to the ground. As Castro morphed a somber event into a high-energy pep rally, Cuba's oft-frustrated quest for national sovereignty felt palpable to all gathered at the cemetery. The same was surely true for many thousands watching on TV.[32]

Another important event bookended the initial cycle of mobilization and commemoration unleashed by the invasion: May 1. Falling just twelve days after hostilities at the Bay of Pigs concluded, May Day celebrations in Havana in 1961 were the most extravagant then on record, with a reported 2 million citizens participating or observing.[33] If accurate, that would mean fully one-third of the island's population at the time. Surveying the festivities, Fidel Castro praised observers for having "endured" a fourteen-and-a-half-hour parade, with marching brigades divided into divisions of workers, students, women, soldiers, and teachers. Popular slogans chanted en masse suggest the degree of revolutionary commitment on display, but also joy and comedy: "¡Somos socialistas! ¡Pa'lante! ¡Pa'lante! ¡Y al que no le guste tome purgante!" ("We are socialists! Forward! Forward! And whoever doesn't like it can take a laxative!").[34] In an act pregnant with patriotic meaning, that same day cranes removed a marble statue of an eagle from the top of Havana's Monument to the *Maine*, fulfilling a government decree from several months before.[35] For Cuban nationalist purists, the monument erected in 1925 had always stood for a false narrative of history, one in which the United States was Cuba's partner, rather than interloper, in its struggle for independence and national dignity.

May 1 rounded off what was to become a potent triumvirate of annual tributes, all of which continue to occupy a privileged space on the Revolution's list of official holidays: April 16, the declaration of socialism; April 19, victory at Playa Girón; and finally, International Workers' Day. On each of these occasions, Castro would deploy a rhetorical paradox that came to typify memory discourse about the Revolution in general, but one that could only be mastered in the wake of the victory Girón represented. On the one hand, Castro argued, Cuba was a "small country," with little resources or military strength, persecuted historically by an imperial aggressor with no compunction about keeping the weak under its thumb. The Revolution was "of the poor, with the poor, and for the poor," with the Spanish word *humilde* (humble) suggesting innocence as well as material want.[36] On the other hand, Castro emphasized that "the Revolution [was] too strong to have fear, the Revolution [had] too much support," particularly at its grassroots.[37] "That is what they cannot forgive us for," Castro had proclaimed on April 16, "that we have created a socialist Revolution right under the noses of the United States!"[38] This famous statement of the Revolution's socialist affiliation — Fidel's grand ideological reveal — almost reads as a note in passing. In further cementing insurgent feelings of confidence, the "total," "crushing" victory at the Bay of Pigs invited active engagement not just with a spirit of revolutionary possibility but with an anti-imperialist reading of Cuba's past that had become ever more prominent in revolutionary discourse since 1960.[39]

Mass rallies and other public acts in the aftermath of the crisis were about more than populism, securing legitimacy, or selling the Revolution's new ideological label. They made manifest the march of history, one and the same as the Revolution itself. In squaring off against and defeating the forces of U.S. might on the battlefield — something Cuba had never achieved — Cubans became protagonists of a revolutionary future that, in many respects, had already arrived. The exploits of Yuri Gagarin, covered extensively across the Cuban media, may have provided proof of socialism's destiny to "triumph."[40] Yet only Cuba had faced the imperialists head on, turning April 19, 1961, into a date for posterity, "the day imperialism suffered its first defeat in the Americas."[41] For those Cubans who had not participated directly in combat, meanwhile, highly mediated experiences of the invasion through public spectacles, the press, television, and documentary film would profoundly shape recollections of the event in years to come.[42] Whether the broadcast of government communiqués updating citizens on the status of the battle, constant exposés in state newspapers, or an extended television appearance by Fidel Castro to explain to Cuban citizens what had transpired (in front of a blackboard no less), such fragmentary portions of public discourse became as much a part of public memory of the event as accounts of the battle itself.[43]

Naturally, the Bay of Pigs generated a long roster of heroes for the revolutionary government. But the martyrs and survivors of the violence who left the biggest mark were those whose individual accounts entered a mode of "mnemonic reproduction" in the press, on the radio, and on television screens.[44] Among the first cases was that of Eduardo García Delgado, one of the young militiamen killed at Camp Columbia on April 15, 1961, when a B-26 bombed the airfield in advance of the invasion itself. Before dying, he marshaled enough strength to write the word "FIDEL" on a wall nearby, using his own blood as ink. On April 18, with fighting at the Bay of Pigs ongoing, *Noticias de Hoy* published poet laureate Nicolás Guillén's "La sangre numerosa" ("Ample Blood"), the first public elegy to García Delgado's memory.[45] Quickly, his story and the image of the bloodied wall spread. Whether physically removed from the rubble or converted into a blown-up photograph (published images make it hard to tell), marchers carried García Delgado's last political testament during the funeral procession for the deceased and displayed it on his casket while his remains lay in state.[46]

The fate of innocent civilians caught in the crossfire, particularly youth, weighed heavily in emblematic accounts as well. The story of Nemesia Rodríguez Montano, a thirteen-year-old girl, became one of the best known. Born to a family of *carboneros* in the town of Soplillar—the very town where Fidel Castro had spent Christmas Eve in 1959—Nemesia evacuated with her family on April 17, 1961, heading north in a flatbed truck as the invasion began. As they drove toward the municipality of Jagüey Grande, an enemy B-26 flew overhead, first passing without incident, then returning and opening fire. Nemesia's mother died in the attack, while Nemesia and the rest of her family survived. Soon poet Jesús Orta Ruiz arrived in Jagüey Grande to report on the incident for the press. Among the girl's belongings, he discovered, were a pair of damaged white shoes that Nemesia's mother had gifted her a few weeks before thanks to fatter revolutionary-era earnings. Moved by the object, the widely read author of the "Al son de la historia" ("To the Rhythm of History") column in *Noticias de Hoy* returned from his trip with a poem. On April 19, "Elegía de los zapaticos blancos" ("Elegy to the Little White Shoes") made its debut in a dramatic reading on now state-run CMQ Radio.[47] Children in schools would learn its lines, and Nemesia's bullet-hole-filled footwear, like Delgado's bloody uniform, would be photographed and displayed in a museum dedicated to the invasion's memory.[48]

And then, of course, there were the countless photographs of nameless and named soldiers at the Bay of Pigs front lines splashed across the revolutionary press. Like images of popular mobilizations writ large since 1959, the visual records of militiamen in battle had "a duty to perform": to render not only power but also popular memory of major revolutionary events "aesthetically," as scholar José Quiroga has put it.[49] Photographs of Fidel Castro in battle also appeared in glossy Cuban magazines. In two

Figure 3.1. Eduardo García Delgado's last statement of revolutionary devotion. Mnemonic reproduction at work. *Bohemia*, April 23, 1961, 62. Image reproduction courtesy of University of Florida Digital Collections and Digital Library of the Caribbean, George A. Smathers Libraries, University of Florida, Gainesville, FL.

particularly famous images, he appeared jumping from a tank and directing operations from a military jeep. Outside of Cuba, the degree and significance of Fidel Castro's actual role in the fighting was contested, with some saying that Castro fired on a U.S. troop and supply vessel only after the boat was already in flames. Yet even if such widely photographed scenes were photo ops, their dissemination made them into a veritable revolutionary truth.[50] Here was a leader, they indicated, not afraid to put his own life on the line alongside his troops.

Conversely, descriptions of the invaders' backgrounds made for a compelling portrait of the malicious Cuban past that the Revolution had boldly overcome. "Together War Criminals, Former Military Men [of Batista], Large Landowners, and Stuck-Up Kids," proclaimed *Revolución* over an ongoing series of articles, each featuring multiple pages of mug shots and brief descriptions of detained exile fighters. While at times referencing their varied pre-1959 political affiliations, the revolutionary press nonetheless depicted members of the Brigade 2506 as little more than scions of the dethroned Batista regime or of Cuba's former elite. "José Hernández Tomeu ... also known as Pepe ... as inheritor of Enrique Tomeu Hidalgo, owner of an 8,290 acre farm." "Humberto Chamizo Quintana ... belonged to Batista's police and army until 1959."[51] High-profile invaders with some connection to "the Revolution's" past, like the son of exile political leader José Miró Cardona, became targets of especially strong opprobrium for getting in bed with pro-Batista elements.[52] Meanwhile, *Revolución* noted that alumni of the soon-to-be-closed Villanueva University, a private Catholic institution deemed a "center ... for counterrevolutionaries and terrorists," had figured prominently among the exile brigade's leaders.[53] Speaking to Ciénaga de Zapata residents later in July, Fidel claimed that the invaders had even included a former landowner under whom the *carboneros* had once toiled.[54]

But even more damning was the invaders' evident collusion with, and evident subordination under, Washington's plans to turn back the revolutionary clock. "1,500 men contracted in Miami, trained in the United States and its bases in Guatemala and Puerto Rico," intoned the narrator of the rapidly made ICAIC documentary *Muerte al invasor* (*Death to the Invader*). "Their instructors were named Frank, Bill, Pat, and Les." At stake, the film emphasized, was the possible reestablishment of a past "regime of terror and injustice" that the Revolution had replaced. "Mercenaries ... supported by an empire that they judged invincible" could hardly call themselves Cuban. "Wearing the camouflage uniform of the Yankees, sponsored by the Yankees, and *almost Yankees themselves*, [they] had no moral strength to resist the advance of the people." In the background, the notes of a U.S.-style secret agent television theme song sarcastically cast Brigade 2506 fighters as little more than actors in a Cold War farce.⁵⁵

Fostering dystopian visions of exile interlopers turned foreign agents, and urging Cuba's citizens to honor martyrs' unrealized dreams, authorities and cultural producers thus capitalized on victory at the Bay of Pigs for its national mobilizing potential. In the weeks and months following the invasion, frequent invocations of what had transpired would serve as potent reminders of the wider Revolution's stakes. Not surprisingly, when teenage members of the Conrado Benítez Brigades—the dominant public face of a still burgeoning national literacy drive, if not its numerical majority—set out to bring education to an impoverished countryside, cameras covered their work in the Bay of Pigs region insistently.⁵⁶ On June 12, the nationalized CMQ television network broadcast live from the area all day, inviting viewers to "get to know the historic stage where the fighting [Cuban] people defeated imperialism."⁵⁷ Then, in what can only be described as one of the more creative media spectacles undertaken by the revolutionary government, authorities staged additional literacy volunteers' arrival in the region as a symbolic reinvasion of the surrounding beaches, complete with airplanes dropping reading materials and booklets rather than bombs and youthful "soldiers of literacy" wading ashore brandishing gigantic pencils.⁵⁸ The swamp was symbolically rebaptized not just as a memory site of heroic battle or mourning but also as the incarnation of a new hope.

History Debates on Live TV

And yet, there were moments when the stark lines dividing turncoats from loyalists, Cuba's past from its revolutionary present, seemed to blur. Although exile participants in the invasion came face to face with evidence of popular support for the Revolution, some of those same exiles tried to contest Cuban officials' efforts to define how they should be remembered—that is, as simple sellouts and Washington lackeys. Even as officials labeled the defeated enemy "imperialism," one could not escape the fact that those who had perpetrated the invasion were Cubans themselves. The invaders also had sympathizers on the island, at the very least at the level of family. Buried among postinvasion press coverage were periodic notes informing relatives when, and with what frequency, they could visit "mercenary" loved ones in jail.⁵⁹ Clearly, the fissures between Cubans on and off the island were messier than the all-or-nothing terms in which revolutionary discourse tended to speak.

Such untidiness came to the public's attention most dramatically over the course of five days immediately following the attempted invasion. In television broadcasts on April 21, 22, 24, and 25, a group of well-known Cuban intellectuals and journalists identified with the revolutionary government interviewed some three dozen of the first Brigade 2506 captives. Gathering at the halls of the Confederation of Cuban Workers, the panel included Carlos Franqui, director of *Revolución*, official paper of the 26th of July Movement; Carlos Rafael Rodríguez and Raúl Valdés Vivó from the PSP's *Noticias de Hoy*; and Guillermo Jiménez, a veteran of the Revolutionary Directorate and editor of its paper *Combate*. Mario Kuchilán, a well-known TV commentator and columnist who stayed on to direct the paper *Prensa Libre* after it was "intervened" by its workers in 1960, also took part in the questioning. Subsequently, on April 26, Fidel Castro presided over his own "dialogue with the prisoners" from the principal Havana sports arena, "La Ciudad Deportiva," where growing ranks of defeated brigade members were being detained. Taken as a whole, these proceedings represented a golden media opportunity to reinforce the revolutionary government's depiction of the invaders but also a unique moment when multiple narratives about recent Cuban history would square off in revolutionary Cuba's condensing public sphere.

The interrogations riveted domestic and international observers alike. As visiting U.S. radical Leo Huberman wrote somewhat flippantly for the *Nation*, "The most exciting event of the invasion season was the nightly TV program of interrogation of the prisoners by the editors of the leading newspapers—a spectacle unlikely to have been put on anywhere else in the world."[60] Still, it is not as if both sides faced off on equal footing. For one thing, Brigade 2506 members faced the difficult, if not impossible, task of justifying their paradoxical subordination within a U.S. plot in the name of rejecting Cuba's supposed "colonization" by the forces of international communism. Given the setting, it is no surprise their attempts did not convince.[61] Emotional scenes of Batista enforcer Ramón Calviño, a Brigade 2506 soldier, confronting the relatives of former victims of his crimes left an indelible mark on viewers' impressions of the invaders as a whole.[62] For their part, Fidel Castro and other government questioners repeatedly rubbed in the fact that Washington patrons had abandoned exile fighters. In this way, one of the anchors of exile memory in later years as we saw in chapter 2—namely, the idea that Washington had abandoned the Brigade 2506 to its fate—took root as a feature of revolutionary rhetoric first.[63] Needless to say, for Brigade 2506 members, the interrogations did not provide a fitting setting for mourning casualties among their own, including nine who had suffocated to death in a truck after being captured.[64]

Nonetheless, the questioning thrown at them indexed two contradictory imperatives in revolutionary retrospective discourse about the invaders, and about all Cubans leaving the country in general. On the one hand, interrogators attempted to denationalize the growing number of prisoners along with all opponents of the Revolution. Simultaneously, government representatives held the defeated up as clear examples of *Cuban* citizens who had exceeded the boundaries of discourse and action that the Revolution would permit. Fidel Castro's insistence at one point that the brigade had invaded precisely a region of the island where the Revolution was most needed both revived the Ciénaga de Zapata as memory synecdoche and presumed knowledge on the part of the interrogated as to what the swamp had been like before.[65] As Huberman noted, "The parade of witnesses was fascinating" precisely because "their names and faces [were] familiar to the millions who sat [watching] breathlessly before the [TV] screen" at home.[66] Vestiges of the past, however recent, had returned.

The attempt to deny prisoners a legitimate claim to *cubanidad*, or Cubanness, proceeded on several fronts. The most basic strategy involved the label constantly pinned on the Bay of Pigs invaders: mercenaries. In many ways, of course, this depiction fit the profile of the accused. All had participated in a military plot organized and funded by the CIA. President Kennedy's formal admission of U.S. responsibility in the days following the invasion's defeat only confirmed what most Cubans already knew.[67] Yet, in addition to compelling the prisoners to confess the extent to which the United States had overseen the operation, most interrogations also began with a preposterous question: What is your nationality?[68] Such a line of inquiry immediately cast doubt on the accused's claim to "true" Cuban origin. When prisoner Mario Freyre responded to an unrelated query with an incorrect, anglicized expression in Spanish ("Estaba supuesto" to mean "There was supposed to"), his interrogator went on the offensive: "Were you educated in the United States?.... This 'estaba supuesto' is a terminology not of our own making."[69] In this way, revolutionary sympathizers cast the invaders as "foreign," not only in their alliance with the United States but also as somehow detached from "true" Cuban culture or under the spell of external influences.

Further scrutinizing the prisoners through a politics of national and revolutionary authenticity, Fidel Castro asked assembled brigade members to raise their hands if they had ever cut sugar cane. The sparse response made abundantly clear the nature of the gendered accusation: Castro was both impugning the prisoners' masculine character and excluding them from a vision of socialist Cuban citizenship for which experience in the countryside—specifically, the symbolically resonant cutting of

Figure 3.2. Scenes from the televised interrogations of Brigade 2506 prisoners. "The Fauna of the Captured Mercenaries," *Bohemia*, April 30, 1961, 82–83. Image reproduction courtesy of University of Florida Digital Collections and Digital Library of the Caribbean, George A. Smathers Libraries, University of Florida, Gainesville.

cane as volunteer labor—would increasingly constitute a rite of passage and badge of honor across the 1960s.[70] Prior to 1959, Castro could not lay claim to this important signifier of revolutionary virtue either. After all, he hailed from the upper middle class too. Such complexities, however, were beside the point. Privileged Cuban origins combined with evident U.S. collusion reinforced a dominant memory narrative of Brigade 2506 members as enemies at the proletarian gates.

But obviously, most prisoners *were* Cuban and still identified as such. In fact, exchanges between revolutionaries and prisoners at times had the ring of a family affair. At one point, PSP leader Carlos Rafael Rodríguez admitted not wanting to interrogate prisoner Manuel Pérez García, citing his "profound respect for your family, whom I know."[71] Later, Mario Kuchilán approached the son of Cuba's former vice president (under Prío) Guillermo Alonso Pujol, slipping the prisoner and family friend two boxes of cigarettes as a gesture of care.[72] Even more confusing for the initial panel was the appearance among the accused of Cándido Mora Morales, the brother of Menelao Mora Morales, one of the celebrated revolutionary martyrs of the failed Revolutionary Directorate attack on the Presidential Palace in 1957. Interrogators paused to assure the audience that, despite Cándido's treason, Menelao's memory remained untainted.[73] All in all, such scenes brought inconvenient, at times private recollections to the fore, revealing the interpersonal knowledge that linked prominent exiles and revolutionaries. The unfolding bifurcation between "revolutionary" and "counterrevolutionary" factions defied simplistic divisions of history, citizenship, or class.

Yet class provided a crucial anchor around which revolutionary authorities repeatedly attempted to cement audiences' understandings of who the exiles were and the kind of past they represented. In his May 1, 1961, address to the nation, for example, Fidel Castro highlighted the financial interestedness of the invasion's perpetrators as a key takeaway from the interrogations, providing a detailed list of the cumulative economic assets brigade members' families had controlled before 1959:

> Who were those that fought against the workers and the farmers? . . . Doing an analysis of the social composition of a thousand of them, we have the following: approximately 800 were from well-to-do families, and within these 800, a portion of them together accounted for land properties equivalent to 27,556 *caballerías* [more than 900,000 acres] affected [i.e., nationalized] by the Revolution; 9,666 homes, 70 industries, 10 sugar refineries, 2 banks, 5 mines, and 2 newspapers. Moreover, more than 200 of those 800 were members of the most exclusive and aristocratic clubs of Havana, and of the 200 remaining, 135 were ex-soldiers from Batista's army.[74]

Complicit in prerevolutionary inequalities, Brigade 2506 members did not belong in Cuba's selfless society to be. Here, though, we might return to the epithet "mercenary" and begin to discern its slippery significations. "Mercenary" generally references a soldier of fortune with only an external pecuniary stake in armed conflicts. Castro outlined quite the opposite: the deep social embeddedness of these exiles' class advantages *within* Cuban history. Cubans opposed to the Revolution were cancers to be expunged from the national body not strictly for selling their military skills to the highest bidder but precisely because they sought to restore Cuba's submission to imperialist mandates in exchange for past privileges.

In real time, however, the exile prisoners' interjections into their interrogators' lines of questioning disrupted rather than reinforced any easy partition between Cuba's prerevolutionary elites and its deserving socialist citizenry. Upon entering the hall for his "dialogue with the prisoners" on April 26, for instance, Fidel Castro commented to one of the few Afro-Cuban prisoners present, "And you, what are you doing here?" Castro's assumption, visible to all, was that a black Cuban did not fit in an exile force composed of largely white Cubans from the upper and middle class. Most black Cubans had indeed aligned with a Revolution that moved in early 1959 to abolish formal manifestations of racism on the island, including by nationalizing the elite's former whites-only private beaches and clubs. In response, the soldier in question, Tomás Cruz, a rank-and-file veteran of Batista's armed forces, insisted that racial difference in prerevolutionary society existed primarily along economic rather than social lines.[75] However questionable this assertion—de facto and cultural segregation did exist in prerevolutionary Cuba—fellow exiles would remember Cruz as a hero, whereas revolutionary loyalists would herald Fidel for deconstructing Cruz's racial relativism.[76] All the same, Cuba's leader was forced to concede that humble "ex-soldiers [of Batista]" like Cruz—"even though not all were at fault"—"had trouble finding work" after the Revolution, turning some into counterrevolutionaries by circumstance rather than class interest or individual choice.[77]

Other prisoners proved vexing for interrogators because they staked out heterodox ideological positions. In this regard, Felipe Rivero Díaz proved the hardest nut to crack. On the one hand, Rivero Díaz freely admitted to leaving Cuba in early 1959 due to the alleged persecution he faced as relative of both Batista confidant Andrés Domingo y Morales del Castillo and noted Cuban conservative newspaperman Pepín Rivero, owner of *Diario de la Marina*. On the other, Rivero Díaz defined himself fervently as a nationalist, not a communist or imperialist. He even invoked the purported "Third Way" between communism and capitalism of Egyptian leader Gamal Abdel Nasser's nationalist state. Interrogators repeatedly tried to back him into a corner: "Well, and you who are concerned with the 'Third Way' and nationalism, why did you only begin to be 'nationalist' now that Cuba is really nationalist and not during the era when all of your family ... dominated in Cuba?" Yet while government interrogators scored some points, Rivero Díaz failed to lose steam. "During the Revolution, and here I already admitted it, if I had any sin it was of having lived on the margins of circumstances; I didn't think *that* Revolution was going to win." He went on to readily agree with his questioners' description of the United States as an empire, describing its politics as "dreadful" [*nefastas*] and arguing that Cuba "demanded a more just distribution of wealth." Asked whether participating in a mission funded by the United States and supported by the military regimes of Guatemala and Nicaragua was in any way "nationalist," he insisted, "the Somoza regime is monstrous," but "we had to swallow that pill." Such explanations hardly rationalized the hypocrisies and faulty assumptions driving the invasion. Yet transcripts make clear that interrogators felt frustrated by Rivero Díaz's ability to dodge caricature. "You are a very strange nationalist because you definitely should have been in agreement with us," confessed one of the government panelists, sarcastically. "I understand nationalism," Rivero Díaz replied, "as not only nationalizing businesses and private properties; I understand that nationalism does not have to be something precisely of the left or of the right."[78]

The tensest sequences, though, were those in which prisoners turned the tables, challenging Castro and other interrogators to answer more politically grounded accusations about *their* pasts. Specifically, several Brigade 2506 members took advantage of the exchanges to openly indict the Revolution for abandoning what they saw as its original democratic goals. For example, Carlos de Varona, son of exiled Partido Auténtico leader Antonio de Varona (a key figure of the Cuban Revolutionary Council in Miami), maintained during his questioning that the brigade's mission was to install a "constitutional government, based on free elections, to take place in less than eighteen months," what Castro himself had once vowed. "How many counterrevolutionaries voted for you?," noted Carlos Franqui, editor of *Revolución*, offering an acerbic and fair retort.[79] But despite the brigade's own lack of democratic credentials, de Varona insisted that he was not "in disagreement with all" the Revolution had done.[80] "The agrarian reform," for example, "was something completely necessary in Cuba."[81] But "if you had the whole nation on your side," he implored, "why not bring [the country to elections]?" "Do you know [Dominican dictator Rafael] Trujillo holds elections?," replied interrogator Gregorio Ortega, of *La Calle*, "Do you know that [Nicaraguan dictator Anastasio] Somoza holds elections?" "OK, so what? I didn't come here so that elections would be held like those of Trujillo or Somoza," de Varona answered back.[82]

Evidently, Fidel Castro felt the need to answer these and similar charges in his May 1 address to the nation. In that speech, the Revolution's leader responded to brigade members' accusations of hypocrisy with his own:

> And they say they came to defend the Constitution of 1940. And the curious thing is that they did nothing when the 1940 Constitution was torn to bits by the Batista tyranny.... It is truly cynical to see one of these "señoritos" [dandys] come here accompanied by a series of *politiqueros* [corrupt politicians], mayors, and representatives from the era of Batista.... [And] that Constitution said that the latifundio would be pro-

scribed.... it said that there would be established a maximum amount of property that any agricultural or industrial enterprise could own. Clearly no one complied with this Constitutional law. Why? Because it had to be implemented in a secondary law in Congress. And who was in Congress? ... These gentlemen talk about elections. What elections did they want? Those elections of the bad politicians that bought votes and that had dozens of agents dedicated to corrupting consciences?[83]

Here, then, was Fidel's defining take on the irrelevance of the constitution he had once pledged to restore and in fact bring to full fruition. In this passage Castro no longer located exiles' unfitness for revolutionary *cubanidad* in any inherent class positioning, or even in their work as "mercenaries." Rather, it was the invaders' duplicity and ahistorical outlook *as Cubans*, and some of their false idealizations of parts of the *pre-Batista* political order, that disqualified them from a legitimate claim to the revolutionary present. It is true that Cuba's leader did not give sufficient credit to the anti-Batista, proreform credentials of some Brigade 2506 members. Nor did he exactly explain his changing views on the constitutional framework that he had once invoked in his own defense (following Moncada in 1953). But he was right that the full promise of the Constitution of 1940, embodied in its social guarantees, had never truly come into force. Thus, if Castro was vulnerable to the accusation he had broken pledges to restore it, he also compellingly questioned the integrity of an operation including in its ranks individuals whose commitment to the political principles, let alone the full social doctrines, of the Constitution of 1940 might have been insincere or incomplete.

We can only guess how television viewers interpreted such remarks at the time. In terms of public representations, Fidel Castro's May 1 address probably offered the definitive, or at least most influential word on who the invaders were and what they were about. But for at least some watching at home, the awkward exchanges between prisoners and journalists on television might have been as striking as Fidel's evaluation. In light of deep webs of past collaboration and political affiliation linking Cubans across the Florida Straits, just the reminder of Castro's well-documented commitments to hold elections—not even a year after the nationalization of the private press—broke still emerging revolutionary memory taboos. On balance, abundant evidence of the exile brigade's subordination to a CIA-designed plot overwhelmed most prisoners' pretenses of nationalist legitimacy. Still, a number of prisoners successfully resisted efforts at pigeonholing, putting forth their own narratives of what the Revolution was supposed to be about and where it had gone off course. That interplay made the interrogations a significant and, as we will see, memorable stage of retrospective debate.

Ambiguous Echoes

The members of Brigade 2506 made one more public appearance in a mass trial held in March 1962. Some Bay of Pigs veterans would later claim that allowing them to speak directly after the invasion had been "an error" on the part of revolutionary authorities.[84] Regardless, just shy of their landing's one-year anniversary, officials summoned the captives to the courtyard of Havana's Castillo del Príncipe jail for a repeat spectacle, calling on them to testify. With two exceptions, brigade members refused, fearing a ruse. This time, the proceedings would not be broadcast live, only photographed and reported in the news. A damning summary judgment condemning brigade members for high crimes and treason appeared in the state press. Based on the prisoners' degree of leadership in the operation and past political trajectories, revolutionary authorities assigned each a ransom price.[85]

It would be nine more months, as referenced in chapter 2, before an indemnity of $53 million in canned foods and medicines secretly negotiated by a Kennedy administration emissary brought the Bay of Pigs prisoners back to the United States. In the interim, mention of the invasion in Cuba served to reinforce the need for continued national vigilance and unity in the revolutionary ranks. When the now nationalized *Bohemia* magazine celebrated the first anniversary of the invasion's defeat three weeks after the Brigade 2506's trial, cartoons submitted by elementary school children depicted the invaders as anthropomorphized *gusanos*, or worms, the most frequent epithet used by this point to describe counterrevolutionaries and all Cubans departing for the United States.[86] When they were released, Fidel Castro drew the bulk of national media coverage by inaugurating Cuba's first "Charcoal Festival" in the Ciénaga de Zapata. As exile families prepared to greet rescued brigade members in Miami, the Cuban state astutely revived the swamp's history as national memory trope.[87]

Thereafter, anniversary speeches celebrating victory at Playa Girón each year reminded the Cuban public that Yankee imperialism was still plotting to bring about the Revolution's demise.[88] For much of the 1960s, as economic sanctions, exile incursions, and CIA plots against the island continued—however ineffectually—leaders no doubt had a point. Even so, invocations of the invasion's legacy soon bumped up against worrisome developments on the home front. For starters, the now self-advertised "socialist" economy was struggling to live up to its utopian promises. At the same time, repeated calls to duplicate the example of the nation's principled self-defense were interrupted by occasional reminders of the revolutionary coalition's older memory divides. In this context, the memory of the invasion could remain both a source of inspiration as well as a metric against which to compare ongoing challenges. If Girón was to be remembered as the nation's ideological and anti-imperialist turning point, the results of that transition could also disappoint.

Continued signs of factionalism dated to the time of the Brigade 2506's mass trial in 1962, reviving some of the memory feuds of 1959 and 1960. Following the invasion, as noted in chapter 2, the principal political remnants of the anti-Batista coalition—the 26th of July Movement, the PSP, and the Revolutionary Directorate—began to fuse, culminating in the establishment of the Cuban Communist Party as the guiding force of the revolutionary state in 1965. However, this process was by no means seamless, and early on the political unity that Girón seemed to manifest showed signs of remaining incomplete. In March 1962, just days before Brigade 2506's public trial, Fidel Castro publicly accused a group of former PSP militants of "sectarianism" after they attempted to wrest control of the so-called Organizaciones Revolucionarias Integradas, founded in late 1961, from representatives of the 26th of July Movement and the Revolutionary Directorate. Bringing the PSP into the fold after 1959 did not mean that Castro was willing to let them run the show. "We have to stop with this 'I was here or there,' 'I did this or that' business," he fumed in a televised appearance, referencing old legacy battles over who had done the most to bring about the Revolution in the first place. "What is important is not what we have done separately, but what we do together."[89] In this context, the timing of the mass trial of Brigade 2506 members just days later was perhaps coincidental but conspicuous. Against ongoing evidence of factional and memory infighting in the revolutionary ranks, it reminded audiences that the Revolution's external enemies were still waiting in the wings.

Economic difficulties, meanwhile, also undermined, or complicated, the premise that the Bay of Pigs enshrined Cuba's triumphant transition to openly socialist politics and commitments. After early boom years when the government's redistributive measures lifted many boats, between 1962 and 1965 Cuba registered negative rates of economic growth with the exception of one year. The effects of the U.S. economic embargo played a large role. But efficiency, quality control, and workplace morale also took significant hits as most nonagricultural economic activities fell under state control. Nationally, absenteeism and the pilfering of goods combined with the effects of U.S. economic isolation to make necessary the institution of a rationing system in March 1962—again, the same month as the Brigade 2506 mass trial. In the agricultural sphere, where small private farmers remained important players outside of the sugar sector, increasing requirements that they comply with state production and collectivization schemes generated passive and sometimes violent forms of resistance to revolutionary designs. Particularly in Cuba's central Escambray Mountains, grievances among small landholders fueled local sources of support for isolated anti-Castro insurgent groups operating with on-and-off backing from the CIA through 1965. The Revolution's so-called (and euphemistic) Lucha contra Bandidos (Struggle against Bandits), initiated in 1960, only succeeded through the sustained mobilization of thousands of Cuban troops and the forced relocation (and thus silencing) of peasants demed susceptible to counterrevolutionary ideas.[90]

In this context, references to, and analyses of, the mass-mediated public questioning of mercenary invaders could serve as potent reminders of the "bourgeois" mentalities that exemplary laborers and farmers of a more spartan socialist present were expected to reject. In 1963, for example, just as Cuban policymakers were debating the merits of "material" over "moral" incentives as a way of boosting output among workers, Argentine intellectual León Rozitchner—then teaching at the University of Havana—published *Moral burguesa y revolución* (*Bourgeois Morality and Revolution*), an influential Marxist dissection of the Bay of Pigs interrogations that first appeared in the *Revista Universidad de la Habana* and later circulated in book form.[91] Drawing on his work with Cuban students who studied the interrogation transcripts, Rozitchner argued that brigade members' testimonies revealed little more than a series of hidden economic motives "structured in the bosom of a determined social class." Past privileges, he contended, were merely the necessary "price" of exiles' imperialist allegiances, making them "mercenaries" after all. Several prisoners' deceptively "apolitical" narratives about "losing" and seeking to "recover" the homeland, Rozitchner insisted, barely concealed their vested interest in recouping properties and businesses. Lest any disgruntled Cuban worker in the mid-1960s get ideas about sympathizing with counterrevolution, or becoming enchanted with the false memory of capitalism amid the revolutionary present's difficulties, the Argentine writer reminded audiences to think twice. The ideological link prisoners expressed between property and nation, he emphasized, excluded from their ideals of citizenship the many Cubans before 1959 who had never possessed property of their own.[92]

Yet if such theorizing associated counterrevolutionary forces with capitalist sensibilities that were no longer valid, even working-class citizens devoted to the Revolution's cause were soon contending with degrees of scarcity that before Girón some had never known. Through the mid-1960s, shortages of goods worsened, compounded by the effects of U.S. sanctions and continued domestic mismanagement. In this context, calling production campaigns in the sugar fields or on the factory floor "new Giróns" became a repeated refrain to channel the gusto with which Cubans had defended the island from military incursion several years before.[93] Rather than undertaking a deep self-diagnosis of central planning, the government accelerated its course. Most notably, in March 1968, the so-called Revolutionary Offensive led to the confiscation of all remaining private small businesses in urban areas on the island—corner stores, bars, barbershops, some piecework manufacturing, and artisanal work in cities. Meanwhile, economic authorities sidelined once ambitious plans for industrialization and agricultural diversification that many Cubans remembered as central to the Revolution's original hopes.[94] Back in the Ciénaga de Zapata, the once highly publicized, symbolically important idea of draining large portions of the swamp and converting it to rice acreage had long since been abandoned.[95] Sugar cultivation reassumed its vexed historic place as Cuba's economic heart, due to generous Soviet terms of trade. Arguably, economic ghosts of the "pseudo-republic" were close enough for anyone prepared to look.[96]

At the same time, the Revolution's evolving project of not just economic but social transformation—crystallized in an influential 1965 essay by Che Guevara on the need to forge a socialist "New Man"—was abetting increasingly exclusionary discourses and political practices.[97] Cuban authorities began monitoring and imprisoning suspected members of CIA-financed anti-Castro underground groups and their accused sympathizers in the early 1960s. But in the mid-1960s, the force of the revolutionary state also targeted gays, religious minorities, consumers of Western music, or the overly intellectual under the cover of a "moral" drive to promote asceticism and productivity. Particularly by the second half of the decade, those who matched these descriptions risked public ostracism, dismissal from their university, or firing from their jobs. In one of the worst episodes, between 1965 and 1968 as many as 30,000 suspected homosexuals, Jehovah's Witnesses, and other "antisocial" men were sent to fulfill obligatory military service (instituted nationally in 1963) in forced agricultural labor camps called Unidades Militares de Ayuda a la Producción (Military Units to Aid Production, UMAP). Such practices, together with the subsequent silencing of the UMAP's existence and severity after they were closed in a hurry, left deep and, to this day, largely repressed memory wounds.[98]

Nor did the memory wars within the Revolution's political fold go away. At no time was this clearer than when authorities put twenty-six-year-old Marcos Rodríguez on public trial in March 1964. A former affiliate of the Revolutionary Directorate, Rodríguez stood accused of ratting out to Batista's police several survivors of the organization's famed Presidential Palace attack in 1957, leading to the murder (and martyrdom) of Joe Westbrook Rosales, José Machado Rodríguez, Juan Pedro Carbó Serviá, and Fructuoso Rodríguez Pérez in their hiding place at 7 Calle Humboldt. Yet beyond the intrigue and treachery involved in the case, what really riled opinion was that, by Marcos's own confession, he had evaded justice ever since thanks to the protection of influential members of the PSP. This raised the possibility that, within the Revolutionary Directorate, he had really been acting as a PSP mole at a time when the PSP opposed the Revolutionary Directorate's armed tactics, and perhaps he had given up his comrades at their behest.[99]

Old feuds between the Revolution's insurgent factions thus resurfaced in vivid fashion, threatening the ideal of unity that the primary struggle against U.S. imperialism, and the proximate shadow of Playa Girón, demanded. Lest battles over the PSP's past opposition to armed insurrection once again bubble over, Fidel Castro intervened in the trial, broadcast to rapt radio and television audiences nationwide. "We have made a Revolution that is bigger than ourselves," he affirmed. Cubans must not fall prey to "Saturn's Law" — "the classic law ... that says that revolutions, like the god Saturn, devour their own children."[100] And yet, just four years later, Castro would find himself intervening in a similar episode, when he purged from the governing ranks a broader *microfracción* of former PSP members. Some of the same individuals accused of sectarianism in 1962 — and subsequently reintegrated into government functions after making amends — were again conspiring with allies in Moscow to do an end-run around the revolutionary leadership's authority.[101]

Difficulties were equally pronounced in the foreign policy realm. Che Guevara is well known around the world for giving up his roles in socialist Cuba's economic restructuring internally by the mid-1960s to dedicate himself to the task of spreading revolution abroad (notwithstanding significant Soviet opposition to such "adventurism"). However, the fact that Guevara met his death at the hands of U.S.-backed forces in Bolivia in the fall of 1967 meant that Cuban leaders' ambitions to spread their model of guerrilla struggle across the region had hit a wall.[102] Meanwhile, the goal of national sovereignty, ostensibly a lasting achievement of Cuba's break from the United States, at times seemed compromised. In October 1968, Fidel Castro famously linked the 100th anniversary of the beginning of the island's first failed independence war to a teleological "100 years of struggle" for true independence that the Revolution now had fulfilled.[103]

But a few months earlier, Castro defended the Soviet Union's invasion of Czechoslovakia to end the Prague Spring, even though it appeared to many Cubans to contradict the principle of self-determination they remembered as the Revolution's own.[104] If external dependence was one of the chief historical legacies with which the Revolution was supposed to break, Castro's decision hinted at the ways Cuba had traded its historic dependence on Spain and the United States for a similarly symbiotic, if never entirely submissive, relationship with the USSR.[105]

By the mid- to late 1960s, therefore, the Revolution's future in many ways stood in the balance, even as overt challenges to the Cuban state from Miami, and internally, had receded in strength. Out-migration had begun again in earnest, too, as after opening the port of Camarioca in 1965 to anyone wanting to leave, the U.S. and Cuban governments hastily negotiated an air bridge of twice daily flights, five days a week. The so-called Freedom Flights would bring 297,318 new Cubans to the United States before they ceased in 1973. Only now the Cubans opting for exile were not so easily lumped in with the Brigade 2506 as vengeful members of the prerevolutionary elite. Many were elderly, many were working class, and, by the late 1960s and early 1970s, many were the owners of small businesses that the government had nationalized in 1968.[106] All told, these migrants had known and lived Cuba's transition to socialism, and some had even sympathized with it longer than those who left the island previously. Indeed, there is a strong possibility that some of those joining the émigré community in the late 1960s might have opposed or even directly fought off the U.S.-backed exile invasion in 1961, defending a Revolution in which, several years later, they had lost faith.

For all of these reasons, it is telling that memories of the Bay of Pigs prisoners' words, and of the invasion generally, began to resurface in Cuban cultural production precisely in such trying years of internal and external turmoil. Even well-known "revolutionary" voices in the Cuban arts turned to the memory of Girón not only for a reminder of moral clarity or better times but also to channel their contemporary doubts. As the Revolution entered its most radical phase, Girón was a parable that could still motivate and stir revolutionary passions. Celebratory texts continued to be published and consumed.[107] But the victory against Cuban exile forces was also a vehicle through which writers, filmmakers, and playwrights increasingly began to reflect more somberly on the Revolution's costs.

Consider the seminal 1968 ICAIC film *Memorias del subdesarrollo* (*Memories of Underdevelopment*), directed by Tomás Gutiérrez Alea and based on a 1965 novel of the same title by Edmundo Desnoes. Set between the Bay of Pigs invasion and the Cuban Missile Crisis in 1962, the film revolves around the character of Sergio, the son of an upper-middle-class clothing store owner who opts to stay behind in Cuba while his own family and wife flee the Revolution's advance to Miami. As critic John Mraz has argued, Sergio struggles to come to terms with the "inescapable fact of historical transformation." He simply cannot reconcile inherited bourgeois mores with the Revolution he theoretically wishes to embrace.[108] Gutiérrez Alea claimed to have envisioned Sergio as a self-absorbed protagonist that spectators would hate. But the film embraces a perspective internal to his psyche, offering the potential for a sympathetic reading of his failure to resolve old and new (despite his repugnant womanizing).[109] The film thus memorializes the seismic events of 1961–62 not as triumphs of revolutionary resistance but as alienating spectacles symptomatic of a nation that has lost its bearings. Significantly, it debuted in Cuban theaters in August 1968, one week before Fidel Castro made known his position on the Warsaw Pact invasion of Czechoslovakia.

Because the film was released in 1968, it can be read as inviting Cubans to reexamine their recent past in order to find answers to the contradictory forces that persist in their present. "In socialism," Sergio says subversively at one point, "nothing has continuity. Everything is forgotten." It is in this respect that references to the Bay of Pigs interrogations in the film acquire significance. They invite viewers to revisit a major anti-imperialist milestone—and, by proxy, the more conditional terms of Cuban anti-imperialist commitments in the present, at least vis-à-vis the USSR—with a more discerning, even slightly jaundiced perspective. In one crucial sequence, Sergio reads a passage to himself from León Rozitchner's above-mentioned analysis of Brigade 2506 members' televised declarations in 1961. Footage of the prisoners responding to government questioners rolls in the background. If Rozitchner's interpretation of the "mercenaries" tempts the viewer to criticize their pecuniary motives, his dry Marxist assessment seems woefully out of touch with Sergio's plight.[110] The scene thus serves to question the overconfidence in revolutionary ideals that victory at Girón or texts like Rozitchner's had once fueled. "At the end of ten years," Gutiérrez Alea himself concurred at an early presentation of the film in June 1968—ironically in Czechoslovakia, several weeks *before* the Soviet invasion—"we have learned that our condition as an underdeveloped country . . . has not been overcome. . . . It has not been easy to arrive at this conclusion, because in the first years, the happiness of triumph made us believe that paradise was around the corner."[111]

Just as *Memorias* recast the Revolution's recent history in darker colors more fitting for its less bullish present, other Cuban writers also began to look back on the Bay of Pigs with wearier hearts and minds. In the short story collection *La guerra tuvo seis nombres* (*The War Had Six Names*), winner of a 1968 prize from the government-linked Unión Nacional de Escritores y Artistas de Cuba (Cuban National Union of Artists and Writers, UNEAC), Girón veteran Eduardo Heras León did not directly contradict the revolutionary memory canon. But he did challenge the premise that moralistic tales of self-sacrifice and bravery were the only stories about the invasion worth being told. In one tale, a soldier reacts angrily when a lieutenant orders him to fire mortars toward an area where an advance team from their own battalion is already fighting. In another, the leader of a squadron despised for his vindictive belittling of troops in training fails to provide adequate leadership in a firefight, faking a wound to get out of harm's way. It is the last, autobiographical story, however, that is the most powerful, as Heras León uses it to reveal shameful memories of his own. After spending the entire battle waiting to be ordered into action at a nearby sugar mill, the main character is embarrassed to be feted as a war hero as militia caravans of those truly hardened on the front lines make their way home. For Heras León, recollections of fear, guilt, and opportunism hid behind the public memories of audacity so often repeated and figuratively etched into marble walls.[112]

The most ambitious and controversial work that revisited the memory of Girón in 1968 was the play *Los siete contra Tebas* (*Seven against Thebes*). A successful and well-regarded playwright in the revolutionary-era cultural scene, Antón Arrufat set out seemingly innocently to adapt the classic Greek tragedy of the same name to a Cuban frame. But parallels between Aeschylus's drama and the plot of the Bay of Pigs invasion were so striking as to be impossible to ignore. Like the original, Arrufat's version follows the conflict between Eteocles and Polynices, brothers and heirs to the throne of Thebes. Yet when Eteocles takes power, Polynices flees to distant lands, betraying Thebes and collaborating with "foreign chiefs" in order to lay waste to the city by siege. The allegorical subtext—Eteocles *equals* Fidel Castro, "foreign chiefs" *equals* U.S. imperialism—was quite overt.

The problem was that Arrufat's script, even while condemning Polynices as a selfish revanchist, remained a tragedy. The Revolution's victory over brothers turned enemies, the play suggests, should not be commemorated but mourned. While Eteocles accuses Polynices of "hand[ing] himself over to other people" (an obvious reference to Cuban exiles' collaboration with the U.S. government), Polynices claims to represent the return of "law" and "right." "I remember the pact we made three years ago," he alleges, "to govern for a year each one, sharing command of the army and the paternal house. You pledged to fulfill it. And you have violated the oath and your promise."[113] Parts of the play thus conjured memories of not only the ideological conflict between Cubans generally after the Revolution, but specific allegations of revolutionary "betrayal" that defined the memory fabric of the exile community and popped up during the Bay of Pigs interrogations themselves. "Our time is a different time," Eteocles declares, refusing to "submit to the memory of his own blood."[114] Still, even as Eteocles's side is victorious in battle, he and brother Polynices kill one another in the end, consummating a metaphor of the Revolution as national fratricide.

In this way, Arrufat captured what most celebratory commemorations of events in 1961, or since, missed—namely, the ways the Bay of Pigs proved that the Revolution had not immediately eliminated deep divisions among Cubans but in some ways exacerbated them even more.[115] A political project intended to "unite with equal ties" had been "cut by blood and iron."[116] Although the play received the 1968 UNEAC prize for theater (albeit with a divided international jury), UNEAC officials promptly condemned its contents. "Here ... there is a pretend reality," they wrote, seeking to reassert revolutionary retrospective discourse: "Those who abandon their country to stock up in the house of the enemy, conspire against it, and prepare to attack it, stop being brothers and become traitors."[117] UNEAC pledged to publish the work with this clarifying note indicating their disapproval. But according to the author, only scarce copies of the edition circulated, either in Cuban diplomatic legations for show or after being stolen from the printers.[118]

Conclusion: Hidden Giróns

Throughout the 1960s, Cubans turned to the Bay of Pigs as a palimpsest on and against which to rewrite and measure their presents. Two years into the Revolution, victory at Girón invested a still incipient political process with the most dramatic evidence yet of its historic, anti-imperialist purpose. At the same time, interpersonal links between Brigade 2506 members and their interrogators offered inconvenient evidence that the line between revolution and counterrevolution had in fact been blurry. By the late 1960s, the Bay of Pigs retrospectively represented a high point of the nationalist vision that for some Cubans no doubt remained worthy of defending, despite revolutionary hardships since. For others, however, it served as a reminder that impediments to achieving revolutionary goals, and divisions in the revolutionary ranks, had been present from the beginning.

Even early attempts to figuratively fix the invasion's retrospective meaning encountered difficulties. Fidel Castro first announced his government's intention to erect a monument to the martyrs of Girón in the summer of 1961. Yet, after an international design competition for the monument was held in 1963, the winning proposal—one of 274 sent from all over the world—was never built. The work of a Polish team of architects, it consisted of large, reddish concrete blocks meant to be positioned just off the coast at Girón beach, as if rising from the sea and crashing onto the shore. Some officials were skittish about the abstract form and complex technical requirements of the design. But the proposal's unconventionality also lent itself to politically vague readings, placing more emphasis on the fact of external aggression rather than Cuba's successful effort to repel it. After several members of the design team defected to the West, what would have been one of the first artistically significant monuments of the revolutionary era was scrapped.[119] In the end, only a small museum—featuring Nemesia's "little white shoes" among other items—and a rather traditional memorial wall were erected, the latter inscribed with the names of revolutionary soldiers who gave their lives.

Similarly, beyond the late 1960s, the Bay of Pigs invaders' political agency was gradually written out of most versions of the story, as were any retrospective ambiguities about the invasion's legacy. Thus, by the time Víctor Casaus's book *Girón en la memoria* (*Girón in Memory*) was published in 1970, it appeared to be one more among many celebrations of revolutionary heroics.[120] Still, amid his collection of testimonials from soldiers who had defeated the exile invaders nine years before, Casaus also interspersed provocative fragments of exile declarations lifted from the interrogation transcripts, without deconstruction or critique.[121] No wonder that, as writer Eduardo Heras León subsequently recalled, access to Casaus's book at Cuba's National Library was soon restricted, lest its inclusion of exile interpretations of the operation exercise an untoward influence on the revolutionary reading public.[122]

Silences did not haunt the public memory of Girón on the island alone. They also trailed former revolutionaries who now joined the renewed exodus of Cubans heading abroad in the mid- to late 1960s. Such was the case of Carlos Franqui, a key member of the 26th of July Movement underground, founder of the guerrilla radio station Radio Rebelde, and editor, as we have seen, of the 26th of July Movement's official newspaper *Revolución* beginning in 1959. It was in the latter role that Franqui had participated in the televised interrogations of Bay of Pigs prisoners in 1961. Just two years later, however, he lost his job due to mounting ideological differences with the revolutionary leadership, particularly members of the old PSP. In 1968, after several years spending as much time in Europe as on the island, Franqui broke publicly with the socialist state. But if his disappearance thereafter from accounts of the Bay of Pigs on the island, or even the anti-Batista insurrection, was typical of the Revolution's memory machinations, Franqui could also be accused of historical elusiveness of his own. In subsequent anti-Castro writings from exile, the former 26th of July Movement leader devoted scarce attention to his energetic participation in the Bay of Pigs interrogation, alongside representatives of the PSP, no less. Perhaps this explains his decision to settle in Italy, not Miami.[123]

And yet, beyond an increasingly narrow official memory script on the island and the burdened consciences of exiles new and old, one wonders about the missing voices of average island citizens caught in between. Did the memory of Playa Girón really matter? How? And to what degree? Among older Cubans, a joke still circulates that offers one kind of response. When news of the exile-led invasion arrived, some on the island purportedly walked out to the street and shouted, "I'm with you!," at the top of their lungs with purposeful ambiguity.[124] If that was true, perhaps other politically malleable Cubans, ready to ingratiate themselves to any victor, might have forged more politically equivocal relationships to one of the Revolution's signature victories.

For another indirect route to such possibilities, we might turn to a songwriter who, ironically, later became a luminary and defender of Cuban socialism in the 1970s. In 1961, Silvio Rodríguez was fourteen years old. He was a child of poor farmers in San Antonio de los Baños, the same town on the outskirts of Havana whose airfield had been bombed days before the Bay of Pigs invasion. Rodríguez participated in revolutionary student militias and even Cuba's literacy campaign as a young man. By the late 1960s, however, long hair and a hippy-like appearance resulted in numerous clashes with defenders of an orthodox vision of revolutionary morality. Thus, despite the notoriety he had already started to garner for his songwriting, Rodríguez did not escape the effects of an increasingly conformist cultural politics promoted by socialist authorities.

Fired in 1969 from his job as a performer at the Instituto Cubano de Radio y Televisión (Cuban Institute for Radio and Television, the umbrella organization for now state-run TV and radio), Rodríguez was sent to work on a state-owned fishing vessel—incidentally called the *Playa Girón*. He returned from a five-month journey along the African coast, alongside other wayward revolutionary citizens also working as crewmen, having written scores of new songs.[125] Among them was an implicit critique of platitudinous elegies to revolutionary martyrs, a call to consider other heroes "outside of the vanguard." Equally worthy of remembrance, Rodríguez sang, were the imperfect Cubans who did not give their lives on Girón the beach but instead labored out of sight on *Playa Girón*, the boat.

Comrades of history,
keeping in mind how implacable
the truth should be, I would like to ask,
—it urges me so much—
What should I say?
What borders should I respect?
If someone robs food,
and then gives his life, what to do?
Until when should we practice truths?
Until when do we know?
Let them write, then, the history, their history
The men of the *Playa Girón*.[126]

In tough times, the memory of the Bay of Pigs could still inspire. Even more than some events of the anti-Batista insurrection itself, Girón was the feat of revolutionary resistance to which subsequent endeavors would be compared. But over time increasingly repetitive paeans in public to revolutionary heroism also overshadowed, or even implicitly denied, the more mundane, less uniformly celebratory experiences and memories of everyday Cubans themselves. On the island and in exile, too, as it turns out, not just adults, but younger Cubans in the following decade would have reason to look back on seismic events from the early 1960s with less reverence and through more inquisitive eyes. For those who were still children in 1961, the fratricidal conflict that the Bay of Pigs invasion made manifest, and which the invasion's results did not fully bury, represented inherited trauma, a legacy that they would struggle to make their own.

4

Antinostalgias in an Exile Age of Fracture

On March 13, 1971, sixteen members of Agrupación Abdala, a relatively new Cuban exile student organization founded in 1968, staged an act of civil disobedience at UN headquarters in New York. Taking their name from an early dramatic poem by independence hero José Martí, the young men and women made their way to the chambers of the Security Council, posing as sightseers and following the route of regularly scheduled tours. When a guide asked assembled visitors if there were any questions, the students fell into rank, declaring their intention to occupy the room until they could speak to a high UN representative regarding the plight of their homeland. Chaining themselves to the chairs from whence, less than ten years prior, superpower diplomats had squared off during the Cuban Missile Crisis, the group held its ground for several hours before being forcibly removed and arrested.[1]

More than age and protest tactics set Abdala apart from predecessors in Cuban exile politics. In the first edition of its monthly newspaper, published one month after the UN demonstration, the organization not only lambasted Cuba's "Marxist-Leninist dictatorship" but also took potshots at exile brethren with a history of allying with the U.S. government: "Against us, the 'champions of democracy' will rise. Those who speak about Latin America with a check from the CIA in their pockets. Those who modified the Monroe Doctrine, changing it into 'Latin America for the North Americans.' Those who dream that upon returning to Cuba, they will be received at the airport with a car and a furnished house so they can go and save the homeland."[2]

Sarcastic criticism of an older exile generation's sense of entitlement, acquiescence to U.S. meddling, and alleged historical paralysis only continued. "For many, Cuba only exists in the past," wrote founder Gustavo Marín Duarte, "but we must not forget that if we want to be free we have to incorporate ourselves into the present in a combative and energetic form."[3] While by the late 1960s influential strains of nostalgia had led many in the Cuban exile community to commiserate over shared longings for a "Cuba of yesteryear," Abdala boldly claimed a stake on the Cuba of tomorrow. "¡El futuro será nuestro!" ("The Future Will Be Ours!"), they declared.[4]

At the time Agrupación Abdala burst onto the scene, a first era of continuing exodus and sustained exile mobilization to bring down the revolutionary government appeared to be winding to a close. Anticommunist dreams died hard, of course—or not at all. But bitter recollections of recent political failures, coupled with Washington's new efforts in an era of détente to ease tensions with the socialist world, would convince some of the need to retreat if not move on. Others refused to countenance such a possibility, denouncing those who did so with intensifying anger and resentment, or even getting involved in more violent anti-Castro pursuits. Still, two years after Abdala's headline-grabbing UN action, the arrival of the last "Freedom Flight" from Cuba on U.S. soil (out of more than 2,800 since 1965) seemed to mark a turning point in the community's growth and political evolution. Shorn of a stable flow of newcomers after 1973, more Cubans in the United States began to buckle down and count their blessings, as many thought they should.

Not that the Revolution was free of problems that exile activists could point to and hypothetically exploit. By the late 1960s, as we saw in chapter 3, economic disappointments, continued dependence on sugar cultivation, and ideological and other forms of repression had revived and conjured up their own retrospective ghosts on the island. A last burst of mass economic mobilization at the end of the decade—a quixotic plan to harvest more than 10 million tons of sugar, as a way of finally spurring Cuba's definitive leap toward economic development—had left much of the Cuban economy in tatters, as we will see. Yet, despite the country's ongoing economic and existential quandaries, the stability of the Cuban government appeared in little doubt—especially when, after 1970, the island moved to become more closely integrated into the Eastern bloc and began to receive greater Soviet economic support. In this context, a "Cuban American" future began to dawn, as the affairs of the homeland increasingly gave way to the realities of immigrant adjustment. What was once conceived as temporary exile was evolving for more and more Cubans in the United States into permanent settlement, if only by default.

This left younger members of the exile community with a choice. Either they could join remaining activists endeavoring to carry the cause forward—sometimes violently—or they could acquiesce to the Cuban exile community's transition into just another U.S. immigrant group. The question was no longer just *which* exile memory camp to back, as it had been during the 1960s, but whether the Cuban past mattered much anymore and, if so, how. By the mid-1970s, militant holdouts, including embittered former U.S. intelligence assets, had accumulated a considerable record of terrorist attacks on Cuban diplomatic, commercial, and, infamously, civilian targets, including dissenting voices in the exile community itself. Maybe everyone would be better off, others suggested, if Cuba were relegated to the dustbin of history. The island could remain a source of pride, personal ties, and cultural traditions, perhaps, but no longer the focus of all political involvements or emotional investments.

Other young people in the diaspora resisted such fatalism. The lure of the island's past remained strong, not only for groups committed to actively pursuing Castro's demise, like Abdala, but also for a smaller set of left-leaning scholar-activists questioning the historical wisdom they had inherited about the Revolution. Caught between the social unrest of their adopted country in the era of Vietnam and the political legacies of their parents, select exile youth yearned to leave their own marks on a national saga inherited by birthright. Conscious of the ways history had happened *to* them as children, many clamored to make history of their own. Doing so began by critically revisiting the traumatic memories associated with their cultural uprooting from the island as children as well as reexamining Cuba's and the exile community's history to that point.

In addition, then, to narrating Agrupación Abdala's own widely forgotten history and unique interventions in the Cuban memory wars, this chapter also tells the story of the group's chief rivals: the radical students and young intellectuals gravitating around the journal *Areíto*, first published in 1974. *Areíto* contributors became pariahs for rejecting the exile community's most basic retrospective premise: that the Revolution after 1959 had "gone wrong." Instead, they sought to accept Cuban socialism on its own terms, convinced that leaving the past behind meant not abandoning the nation and its history but breaking a cycle of exile delusion and confronting the reality of the Revolution's permanence. Yet though loath to recognize it at the time, they and Abdala articulated similar criticisms of their forebears along generational lines. As young people unburdened by direct implication in the calamitous events of the Cuban 1960s, but nonetheless marked by them, *abdalistas* and *Areíto* contributors freely denounced their parents' choices, nostalgic ruminations, and misguided faith in Washington.

The counterpoint of the two groups thus illuminates a juncture in which exile youth challenged zones of consensus in exile memory culture in the service of political visions they could call their own. Their story helps to recover generational contours of Cuban memory struggle that, like the 1970s as a whole, contemporary narratives of exile history as a unitary tale of immigrant resilience tend to overlook. To this day, the exile community's own retrospective imaginary, as noted in chapter 2, is dominated by celebratory, if tragic, accounts of exodus and uplift in the 1960s. But the 1970s, this chapter shows, proved to be critical years of both heightened community consolidation and in some ways even sharper political and memory disputes. Those disputes involved new disjunctures between young exiles' personal memories and dominant narratives of exile history, as well as, in the case of *Areíto*, new encounters between the testimonies of exile youth and the retrospective truisms associated with the revolutionary state.

"Identities," the late Stuart Hall reminds us, "are the names we give to the different ways we are positioned by, and position ourselves in, the narratives of the past."[5] In their own ways, both Abdala and *Areíto* disrupted the identity categories undergirding more established, if still fractious, exile memory claims. Drawing as they did on a combination of personal memory and more empirical historical arguments, their efforts again show us the intertwined role of "history" and "memory" in Cuban retrospective politics. Although countless Cuban diaspora actors in the 1960s had wrangled over who bore greatest responsibility for Cuba's communist takeover, few had disassociated from the identifier "exile" itself. Now, young people were pulling such labels apart, in some cases questioning the presumed "forced" nature and wisdom of their parents' departures (another truism of exile retrospective culture), and in others worrying that a new identity as "Cuban Americans" might signal permanent indifference to the island's fate.

Forward to the Future, Exorcising the Past

Gustavo Marín Duarte's political education began at home, under the influence of his father. An accountant and professor at Havana's Villanueva University, Gustavo Marín Sr. welcomed the onset of the Revolution in 1959 like many middle-class professionals frustrated with Batista-era politics, Cuba's rural poverty, and the island's recurring cycles of national frustration. Yet despite being swept up in the spirit of reform pervading all corners of Cuban life, and even landing a job at Cuba's Ministry of State, Marín Sr. soon grew disillusioned with the radicalization of government policies, signing a declaration ratifying the expulsion of allegedly procommunist students from Catholic Villanueva in late 1960. As part of the roundup of an estimated 100,000 suspected anti-Castro fifth columnists in the days preceding the Bay of Pigs invasion (most of whom were quickly freed), Marín Sr. was arrested. Released several months later, the erstwhile civil servant quickly found his way out of the country. Within two weeks, thirteen-year-old Gustavo also boarded a plane.[6]

Marín Duarte's early life experiences paralleled those of other future contributors to Agrupación Abdala. Like other members of what sociologists would later call the 1.5 generation, *abdalistas* were born in Cuba but saw their childhoods and adolescences interrupted when parents rubbed up against intensifying revolutionary government centralization and felt compelled to take their families abroad.[7] Yet, while many of their elders had sympathized with the Revolution in its presocialist phase, what most linked Abdala participants was not straightforward class, political, or ideological inheritance but a deep desire for political protagonism born of the cultural uprooting they endured as children.[8] They were tired of just hearing stories about Cuba. They wanted to make "the cause," and the country, their own.

Coming of age in or near New York City during the 1960s and 1970s left a particular mark on the organization's founders. Miami remained the capital of Cuban diaspora life. However, the greater New York metropolitan region came second, with more than 100,000 Cubans spread across New York and New Jersey, especially Hudson County (bordering the Big Apple), by 1970, some of whom had been in the area since before 1959.[9] While in some sense bearers of an inherited anticommunist torch, founding *abdalistas* drew from the New York area's unique political and social landscape in ways that distinguished their influences from Miami's increasingly conservative ideological norm. The idea for the organization, for example, emerged after a group of young Cubans erupted in anger at the pro-Castro comments of an invited speaker at a Socialist Workers Party meeting.[10] Such outrage may have been unsurprising. Yet that a contingent of young Cuban exiles would even be present at the gathering of a Trotskyist organization—and not just to cause a stir—hinted at the group's exposure to alternative political currents.

By the time Abdala came about, the social and class composition of the Cuban exile community itself had also changed. A significant number of Cubans fleeing the island in the late 1960s continued to trace their roots to the island's prerevolutionary middle and professional classes. But as noted in chapter 3, the Freedom Flights between 1965 and 1973 also brought significantly more working-class and even rural Cubans to the diaspora than before. This would shape not only Abdala's membership but also the organization's views. Some of the new migrants were among the Revolution's imagined beneficiaries. As such, they were at times treated suspiciously—ironically by the same exiles whose early belief in the Revolution had similarly been questioned by pro-Batista foes in the early 1960s. Yet Abdala never uniformly questioned recent arrivals' retrospective complicity or political pedigrees. While some Miami voices accused the new exiles of being *"Patria o muerte* [fatherland or death] types" (i.e., hardcore revolutionaries who had only just flipped), or being imbued with "a very sad communist morality," Abdala members saw their struggles as part and parcel of their own.[11] They, and not necessarily the exiles of the early 1960s, had truly experienced life under communism. They could testify to its ills with the greatest moral and memory authority.[12]

Thus, even as most of its leaders traced their origins to the first exile wave before October 1962, Abdala went on to build part of its early strength on a series of left-leaning and working-class alliances, within and without the exile community. To wit, after founding the organization on January 28, 1968 (also the anniversary of José Martí's birthday in 1853), early members began gathering at the Woodstock Hotel, a once luxurious midtown establishment converted into a single-room occupancy lodging house and union haunt. Group leaders forged lasting ties with both Harlem-based civil rights leader Bayard Rustin, coorganizer of the 1963 March on Washington, and the Young People's Socialist League (YPSL), the youth wing of the Socialist Party of America (later, Social Democrats USA). The latter had roots in anti-Stalinist, prolabor, democratic socialist currents in U.S. leftist thought. Women, while outnumbered in Abdala's leadership, played more than supporting roles, bucking the gender dynamics of most exile organizations past. Drawing both on their own parents' economic difficulties in the United States (irrespective of prior class origins in Cuba) as well as the more recent, economically diverse arrivals from the Freedom Flights, Abdala positioned itself as the voice of a struggling Cuban émigré working class. And despite the establishment of a formidable Miami chapter, the organization's heart remained in what members called the *Zona Norte* (Northern Zone), with deindustrialization, sustained economic discontent, and racial tensions in the backdrop.[13]

This setting attuned *abdalistas* to social issues in a way not as common to many exile organizations in Miami. Still, whether experienced from outer-borough neighborhoods like Jackson Heights, Queens (where Marín's family settled) or working-class enclaves like Elizabeth and Union City, New Jersey, persistent signs of greater New York City's malaise in the late 1960s ultimately catalyzed a sizeable turn *away* from the affairs of the adopted home toward the fraught history and dreamed-of redemption of the homeland—notwithstanding the exile community's failures to achieve such a goal to that point. Despite the organization's contacts with non-Cuban political groups, Abdala's published materials included little commentary on U.S. national or local politics.[14] In 1970, a short story in Abdala's ephemeral magazine cast the death of one exile family's son in Vietnam (on the same day that his father received approval of an application for U.S. citizenship) as a tragic wakeup call for renewed Cuban nationalist commitment. Blunt as the narrative device may have been, the message was clear: exile youth should embrace, not forget, their Cuban roots.[15]

Progressive commitments, in turn, deeply shaped the lens through which Abdala members understood their Cuban past. Founder and polemicist in chief Marín Duarte led the way, devouring classics of Cuban nationalist thought during weekly visits to Spanish-language bookstores in New York.[16] Among the works that proved influential was Gustavo Pittaluga's *Diálogos sobre el destino* (*Dialogues about Destiny*), a terse, penetrating diagnosis of Cuba's pre-1959 economic and cultural dependency on the North. First published in 1954, the book would be reprinted in Cuba in 1960 as an effective sounding board for revolutionary ambitions at the time.[17] Equally noteworthy was Emilio Roig de Leuchsenring's *Cuba no debe su independencia a los Estados Unidos* (*Cuba Does Not Owe Its Independence to the United States*), a concise primer from 1950 on the struggle for Cuban independence in spite of U.S. imperial impositions in the late nineteenth century—also reprinted several times during the post-1959 era. (A veteran of the anti-Machado struggles of the 1920s and 1930s, Roig de Leuchsenring had served as Havana's official City Historian at the Revolution's start.)[18] Abdala's stated positions and public profile thus came to reflect serious intellectual engagement with the dominant motifs of Cuban nationalist thought pre- and post-1959: effective independence, anti-imperialism, political sovereignty, and sacrifice for the greater good. Such ideas necessarily drew on a canon of writing and historical literature that overlapped with significant portions of the Revolution's own.

Admittedly, Abdala's founders may have been more intellectually precocious than rank-and-file affiliates happy to find a network of young people with common cultural backgrounds.[19] But whatever the social function of the group's activities for its growing base of 200-plus members and more casual hangers-on, Abdala's mix of associational life, political militancy, and vaguely countercultural aesthetics recalled in its own way the broader swirl of influences characterizing Latin American and U.S. New Lefts.[20] While fiercely anticommunist, Abdala crafted a brand of politics attuned to historic Cuban progressivism. Programmatic documents envisioned a future republic with agricultural cooperatives, nationalized public utility and national resource companies, and a banking sector free of foreign control.[21] As the organization expanded into a wider network of delegations spread across college campuses throughout and beyond the

United States—eighteen in total, including chapters in Spain and Puerto Rico—leaders strenuously rejected accommodation with the proverbial anticommunist middle ground.[22] "Those who lived from dirty business during the years of the past Republic," they warned, "those who gambled with the fate of the nation [*los que comerciaron con la Patria*], could try to do it again."[23] Even while adopting the amnesia-laden language of a singular "lost Republic," Abdala rejected phony glorifications of the Cuban past as idyll by others in the exile community, as well as the false sense of security afforded by anti-Castro boilerplate.

To put such attitudes into practice, *abdalistas* naturally needed to marshal historical reference points and heroes of their own. Thus, it was no coincidence that they staged their debut UN action in 1971 on March 13. It was on that date in 1957 when members of the Revolutionary Directorate, led by José Antonio Echeverría, had attempted to assassinate Fulgencio Batista in his office. Though the activists killed then—especially Echeverría—were duly incorporated into the revolutionary government's pantheon of martyrs, Abdala, too, claimed the Revolutionary Directorate's school of direct action as its own. The group would inscribe its own protest activities within a wider legacy of Cuban student activism over which they believed Castro government institutions had attempted to assert an exclusive, sanitized claim. *Abdalistas* knew, for instance, that in his time Echeverría had been no fan of the communist party (the PSP) that joined the revolutionary government after 1959.

To be fair, Abdala's political platform did echo significant earlier sources of left-leaning exile thought. As we saw in chapter 2, several organizations making up the Cuban Revolutionary Council in the early 1960s embraced social democratic, even "revolutionary" aims on paper. Members of the CRC also included partisans of the so-called Directorio Revolucionario Estudiantil en el Exilio (Student Revolutionary Directorate in Exile, DRE), a Miami-based organization that claimed to be the anticommunist and thus true incarnation of what the original anti-Batista Revolutionary Directorate in Cuba had been all about. As an anti-imperialist, of course, Revolutionary Directorate founder José Antonio Echeverría might have rolled over in his grave at the thought that an organization receiving CIA funds was claiming to be his political and ideological descendant. Nonetheless, the celebration of Echeverría's legacy in Miami could not have gone over well with former partisans of the man, Fulgencio Batista, whom Echeverría's organization tried to assassinate.[24]

The mid-1960s saw other progressive voices persist and resist the community's predominant rightward drift, too. In 1965, the simple, inexpensively made magazine *Nueva Generación* debuted in Miami as "The

Voice of Cuban Youth."[25] It raised suspicion in conservative corners for its insistence on recovering a "humanist" progressive tradition at a time when dominant exile political thought had moved to the anticommunist right. *Réplica* (*Reply*)—a longer-lasting Miami newspaper founded in 1963 by Max Lesnik, a former youth leader for Cuba's Partido Ortodoxo—foreshadowed Abdala's combination of robust anticommunism and reformist ideas. In this way, even through the late 1960s, exile politics continued to encompass a confusing and often contradictory mixture of positions and memory claims. The draw of a common, uncritical nostalgia was powerful for many, but not universally embraced.

Abdala's views, however, went beyond the liberal anticommunism of such forebears. In articles like "Why We Are Revolutionaries," *abdalistas* attempted, not unlike several exile actors before them, to reclaim "revolutionary" politics from their tainted association in popular memory with Fidel Castro. They also echoed a vocal, previously influential strain of nationalist militancy that had once defined sectors of the 26th of July Movement itself. "Cuba needs a revolution, not a revolt," they wrote. "Revolution means destroying unjust, oppressive structures and building a new order.... [And if] we do not prepare to face the constructive phase that comes immediately [following Fidel Castro's defeat], we will incur the same errors of past eras, wasting the hopes of an entire people."[26] A repetition of the more conservative version of the well-worn betrayal thesis from the early 1960s this was not.

The nature of Cubans' past mistakes was clear in Abdala's view. As Marín Duarte wrote in September 1971, "Cuba's is a revolution murdered by the two great failures of our time: the representatives of a middle class incapable of comprehending the message of the true revolution; those that never sat at the table of the black man or the farmer and now take portraits of themselves in his embrace, and call him brother and the great hope [*proeza*] of the future. And [secondly], the communists, the merchants of hate and deceit, who ride upon the backs of the poor with their flags of destruction and death."[27] Notably, a run-of-the-mill, if vitriolic condemnation of Cuba's communists comes second in this passage. The open-ended denunciation of false revolutionaries, in contrast, seems to target a diverse cast of characters, notwithstanding an instrumental (and, for Abdala, rare) invocation of antiracist ideals. By formally allying with the Castro government's ideology, Marín implied, opportunistic individuals had found ways to maintain past privileges. Yet equally worthy of reproach were those armchair reformers, perhaps even *abdalistas*' parents, who too easily in the past, and again in the exile present, paid lip service to the concerns of common citizens.

Where Abdala's politics did overlap more consistently with what had become the exile mainstream was in their consistent criticisms of the United States. As we saw in chapter 2, varied voices in the exile community had arrived at bitter conclusions about alleged U.S. hypocrisy by the dawn of the 1970s. Abdala in many ways partook in the broader anticommunist, anti-Washington sentiment slowly percolating across U.S. Cuban communities as a new anchor of collective memory in response to a litany of perceived U.S. betrayals—from botched air cover at the Bay of Pigs to the fabled (and phantom) "Kennedy-Khrushchev Pact" of 1962. The move toward global détente in the 1970s only confirmed some exiles' worst fears: when push came to shove, the White House had bigger fish to fry. As one political cartoon of the era put it, "El Tío: Ni me saca del lío, ni me cruza el río" ("Uncle Sam: He won't get me out of a jam, or get me across the river").[28] The beginnings of U.S. withdrawal from Vietnam, Nixon's announcement of plans to visit China, and, later, the negotiation of a 1973 antihijacking accord with the Cuban government (following the attempted diversion of more than ninety U.S. planes to Havana between 1968 and 1973, mostly by U.S. radicals) all appeared to augur the unmooring of U.S. interests from anticommunist ideals.[29]

Nonetheless, while many Cuban exiles had grafted a tenuous convergence of their identities upon shared memories of communist *and* U.S. victimization since 1959, Abdala's leaders proved unique in the degree they indicted predecessors for ever having gotten in bed with Washington in the first place. As students of the island's troubled past under a profound U.S. shadow, *abdalistas* insisted that prerevolutionary Cuba had been "mediated politically, alienated economically, and humiliated socially"—not only during the most clearly interventionist period of U.S. dominance under the Platt Amendment (1902-34) but also throughout the years that followed (1934-58).[30] The use of Cubans as expendable pawns in a greater play for global power did not strike the organization's leaders as a Kennedy- or even Nixon-era invention. On the contrary, they argued, such treatment was consistent with a deep record of U.S. meddling and obstructionism in Cuban affairs. "One of the most destructive effects of the Platt Amendment," *Abdala*'s editorial board noted in 1973, "had been the forced political dependence of the first years of the Republic." "But even worse," they continued, "was the fact that after the abrogation of said Amendment [in 1934], a mental dependency remained that has plagued our struggles for a better Cuba ever since." Such statements represented not-so-subtle swipes at the exile community's predominant modus operandi during the 1960s, while also referencing anti-imperialist historical precedents most exile groups by the 1970s were more hesitant to invoke.[31]

Abdala thus distanced itself from attitudes, personalities, and legacies in exile smacking of submissiveness to great power politics—*plattismo* in Cuban historical shorthand. In the process, they echoed some of the Cuban state's own historical tenets and obligatory reference points while also advancing a deeply critical view of exile history itself. Because of an ingrained "political-psychological" deference to U.S. power, the organization alleged, it remained common to hear exiles passively affirm "without the Americans, nothing."[32] A truly "independent mentality" meant "understanding that like 1,500 men on the beaches of Cuba twelve years ago"—a reference to the Bay of Pigs—"we are alone."[33] While showing a certain respect for the men who took part in the CIA-organized debacle a decade before, the group also dared to call veterans of the invasion "naive" and "gullible," breaking commemorative taboos.[34]

Abdala likewise made a point to emphasize that its opposition to Fidel Castro stemmed from not his nationalization of "U.S. interests" but his willingness to serve as a "puppet of global Soviet aspirations."[35] Such arguments ignored the grassroots logics accompanying Cuba's radical transformation between 1959 and 1961, not to mention recurring sources of friction between the island and Moscow in the 1960s, particularly in the realm of foreign policy.[36] But the organization was nonetheless distinct in marrying this assessment to a powerful, historically informed denunciation of U.S. power. At one point members canvassed university campuses in Miami with flyers reading "¡Abajo los imperialismos!" ["Down with Imperialisms!"].[37] No wonder Abdala's leaders also found inspiration in diverse, classically "leftist" international struggles and organizations—the early Sandinistas, the Irish Republican Army, and the Palestinian Liberation Organization, but not, significantly, Puerto Rican nationalists, given their ties to revolutionary Cuba—even as they were embraced as anticommunist darlings. Ingenuously perhaps, but convincingly, they saw the purported requirement of deigning to U.S. influence as a false choice.[38]

Opting for "the Cuba That Exists"

Uptown from Abdala's first offices near Times Square, editors of the journal *Areíto* might have agreed with aspects of Gustavo Marín Duarte's criticisms of past exile politicking. First published in April 1974, the magazine brought together a distinct, geographically diffuse network of young Cuban exiles equally committed to breaking free of the right-wing political leanings and nostalgic obsessions of their forebears. The present, however, demanding these scholar-activists' attention was what one writer labeled "the concrete Cuba that exists"—revolutionary Cuba, where the apparent permanence of Cuban socialism, despite its difficulties through the late

1960s, at least seemed to warrant a pragmatic effort to better understand its origins, inner life, and ostensible sources of legitimacy.[39] For most Cubans in the United States, any suggestion that the Revolution be taken seriously represented the ultimate political and memory heresy.

From the moment of its debut, then, *Areíto* attracted a degree of attention and animosity beyond what its relatively limited readership probably deserved. As a result, the magazine represents much more than a blip in diasporic intellectual history, as other scholars have emphasized.[40] Detractors have alleged that *Areíto* was little more than the work of Cuban intelligence and disinformation agents, and they have treated it as simply a propaganda ploy.[41] Yet, while one cannot deny the likelihood that the magazine's existence would have been of interest to Cuban diplomatic and intelligence circles, in reality nothing about its contributors' political trajectory was preordained. A more thoughtful treatment of the magazine—and the community built up around it—must engage its contents deeply, and it must excavate the kind of implicit and controversial memory work its contents performed.

By birthright and class background, several members of the *Areíto*'s editorial board might very well have ended up to Abdala's political right. Marifeli Pérez-Stable, a leader of the project, came from a well-known family of doctors whose relatives included the owners of an elegant department store in Havana. Siblings Mariana and Mauricio Gastón were the children of an influential architect, spending weekends as kids at the Havana Yacht Club and traveling as far as Fort Lauderdale for competitive swim meets. Burgeoning literary scholar Román de la Campa was the son of a judge and university professor, growing up in Havana's up-and-coming Nuevo Vedado district.[42] Accordingly, *abdalistas* pilloried their *Areíto* rivals as descendants of "bourgeois," "well-off" families—ivory tower academics disconnected from the true struggles of Cubans at the grassroots.[43]

Yet even if such caricatures were generalizable to all—which they were not—the personal and ideological genealogies of both groups crossed in interesting ways. Lourdes Casal, a woman of color who was slightly older than other members of the group, served as the *Areíto* collective's primary mentor and organizing force. A closeted lesbian and former Villanueva University student who descended from Cuba's black middle class, Casal had been deeply involved in left-of-center but fiercely anticommunist exile organizations in the 1960s, like the DRE mentioned above. By mid-decade, she began moving to the left while working as a New York City social worker and literary scholar, completing a PhD at the New School for Social Research in 1975. Still, she remained part of a wider network of exile academics who, beginning in the late 1960s, had started to advocate for serious studies of Cuban revolutionary society rather than predictable anti-Castro broadsides. From the pages of the aforementioned and progressive (but, again, still anti-Castro) *Nueva Generación*, Casal had echoed those calls. As a result, many *abdalistas* knew her, crossing paths at events, and at times engaging in debate and conversation. In fact, as cofounder of the Instituto de Estudios Cubanos (Institute for Cuban Studies), an academic body established in 1969, she collaborated with two of Abdala's most important intellectual mentors: the exiled philosopher Humberto Piñera Llera, professor at New York University, and Catholic journalist Andrés Valdespino, former anti-Batista correspondent at *Bohemia* magazine and professor at Hunter College after leaving the island in the early 1960s.[44]

For younger *Areíto* contributors, the journey toward open revolutionary sympathy proved even more indirect, beginning in vibrant, decidedly non-Cubacentric activist milieus on and off university campuses of the late 1960s. Before ever turning toward the island of their birth, most future members of the *Areíto* collective cut their political teeth in diverse manifestations of the antiwar, civil rights, and other social movements marking the era. The University of Florida was an important site in this regard, as it was a public institution accessible to many from Miami but seemingly worlds away from the exile community's political norms. Yet even on the private, refined grounds of Catholic schools like Manhattanville College in New York's Westchester County, ideas of liberation theology, the organizing of Students for a Democratic Society, protests against U.S. military intervention in the Dominican Republic in 1965, and the Marxism-inflected languages of black and Puerto Rican nationalism all made their presence felt. Revolutionary Cuba entered these conversations as an idealized and frequently referenced foil. Early interactions with returning members of the first Venceremos Brigades, groups of U.S. leftists that started to travel to Cuba for solidarity work in late 1969, further inspired these same exile youth to question whether their own positions on Cuban issues relied more on inherited, simplified memory than sound knowledge of the historical or present truth.[45]

That said, nothing guaranteed that an embrace of Cuba and the Revolution would prevail over competing issues and attentions in the United States. Communal taboos stood in the way, for one thing. Traumatic recollections of their own experiences in Cuba might have proved an impediment too. Later *Areíto* contributor Albor Ruiz saw his father jailed, like Abdala founder Gustavo Marín Duarte's own, in the preventative sweep-up of suspected government opponents in advance of the Bay of Pigs.[46] That he ended up adopting different political views thus appears a matter less of destiny than intellectual choice. Because of these complexities, it is not surprising that a competing progressive publication also emerged, urging left-leaning Cuban exile youth to identify their fates first and foremost with other Latino and oppressed minority populations within the United States. Often writing under pseudonyms, contributors to *Joven Cuba* contended that Cuba was too far in their past to warrant claiming much of a stake in its present or future. "We that came to the United States speak English as well as, or better than, Spanish," they acknowledged. "Some might be more 'Americanized' than others, but what we have to understand and accept is that our future as a community is to be part of the history of *this* country."[47]

Joven Cuba, though, would last just six issues, folding after April 1976. In its place, *Areíto*, under Casal's leadership, would increasingly link radicalizing Cuban exile students in Gainesville to twenty-something counterparts in New York, Boston, San Juan, and beyond. Their common interest was exploring the history and reality of the Revolution they had been forced to exit rather than personally live. With Casal already an intellectual rising star, it was only natural that students were drawn to her example. Equally important was a defiant and ultimately enduring anti-U.S., antiassimilationist posture. "The reality is that in spite of fifteen years of revolution and a few less of exile, we are Cuban," *Areíto*'s opening 1974 editorial declared. "And it is precisely the force of our national identity that propels us in a new quest." "It is illusory," the piece continued, "to think that our national traditions can be maintained for an indefinite period of time in a piece of Miami, New York, or New Jersey. Our national tradition is intimately rooted in Cuba, its history, its heroes, its martyrs, its people."[48] A number of former *Joven Cuba* and even *Nueva Generación* contributors eventually joined *Areíto*'s intellectual and progressively pro-Revolution political fold.

In these ways, the results of the *Areíto* group's memory work led contributors to diametrically different conclusions about revolutionary Cuba than the nonconventional, but still strongly anti-Castro positions of the *abdalistas*. *Areíto* contributors not only identified as Cuban but also felt compelled to examine—allegedly without bias—the emergence and existence of the Cuban Revolution without recourse to typical anticommunist arguments and complaints. But in retrospect, the degree to which *Areíto*'s antiassimilationist identity politics echoed Abdala's own is as notable as their political differences. Both groups' viewpoints reflected comparable estrangements from the U.S. mainstream in an era of declining economic fortunes and post-Vietnam political disenchantment. Even blunter in their rhetoric, Abdala members, too, expressed frustration with exile youth who preferred to "spend $50 on a Saturday night to go to a party, buy a color TV, or a new car."[49] *Areíto*'s editorial board worried that "young Cubans in exile are denationalizing and depoliticizing at a rapid pace. The problems that move and worry them are not those of Cuba, with or without revolution, but those concerning adaptation to their respective communities."[50] In both cases, keeping the memory of the homeland alive, in order to claim a legitimate stake on its present, was paramount.

Abdalistas and contributors to *Areíto* also drew inspiration from the common displacements they endured as children. *Areíto* was most explicit in this regard, directly indicting elders' supposed sacrifices on young Cubans' behalf. Phrases like "they sent us off to an unknown country" not only conjured a collective sense of loss and alienation; they transformed the generic claim of *forced* migration at the center of prevailing narratives of exile collective memory into a stinging condemnation of parents' *choices* to depart (all while *forcing* their kids to go with them).[51] Consistent with their own fiercely nationalist posture, Abdala members also struggled to understand the reasons why they had ended up in the United States even as plenty of other people their age had remained behind. A July 1971 article offered sardonic advice to prospective attendees at Abdala's first national congress: "If [your parents] ask ... why you're wasting time doing something for Cuba, tell them that you want what is yours and what they did not want to give to you." "Your parents were born and raised in a Cuba that had many problems—economic depression, robber politicians, and ambitious military men," the author, Antonio García-Hernández, continued. "But when it was their turn to fight for what was theirs, they took the easiest decision: FLEEING CUBA."[52] The iconoclasm of such criticisms of exile *choice* in light of prevailing narratives of the community's *involuntary* origins—not to mention the gratitude many expected younger exiles to feel for having escaped a communist upbringing—cannot be overstated.

Even more sensitive were *Areíto* contributors' and *abdalistas*' memories of Operation Pedro Pan, the U.S. government-backed, Catholic Church-supported airlift of more than 14,000 unaccompanied Cuban children to the United States between 1960 and 1962. Today, as briefly noted in chapter 2, the program is most often celebrated in Cuban American lore as an altruistic undertaking.[53] Thanks to the work of a devoted clandestine network, thousands of children were "saved" from communism. Members of the *Areíto* circle, however—some of whom had endured prolonged separations from their parents in Church-sponsored camps and foster homes across the United States in the 1960s—came to see the airlift as a swindle, the result of a propaganda ploy on the part of the U.S. government to drum up anticommunist fervor on the island by spreading false rumors of Cuban government plans to send children to Russia. (This view both drew from and strongly influenced later Cuban government characterizations of the program along the same lines.)[54] Most in the exile community, then as now, equated such allegations with blasphemy.[55] Still, Abdala members also questioned the traumatic consequences of their parents' decisions. In May 1971, several years before members of the *Areíto* group would articulate a view on the subject, twenty-one-year-old Abdala member Luis Reina described his own departure as part of the secret children's exodus. If Reina had been sent to live with a family in the United States in order to escape "Murderous and Traitorous Communism," the cultural confusion clouding his upbringing represented a tragic loss for the nation—a loss, that is, until Reina recuperated "the Cuba he carried within."[56]

For all of their differences, then, *Areíto* and Abdala were in many ways two sides of the same generational coin. Each channeled a common impulse among alienated Cuban exile youth to define and reclaim a vision of national belonging and memory for themselves. In the process, they revised standard narratives of Cuba's past and the exile community's history that they had been taught or assimilated over time. *Areíto* provided a forum for exile students so radicalized by the left that they were willing to question inherited assumptions about the nature of the Cuban Revolution itself. Still, that group's more direct criticisms of the political instrumentalization of Cuban children during Operation Pedro Pan did not, in the abstract, represent such a dramatic departure from Agrupación Abdala's own denunciations of Washington's historic bad faith.

Activist Ambitions, History's Traps

Talk, as the old adage goes, is cheap. Novel takes on the historical record may have helped *Areíto* and Abdala solidify their respective senses of group identity. Yet in order to leave a concrete mark, the young exiles in both circles, particularly the *abdalistas*, were determined to put words into action in the present. In different ways, *Areíto* and Abdala set out to take their messages off the page, and because each group had arrived at such opposing views of the Revolution in power, they inevitably found themselves on a collision course. Writers and activists in both camps wrestled with the past not only as part of their personal quests to throw off its shackles, but also to delegitimize their opponents as caught in historical and ideological traps.

Starting with its intervention at the United Nations in 1971, Abdala devoted itself to aggressive anti-Castro public demonstrations as much as consciousness-raising through the written word. Whether chaining themselves to the Statue of Liberty to draw attention to the plight of the Cuban people or participating in "Marches of National Reaffirmation" to assert the exile community's refusal to accept "coexistence" with the Castro government as heralded by U.S. policies of détente, Gustavo Marín Duarte and colleagues were uncompromising in their efforts to advocate against the Cuban government without U.S. support.[57] In addition to organizing elaborate letter-writing campaigns to the island and strategizing ways to establish cells on Cuban soil, the organization ran a clandestine radio broadcast beamed toward Havana listeners.[58] Nonetheless, very much like the conservative exiles they criticized, *abdalistas* also employed tactics resembling the butt of a contemporary Miami joke: "Here in a democracy, we have the right to not permit communists to speak."[59] In 1972, thirty Abdala members infiltrated an exhibition of cinema from revolutionary Cuba in New York City, releasing concealed mice and stink bombs to cause panic in the theater.[60] Just over a year later, fifty took part in, in their own words, an "extremely violent" confrontation with "castristas" (or local Cuban government supporters) in a Queens College auditorium where Cuba's then-ambassador to the United Nations was delivering a speech.[61]

For *Areíto* contributors, such incidents placed Abdala firmly within an increasingly prominent exile tradition of silencing voices dissenting from baseline anticommunist positions. In fact, that tradition was becoming more violent. Exile attacks against Cuban government targets were nothing new. Dating to the 1960s, rogue actors occasionally targeted Cuban officials on U.S. soil (at the United Nations, for example) and *without* U.S. government support, especially following the drying up of covert action funding in the middle of the decade.[62] Yet in the 1970s, the continuation and intensification of such actions by fringe groups was accompanied by evidence of increasing political violence *within* the exile community itself. This turn of events responded to the unique frustrations and circumstances of the time. Exile-owned businesses, institutions, and local interests—what would later be described as the Cuban "enclave," especially in Miami—had begun to thrive, and, along with this drift to immigrant adjustment, some had started to question the tenets of economic and political isolation that had defined Washington's and most exiles' preferred foreign policies toward Cuba to that point. Still, much like Abdala's leaders, others rejected any perceived signs of complacency, or compromise, to anti-Castro principles, however defined. The 1970s thus proved to be years of unparalleled controversy and tension within the Cuban exile community, as some extremist groups embraced desperate, deadly, and openly terrorist tactics to keep the memory and reality of the anti-Castro struggle alive.

These "Cuban exile wars," as José Quiroga has described them, left a bloody trail of victims in Miami and beyond.[63] In February 1975, Miami anti-Castro activist Luciano Nieves was gunned down after suggesting he would vote were Castro ever to convene open elections. In late April 1976, a car bomb blew off the legs of radio commentator Emilio Milián after he dared to criticize militants' attacks on other exiles who questioned the wisdom of continued U.S. sanctions against the island. Even the head of the Bay of Pigs Veterans Association at the time was assassinated in January 1977 after denouncing colleagues who countenanced terrorism within the community. By one count, more than 100 bombs exploded in Miami alone between 1973 and 1976, while others were detonated in New Jersey and New York. Internationally, covert exile organizations and actors perpetrated a wave of bombings and terrorist attacks exceeding anything similar from the 1960s, many targeting Cuban diplomats.[64] Most notoriously, on October 6, 1976, a bomb planted aboard Cubana Airlines flight 455—traveling between Barbados and Havana, with a scheduled stop in Jamaica—exploded shortly after the plane took off, killing all seventy-three civilian passengers on board. The likely masterminds were Luis Posada Carriles and Orlando Bosch, both Cuban exiles with prior ties to the CIA.[65]

Members of the *Areíto* circle were lucky to escape this wave of violence unscathed. Nevertheless, by mid-1976 journal affiliates reported being subject to three attempted or threatened bombings.[66] Given these experiences, the *Areíto* collective came to see Abdala as not just the latest mouthpiece for tired anticommunist ideas but part of a fanatical underworld perpetuating entrenched forms of political intolerance echoing the worst McCarthyite impulses of prerevolutionary Cuban political life.[67] Despite their "progressivism," Abdala members publicly harassed contributors of *Areíto* and similar intellectual circles in ways that scarcely differed from the opprobrium thrown their way by more ideologically conservative exile groups.[68] The organization's leaders also openly discussed violence as a necessary and justified tool in the struggle against communist tyranny. Making a reality the dream of a Cuban anticommunist but anti-imperialist future, they argued, meant sooner or later reviving the defunct anti-Castro armed struggle, perhaps in their own hands. While declassified FBI reports tend not to implicate Abdala in deadly attacks against others in the exile community, we know that the organization's leadership flirted with violent and even protofascist actors involved in terrorist plots outside of the United States. For a short time, several members of Abdala participated in the so-called Frente de Liberación Nacional Cubano (Cuban National Liberation Front, FLNC), which planted bombs at Cuban diplomatic installations abroad.[69]

Yet even as their affiliations and alliances were troubled by ideological contradiction and moral hazard, Abdala members' views of "legitimate" violence did not simply stem from the nefarious impulses of a transhistorical "Cuban right," as *Areíto* contributors were wont to suggest. Rather, they drew on their own retrospective reference points—namely, the radical actions that had marked Cuban insurgent politics in the late 1950s. In its heyday, the urban underground of Fidel Castro's 26th of July Movement had engaged in what it called "action and sabotage" operations. The Revolutionary Directorate had assassinated several Batista administration officials in addition to carrying out the failed 1957 attempt on Batista himself.[70] For *abdalistas* like Blanca Bianchi, Revolutionary Directorate founder José Antonio Echeverría's cousin, *Areíto*'s blanket condemnation of "violence as a means for imposing ideological positions" sidestepped the memory of how the very revolution that the magazine claimed to admire had come to be.[71] Some Abdala members' choices of partners and targets were no doubt deeply flawed and ethically compromised. But on historical memory grounds, they in part had a point.

If *Areíto* contributors saw the *abdalistas* as just another anti-Castro group perpetuating the failed constructs and right-wing violence of the past, the latter felt justified in seeing the former as out of time in their own way. For as long as the Revolution had been in power, Cuba had served not just as a launching point for exodus but also as a site of international inspiration and refuge. In this regard, the *Areíto* collective was in some ways no different from other fellow travelers of the Cuban Revolution over the 1960s. Yet *Areíto* and Abdala members were also aware that by the early 1970s, many early international friends of the Revolution were turning away, or at least looking at Cuban socialism more apprehensively. If some of the Revolution's longest and most influential admirers had begun to lose faith, Abdala argued, this made *Areíto*'s gradually more sympathetic engagement with the island's government over the 1970s a historical relic in its own right.

Abdalistas were not wrong to point out the contradictions of the moment. Following the Revolutionary Offensive of 1968, the Cuban government began to mobilize the nation's workforce to achieve a record 10-million-ton sugar harvest in 1970. With significant areas of the economy left unattended, the project ended in disarray, as Cuba neither met the desired 10 million metric tons nor created the conditions for a definitive leap forward into economic development, the stated goal. Thereafter, the

Cuban government initiated a process of socialist "institutionalization" whereby it restructured government institutions and practices in a more Soviet-inspired mold.[72] But if such moves did help the economy improve, particularly after Cuba formally joined the Soviet Union's trade bloc in 1972, the petering out of utopian mass campaigns from the 1960s also worried international sympathizers who had long admired Cuban socialism's supposed autonomy from Soviet ways.[73] (We will return to Cuban economic developments and improved ties to the Eastern bloc in the 1970s in chapter 5.)

Ideologically, meanwhile, the parameters of "revolutionary" thought and permitted cultural expression internally had further narrowed. Back in 1968, Cuban authorities censored an introspective volume of poetry by the well-known writer Heberto Padilla alongside Antón Arrufat's dramatic allegory of the Bay of Pigs mentioned in chapter 3. But in 1971, the scandal acquired international proportions when Padilla was arrested and forced to perform an embarrassing "self-critique."[74] Like other intellectuals abroad who broke ranks with the Revolution as a result, *Areíto* founder Lourdes Casal wrote critically about the Padilla case.[75] In 1973, moreover, she acknowledged that the island seemed to have "entered a less romantic and more pragmatic period," even though the economy had picked up on the backs of greater Soviet support.[76] A move to "state socialism" perhaps had its attractions in stability and better functioning social welfare systems. But an era of massive military parades, increased Soviet dependence, and greater censorship did not necessarily seem the most obvious juncture for young diasporic children of the U.S. counterculture to fulfill their anti-imperialist dreams.

Abdala thus saw *Areíto*'s increasing sympathy for the Revolution in the mid- and late 1970s as historically out of place—a denial of what even many former international friends of the Revolution had gleaned from its recent history. To make their point, the group's members invoked not only the more familiar story of the Revolution's "turn to communism" in the early 1960s but also the "victims" of Cuba's late 1960s and early 1970s internal hardening. Significantly, the organization established contact with former *Revolución* editor Carlos Franqui, eventually publishing a lengthy interview with the man whose affiliation with the Castro government through 1968 made him taboo in many corners of the exile world. Describing himself as still "revolutionary," Franqui told Abdala's newspaper that the radical project in which he had once believed had fallen too much under the weight of Fidel Castro's cult of personality.[77] Likewise, Abdala's newspapers covered the reverberations of the "Padilla case" closely.[78] To look sympathetically upon the Revolution in light of such recent events, or to flirt with its officials, could not be a product of ignorance in Abdala's estimation. *Areíto*'s posture, they alleged, reflected the blind loyalty of opportunists and lackeys.[79]

Yet it would be a mistake to see *Areíto* as nothing but a vehicle for unthinking and intensifying revolutionary adulation, or a retrospective idealization of the Revolution's past. Some magazine contributors' views of the Revolution did fall prey to nostalgic simplifications of what it had represented and achieved. Nonetheless, if the magazine's exploration of Cuba's post-1959 history at times seemed superficial, neither did *Areíto* entirely shy away from the record of conflict attending Cuba's transition to socialism.[80] In a poem dedicated to a friend who was executed for participating in anti-Castro underground activities in the early 1960s, Albor Ruiz thoughtfully broached the buried emotional, political, and generational traumas of that decade.[81] In a published interview with a Cuban Baptist minister still living on the island, *Areíto* offered a surprisingly detailed account for the time of the still not widely known forced labor camps to which gay men and religious practitioners in Cuba had been sent only a few years before.[82] Most important, with regard to the process of "revolutionary institutionalization," the magazine provided an outlet for critical (if still generally sympathetic) academic analysis as much as blind praise.[83]

For *Areíto* contributors, therefore, the effort to comprehend "the Cuba that exist[ed]" in the 1970s required not only dismissing the nostalgias for "the Cuba that was" of their parents, or the anticommunist, "revolutionary" delusion of the *abdalistas*. At its best, the magazine invited contributors to analyze an economically improved yet tepid socialist present in which Cubans' daily concerns were devoid of the epic character accorded to earlier struggles. Even in the magazine's more preening moments, retrospective sycophantism could provide a language for present doubts. "Will [the process of Cuban institutionalization]," José Villalón asked in 1976, "mean the abandonment of that beautiful project to construct the New Man (seen as the objective of the Revolution in the earlier phase) in favor of the construction of a society according to a copy and not its own inspiration?"[84] *Areíto*'s idealization of the revolutionary project spoke in some ways to the depth of its contributors' identity anxieties in the United States more than any intrinsic political romanticism the island inspired at that particular historical juncture. Intellectually, however, the magazine's work still stood apart from Abdala's tendency to paint life on the island as a totalitarian black box. Some analyses also departed significantly from the kinds of assessments that were possible in the island's own media outlets.

In this regard, *Areíto*'s reflections on Cuban politics and history, whatever their ideological blinders, are indeed worthy of attention. But so are magazine contributors' activist efforts. At their core, *Areíto* writers mostly sought to understand Cuba—past and present—rather than change it. Yet the magazine would also become a crossroads for young Cubans abroad who began lobbying for concrete causes: the normalization of U.S. relations with Cuba (something increasingly floated in Washington in the context of détente in the 1970s), and the right of Cuban exiles to travel back to the island as visitors, both developments we will return to in chapter 6. For its part, Abdala did not oppose the possibility of U.S.-Cuba normalization either, even as other anticommunist activists in the community denounced the prospect as yet another sin in a long history of Yankee deceit. Drawing once more on his anti-imperialist, anticommunist version of exile history, Gustavo Marín Duarte argued that the United States had already abandoned Cuba's interests by pursuing a policy of effective "coexistence" with Castro since the mid-1960s. Better to avoid making support for continuing U.S. diplomatic or economic isolation the litmus test for loyalty, lest exiles once again be played for *plattista* fools. "We have never fallen victim to the almost neurotic preoccupation that sees the formalization of [U.S.-Cuban] relations as the end of all efforts to defeat the Castro tyranny," Abdala's leaders insisted.[85]

Toward Ethnic Transition and Homeland Forgetting

And yet, for all of their efforts to break free of the constraints of inherited pasts and their parents' retrospective obsessions—for all of Abdala's protest activities and *Areíto*'s deployment of the written word—by the late 1970s neither group's objectives seemed particularly achievable. Abdala's goal of unseating the Cuban government was no closer than when the organization was first founded. With Soviet financial support to the island in full bloom and the United States moving toward a posture of open rapprochement under President Jimmy Carter, anti-Castroism still appeared to be losing steam. But most young Cubans in Miami were also unwilling to explicitly repudiate, in *Areíto*'s mold, the historical understandings they inherited from their parents. The magazine's contributors would continue to carve out a voice, but they represented a small minority. In this context, the surest way to break with the past may have been to turn *away* from Cuba's history and memory to a significant degree. As the 1970s progressed, antinostalgia as lived reality often meant leaning in to a burgeoning "Cuban American" present, whether by default or as a conscious exit strategy from the island focus of the exile community's traditional politics.

One of the most influential models of what this transition might look like—what it already looked like in practice in many homes—appeared in an unlikely place: on television. In 1975, sociologist Manuel Mendoza, a young Cuban professor at Miami Dade Community College, was worried that average Cuban youth in the United States felt "trapped" between the nostalgic outlooks of their parents and the U.S. social norms and cultural influences they encountered in daily life. Rather than ostracize sellouts who reneged on national inheritance, he dreamed up a bilingual TV program wherein the inevitable melding of old and new could be depicted as not only hilarious but a positive good.[86] With an appealing multicultural, yet in many ways assimilationist, bent (the bilingual format was meant to aid English fluency), Mendoza's proposal found eager support from the local public television station, WPBT2, and a Miami nongovernmental organization, the Community Action Foundation. The U.S. Department of Health, Education, and Welfare agreed to provide an initial round of funds, the first of several, which helped get the project off the ground.[87]

The resulting series, ¿Qué pasa, U.S.A.? (What's Up, U.S.A.?), debuted in 1977 and became an overnight sensation in Cuban exile living rooms in and outside Miami. Centered around the high jinks of the fictional Peña family, the show treated the "Cuban Americanization" of the quintessential Cuban immigrant household not as a liability but as nature's course. Extended, nonironic reflections on the lost *patria* were few and far between. Retrospective polemics perennially rocking exile politics were referenced elliptically if at all. Insofar as the show dealt with political or social themes, episodes revolved around issues germane to Cubans' futures in the United States: relations with "Anglo" neighbors, language confusions, gender politics, generational tensions, and "ethnic" and race relations in South Florida. It was a show focused on the here and now for Cuban migrant families, not their homeland dreams.

Compare the show's tendency to ignore Cuba's past and present to calls by both *Areíto* and Abalda to confront them head on. "As a group and as individuals," one early *Areíto* contributor asserted in 1974, "we cannot see a future in being 'Cuban-Americans' in integrating into the U.S. society of consumption. We reject 'the American way' as a path to resolving all problems. Among us there is a primordial interest in our history, in our culture of the past and the present, and we feel a real concern for its future."[88] *Qué pasa* audiences instead roared with laughter when the Peña grandparents, barely speaking a word of English, came back humming the Mickey Mouse anthem after their first trip to Disney World. One draft poster found in a vertical file of Abdala materials went so far as to ask, "Are You a Yankee Cuban? Be Cuban Cuban. Try It."[89] The *¿Qué pasa, U.S.A.?* theme song—echoing the show's title—announced the exact opposite: "Say helloooo America, we are part of a new USA."

Attracted by the show's upbeat focus on immigrant incorporation, more than 130 public television affiliates from Idaho to San Juan (and of course New Jersey and New York, given their sizeable Cuban communities) picked up the series for their markets.[90] Commentators, in turn, emphasized not the Peñas' Cuban particularities but their ongoing journey to U.S. immigrant integration.[91] "This house is provisional!" father Pepe angrily reminds his daughter Carmencita in one early episode, channeling an exilic sensibility. "Here in Miami we're just passing through!" Yet the fact that Cuban studio audiences laughed uproariously at these lines revealed a clear conviction: there was, in fact, no going back. Hopes of permanent return to the island, once a unifying thread in an otherwise divided memory culture in the exile community, had become a hilarious punch line.

Occasionally the show's creators also sought to advance this message in less sarcastic forms. In one abbreviated treatment for a script dated January 1977, a coworker of Pepe's asks him to look after his small boat while he is away on a trip. To get away from daily stress, the family members convince Pepe to take them out for a joy ride. The entire family seems to be having a fun time, until the motor dies.[92] Panic ensues among the elders when the grandchildren suggest they might float all the way back to Cuba. Suddenly, the grandparents, well known on the show for constantly groaning about how nothing in Miami is as good as it was in Cuba, become fixtures of gratitude for their slice of the American dream. Eventually, grandson Joe spots a U.S. Coast Guard vessel approaching in the distance. The next day's newspaper headline captures the family's feelings: "Cuban-American Family Rescued Yesterday as Their Boat Drifted toward Cuba ... They Are Very Happy ... to Be Home Again." "Home," says grandmother Adela to her husband. "Yes," replies Antonio, the grandfather in the family. "I think this is our home."

According to surviving notes in the chief writer's archive, however, this episode was never made. Producers worried that it treated the idea of the past being left behind *too* cavalierly.[93] Undeniably, *¿Qué pasa, U.S.A.?* depicted a world in which it was Cuban exiles' destiny, like that of their Cuban- or U.S.-born children, to become contributing citizens of the society in which they had come to live. But the show also had to strike a balance between advancing this position and respecting the exile community's refusal to forget.

The most lasting example of the show's promotion of immigrant adjustment can be found in an episode called "Citizenship," uncharacteristic and beloved by fans for its somber tone. At the top of the show, viewers learn that eldest son Joe wants to apply for U.S. citizenship to become eligible for a college scholarship. Because he has not turned eighteen, however, he also needs his father to apply, who refuses on patriotic principle. Frustrated, Joe performs a song he has composed to express his feelings. Sympathetic, his mother, Juana, sings along:

[Juana, in Spanish:]
What's happening to our customs? ...
The old folks cultivate them
The young look for a reason
And what was once exile,
is becoming immigration.

[Joe, in English:]
How can I yearn for what I hardly knew?
How can I feel the same way you do?
I don't remember what I didn't live.
What I never had I cannot give.

[Chorus, together, in Spanish:]
And we keep walking,
Time keeps passing,
Kids are growing up
Old folks are dying.
And the dreamers,
are growing weary.

The favoring of ethnic transition over exilic retrospective obsession could not have been clearer. But as the credits prepare to roll, Pepe contemplates an unopened, spoiled bottle of champagne purchased in the early 1960s to celebrate his family's "imminent" homecoming. "If I ever become an American citizen, I will buy another bottle," he declares emotionally, leaving the question of his citizenship unresolved, "Pero ésta, ésta es para Cuba" ("But this one, this one is for Cuba").[94] At a time when Abdala and the *Areíto* collective were putting their own imprints on long-pitched debates over the island's history within the exile community, *Qué pasa*'s overall underemphasizing of battles over national memory and the homeland concerns of exile politics represented a bold choice. But the Peña children could nonetheless learn to respect their Cuban past as vague, historically simplified tradition. Neither mere model minorities nor exile intransigents, the show's characters inhabited an appealing and, in the end, more resilient intermediate space.

Conclusion: Generational Memory Fractures

Historian Daniel Rodgers has characterized the 1970s as an "age of fracture" in the United States, an "era of disaggregation" in which increasingly plural identities appeared to shrink the "imagined [national] collective."[95] Within the Cuban exile community, too, the 1970s were years of new divisions, as already fractious claims on collective memory from the 1960s collided with new generational rifts. Still, as this chapter has also revealed, underneath the counterpoint of Abdala's and *Areíto*'s divergent conceptions of the Cuban past lay, paradoxically, parallel searches for Cuban completeness—explicit reactions against the fragmentation of "ethnic" life in the United States and a perhaps naive, at turns wistful embrace of a "true" national memory and culture as somehow a reparable whole. *Areíto* contributor Román de la Campa would later conclude that the magazine's contributors had been guided most "by the affective inventory of traumatized memories" and "profound nostalgia[s]" of their own.[96] The same could probably be said about the vicarious desire to make up for missed historical participation that in part drove Abdala's political work.

If *¿Qué pasa, U.S.A.?*'s popularity is any indication, by the end of the 1970s, reckoning with the vagaries of a "Cuban American" present represented the path of least resistance for many Cubans in the United States over projects of exilic vindication. Still, that transition would have consequences for the exile community's memory landscape that could be troubling in their own way. In casting an endearing light on Cuban émigrés' place in a multiethnic U.S. landscape, *¿Qué pasa, U.S.A.?* became a new and, over time, beloved mirror for exiles' own sense of their community's collective story. Yet by reducing that story to a tale of integration and multicultural comedy rather than contentious political struggle, the show—still playing on reruns to this day—also made Cuban exile history look deceptively harmonious and neat.

In truth, the Cuban diaspora in the 1970s remained an evolving "palimpsest" of viewpoints and subject positions more than a straightforward crucible of immigrant assimilation.[97] Cubans expatriates would continue rewriting their pasts and futures vis-à-vis ongoing events on the island in the years to come. In particular, the possibility of traveling back to Cuba in the late 1970s—beginning with members and friends of the *Areíto* group— would bring the disjuncture between memory and the island's reality into closer view. But before we assess that turning point, we must examine in more detail what the Revolution had become. In Cuba during the 1970s, an "age of fracture" had also set in, full of retrospective (over)confidence and anxiety, as well as parallel questions about the relationship of past to present, especially for Cuban youth. If *Qué pasa*'s basic position on the Cuban memory wars was to bury them under a more presentist vision, little did the show's creators know that citizens on the island were confronting a similar choice.

5
Anniversary Overload?
MEMORY FATIGUE AT CUBA'S SOCIALIST APEX

Flip through any Cuban periodical from the 1970s and a recurring feature assaults the senses: anniversaries. State-sponsored newspapers and magazines of the era fixated on the commemoration of events big and small, domestic and international. Between 1972 and 1973, the journal *Revolución y Cultura* included special coverage of the fifth anniversary of Che Guevara's death, the fifty-fifth anniversary of Russia's October Revolution, the 120th birthday of José Martí, and the seventy-fifth birthday of Bertolt Brecht (the East German playwright).[1] In 1974, the covers of *La Gaceta de Cuba*—the chief publication of Cuba's National Union of Artists and Writers (UNEAC)—referenced the fifteenth anniversary of the Cuban Revolution, the 100th anniversary of the death of national founding father Carlos Manuel de Céspedes, the thirteenth anniversary of the Bay of Pigs invasion, and the thirtieth anniversary of the "Liberation of Romania" (from fascism by Soviet troops).[2] Arguably the biggest occasion of the decade was the twentieth anniversary of Fidel Castro's attack on the Moncada Barracks, the ill-fated start to his insurgent career. That milestone in 1973 generated articles, books, posters, and retrospective paeans too numerous to tally.[3]

Historical pomp was nothing new in revolutionary Cuba, of course. Dating to before and certainly during 1959, revolutionary leaders had framed their campaigns as "historic" before they were even complete. Starting in the early 1960s, each year of the Revolution in power was given a thematic or commemorative title—the Year of Agrarian Reform (1960), the Year of Education (1961)—not only to register the sense that Cubans were living in a distinct revolutionary time, but in anticipation of the ways their present would be remembered later on.[4] Authorities, likewise, had engaged in important, if uneven, efforts across the Revolution's first decade to appropriate important pre-1959 landmarks, mark sites of historical significance, and otherwise resignify portions of public space.[5] And, as we have seen, the dates of important revolutionary events like Fidel Castro's attack on the Moncada Barracks in 1953, or the victory at Playa Girón, became annual holidays.

Yet in the 1970s, commemoration bordered upon obsession. Something like an anniversary overload set in, not just in the press, but in the commemorative practices and rhetoric of officials and institutions. Existing museums were refurbished and expanded. Dozens of new historical displays and plaques popped up in remote towns and provincial cities. With the Revolution's insurgent "glory days" behind it, memorialization, now sprinkled with increased Eastern bloc frames of reference, implied an urgent effort to keep the spirit and loyalties of the early 1960s alive. After the tribulations of the mid- and late 1960s, perhaps the Cuban population, and especially its young people, needed to be reminded of the reasons for the Revolution's existence, so that Cuban socialism might finally find a way to thrive.

With commemorative excess, though, also came renewed confidence in a modernizing present. As we saw in chapter 4, the 1970s began ominously, with economic disarray as a result of the failed 10-million-ton sugar harvest. Unparalleled political and ideological dogmatism also set in, due not just to the aforementioned Padilla case but even more as a result of the strict pronouncements of the 1971 National Congress of Education and Culture, which came on the heels of Padilla's arrest and set the agenda for cultural and educational policy for the decade.[6] Nevertheless, despite the initiation of a period of greater artistic orthodoxy and censorship later dubbed the *quinquenio gris* (five gray years) or *decenio amargo* (bitter decade), the 1970s also saw Cuba successfully "convert [economic] defeat into victory" in many ways, just as Castro had pledged.[7] Thanks to formal integration into the Council of Mutual Economic Assistance (the Soviet-backed trade bloc of mostly Eastern European countries) in 1972, the island's aggressively subsidized economy grew at an average annual rate of as much as 14 percent.[8] As scholar Susan Eckstein has noted, "for every hundred homes with electricity, the percentage with television sets ... rose from 33 to 74, with refrigerators from 15 to 38 percent, with washing machines from 6 to 34 percent."[9] From a reliance on moral mobilization and mass campaigns, state economic policy pivoted to more practical terrain, compensating productive employees with imported material goods. In such an environment of improved economic indicators and ideological narrowing, hard work and identification with the Revolution's memory canon could provide a path to trips abroad, Soviet-made appliances, and other forms of political and pecuniary gain.[10]

On the one hand, then, the onslaught of dates, references to heroic figures, and new commemorative spaces in the 1970s may have reflected a spirit of fresh revolutionary optimism as the material conditions of Cuban life stabilized. Yet on the other, such practices could also represent ground zero for a potentially cynical brand of revolutionary citizenship, whereby the *performance* of loyalty became more of a conscious strategy to receive material rewards. Both the repetition and simplification of state origin stories in this period may have cemented increasingly passive, rote citizen engagement in state-led memory work. In that case, examining retrospective politics would require not just analyzing the shifts in commonly used memory narratives during the period in question but also gauging their instrumental use. However, ascertaining the degree to which "emblematic frameworks" of revolutionary remembrance actually ceased to resonate with the personal sentiments of Cubans in the 1970s presents a challenge.[11] Detailed reports of the attitudes, complaints, and private jokes that greeted daily life during the Revolution's second decade do not abound in the largely closed Cuban archival record.[12] And where the documentation of state institutions involved in commemorative work is within reach, we lack the means to accurately access how everyday and particularly younger Cubans' relationships to and understandings of their history may have changed.

Nonetheless, within official statements and sanctioned cultural production of the era, one can trace the evolving contours and contradictions of historical narrations that would have shaped Cubans' impressions. One can also see how the wider triumphalist spirit pervading public retrospective discourse in the 1970s proved a double-edged sword. Short of new events to rekindle the fires of revolutionary hopes, commemorative repetition risked converting the state's grand narrative into stale slogans. Cubans saw signs of social progress and relative prosperity that made aspects of the present more attractive than the recent past. But young Cubans in particular also confronted an increasingly streamlined revolutionary epic to which their more modest efforts in the here and now could hardly compare. Rather than providing fulfillment, the activities expected of citizens might very well have yielded a gnawing sense of frustration. The result, paradoxically, was a cultural climate in which invocations of memory and history appeared everywhere, yet everyday existence could seem unremarkable, *forgettable*—at best the evidence of a future already constructed and a prerevolutionary past left behind.

From the "Time of History" to Futurity's Past

"They asked this man for his time / to be added to the time of History," wrote Heberto Padilla in 1968. "They asked him for his lips, / his dry cracked lips, to affirm / and with each affirmation to build up a dream."[13] In his controversial 1968 collection *Fuera del juego* (*Out of the Game*), Padilla's critical reflections on the binding of individual subjectivity to national epic had marked his emergence as an intellectual bête noire within the Revolution's cultural establishment. Like Antón Arrufat's play *Los siete contra Tebas*, *Fuera del juego* received a UNEAC prize but was only printed with a foreword noting UNEAC's protest against the "antihistoricism" and "ambiguity" of its contents.[14] By 1971, as we saw in chapter 4, the poet's growing dissidence had culminated in arrest and an internationally denounced public "self-critique." Oddly, however, had Padilla's lines continued circulating, they might have taken on the powers of nostalgic incantation. As reliance on moral mobilization shifted toward more mundane patterns of central planning, the true "time of History" for Cubans in many ways seemed to have come and gone.

In the 1970s, the stakes of Cuba's past, present, and future no longer seemed quite as immediate, intimately intertwined, or dangerously in the balance as in the decade before. Of course, the national saga continued to impregnate public rhetoric. In addition to signaling a new age of cultural orthodoxy, the final declaration of the 1971 National Congress of Education and Culture insisted that Cubans were living "true history," the era in which "the masses" were the protagonists of social life.[15] Official media likewise cast the bureaucratic "institutionalization" of the state along Sovietizing lines in this period as a new front of urgent battle, while cases of Cuban exile terrorism suggested that the Revolution's opponents still presented an existential threat.[16] Yet, whereas through the late 1960s many Cubans still believed that they were consummating the island's history in real time—notwithstanding that others harbored real doubts—by the next decade the joyfully chaotic, unpredictable rallies that characterized the Revolution's first years had long since morphed into routines of mass organization. When Leonid Brezhnev became the first Soviet premier to visit Cuba in 1974, the island's political leadership greeted him with a full military review, a spectacle of state order, not popular euphoria, to seal Cuban-Soviet goodwill.[17]

Officially, any note of retrospective melancholy remained taboo in revolutionary political culture. Cuban literary giant turned cultural diplomat Alejo Carpentier wrote fawningly in 1979, "I have to profoundly thank the Cuban Revolution for the fact that ... due to its energetic impulse toward the future, I have become immune to the aging, morbid fascination of nostalgia. I have been lucky to belong to a generation of Cubans that, from the first of January 1959, has been cured forever of empty longings, convinced by visible and tangible achievements that, for us, no past was better than the present."[18] Fidel Castro, too, denied that time had sapped the public's spirit. "What has experience taught us?" he asked in 1975. "That [the people's] energy has not fallen, that enthusiasm does not weaken, that if the Revolution had a heroic stage in the fight for liberation and a historic stage in the fight to defend the nation [i.e., the 1950s and 1960s], it also has a very heroic, dignified stage [dedicated to] the work of creation."[19] After a decade of conflict, mass mobilizations, and material shortages, some semblance of stability might very well have been welcome. Even if plagued by continued problems and the greater "Sovietization" of Cuban politics and culture in a variety of ways, socialist "normalcy" in the 1970s no doubt held considerable appeal.[20]

Still, as the urgency of improvisation gave way to more consistent five-year plans, some wistfulness for lived drama may have proved unavoidable. Poet Raúl Rivero hinted at such dilemmas in his award-winning 1972 collection *Poesía sobre la tierra* (*Poetry about the Earth*). "Nothing will stain what we will call the struggles of the past /," he wrote, "and it is nothing less than our time / this day, this exact hour / during which, leaning against the machine / [or] only looking out of the window / I am witness to the yesteryear of future generations / that will have to look up in history books / the battle of Playa Girón."[21] Rivero foresaw a time when history would be less lived in the day-to-day than reflected upon from a distance. Yet, as he suggested, such a prospect conjured feelings of both pride and longing. To wit, in the poem "Historia viva" ("Living History"), Rivero described spotting an old friend in footage of young rural literacy teachers returning as heroes to Havana in the early 1960s. "Never again will my friend Oscar Granados enter triumphantly in Havana," he pondered, sentimentally. "Simple and clean, he will step down from a bus / as a worker coming back from vacation / always having left, in another year of turns at neighborhood watch / and meetings, the light of his pupils atop the desk."[22] If for Rivero such a peaceful destiny represented a source of satisfaction, the closing image of the activist now wed to routine suggested that the rhythm of historical change for Cubans in the present had slowed.

The winding down from the high points of external conflict and internal revolutionary mobilization registered in other ways. It is telling, for example, that over the Revolution's entire second decade in power, only one event—the notorious bombing of Cubana Airlines flight 455, masterminded by Cuban exiles in October 1976—found an immediate and permanent place on the island's national memory calendar. On that occasion, tens of thousands of distraught mourners flooded Havana's Revolution Square, waiting in long lines to file past coffins of the deceased. In moments of real crisis, nationalist convictions remained as palpable as ever.

The rawness of the tragedy required little embroidery.[23] Significant as well was the beginning of what would become a sustained Cuban military engagement in Angola in 1975—though as a secret operation at first, with few details publicly reported.[24] For the most part, then, older patriotic holidays (like José Martí's birthday) continued to dominate the commemorative schedule, while anniversaries from the anti-Batista insurgency rounded out the list. As already noted, the July 26, 1953, attack on the Moncada Barracks, the namesake for the 26th of July Movement, remained both the Revolution's most important national holiday (especially in the twentieth anniversary year of 1973) and a frequent subject of retrospective hagiography.[25]

The writer Dariela Aquique remembers the month of October as particularly ripe with ritualized national memory significance during these years.[26] Every October 10 Cubans recalled Carlos Manuel de Céspedes's declaration of war against Spain in 1868, the opening bell in the long struggle for independence and the "100 years of struggle" (as Castro had put it in 1968) that followed. The days preceding, however, revolved mostly around recent occasions of national mourning: the memory of Hurricane Flora in early October 1963 (a devastating storm that took the lives of 1,200 Cubans), the "Crime of Barbados" (as the Cubana flight 455 bombing became known) on October 6, 1976, and the death of Che Guevara in Bolivia on October 8, 1967—though, as was later confirmed, his execution actually took place on October 9.[27] At the end of the month, thousands of schoolchildren gathered at seashores across the country, as they had since the 1960s, to recall the mysterious airborne disappearance of charismatic revolutionary hero Camilo Cienfuegos on October 28, 1959, placing flowers atop his presumed maritime grave.[28] Cienfuegos's routine flight from the central city of Camagüey to Havana had simply disappeared from radar screens, and rescue personnel never located his remains. By contrast, on July 26, 1970, Fidel tempered his reflections on the failure of the 10-million-ton harvest by revealing that Guevara's hands, severed by his executioners to identify his fingerprints, had been returned to Cuba "perfectly conserved." Next October, Castro pledged, on the anniversary of Che's death, the government would display the heroic guerrilla's preserved appendages in crystal urns to appear as if protruding naturally from his original olive green uniform. A more dramatic totem of not just revolutionary memory but quasi-religious faith could scarcely have been conceived.[29]

Fortunately, perhaps, this morbid spectacle never came to be. But the 1970s did witness a boom in the construction, expansion, and refurbishment of museums across the island. Early on, revolutionary authorities recognized the importance of conserving the history they were making and shaping its telling. Decree-Law Number 17, signed by Raúl Castro on December 12, 1959, authorized the creation of a museum of the Revolution—a project that, in fact, guerrilla confidante Celia Sánchez had first envisioned before the rebel victory. The institution was first housed in provisional offices in Havana's Vedado district before being officially inaugurated in the Castillo de San Salvador de la Punta in Old Havana under the direction of the Ministerio de las Fuerzas Armadas Revolucionarias (Ministry of Revolutionary Armed Forces, MINFAR) in 1961. It was then transferred to the base of the José Martí monument in Revolution Square (the former Plaza Cívica) in 1963, where it remained opened to the public until 1968.[30] Not until January 4, 1974, however, did the Museum of the Revolution open its doors in what would become its permanent location, the former Presidential Palace, after a significant exhibition expansion and redesign. Officially, the revolutionary "process" remained eternal and ongoing in its sixteenth year. Still, the fact that the museum now had a secure home seemed to say something about the Revolution's core struggles being "complete." As they had done on numerous occasions in the early 1960s, authorities once again rebaptized a site of pre-1959 infamy—the headquarters of so many corrupt Cuban presidents, including Batista—into a vessel of revolutionary mythmaking.[31] Two years later the glass-enclosed *Granma* memorial, displaying the famous yacht Fidel Castro and other rebels used to reach the Sierra Maestra from Mexico, opened across the street.[32]

Museums dedicated to individual revolutionary heroes and episodes also proliferated. Here, too, roots of the initiative reached back to the 1960s. In 1966, Raúl Castro and MINFAR put together "a nationwide plan to heritagize revolutionary sites of memory."[33] But only in the 1970s did that original ambition begin to bear considerable fruit. In October 1973 the Museo Casa Natal de José Antonio Echeverría, dedicated to the most famous martyr of the Revolutionary Directorate's failed attack on Batista's Presidential Palace in 1957, officially opened its doors in the city of Cárdenas (where Echeverría was raised).[34] Several months earlier the Museo Casa de Abel Santamaría, the most venerated activist to die in the 1953 Moncada attack, debuted in Havana with similar fanfare and a visit from schoolchildren.[35] Reflecting the extensive cult of Moncada in the year of the attack's twentieth anniversary, a second museum and park dedicated to Santamaría in Santiago de Cuba also opened on July 26, the anniversary of the attack and his brutal death at the hands of Batista's police.[36] Several days later the panopticon-style Presidio Modelo on Cuba's Isle of Pines (officially renamed the Isle of Youth in 1978) welcomed its first visitors to the refurbished cells where Fidel and other survivors of the Moncada debacle had been imprisoned between late 1953 and the spring of 1955. Left off the displays, though, were mentions of the facility's continued use as a jail for accused counterrevolutionary insurgents after 1959, including prisoners from the Bay of Pigs. Also missing were references to what one rare text later called the "unintegrated" *moncadistas*—those Moncada fighters who after 1959 had, at varying points, found their way out of the country, back to prison, or into "internal exile" after falling into conflict with the socialist state.[37]

But the most noteworthy expansion of museum spaces by far occurred at the provincial and municipal level. As anthropologist Pablo Alonso González has documented, Law 23 from 1976 charged Cuba's Consejo Nacional de Patrimonio Cultural (National Council of Cultural Heritage, CNPC), under the recently created Ministry of Culture, with overseeing the development of generalist historical museums in each of the island's municipalities and provincial capitals. Many of the latter were new, as the "institutionalization" of the Cuban state in the mid-1970s brought a significant reorganization of its administrative divisions and territorial boundaries. The project was not only massive in scope; it also fulfilled one of the 1966 plan's other unrealized goals. As González puts it, the new museums "enacted a top-down 'localization' of national history, instead of opening a path for local histories to make the national from the ground up."[38] While municipal officials were encouraged to highlight revolutionary heroes, events, and martyrs specific to each locality, the overarching organization and format of each museum were centrally controlled. A team in Havana produced the pictures, panels, and historic texts sent to each institution, and where local evidence of participation in a significant event could not be identified, other examples would substitute. In cases where existing local historical museums were renovated to fit new parameters, their exhibitions and designs had to be submitted to Havana for approval. In the illustrative case of La Periquera museum in the eastern city of Holguín, the CNPC even ordered that the display be rearranged in a clockwise direction, "symbolically equating the historical evolution [of Cuba] from political 'right' to 'left.'"[39]

The significance of the municipal and provincial museums, however, was not just their existence. The narrative of Cuban history they standardized—and apparently even its directional orientation—was itself symptomatic of gradual shifts in how the nation and the Revolution's history were being told. While spaces like the Museum of the Revolution or individual "home museums" continued to emphasize a nationalist historic canon of "great men" and revolutionary events, provincial and municipal museums increasingly approached Cuba's past in a more structuralist mode. This reflected the now institutionalized influence of Marxist historical concepts—especially those derived from the "scientific" Marxism-Leninism of the Soviet Union. Accordingly, Cuba's indigenous history, the history of slavery during the colonial period, and the independence struggle were all depicted as discrete historical phases in Cuba's history of class struggle. The period after Cuba's independence, in turn, was no longer labeled just "the pseudo-republic," an indictment of the era's moral corruption and failings already canonized to a degree in the 1960s. Instead, "neocolonial republic" or simply "the neocolony" became the much more common terms du jour to emphasize overt and indirect forms of imperialist submission. Which of these imperatives to prioritize—the nationalist-heroic (associated with the trope of the "100 years of struggle") or the structural stages of Cuba's historic progress (per Marxist logic)—would remain a source of tension and debate. Nonetheless, heritage professionals on the island also found ways to fuse them, regimenting an increasingly clear "official history" over the course of the decade.[40] Needless to say, when it came to narrating the emergence of the Revolution itself, these spaces and narratives studiously avoided the political diversity of the original anti-Batista coalition, let alone the ideological disputes within that coalition at the Revolution's start.

The numbers on museum expansion speak for themselves. Excluding the provincial and municipal museums housed in towns and cities, of the 154 other functioning museums on the island today, 38—roughly a quarter—opened in the 1970s. Compare this to the 18 similar museums that opened the decade before.[41] More than 150 municipal and provincial museums, meanwhile, were created between 1968 and 1983.[42] Significantly, preexisting specialized museums also underwent renovation—not only the aforementioned Museum of the Revolution but also the museum at Playa Girón dedicated to the Bay of Pigs invasion, first opened in 1964 and reinaugurated in 1976 after undergoing an expansion.[43] Cuba also saw the beginnings of a monumental push. The 1977 creation of a National Commission of Monuments as part of the Ministry of Culture (following Law No. 2, dated August 4) formalized a more ad hoc process for commissioning and designating monuments prior to that point. And though the creation of new physical monuments in public space would not reach its peak until the 1980s, sixteen sites associated with the anti-Batista insurrection and post-1959 events of significance were designated national monuments in 1978 and 1979, together with a number of others related to various heroes and happenings of Cuba's independence struggle.[44] At the risk of simplification, whereas the Revolution focused in its earliest years on the "resignification of a preexisting heritage"—the conversion of Batista's barracks into schools being a prime example, or Plaza Cívica into Revolution Square—in the 1970s the Cuban state increasingly codified, standardized, and institutionalized new heritage spaces of its own.[45]

Meanwhile, filmic and other cultural monuments to canonical revolutionary events abounded in the backdrop. Cuba's victory at Playa Girón, predictably, continued to occupy a prominent place, indexing a wider history of resistance to U.S. imperial designs. Manuel Herrera's 1972 experimental documentary *Girón*, for instance, in theory aimed to do more than repeat a familiar hagiography.[46] By showing veterans of the invasion on film directing the movements of historical reenactors, Herrera sought to highlight the fuzzy line between individual memory and mass-mediated narrative reconstruction—a potentially interesting, even subversive point. For the most part, however, bombastic reenactments overshadowed such "alienation techniques," sweeping "the audience up and [forcing] it to accept without question a glorification of war, of tanks, guns, and planes," as one reviewer outside of Cuba put it at the time.[47] For its part, Raúl Macías's 1971 play *Girón: La verdadera historia de la Brigada 2506* (*The True Story of the Brigade 2506*) revisited the Bay of Pigs interrogations that we analyzed in chapter 3. But the farcical drama stripped the most famous exchanges of their argumentative feel, rendering now nameless exile prisoners as the objects of pure ridicule and uniform distaste.[48]

In a complementary fashion, artists and filmmakers cast their depictions of the prerevolutionary "before" of Cuban history into ever simpler, more caricatured terms. Take the long-form 1972 documentary *¡Viva la República!* (*Long Live the Republic!*), sarcastically titled to rebuke the simplified "lost Republic" that the Revolution's most conservative enemies tended to celebrate.[49] Meant to provide audiences with a crash course in pre-1959 Cuban politics, the movie situated U.S. geopolitical influence in Cuba immediately before the Revolution within a longer genealogy of North American meddling. Curiously, after depicting the pre-1959 period as a schizophrenic whirlwind of corruption and inequality, the film concludes with only the briefest fragment of silent archival film featuring Fidel Castro in the Sierra Maestra, interacting with a nameless girl and boy. So ingrained was the officially accepted legend of what came next that the film's director, Pastor Vega, evidently felt no need to rehash what his audiences already knew. And once again, that assumed knowledge erased or minimized any recollection of factional memory disputes and political tensions at the Revolution's start.

All the same, one wonders whether such diverse exercises in museumification, screen memorialization, and literal and figurative "memory prosthesis" (to return to the case of Che's hands) reflected broader confidence in, or a vulnerability of, the official historical canon. Alison Landsberg defines "prosthetic memory" as that emerging "at the interface between a person and a historical narrative about the past, at an experiential site such as a movie theater, a monument, or a museum." "In this moment of contact," she writes, an individual "sutures himself or herself in a larger history."[50] Revolutionary leaders had proven adept at this strategy during mass rallies and in the media in the early 1960s. It remained their goal in the 1970s, as municipal and provincial museums "became places of initiation and ritual for schoolchildren, ... members of the pioneer movement [as all schoolchildren were known] swearing oath, and university graduates."[51] A decade later, though, authorities needed to connect to a generation that had not been witnesses, let alone protagonists, of the history represented. Though less "tainted" than their parents by selfish prerevolutionary attitudes—or "rezagos del pasado" (holdovers of the past)—young people might also have been more likely to take the Revolution's achievements for granted.[52] Could they be enlisted as true revolutionary subjects? Would their loyalty be genuine or the product of social and political expectation? Would they be inspired by museum exhibitions or bored?

One might also surmise that, more than a defensive effort, the construction of museums represented an expected response to a renewed rhythm of modernization. The French scholar Pierre Nora famously theorized that societies preserve national history in "memory places" like monuments only when the shape of social life makes memory no longer "a real part of everyday experience."[53] Something similar, perhaps, was afoot in Cuba during the Revolution's second decade. It was in these years, after all, that the original industrializing ambitions of revolutionary officials regained force after years of officially valorized rural asceticism culminating in the failed 10-million-ton harvest of 1970. Following Cuba's insertion into the Council of Mutual Economic Assistance in 1972, newly imported mass consumer goods from the Soviet bloc helped resuscitate visions of productive utopias first imagined in the early 1960s.[54] Nonfiction films like *No tenemos derecho a esperar* (*We Don't Have the Right to Wait*) took viewers on sweeping tours of infrastructure projects, medical advances, and other social welfare programs finally coming into their own.[55] East of Havana, meanwhile, construction on the planned seaside town of Alamar, and the equally celebrated model settlement of La Yaya in the Escambray, presaged a prosperous residential future made of prefabricated Soviet cement.[56] By the middle of the decade, the slow introduction of a series of "parallel markets" offered consumer and manufactured goods for sale outside of the ration system.[57] "Cuba goes forward!"

professed one of the more famous songs of the era, as higher standards of living and "material comfort" became legitimizing features of a modest but more stable socialist "dreamworld" with which plenty of Cubans might have found reason to identify.[58]

The promise of material plenty, though allowing for modest new consumption distinctions, went hand in hand with admiration for the leveling potential of Soviet technology. Whereas in 1966 then "President [Osvaldo] Dorticós declared that communism would not be possible as long as there existed work as brutal as [cutting sugar cane]," by the end of the 1970s mechanized Soviet- and Cuban-designed KTP-1 harvesters (fabricated outside the city of Holguín) accounted for half of all sugar cultivated on the island.[59] In the mid- and late 1960s revolutionary officials and authors alike celebrated manual labor in the sugar field as the purifying forge of revolutionary consciousness.[60] Now, grandiose "Schools in the Countryside," depicted in Jorge Fraga's 1974 film *La nueva escuela (The New School)*, were helping to modernize the backlands as much as expose young urbanites to the rigors of rural life.[61] More dramatically, a celebrated 1976 accord with the Soviet Union portended Cuba's entry into the nuclear age thanks to the promised construction of two 440-megawatt reactors on the outskirts of the city of Cienfuegos.[62] And while *Casa de las Américas* magazine once promoted "testing one's bones against underdevelopment" over the arrogance of a Yankee moon landing, by 1978 the Cuban pilot Arnaldo Tamayo Méndez was on his way to Moscow to begin training as the first Cuban cosmonaut.[63] In 1976's "Introduction to the History of Cuba," poet Víctor Casaus, author of the controversial *Girón en la memoria* at the beginning of the decade, went so far as to imagine a fictional antimonument as the ultimate testament to the age: a housing project that, unbeknown to residents, covered the hallowed grounds where the bones of Martí and other Cuban political martyrs lay buried. In this view, the privilege of enjoying the fruits of socialist modernization involved, heretically, a certain right to forget.[64]

But if such images suggested to Cubans that their lives were already free of worries, Cuba's political leaders constantly reminded citizens—and young people especially—of the sacrifices that had made it possible and against which their efforts would be measured. "If one looks at the age of those who waged the Ten Years War," Castro told members of the Cuban Communist Party's youth branch, the Unión de Jóvenes Comunistas (Union of Young Communists), in 1972,

> the age of Maceo and the great combatants of that era—the ages of revolutionaries of all eras of the history of our country—one would see

that they could have been members of the Union of Young Communists if they were living today. That is to say, historically, in our country men of your age were the agents and executors of the great revolutions.... But today you do not have to fight to take power that the people conquered from the exploiters. You no longer have to shed blood in our country to make a revolution. You have a revolution in your hands![65]

Instead of consigning the past to marble simulacra, "institutionalization" in the Cuban 1970s regimented the place of commemoration in daily life, setting up a series of expectations that all Cubans, and young people in particular, could scarcely hope to meet. "The new generations will have to be superior to the older generations," Fidel intoned.[66] "Run" to the future, the now popular, officially embraced singer Silvio Rodríguez advised his idealistic fans, lest it "fall down" without their help.[67] The activities demanded of young people, however, could hardly equal the great deeds students were told to admire. Amid signs of socialist progress, the past could seem more heroic and monumental, but also out of reach.

Origin Stories: Revise and Repeat

Abetting such possibilities for disidentification between ordinary Cubans and political legend was a subtle, in some ways contradictory shift in another feature of state historical discourse: the ways revolutionary leaders specifically narrated their own ideological roots and political evolution between the insurrection in the 1950s and the turn to socialism in 1961. Commemorative surplus in the 1970s may have resulted in the repetition of many familiar story lines and anniversary markers. But whereas Marxist-Leninist orthodoxy shaped the emphasis of new municipal history museums, revolutionary officials began to revise elements of the Revolution's origin story in ways that partially wrote out both structural explanations and everyday Cubans. By the middle of the decade, the First Congress of the Cuban Communist Party (PCC) provided the stage for institutionalizing not only a more Soviet-style structure of government in a socialist constitution (approved in 1976) but also a newly simplified narrative of the Revolution's coming-to-be in the 1950s and 1960s. The resulting account contradicted a previous emphasis on citizen protagonism in the nation's transformations but curiously did not replace it with a depersonalized account of class struggle. Instead, officials emphasized the prowess of the Revolution's leaders, suggesting that Cubans had been beneficiaries of their wishes and foresight.

Since the early 1960s, explanations of the anti-Batista insurrection and the Revolution's subsequent evolution in power had followed a foreseeable script. Starting in late 1961, high-placed intellectuals-cum-politicians like Carlos Rafael Rodríguez, Aníbal Escalante, Blas Roca, and Che Guevara (all important leaders of the old PSP, with the exception of Guevara) had taken it upon themselves to explain how the revolutionary project had gone from "olive green," as Castro characterized his ideology at one point in 1959, to "red," or openly socialist, by April 1961.[68] This "transition to socialism," Marxist theorists argued—implicitly rejecting the thesis of "betrayal" proffered by their more moderate exile foes—grew out of a process of radicalization forged at the crossroads of domestic class mobilization and foreign (read: U.S.) antagonism. The victory, in other words, of a radical but at first admittedly nonsocialist political project had unleashed both internal and external tensions that eventually "pushed" revolutionary officials into casting off lingering bourgeois beliefs.[69] In this reading, the Revolution's ideological transformation did not so much depart from its original intentions as it responded to the demands of the populace itself and the exigencies of conflict that took on a logic of their own.

Notably, Fidel Castro echoed such views during a highly public visit to the Chile of Salvador Allende in late 1971. In 1970, Allende had been elected to the presidency in Chile on the basis of a novel promise: bringing about socialism by the ballot box. Yet if in Cuba Allende's electoral victory was said to be evidence of an unstoppable "revolutionary wave that is making Latin America tremble," it also represented a challenge to the Cuban historical model of taking power by insurrectionary force.[70] Three years after the death of Che Guevara—and, with him, the denouement of radical guerrilla dreams in the hemisphere for a time—the memory of Cuba's armed struggle risked losing some of its sheen when measured against Allende's more peaceful alternative. Fidel Castro thus had a strategic reason not only to explain why Cuba's experience had differed, as interlocutors frequently asked him, but also to portray all revolutionary outcomes as the result of nationally specific circumstances and evolutionary processes reflective of specific historical moments in time.

In Cuba's case, argued Fidel, the inevitability of an armed path to victory stemmed from the island's weak tradition of electoral politics compared to Chile's. While true, that argument conveniently elided demands for constitutional and electoral restoration that Fidel Castro and other anti-Batista activists had once embraced as personal and programmatic goals. Still, Castro acknowledged the original hesitance of his own ideological point of view. "I was not yet a communist, no," he admitted to Chilean audiences about his thinking in 1959. "The program of the 26th of July Movement was not yet a socialist program."[71] Cubans, he claimed, thus understood "that Revolution"—whether in Chile or Cuba—"is a journey, that Revolution is a process." Revolutions, Fidel proclaimed, "could not even be preconceived."[72] Contrast this with Castro's 1966 prophecy, when speaking to a gathering of revolutionary movement leaders from across the Third World, that "sooner or later, all people, or almost all people, will have to take up arms to liberate themselves."[73]

Ironically, though, as the 1970s progressed, it was precisely a more "preconceived" view of Cuba's recent history that began to take hold. Take Castro's speech on Moncada's twentieth anniversary in July 1973. On that occasion, he claimed that "some of us, even before March 10, 1952 [the date of Batista's coup], had arrived at the intimate conviction that the solution to Cuba's problems had to be revolutionary ... and that the objective had to be socialism." Here, Castro did not refer to himself specifically, or even to the attackers at Moncada. He also went on to repeat the idea that Cuba had "awakened" to a socialist trajectory after 1959.[74] Still, in contrast to his remarks in Chile two years before, the Revolution's leader now seemed to be hinting that members of his inner circle may have been envisioning a socialist project all along.

It was really in the lead-up to the First Congress of the Cuban Communist Party in 1975—two years after a coup d'état led by Augusto Pinochet had violently removed Allende and, with him, the Chilean comparative threat—that authorities ditched previously dialectical, materialist, if still selective modes of analysis for a more conspiratorial vision. A socialist makeover, the PCC now insisted, in fact had been the secretly held desire of the Revolution's core leadership, including Fidel, from the start. Reflecting upon the significance of the Moncada attack on July 26, 1975, Castro amended his words in Chile four years before. "At the beginning we were few," he stressed, "[And] although our program as the 26th of July movement was not yet a socialist program, *we, the 26th of July, were socialists.*" Castro thus skirted the memory of 26th of July Movement members in the late 1950s who clearly did not think in such terms. "Our books were the works of Martí, and Marx, and Engels, and Lenin," he continued. "And these ideas, even in the most difficult of circumstances, brought us to victory."[75] Back in 1961, by contrast, Fidel was only prepared to argue that "the socialist germ of the Revolution was already present in the Moncada movement." What had once been treated as retrospective revelation had suddenly morphed into a deliberate goal.[76]

Revolutionary officials also returned to, but dramatically simplified, the controversial history of the PSP's role in the anti-Batista insurrection, painting it as simply one of three main political factions that had become seamlessly integrated into the revolutionary government after 1959. "And there was also in our country a communist party," Castro professed, "and those militant communist revolutionaries were closely united, throughout the struggle, with the combatants of the 26th of July revolutionary movement."[77] As we saw in chapter 1, certain members and collaborators of the 26th of July Movement did have ties to the PSP going back to the early 1950s. Officially, though, the PSP leadership both repudiated Fidel's attack on the Moncada Barracks in 1953—ironically, the very event being commemorated in the above-cited speech—and failed to reach a definitive understanding with his 26th of July Movement until the summer of 1958. After 1959, this legacy made it difficult for many noncommunist rebels to accept the revolutionary government's move to bring them into the fold, eventually sending many into exile. Now, in one swift allocution, the Revolution's leader had rendered that history of political and retrospective conflict null and void. His words also expunged the sequence of "sectarian" conflicts referenced in chapter 3 that had continued to fracture the revolutionary leadership ranks in the 1960s, all of which stemmed from lingering pre-1959 competition among anti-Batista groups.

The culmination of such revisionism came at the First Congress of the PCC in December 1975. Ironically, what conservative, pro-Batista elements of Miami's Cuban exile community had long alleged—that Castro had always been a clandestine communist—became enshrined as official state wisdom. The Revolution of 1959, the party's widely printed *Historical Analysis of the Cuban Revolution* intoned, "had to be the work of new communists, in essence, because they were not known as such." "If it is true that [socialism] was not the general thinking of all of those who initiated the path of revolutionary armed struggle in our country," Fidel backpedaled slightly, "it was for its principal leaders." Isolated, repressed, and politically paralyzed, Cuba's PSP had not been in a position to lead. Only a younger generation, recognizing that "the proclamation of socialism during the insurrectional stage would not yet have been understood by the people," proved capable of assuming the undercover vanguard.[78] "Before March 10 [Batista's coup]," Castro said even more bluntly in a published 1978 interview, "I was already a communist."[79] Prominent Castro biographers today disagree.[80]

The result of these rhetorical gymnastics was a remarkable shift from a dynamic to a more oracular vision of the Revolution's history. Whether a product of Cuba's new strength under Soviet support or residual fears that retrospective what-ifs could prove a Trojan horse, this recasting painted revolutionary socialism as the outcome of premonition and design. "History transpires as a function of objective laws, but men make history," Castro stated at the party congress in 1975, oddly inverting the emphasis of Marx's old adage, "Men make their own history, but they do not make it as they please."[81] In this case, though, the men making the most consequential history were a chosen few. Party documents continued to speak of an "inevitable objective process" by which a "democratic-popular, agrarian, anti-imperialist" phase of the Revolution progressed to a stage of "socialist construction."[82] Yet, whereas Fidel and other leaders had previously remembered the masses driving the revolutionary administration to these ideological heights, now the all-seeing leadership assumed primacy of narrative place and political authorship. No longer the principal agents of revolutionary transformation, the Cuban people seemed to be the objects, or at best partners, of a calculated plan.

History as Melodrama, November Doubts

The seeming incontestability of these claims appears dumbfounding from the vantage point of today. Surely many Cubans privately recalled a more complex pattern of historical change. Yet in a decade that was at once past-obsessed and forward-looking, one can almost understand the attractions of amnesia. Besides, save for those paying academic attention to Castro's every word, gradual mutations in public rhetoric probably registered less powerfully than dramatizations of Cuba's story as consummated epic—particularly in the media. If on screen and television the Revolution's true purpose, orientation, and protagonists were represented as broadly unchanging, or undisputed truths, then the finer points and contradictions in state leaders' own shifting narrative on these questions may have passed unperceived. We have already seen some examples of these kinds of discourses. But they are only the beginning.

Contrast, for starters, the Communist Party's changing description of the Revolution's ideological evolution with additional documentary representations of Cuba's and the Revolution's history geared for popular consumption. Regardless of the ways officials explained the government's trajectory in power, the idea that the political process inaugurated in 1959 represented the culmination of Cuban history remained unchanged. In the 1970s, there were many exponents of this view, but ICAIC documentary director Santiago Álvarez brought this foundational teleology to new heights. *El primer delegado* (*The First Delegate*), for instance, released in 1975 as the first color film made by ICAIC, posited a suspiciously neat parallelism between Fidel Castro's leadership of the first party congress that year and José Martí's foundation of the proindependence Partido Revolucionario Cubano (Cuban Revolutionary Party, PRC) in 1892. Never mind that Martí did not intend the PRC to be the only political party allowed once Cuban independence was achieved. The PCC was to be understood as the PRC of modern times. "Fidel: History not only absolved you, it placed you in the highest place of honor," reads one intertitle appearing on screen, an obvious reference to the *comandante*'s famed remarks at his trial after the Moncada attacks of 1953. In this way, while Communist Party directives still officially viewed Cuban socialism as "under construction," Álvarez suggested that Fidel was the modern incarnation of Martí who had already succeeded in bringing his dreams to fruition.[83]

Álvarez's *Mi hermano Fidel* (*My Brother Fidel*) tugged even more mawkishly at the heartstrings. Shot in 1976 as an unplanned diversion from the making of a separate documentary on the twentieth anniversary of the *Granma*'s landing (another anniversary of note), the film depicted Fidel Castro visiting the home of Salustiano Leyva, a practically blind, elderly man in Oriente province.[84] As a boy, Leyva had met José Martí shortly after his arrival on the Cuban coast in 1895 to join the war against Spain. At first, then, the Revolution's leader assumes the role of anonymous student in the exchange, eager to touch his political ancestors through the words of a ninety-two-year-old who had actually been in their presence. The plot hinges, however, on the moment when Fidel arranges for his host to be seen by an optician and fit for glasses. Literally and metaphorically, darkness turns to light, and history's privileged witness breathlessly realizes who stands in his presence. "I am Fidel's brother ... because Fidel is Martí's brother, and I am Martí's brother," Leyva professes, going weak in the knees. As if the point were not clear, the film fades out with an image of Castro alone on the very beach where Martí landed to reignite Cuba's independence war in 1895. Once again, Castro stands as the personification of the nineteenth-century hero, though viewers also might have wondered why it had taken the Revolution so long to help Leyva see.[85]

Nonetheless, arguably the most salient historical narratives available for popular consumption in the 1970s were not found in documentaries. In terms of audience size, dramatizations of recent history carried the day, fictionalizing true revolutionary legends. Tellingly, the most beloved Cuban movies of the era—all produced by ICAIC—staged moments of the Revolution's successful conflict against internal and external enemies the decade before.[86] The 1973 thriller *El hombre de Maisinicú* (*The Man from Maisinicú*), for example, famously dramatized the real-life tale of Alberto Delgado, an administrator of a small farm in the Escambray Mountains, a hotbed of counterrevolutionary unrest in the early 1960s. After successfully penetrating anticommunist rebel groups on behalf of state security, Delgado was assassinated by insurgents in 1964.[87] Drawing a record 1.9 million viewers, the film stood as a celluloid monument to a national hero fighting off the designs of Washington and the internal counterrevolution. Director Manuel Pérez may have prepared by speaking with jailed partici-

Figure 5.1. Advertisement for *En silencio ha tenido que ser*,
El Caimán Barbudo 135 (March 1979): back cover.

pants from the former anti-Castro opposition. Viewers, however, would mostly remember the actor Sergio Corrieri's manly tour de force in the lead role—quite a shift from his starring part in the more introspective *Memorias del subdesarrollo* (*Memories of Underdevelopment*) in 1968.[88]

Similar blockbuster productions also made Cuba's defiance of Cuban exile and U.S. imperial plots in the 1960s central features of revolutionary historical memory. *Patty-candela* (1976) reconstructed a real CIA plot to assassinate both Fidel and Raúl Castro in July 1961, successfully foiled and revealed to the public at the time thanks to the work of loyal informers.[89] ("Patty" was the CIA's code name for the operation. "Operation Candela," or "Fire," was the Cuban counterintelligence response.) One year later the coming-of-age story *El brigadista* (*The Literacy Teacher*, 1977) revived a familiar symbolic trifecta from the 1960s, again linking the Ciénaga de Zapata of Cuba's south-central coast, the invasion at the neighboring Bay of Pigs, and the redeeming work of the Revolution's 1961 Literacy Campaign.[90] In the film, fifteen-year-old Mario works as a literacy instructor in the small swamp settlement of Maneadero, transforming from a naive urbanite into a hardened masculine hero as he successfully fights off counterrevolutionary insurgents supported covertly from abroad.[91] At their best, follow-ups like *Río negro* (*Black River*, 1977) provided reasonably complex retrospectives on the line between revolutionary loyalty and counterrevolutionary betrayal.[92] At worst, sequels like *Guardafronteras* (*The Border Guard*, 1980) and *Leyenda* (*Legend*, 1981) substituted melodrama and Hollywood-esque bombast for more serious-minded, if still one-sided historical reconstructions.[93]

What the film scholar Michael Chanan has called a "return to the popular" in Cuban cinema in the 1970s—surpassing operatic ICAIC productions from the early 1960s set during the anti-Batista insurrection—built on similar turns in literature, radio, and television.[94] Bolstered by the Ministry of Interior's support for an annual prize in detective fiction beginning in 1972, a prolific subgenre of counterespionage paperbacks and audiovisual analogues also emerged as a vehicle for promoting "socialist values" and understandings of Cuba's past.[95] Entry after entry made Cuba's record of foiling covert exile and imperial plots a, if not *the*, central thread of the Revolution's history. Luis Rogelio Nogueras's award-winning *Y si muero mañana* (*If I Die Tomorrow*, 1978), for instance, recounted the exploits of a secret agent successfully infiltrated into Miami's "Plan Torres," a fictional plot to attack Cuban shores inspired by any number of real-life occurrences in the 1960s.[96] Other tales of counterrevolutionary intrigue set in that decade, like Enrique Álvarez Jané's *Algo que debes hacer* (*Something You Should Do*, 1977), were remade for Cuban television.[97] Far and away the most popular example of this kind was 1979's *En silencio ha tenido que ser* (*In Silence It Had to Be*), starring, once more, Sergio Corrieri (figure 5.1). A joint production of Cuban state television and the Ministry of Interior, the six-part miniseries followed the exploits of a Cuban double agent heroically informing on counterrevolutionary exiles and the CIA from the early days of 1959.[98] The title and opening credits referenced a passage from José Martí's famous last letter before his death. In this way, the show invited audiences to view state intelligence agents as the bearers of the Cuban hero's ideas. One reviewer hyperbolically called the series a "work of art," a distillation of the "human stature" and "epic revolutionary inspiration" of Cuban history.[99] A sequel airing in 1980, *Julito el pescador* (*Julito the Fisherman*), enjoyed similar success and popular appeal.[100]

In the 1960s, popular troubadour Carlos Puebla famously sang that Fidel Castro's arrival in Havana had brought all Batista-era *diversión* (or frivolous amusement and corruption) to a halt.[101] By the 1970s, the Revolution had itself become a source of entertainment, a spectacle about the past comfortably, even nostalgically consumed from a movie theater seat. More than a mirror for ongoing social transformations, revolutionary action stories fostered a brand of cultural citizenship akin to that nurtured by Cold War spy sagas of the capitalist world. Films like *Patty-candela* may have pushed back against depictions of the Caribbean as an exotic backdrop in the style of James Bond. Nonetheless, Cuban contributions to the genre replicated other Western discursive codes: the prominence of an "individual masculine protagonist" as "the literal embodiment of state and national interests," and a "semi-documentary narrative style" that "articulated a kind of [passive] civic nationalism linked to the institution of television itself."[102] Moreover, just as early spy series in the United States relied on the close collaboration of the FBI, Cuban counterparts in the 1970s often received support from the Cuban military and the Ministry of Interior. Such productions called on viewers to become part of a "virtual community ... of vicarious witness." They fostered an anti-imperialist historical common sense, concealing the significance of state leaders' rhetorical shifts, and likely reinforcing feelings of national pride. But the fact that a core group of male actors dominated each and every cast also made these productions as much vehicles for depoliticized forms of socialist celebrity as (secret) agents of history telling and revolutionary proselytizing.[103]

And yet, off the screen and back in the present, the question "What now?" remained. Even as spectacular portrayals of revolutionary legend provided distraction from the mundane contours of the socialist everyday, the shape and meaning of quotidian rhythms could not always, or even often, live up to the historic epic in which Cubans purportedly lived. It is thus significant that less sensationalist reflections on the place of the past in the present occasionally surfaced in the 1970s, notwithstanding the lack of artistic daring that tended to characterize the period. In particular, ICAIC debuted a film in 1978 whose complex ruminations on memory and trauma openly contradicted commemorative molds of the decade, offering a rare window into simmering doubts.

Humberto Solás's *Un día de noviembre* (*One Day in November*) featured characters struggling to reckon with their histories amid their safely socialist yet somehow ambivalent lives.[104] At the start of the picture, Esteban, a dedicated, though not particularly high-ranking veteran of the anti-Batista urban underground, is diagnosed with an untreatable cerebral aneurysm that could end his life at any moment. Ordered by his doctor to rest indefinitely and confronting his pending mortality, Esteban suddenly feels that his past as an activist and revolutionary lacks the meaning it once held. From his brother and sister-in-law—both selfish types waiting to leave the country for their "little packet of Cornflakes"—to young students at a block party dancing to psychedelic music, the world around him appears superficial. Individuals go through the motions, yet they fail to appreciate the struggles of those who came before. "They have it all," agrees his mother, after an exasperating trip to the corner store to pick up subsidized rations alongside grumpy neighbors. "They have work, school for the kids, food, because here no one dies of hunger, and still they complain."

Nonetheless, Esteban remains wracked by self-doubt. Severe headaches prompt flashbacks to the private demons he carries from the anti-Batista struggle. Visits to former collaborators only sharpen his sense of dislocation. All seem tired of carrying the burden of their heroism, rejecting, in principle, the idea of resting on their laurels. At the same time, they feel alienated from a newer generation that can never understand or duplicate their sacrifice. Meanwhile, younger Cubans who do strive for a sense of purpose—represented in the film by Esteban's love interest, Lucía—must content themselves with the conviction that their generation "would have done the same." Convinced that life should be about "rebellion, dissatisfaction," she and other characters remain paralyzed by the apparent passing of all important political struggles.

In the end, Esteban, once prepared to give his life for a cause, cannot fathom that his real death will be "for nothing." A disabled veteran of Cuba's battles against counterrevolutionary "bandits" in the 1960s urges him to "not die while living." But then the ex-soldier catches himself, acknowledging solemnly "how easy it is to give advice" while hiding from his own inner ghosts. Solás may have intended *Un día de noviembre* as a call to intergenerational dialogue, a revolutionary critique of complacency and retrospective triumphalism. Yet with Esteban remaining as lost at the film's end as at its beginning, it is difficult to read the story as anything but a pessimistic challenge to narratives equating the Revolution's permanence with a virtual end of Cuban history. For this reason, ICAIC's president Alfredo Guevara opted to preemptively shelve the film after it was originally completed in 1971. This was a clear act of censorship, but some have argued it protected Solás from losing his job had the film been shown so close to the polemics surrounding the Padilla affair.[105]

In *Un día de noviembre*, revolutionary Cuba appeared to have reached an imperfect plateau, not a utopia forged on the blood of martyrs. Most troublingly, Solás's Cuba was one in which the thoughts, emotions, and private recollections of Cuban citizens, for all of their revolutionary credentials, departed from the optimistic pronouncements and commemorative practices of the Cuban state. No wonder that after the film finally debuted, seven years after it was made, Roberto José, writing in the cultural magazine *El Caimán Barbudo*, called the production "decadent," "in no way constructive," and "archival footage"—perhaps a double entendre referencing the film's history of censorship. The public, José claimed, "has a hard time seeing itself reflected in characters who try to stop time and live on their memories alone."[106] Maybe he was right. The irony, though, is that official media culture in this era, as we have seen, was largely guilty of the same charge.

Conclusion: Memory Surfeit, Memory Absence

Even more than in the 1960s, memory and history were ubiquitous in 1970s Cuba, from increasingly simplistic invocations of the revolutionary epic in speeches and films to new museums dedicated to venerated heroes. Yet, because the most celebrated campaigns of the 1960s lay firmly in the past, saying what actually *happened* in the Revolution's second decade proved, and remains, difficult. In most history books to this day, including those used in Cuban schools, these years are cast as an interlude.[107] If events, according to Alain Badiou, are defined by their "undecidability" and "ontological disruption," much of the time period examined in this chapter was characterized by the opposite.[108] Authorities recast dynamic revolutionary events from the 1950s and 1960s as part of a predestined plan. Meanwhile, amid a broader move toward "institutionalization," revolutionary government bodies assumed a more solid and predictable form. The economy improved, as more Soviet-made and Soviet-inspired products entered Cuban homes. All the same, for the bulk of the decade, few present-day turning points—especially on the island itself—seemed genuinely capable of firing revolutionary passions anew.[109]

What, though, of the views of everyday citizens navigating this era's contradictory combination of futuristic confidence and retrospective streamlining? Might they, like Solás, have meditated on history's unresolved dilemmas and stagnated hopes? Or had invocations of patriotic legend become little more than a ticket to getting ahead? Advances toward a socialist modernity were welcome. Greater economic stability was proof for many that the Revolution had finally started to achieve important domestic policy goals. Still, to what extent were young Cubans in particular—in many ways like their counterparts in exile at the time—caught between a feeling of gratitude for some of their elders' choices and the nagging feeling of being trapped by a history that they inherited rather than made on their own?

There are, of course, no simple or uniform answers to these questions. Cuban society has never been a monolith, and archival silence still too often prevents us from seeing it in its plurality and depth. At the time, the popular comedy *Detrás de la fachada* (*Behind the Facade*), one of the longest-running Cuban television programs on air (and in some ways a predecessor to *¿Qué pasa, U.S.A.?* in format), invited Cubans to ignore the past entirely. Instead of offering heady reflections on revolutionary history, the show lightheartedly poked fun at the foibles and inconveniences of present-day socialist life.[110] If that was possible, perhaps one of the government's slogans of the era—"We Are Happy Here!"—really was true for many.[111]

But if documenting the everyday doubts of the 1970s remains difficult, a reading of the decade's political and cultural landscape highlights a paradoxical counterpoint with which no doubt many Cubans had to privately contend: the simultaneous *surfeit* of public memory and its absence. Commemoration, in other words, was everywhere, but few new domestic milestones appeared worthy of state-sanctioned remembrance in the future. Reduced to predictable fables and increasingly didactic public scripts, the collective memory narratives of the revolutionary state risked opening themselves to further notes of melancholy, longing, and regret. If still capable of inspiration, "the Revolution"—in its historical successes, shortcomings, and purported omniscience—had also become conspicuously routine. For that reason, its legitimacy was vulnerable to challenge when, at decade's end, some of the walls separating Cubans from on and off the island, from before and after the Revolution's victory, began to come apart.

6

Confronting Return

In 1979, Cubans in the United States started to do the unthinkable: go home. Over the course of that year, an estimated 100,000 temporary visitors from the exile community—in and beyond Miami—descended on the island. Most, if not all, had not renounced the reasons they left ten or twenty years before. Still, when visiting Cuba suddenly became possible in the context of a tentative Washington-Havana détente, for many the pull of family overwhelmed divisions of ideology. Cuban officials, conversely, would not have allowed émigré travelers in had the benefits of doing so not appeared to outweigh previous reasons for keeping them out.

This turn of events departed sharply from not just prevailing policy but also the ways Cuban émigrés had been characterized on the island in public memory. Throughout the 1960s and 1970s, revolutionary discourse depicted Cubans who left for the United States as turncoats. In disparaging mentions in speeches and the press, those who emigrated were cast as deserters, practically non-Cuban, and as such barred, with rare exceptions, from ever coming back. To the extent exiles appeared on Cuban television, in books, or on film—as during the interrogations after the Bay of Pigs invasion in 1961, or in spy novels from the 1970s—tales of Miami malevolence tended to be the natural flipside to fables of socialist progress. In collaboration with the CIA, or as participants in all manner of anti-Castro groups, certainly enough exiled Cubans had played the real-life parts.

The homecoming, therefore, of thousands of Cuban expatriates who had left the island between the early 1960s and the end of the Freedom Flights in 1973 represented an implicit challenge to the revolutionary state's retrospective norms. Their arrival also broke with officials' emphasis on social prophylaxis vis-à-vis the exile community to that point. In a 1972 speech delivered on the eleventh anniversary of the founding of Cuba's Ministry of Interior, Minister of the Revolutionary Armed Forces Raúl Castro highlighted contact with *apátridas*—formally translated as "stateless" but literally meaning Cubans who were "without a country"—

as one of the "subtle weapons" of "ideological diversionism" being employed by U.S. imperialism to sully Cuba's Marxist-Leninist advance.[1] He was referring to sporadic contact through mail and packages. Why, then, did Cuban authorities move at the end of the decade to facilitate face-to-face encounters with individuals synonymous with historical treachery?

Cubans in the United States, conversely, had long presumed going back would only be possible if the revolutionary government fell. With the exception of iconoclastic voices like those appearing in *Areíto*, most had accepted U.S. policies of diplomatic and economic isolation, including wide prohibitions on traveling to Cuba, as either desirable measures or faits accomplis. Over the years, many exiles had sent irregular letters and shipments routed through third countries. Fuzzy phone connections had allowed loved ones to intermittently stay in touch. Still, before the late 1970s, and despite loopholes in U.S. travel restrictions theoretically allowing humanitarian visits, returning to Cuba was basically unthinkable for most émigrés as a matter of Cuban practice and U.S. law.

For these reasons, when it became possible to actually go to the island, and many thousands did so, the results were bound to ruffle feathers. By any political or emotional rubric, the temporary return of close to 15 percent of the exile population in a single year should have constituted a public historical occurrence of the first order. Returning exiles not only embodied the past that the Revolution had purportedly left behind; their arrival brought islanders' buried personal memories of the departed into contact with visitors' recollections of the Cuba they had last seen. But although the euphemistically dubbed *visitas de la comunidad* (visits of the community) were criticized in the diaspora for bolstering Cuban government coffers to the tune of an alleged $100 million or $150 million, relatively little was reported about what the travelers saw, what the experience meant to them, or how the Cuba of 1979 compared to the Cubas of their memories and dreams. Whether in relation to family reunions joyous and fraught, or the jealousies engendered among friends who did not receive gifts from Miami guests, the island's public sphere (to the extent that one existed) was just as mute.

This chapter fills in these gaps, assembling "loose" historical evidence of, and personal recollections about, the return visits of 1979 that largely have been excluded from "emblematic" memory frameworks in Miami and Havana ever since.[2] In this respect, it fits a pattern that has guided analysis throughout this book. The aim here is once again to historicize a significant juncture at which contending versions of personal and public memory encountered and even competed with one another. Yet for this very reason, here we will once again recover a moment in the nation's retrospective strife that should be, but is not, widely or collectively recalled in its own right—at least not in the typical commemorative repertoire of exile organizations or the revolutionary state.

In order to understand just how significant the return visits were, however, we must first revisit and further explore the ways Cuban revolutionary discourse had "remembered" (or misremembered) the departed all along. We must also examine important precedents without which the trips of 1979 may never have taken place. Against the backdrop of economic improvement and socialist modernization in the 1970s, a conspicuous prelude of select exile visitors—some of whom we met in chapter 4—had begun to reclaim a tentative presence on the island. Yet while such developments subjected monolithic public depictions of expatriates to slight shifts, they did not prepare Cubans to confront the more disruptive, memorable wave of 1979 visitors to come.

Disremembering the Gusano

Mercenarios. Apátridas. La contrarevolución. For years, the list of terms used to describe Cubans who decamped abroad in the 1960s and early 1970s had been as potent as it was long. The origins of the most prominent epithet, *gusano* (worm), are still up for debate. Was it a simple insult? Or did it reference the elongated duffel bags that those fleeing the country in the early 1960s tended to carry with them on their way to the United States?[3] Regardless, Fidel Castro and revolutionary loyalists repeatedly used the word to describe those who, whether because of class origins, alleged submissiveness to imperialist influence, or simply insufficient commitment and faith, constituted the Revolution's fifth column. The exodus of the *gusanera* was thus never to be lamented; instead it was celebrated as a catharsis. "Our nation," Castro declared on the Revolution's third anniversary in 1962, "[is] every day more free of worms, every day more free of parasites, every day more free of exploiters, every day more free of traitors."[4] Never mind that the experiences, political trajectories, and class backgrounds of those leaving, say, in 1959 as opposed to 1969 were often quite distinct.

This rhetoric of cleansing was symptomatic of the pathologization of the Revolution's internal turned external enemies. This tendency also had clear parallels in the exile community's colorful phrases to label *comunista* and *castrista* villains over time. Together, such broad labels and characterizations resulted in mutual forms of "disremembering." As defined by Viet Thanh Nguyen, "disremembering is not simply the failure to remember. Disremembering is the unethical and paradoxical mode of forgetting at the same time as remembering, or, from the perspective of the other who is disremembered, of being simultaneously seen and not seen."[5] Just as committed revolutionaries lambasted the betrayal of those of were leaving, no doubt many in Miami showed a lack of sympathy for compatriots who had their own reasons to embrace the revolutionary project or stay behind.

On the island, though, the "disremembering" of the departed was backed by the imprimatur of a state. For a decade or more, the constancy of leaving "structured [Cuban revolutionary] society" in many ways, shaping "its most consequential struggles."[6] Yet if for individual Cubans the brother, aunt, or friend who fled abroad could remain a powerful absent presence with a name and face, government leaders generally treated the burgeoning exile community as an indistinguishable mass, or an illness expunged—that is, when émigrés were talked about at all. For all intents and purposes, those who left consigned themselves to the dustbin of history, and they were not to be mentioned publicly. Nor did the stigma associated with migration change. In the early 1960s, the link that interrogators sought to establish between the Bay of Pigs prisoners and prerevolutionary Cuba's well-to-do exploiters carried over as generalized class descriptors for those leaving the island. But even as it became more difficult to associate those departing with just the former elite or bourgeoisie, emigration continued to represent a deep form of disloyalty. For Cubans of working-class or rural backgrounds, to leave in the mid- to late 1960s was not necessarily a confirmation of inherent class bias but rather a pernicious act of selfishness and ingratitude. After all, it was on behalf of the working class, not the urban professionals dominating the exile wave before 1962, that the Revolution had embraced socialism as its goal.

For individual Cubans who remained, meanwhile, contact with relatives and friends in the United States, or references to public figures who had departed, became a serious problem. Although a considerable degree of communication by mail and phone did continue among some families (especially those waiting for their own chance to leave, and notwithstanding logistical hurdles in the delivery of mail), for those who became "integrated" to the Revolution, whatever their original class position, there were political incentives and indirect pressures to lose touch.[7] For certain positions, corresponding with relatives in the United States was disqualifying. As monitored by local Committees for the Defense of the Revolution, receiving letters or packages from relatives abroad could count against a child's possibilities for academic and political advancement in school. Meanwhile, for artists, writers, musicians, and politicians (including former "revolutionaries") who had become critical of the revolutionary government, relocating abroad precluded not only contact but also most public references to their work. From exile, too, celebrating notables of revolutionary culture could be taboo, just like keeping in contact with one's proverbial "communist" brother or aunt. But on the island, "disremembering," or the pressure to forget classmates, neighbors, relatives, and particular cultural and political personalities, was often a matter of unstated policy, not just a product of political culture or personal choice.[8]

Regulations and practices governing the conditions under which Cubans left the island, and the consequences of doing so, further sealed the link between migration and diverse forms of legal and subjective erasure. As early as 1959, revolutionary authorities began requiring Cubans heading abroad to obtain authorization from the police to use their passports—to prevent the flight of suspected Batista-era criminals.[9] (Ironically, this measure built on legal precedents from the Batista regime.)[10] Then, in late 1961, the government established the more enduring requirement that all Cubans seeking to migrate apply for an "exit permit." From that point on, the request for such a permit triggered a process by which one's property and goods were inventoried, in preparation to be confiscated by the state and then handed over to a new family should said travelers not return to the island in thirty days.[11] From there, the journey from political exclusion to multilayered modes of mnemonic disappearance was short, as houses acquired new residents and nationalized businesses began to bear new names. After 1965, men seeking to head to the United States on a Freedom Flight at times were forced to abandon their jobs and labor on special collective farms first, becoming nonpersons even prior to migrating.[12]

To head into exile, however, was not only to give up a home or a claim to revolutionary subjectivity; the term "apátrida" was an epithet but also a quasi-legal term of force. As consecrated under Cuba's socialist constitution of 1976, any Cuban naturalized elsewhere lost Cuban citizenship automatically.[13] But as early as 1961 Fidel Castro revealed the political criteria that led the government to treat all U.S.-bound emigrants, and Cubans already abroad who refused to return home, as effectively (if not quite formally) stateless all along. "We must take away the citizenship of those people," he said in reference to medical and educational professionals leaving the country at the time. "We must take away their citizenship, because those people one day are going to come begging here at the doors of this country to be allowed to reenter."[14] Convinced that such exiles would eventually regret their decision to depart, Castro rejected the idea that those who abandoned the Revolution in its moment of trial might later be entitled to benefit from its good works.[15]

Given this background, the exile community by the 1970s had become a homogenous abstraction when mentioned in speeches and the island press, just as many exiles had come to treat the island as an inscrutable black box. The idea of return was so far-fetched as to be an oxymoron. Those watching serial representations of past counterrevolutionary malevolence on ICAIC movie screens scarcely could have imagined such a possibility. Yet it was in those years that notable returns of departed exiles started to occur. Quietly at first, and then covered in the state media, "revolutionary reconverts" began to appear on the island's shores with a certain frequency. Such cases were generally treated as exceptions that reinforced otherwise disparaging memory narratives about the majority of those who had migrated. But they also broke retrospective ground by suggesting that not all exiles were unredeemable flotsam of a maligned and vanquished phase of Cuban history.

Select Exile Visitors and Revolutionary Reconverts

As we saw in chapter 4, young Cuban exiles radicalized by the U.S. left in the 1970s significantly challenged inherited narratives of how the Revolution had come about or where it had gone wrong. In these and other ways, contributors to *Areíto* magazine essentially committed exile heresy. But they also took that heresy one step further. As part of their quest to understand the "Cuba that exists," many were eager to see the island with their own eyes. In part, they were inspired by U.S. leftists who had begun traveling to Cuba in the late 1960s, especially the solidarity activists of the so-called Venceremos Brigades.[16] For young Cubans, however, returning to the country of their birth would not be so easy.

As in most things, *Areíto*'s mentor, Lourdes Casal, was a pioneer in probing the possibilities for visiting home. According to one account, Casal's tentative inquiries to this end with Cuban diplomats at the United Nations in New York began as early as 1970.[17] But the next year, she would reaffirm her position as a Cuban government critic, or at least critical observer, by decrying authorities' "Stalinist exit" in the Heberto Padilla case.[18] All the same, between August and September 1973 she spent two weeks touring her homeland at the invitation of the Instituto Cubano de Amistad con los Pueblos (Cuban Institute of Friendship with the Peoples, ICAP), a public diplomacy institution charged with forging ties of solidarity with the Cuban Revolution abroad. Possibly the first exile of the 1960s to travel back to Cuba as a welcomed visitor—albeit on a clearly guided excursion, and likely under the premise of conducting academic research, an exception allowed by U.S. law—she would write about the experience in *Areíto*'s first issue and in many respects considered it one of the raisons d'être for the magazine as a whole.[19]

At the same time, Casal's first return to Cuba also showed that, even for left-leaning exiles, the road to national reincorporation was strewn with potholes. According to two of her close admirers and disciples at the time, Casal's handlers on the island instructed her to identify not as Cuban, but Puerto Rican, in any encounter or site visit.[20] Perhaps they were concerned that the presence of an exile might provoke untoward reactions among interlocutors. But if that was the case, the excuse reflected the degree to which all exiles, as *apátridas*, continued to occupy an uncomfortable place in insular politics and official memory. Exiles were still abstractions and symbols of the past, not subjects to be publicly discussed, let alone spoken to in real life. Casal never wrote about this slight, but to publicly identify herself as an expatriate would have risked prompting conversations about Cuba's history of migration that authorities sponsoring her visit must not have been ready to entertain.

Ironically, the same year as Casal's first trip, Cuban authorities publicly welcomed not another rare exile visitor but a scarcer commodity: a permanent exile returnee. Edith Reinoso Hernández described herself as a former Batista opponent who had subsequently grown disenchanted with the Revolution and participated in armed counterrevolutionary groups on the island through the mid-1960s. Claiming to have departed clandestinely for Miami in 1967, she returned to the island sometime after 1970, reportedly having realized the error of her ways. Her story was not the first of its kind. There had been a similar publicized case in 1965, but it was quickly overshadowed by renewed outmigration through Camarioca and then the Freedom Flights.[21] For this reason, 1974's *Testimonio de una emigrada* (*Testimony of an Emigrant*), Reinoso's politically charged memoir of her years abroad, stands out for its depiction of Miami intrigue and wide circulation. One Cuban, commenting in an online forum, even remembers being assigned the book in school.[22] There is no evidence of how Casal or other members of the *Areíto* group reacted to the case. But by Reinoso Hernández's own later confession, we now know that she was really an agent of Cuban intelligence sent to Miami to inform on exile political groups.[23] That perhaps explains why her false story became well known once her mission was complete, while Casal's visit was kept out of the public eye.

All the same, Cuban authorities might have just as easily preferred to keep Reinoso quiet, lest her account raise suspicion as to her true role. The publication of her book was clearly a calculated affair, and it is thus worth paying attention to the ways her at least partially apocryphal confession of *gusano* misdeeds both repeated old stereotypes and complicated depictions of the exile community in subtle ways. On the one hand, *Testimonio de una emigrada* resembled countless socialist movies and pulp revolutionary fiction in the 1970s, depicting Miami as a nest of immorality and counterrevolutionary plotting.[24] On the other, Reinoso Hernández also portrayed many exiles as victims of economic predation suffering "misfortune" at the hands of the powerful.[25] The result, the prologue claimed, was an intensifying process of "proletarianization" in Miami that would eventually lead more of the exile community's members, like her, to begin "approaching revolutionary positions."[26] If Reinoso Hernández succeeded at "reintegrating" herself into socialist society—according, again, to the dishonest conceit of her memoir—readers on the island might have wondered whether others could do the same.

In practice, the few exiles most disposed to admire the Revolution continued to receive only a selective welcome. Several subsequent individual visitors from the *Areíto* group in 1974 and 1975 were obliged to mask their exile identities in similar ways as Casal. Traveling with the support of ICAP, or to conduct academic research on their own, their trips generated testimonies as well as serious (if sympathetic) analyses of the Revolution's "institutionalization" process in the 1970s, as we saw in chapter 4.[27] But in Cuba their work was kept out of the public limelight and represented an exploratory opening. Meanwhile, in select cases when "regular" exiles sought to return for humanitarian reasons—for example, to see a sick relative, as was also theoretically allowed under U.S. law—they often found themselves blocked. An up-and-coming exile lawyer named Emilio Cueto, for instance, then working for a New York–based law firm in Paris, spent more than four years in the mid-1970s requesting permission by letter and telegram to return to see his ailing mother. Only in the fall of 1977, after getting contacts in French high society to pester Cuba's European diplomats, was he finally granted an audience with Cuba's ambassador to France and a visa to board a plane to Havana via Spain. Not all exiles had such connections. His ultimately successful bid appears to have been a relatively isolated case.[28]

Slowly, the urgency of return began to gain public momentum closer to the heart of the exile community, albeit in fringe circles. One important character in this regard was an eccentric Miami evangelical preacher, the Reverend Manuel Espinosa. His penchant for the limelight and political flip-flops make him a hard character to pin down to this day. A former captain in the Cuban Rebel Army, member of numerous anti-Castro groups, and insurance claims investigator, Espinosa moved from Miami to New York in 1970, where he trained to be a minister in the Bronx. Soon, his religious awakening led to an ideological conversion, as he began using his Pentecostal Reformed Evangelical Church, founded in a Hialeah, Florida, warehouse in 1974, to advocate for Cuban family reunification. This demand earned him a significant working-class, and especially elderly, flock.

But Espinosa did not content himself with preaching the gospel. In March 1975, he boarded a boat for Cuba without U.S. or Cuban government permission. Entering the Bay of Havana hoisting a white flag, Espinosa was immediately arrested and questioned for several weeks. But he returned to Miami triumphant, claiming to have met Fidel Castro personally and encouraged him not only to let in more visitors like himself but also to restart the Freedom Flights—so as to give 48,000 Cubans that had been waiting for exit papers when the flights were closed in 1973 the chance to finally get out. Hardline anti-Castro voices greeted Espinosa's fanciful stories with predictably harsh rhetoric and threats. The Cuban government gave his early efforts no publicity.[29] Still, perhaps Cuba's openness to exile visitors had begun to broaden slightly. A memo from Jimmy Carter's incoming national security advisor two years later refers to a supposed policy already in place by the mid-1970s of allowing a modest 1,000 exiles to visit family annually. However, a former Cuban diplomat with close knowledge of U.S.-Cuban affairs doubts the accuracy of the document or whether such a quota was ever applied.[30]

More salient, for the moment, were periodic public reminders that return was primarily a rare opportunity reserved for those who sought to reintegrate to the Revolution fully. For example, the defection of Carlos Rivero Collado to the island the same year as *Testimonio de una emigrada*'s publication represented an even more dramatic manifestation of Cuba's purported new commitment to welcoming wayward souls back into the fold. As island audiences would have recalled, Rivero Collado was the well-known son of Fulgencio Batista's chosen political successor in 1958. In 1961, he had been one of the discredited members of Brigade 2506 interrogated on Cuban television following the Bay of Pigs defeat. Through the early 1970s, he had also been connected to the Cuban Nationalist Movement, one of several right-wing extremist groups involved in violent attacks against more moderate émigrés and Cuban embassies. Incredibly, now this *batistiano* favorite son was back on Cuban shores, appearing in the media and publishing his own book in 1976 to expose the exile community's dark underbelly of violence and Washington-dependent political decay.[31] Cuban audiences might have understandably wondered whether comparatively innocent relatives caught in the crossfire of the polarized 1960s might also find their way home, at least as visitors.

Like for Reinoso Hernández, however, intelligence connections—openly, if cryptically acknowledged in this case—seem to have been the key condition of Rivero Collado's welcome. As the moderator of a 1976 television appearance stated, after undergoing a process of "political rectification," Rivero Collado had "performed" unspecified "tasks in favor of our Revolution abroad." As he later confessed, these involved informing on the activities of exile groups in which he was involved (starting as early as 1972). Rivero Collado also ran a right-wing Miami newspaper in the early 1970s at the time he was working with Cuban authorities, which opens the possibility that the paper's calls to violence were meant to egg on internecine tensions within the exile community.[32] Clearly, the road to return remained narrow and required a complete political about-face. The decision to emigrate, as Rivero Collado himself put it, still constituted for any Cuban "the biggest error with the most terrible consequences."[33] It would take a broader push from members of the *Areíto* circle, and changing calculus on the part of the Cuban state, to bend this lopsided discourse and further pry open the island's doors.

Going Back to the Future? The Antonio Maceo Brigade

The moment that many Cubans and Cuban government loyalists still associate in public memory with the first real, if in many ways still conditional, opening to the postrevolutionary diaspora was the December 1977 arrival in Cuba of the first Brigada Antonio Maceo (Antonio Maceo Brigade).[34] Founded by members of the *Areíto* collective in the mold of the Venceremos Brigades, the organization represented an extension of the kinds of tentative return visits that some *Areíto* contributors had been engaging in individually. But despite these and other relevant antecedents, the size of the group—fifty-five members—and the wide publicity it received on the island reflected a decision by Cuban authorities to finally and formally embrace their story of revolutionary reconversion as a public triumph. Through their example, Cuba was now reclaiming parts of exile history for revolutionary memory lore. Yet even as the brigade's positive reception was premised on its members' willingness to break with the political truisms of the exile world, it was not unproblematic. For brigade members, too, like Lourdes Casal before them, the idea of "going home" would reveal itself as a rhetorical conceit as much as a tidy solution to the memory and identity anxieties they brought with them from the United States.

The first Antonio Maceo Brigade was largely the work of two figures from the *Areíto* circle: Marifeli Pérez-Stable and Mariana Gastón. While Pérez-Stable and Gastón had already visited Cuba individually, the idea for a group trip first emerged among their colleagues as early as 1974.[35]

The feasibility of such a trip, though, depended on not only courting the Cuban government's support, but also the Carter administration's decision to lift the travel ban for U.S. visitors to the island—part of a broader effort to normalize relations with Cuba described in further detail below.[36] Backers of the Antonio Maceo Brigade within the Cuban state, for their part, saw the trip as an opportunity.[37] While some previous *Areíto* travelers had been compelled to repeat the ruse of identifying as Puerto Rican, in this case authorities gave exile visitors prominent news coverage and even commissioned an ICAIC film crew at the last minute to accompany them during their three-week stay.[38]

Key to the official welcome, though, was the premise that brigade members represented former children taken out of the country against their wishes—which was, after all, how many *Areíto* contributors had begun to identify themselves. This meant that the positive reception the brigade received in 1977 was based on a public reading of members' histories that absolved them from responsibility for their parents' past mistakes. Incidentally, Fidel Castro himself had previewed this logic in 1961: "Maybe one day we will let the children return," he declared at the time. "That is, one day we will let the kids return who are being taken away, because it hurts to see one of these reactionary families impose on their child the path of being without a country."[39] Yet if for some brigade members the Cuban government's willingness to now "rescue" them for the Revolution gave their mission legitimacy, for others the trip's suddenly high profile and the surprise presence of cameras turned what was first and foremost a personal journey into an unexpected mass media event.[40] Whether they liked it or not, arriving brigade members were on the verge of becoming political and memory symbols, and not entirely on their own terms.

It is thus striking to watch the evocatively titled documentary *55 Hermanos* (*55 Brothers*), which covered the trip, and see both just how raw the emotions were and how many moments of cognitive dissonance director Jesús Díaz managed to capture on film.[41] That is, notwithstanding the political interests in play, or the effort to fit the story of the brigade within established parameters of telling the Revolution's history, to view the film as simply a work of propaganda created by the government film institute, ICAIC, is limiting. For some Antonio Maceo Brigade members, their identification with socialist Cuba already appeared complete, reflecting the vicarious search for memories denied to them, as discussed in chapter 4. Yet, on several occasions, brigade members challenged aspects of revolutionary memory discourse. Even at their most "revolutionary," brigade members' ways of apprehending and relating to Cuban history did not always match official or even more grassroots understandings of the recent past on the island perfectly. Signs of mutual incomprehension were as potent as the connections the travelers forged.

One particularly memorable exchange involved Elián Ruiz, a long-haired traveler and one of the more enigmatic members of the group. After attending a screening of the film *Girón*, Manuel Herrera's 1972 documentary about the Bay of Pigs, Ruiz confessed to ICAIC president Alfredo Guevara that he felt sadness, not pride, in revisiting Cuba's preeminent anti-imperialist victory. "They [the members of the invading exile force] are Cuban brothers too," he reasoned, "and although they may have a mistaken ideology, perhaps I can see myself in their position.... Maybe if I were a bit older, I would have ended up in an invasion of that type.... I feel the strangest sensation.... I can't feel happy. I don't have any desire to applaud." By *Areíto*'s own reporting (the film scene cuts off at this point), an awkward silence enveloped the room until Guevara broke the ice: "But yes, we *can* applaud the sincerity and the feelings of this comrade!"[42] Even for young exiles predisposed to questioning inherited historical wisdom, some of the maxims of revolutionary retrospection could seem uncomfortably simplistic and out of touch.

The film also captured divergent memories of lived experience, within and outside of the Revolution, in more oblique ways. At one group gathering, Puerto Rico–based brigade leader (and *Areíto* board member) Carlos Muñiz Varela recounted his impressions upon meeting the brother of a close Cuban exile friend during a previous trip to Havana. The young *habanero* had been complaining about the many material difficulties he faced in Cuba everyday, notwithstanding the economic improvements of the 1970s: poor public transportation, housing shortages, the still relative unavailability of consumer goods, and the lack of clothing options that fit his style. But Muñiz Varela, bowled over by the achievements of Cuba's socialist modernity, saw his complaints as a sign of ungratefulness. "So when he told me that," Muñiz Varela recalled, "I told him, look, I'll gladly swap the problems that you have here for the problems that I have over there!": negligible public health care, an insufficient salary, and physical insecurity. No doubt these were real problems in Puerto Rico at the time. The island's economy was suffering from a protracted bout with capitalist and frankly colonial austerity.[43] But one can also imagine some viewers in Cuba quietly interpreting the activist's comments as an example of outsider moralizing—the shallow complaint of someone who had no real memory of living under the Revolution, let alone purchasing food using a ration card.

Perhaps the predominant tension running through the trip revolved around the dynamics of personal memory—in other words, the place that group members' reckonings with lost childhoods and family histories occupied vis-à-vis their efforts to embrace the revolutionary present. On the one hand, montages depicted brigade members laying cinder blocks and mortar on a housing project for workers at a nearby factory, part of the group's contribution to revolutionary progress. For brigade member Maritza Giberga, however, pride in helping to build Cuba's socialist future was complicated by knowledge that the factory in question used to be her family's property.[44] Scenes of family reunion, meanwhile, were both festive and emotionally painful. Upon approaching her family's former home in the eastern city of Santiago, Regina Casal (no relation to Lourdes) commented on her momentary disorientation when the diminutive size of the neighborhood failed to match her recollections. That the woman answering the door at her former home was black served as an implicit reminder of the divergent racial and class subjectivities distinguishing those who left the island in the early 1960s from those who stayed. Whatever their ideological convictions, brigade members were not immune from the nostalgia that they decried among their elders. Nor could Casal and the other almost all-white exile visitors help embodying the return of a prerevolutionary past that they had sworn to disavow.

The complexities of "reconciling with their past," as group members put it in the film, crystallized most dramatically as several travelers broached the possibility of returning to live on the island permanently. Not all members of the Antonio Maceo Brigade harbored this desire.[45] Nonetheless, a number of them proposed the idea of repatriation to both everyday citizens and high-ranking political officials, including Fidel Castro himself. In perhaps the most talked-about scene in the film, the Gastón siblings (Mariana, Mauricio, and younger brother Juan Luis) asked a twenty-four-year-old Afro-Cuban man for his opinion about permanent exile return. "The majority of us are simply willing to come here to help build Cuba's future," Mariana explained. Polite but firm, the young Cuban rebuffed the proposal: "Between 1960 and 1977, Cuba has developed a great many technicians, many professionals. Perhaps we need a few more, but the help [you can offer] will be minimal compared to all the sacrifices Cubans have made to have what we have here today." At an emotional meeting shortly before the end of the group's journey, the Revolution's commander in chief echoed the young man's snub. Praising brigade members' love of nation and work to demonstrate a new face of the Cuban community abroad, Fidel Castro nonetheless urged them to focus on developing support for the Revolution in the United States.

Despite this setback, members of the Antonio Maceo Brigade regarded their 1977 trip as a resounding success. Far from scaring them off, fierce Miami opposition to what they were doing sealed a commitment to continuing the group's work. "How different / when return is not a return to the past / but a flight to the future," wrote an idealistic Enrique Rodríguez Bocanegra, a future brigade member, in 1978.[46] The brutal murder of organizer Carlos Muñiz Varela—gunned down en route to his mother's home by Cuban exile extremists in Puerto Rico in April 1979—galvanized his colleagues, who returned to Cuba that summer as part of an expanded "second contingent" honorifically bearing his name.[47]

Nonetheless, four years earlier, future brigade member Emilio Bejel may have captured a more prophetic sentiment in a poem published in *Areíto*: "Where are you going / —To Cuba / Why are you going? / —Don't know / What do you hope to find? / —Problems / What are you really looking for? / —My shadow."[48] As future-oriented as they wanted to be, brigade members were also chasing the ghosts of their former selves. The quest to return also revealed the degree to which younger exiles who rejected their parents' political inheritance still remained on the margins of the nation they had come to idealize. Consider the apt reflections of Lourdes Casal on the impossibility of recovering lost time. "When I hear these men and women who lived here all of these years and have been through all of these experiences," she wrote in 1975, "I realize that it is impossible to 'equalize' what we have lived, that there is a brotherhood because of the common history they share that in me and for all of my group will always be missing.... And I feel a certain sadness or pity at not having been able to share certain things, at having lost crucial experiences for understanding the true history of this Revolution, the hidden, underground history ... beneath (or above) the level of facts (such-and-such a campaign or problem)."[49] What Casal provocatively called the "true history" of the Revolution was what exile sympathizers could never get back because it could not be captured in books they read or state ceremonies they attended. Even for exile renegades desperate to feel part of the Revolution's story, divergent lived experiences and memories of those experiences were as noticeable as possibilities for creating a bridge.

And yet, somehow the ground had shifted. Yes, Cuba's official acceptance of the Antonio Maceo Brigade was predicated on a memory narrative of "innocent" migrant children stolen from the magnanimous Revolution's care.[50] But when *55 Hermanos* debuted in the summer of 1978, it drew lines around the block and remained in Cuban cinemas for weeks, and not just because its characters were revolutionary penitents. As much as brigade members aligned themselves with revolutionary commemorative codes (even placing a wreath in honor of those who died in the 1976 bombing of Cubana flight 455), they also broke them, achieving quasi-celebrity status because of their looks, Western fashion, and comparatively carefree remarks. On subsequent visits, Mariana Gastón recalls being stopped by "fans" on the street.[51] Regardless of the political overtones, the documentary allowed many Cubans on the island to literally *see* the disremembered departed for the first time. And while audiences were thrilled, behind the scenes, not all were pleased. According to the film's sound engineer, José León, up until days before the debut, director Jesús Díaz was under pressure from cultural bureaucrats who preferred to not see his documentary on screen.[52] Apparently, some were skittish about incorporating even the stories of remorseful exile children into public representations of the nation's history.

Toward *las Visitas*

So if the trickle of carefully managed, politically delimited exile guests over the course of the mid-1970s did eventually grow into a mass wave of visitors in 1979, it must have been because other needs displaced the more restricted public depiction of return as a vehicle for historical contrition. In this regard, the wider diplomatic context of U.S.-Cuban relations is key. As we will see, a controversial dialogue in 1978 between Cuban government leaders and a broader group of members of the exile community also put the subject of exile visits on the table, although somewhat disingenuously. Indirect evidence suggests, however, that economic motivations were another important driver, if not necessarily the deciding factor, behind the Cuban government's decision to allow the *visitas de la comunidad* to proceed.[53]

Jimmy Carter was not the first U.S. president to contemplate the possibility of normalizing relations with Cuba in the 1970s or even the 1960s. He was, however, the president who got farthest toward the goal. Starting in 1977, his administration opened up a U.S. Interests Section in the shuttered former U.S. embassy in Havana, lifted the travel ban prohibiting most U.S. residents from visiting the island (as noted above), and made the goal of normalization public rather than sticking only to back-channel talks. Nevertheless, Cuba's military involvements in the African continent at the time became major sticking points for national security hawks in the White House conducting negotiations with Cuban counterparts behind closed doors. Cuba not only had sent troops in Angola in 1975; it also had troops in Ethiopia as of 1977 in the context of the Ogaden War.[54] With Cuba refusing to condition further discussions with Washington upon a withdrawal of its forces from both fronts, by mid-1978, progress toward improving bilateral relations had stalled.[55]

It was against this backdrop that the Cuban government turned to the idea of "family reconciliation" as a stratagem for again courting White House graces. Following on the success of the Antonio Maceo Brigade, Cuban authorities had continued to flirt with the political and public relations benefits of welcoming more exile visitors. In early 1978, for example, the Reverend Manuel Espinosa was rewarded for several years of dogged lobbying when Cuban authorities authorized him to begin bringing groups of up to fifty, mostly elderly, members of his congregation eager to reunite with close relatives on the island.[56] That summer, members of the Antonio Maceo Brigade took part in the Eleventh World Festival of Youth and Students (a major event in the socialist world) held in Cuba. Select Cuban American journalists were quietly invited to attend, too.[57] But the more public overture came in September 1978, when Fidel Castro convened a press conference in Havana with representatives of the Miami press and invited an ecumenical group of "representatives" of the newly dubbed "Cuban community abroad" to ostensibly negotiate two weighty issues long on many exiles' wish lists: first, the release of political prisoners in jail for participating in anti-Castro actions and groups on the island in the 1960s (sometimes in collaboration with U.S. intelligence agencies); and second, the broader rights of Cuban exiles to return to the island, if only as temporary guests.[58]

These agenda items did not appear out of a vacuum. Members of the Antonio Maceo Brigade had already helped put the latter demand on the table. So had Reverend Espinosa, as well as a secret exile emissary, the banker Bernardo Benes, who had been acting as a go-between for U.S. and Cuban officials all along, including on the issue of prisoner rights.[59] But Fidel Castro now publicly insisted that a permanent solution to both matters could only be discussed with a wider range of Cubans from the "community abroad." The U.S. government, ostensibly, had no role. More moderate sectors of the exile community were intrigued by the prospect, while many others were shocked and vehemently opposed to entering into negotiations with the Cuban government at all.

With this presumptive mandate, members of the so-called Committee of Seventy-Five, coconvened by Benes and approved by Havana, gathered with high officials of the Cuban government, including Castro, in a dramatic two-day meeting in late November 1978. Participants would grow to more than 140 for a second meeting in early December that included an even more diverse representation of the exile community, albeit still from a minority willing to sit down with the Cuban government to discuss issues of mutual concern. Back in Miami, "the dialogue," as it was known, generated fierce protest and threats of violence against the participants, with many, perhaps most, suspecting a con. Regardless, an *Acta Final*, or final agreement, dated December 8 lent Cuban government commitments to free 3,000-plus prisoners and permit exile visits starting in January an air of diplomatic pomp. The Cuban government would commence prisoner releases quickly and in fact accept more exile visitors before the new year had begun.[60]

Yet, as arrangements were being made for a wider flow of exile returnees to arrive, public representations in Cuba of how the deal had been achieved did not fully match fact. As subsequently declassified documents and memoirs of the principal players reveal, the Cuban government's commitments with respect to both the prisoners and exile visits had been previously outlined in secret negotiations with U.S. officials dating to 1977. In July 1978, two months *before* the dialogue was proposed, Cuban negotiators explicitly told U.S. counterparts that travel restrictions on Cuban exiles would soon be relaxed.[61] The idea of prisoner releases had also long been a U.S. government demand, especially given the Carter administration's wedding of détente to a global focus on human rights. A first release of forty-eight political prisoners had already taken place in October 1978 as a gesture of goodwill, and they had been allowed to leave the island with the full knowledge of U.S. authorities.[62] By calling for the public exile dialogue, then, the Cuban government had endeavored to force Washington's hand on previously agreed pieces of the road map to normalization that had previously become blocked but were continuing to be secretly discussed. While some dialogue participants were aware of these stakes behind the scenes—and as news of negotiations occasionally trickled out to the press—others were not. Arguably, then, the dialogue's critics were partly right when they portrayed the occasion as really a "monologue."[63]

If Cuba's interest in reviving the normalization of U.S.-Cuban relations represented one factor making the broader *visitas de la comunidad* possible, financial exigency likely added to this political drive. Cuba's economy had enjoyed considerable growth in the 1970s, as we saw in chapter 5. The international stature of the Cuban government had also increased, given its successful intervention in Angola (where Cuban forces helped Marxist Angolan leaders repel an invasion from the apartheid government of South Africa) and election to chair the Non-Aligned Movement, even while remaining closely tied to the Soviet bloc. Yet by 1979, plunging world sugar prices, mounting international debt, and agricultural blight had brought Cuba's Soviet-backed economic recovery to a halt.[64] Rather than hide the obvious, news reports confirmed the economic challenges in play, and state media even occasionally took officials to task. "The public has learned that the maximum leaders of the Revolution are interested in putting together a Development Plan for the year 2000, and some ask how it makes sense to plan for a such a long period when up until now, the annual plans themselves have not been fulfilled," inquired exiled Chilean economist Marta Harnecker, married to Cuban intelligence chief Manuel Piñeiro, in a blistering interview with the head of the government's Central Board of Planning. Long and meandering, the official's responses did little to allay a line of inquiry that exposed the formal process of economic management in the country as inadequate if not at times a farce.[65]

Despite, then, a decade of significant material improvement and the "institutionalization" of the socialist state on the domestic and international stage, the Cuban economy was in need of a fix of foreign cash — cash exiles desperate to see and support loved ones might (and did) prove willing to spend. As former Cuban government economic adviser Charles Romeo recently recalled, as early as the fall of 1978 "young officials of the Ministry of Interior" proposed to Fidel Castro the creation of Cuban companies in the "fiscal paradise" of Panama that could operate according to capitalist rules. Their job would be to start redeveloping Cuba as a tourist destination not only for travelers from the West but also for members of the Cuban community abroad. Therefore, before the dialogue with the Cuban émigré community was complete, the pieces that would allow the implementation of its results had begun to be put in place. Most important, authorities gave their blessing to the founding of a Panama-based company that would eventually handle the traffic of the *visitas de la comunidad* through subcontracted travel agencies in Miami: Havanatur S.A.[66]

Nonetheless, a decision to welcome those previously deemed traitors back to the country still involved domestic political risk. According to the memoir of then Union of Young Communists member Abel Rosendo Castro Figueroa, in late 1978 higher-ups of the Cuban Communist Party showed party militants across the country the film of a speech in which Fidel Castro explained the decision to open up to exile travel as a way to bolster a column of sympathy for the Revolution inside the United States. Though at least one other source corroborates this account, it is possible he is referring to an address Cuba's head of state actually delivered in person to members of the Cuban Communist Party behind closed doors at Havana's Karl Marx Theater in February 1979, after the visits were underway. Regardless, the point of Fidel's intervention in both cases was the same: to allay the concerns of party rank and file wondering whether the government's new exile overture was a mistake. Part of Castro's remarks, according to Castro Figueroa, consisted of refuting the letter of a party member who had questioned why those equated for so long in national memory with disloyalty should suddenly be welcomed as dollar-bearing kings. But even if the letter is apocryphal, in excerpts of the February address that are available for review Fidel Castro insisted that his motives were not pecuniary. "The revolution does not sell itself for a plate of lentils." The decision to welcome returning exiles was not a "concession" to earn dollars but a strategic decision to "win over adversaries," just as the Revolution had done at various junctures previously. To make his point, Fidel cited examples of the Revolution's past magnanimity, from the decision to set certain captives of Batista's army free during the insurrection in the late 1950s to the fact that many former members of that same army had since become card-carrying members of the Cuban Communist Party. From the standpoint of revolutionary memory politics, this last point constituted a stunning revelation in its own right.[67]

For Cubans in exile, meanwhile, the anxieties provoked by the possibility of visiting home were often just as strong, albeit in the inverse. For those who remained opposed to the Castro government, did setting foot on Cuban soil entail turning one's back on past commitments? At the very least, the fact that they now could go back struck at the heart of—or even contradicted—part of what being an "exile" had meant to that point. Others worried that after being allowed in to the country, they would not be allowed out.[68] Clearly, from whichever way one looked, the visits of potentially thousands of exiles were a disquieting prospect. For good or ill, they were bound to mark a turning point.

Logistical, Financial, and Moral Conflicts

So how did the *visitas de la comunidad* unfold? Did travelers struggle to navigate the pressures of family, money, and ideology that framed whether going back to Cuba would be a worthwhile, feasible, or moral choice? On the island, how did local citizens and officials respond? Carrying alternate stories and understandings of what had happened to Cuba after 1959, visitors threatened to bring past conflicts home to roost. They also were firsthand witnesses of what life was like in the capitalist world. At the same time, islanders had their own stories to tell, histories that might have contradicted the ways life under the Revolution, or its history, had been abstractly understood and demonized from afar.

Whatever misgivings some exiles felt about the idea of return, they were not enough to impede an immediate rush to make arrangements. By mid-January 1979, *El Miami Herald* reported that the Panama-based, Cuba-linked Havanatur operation for facilitating the visits—at first with a stopover in Jamaica or Mexico, and eventually direct charter flights from Miami and other points in the United States—was up and running. Subcontracted agencies like 747 Travel Agency in Miami, Viajes Varadero in

Puerto Rico, or Marazul in New Jersey (the latter two founded, not coincidentally, by noted members and friends of the Antonio Maceo Brigade), had begun signing up exile travelers for tickets and competing for fares.[69] Even Reverend Espinosa got in the game, spinning off a travel agency from his church operation.[70] At the same time, exiles rushed to secure reentry permits that some would need due to their status as U.S. permanent residents to secure a transit visa to Jamaica and reenter U.S. territory once they left. On one Monday alone, more than 2,000 waited in line for such purposes at the Miami offices of the Immigration and Naturalization Service. Officials ran out of the required forms.[71]

Travelers also confronted improvised Cuban procedures to secure paperwork for entering their country of birth. While the 1976 Cuban constitution stripped Cuban citizenship from any Cuban who had been naturalized in another country (a de facto legal disremembering), exiles who had naturalized and held U.S. passports were not allowed to use them to enter Cuba in 1979. They, and all returning travelers, were required to secure new Cuban passports, which no one had, along with special entry permits that treated them as Cuban nationals, albeit provisionally.[72] As travelers recall, travel agencies assisted with the necessary paperwork, but the newly established Cuban Interests Section in Washington did not take charge of consular services at the start. In the early months, Cuban immigration officials met travelers at their hotels during one-night layovers in Kingston or Mérida, personally handing them their documentation.[73]

Of course, not all exiles were willing to make the trip. "I would not go as long as Fidel Castro is over there," eighteen-year-old Hialeah resident Ernesto Hernández told reporters. His logic—that Cuba's "regime violates human rights"—was typical of the majority, young and old, who equated travel to the island with lending support to the Cuban government. More militant organizations insisted that historical hypocrisy would be the price of visitors' admittance. "Smile at the immigration official who yesterday subjected you to abuse and insults when you left," one ominous broadside declared, "but [who] today receives you for the economic contribution you are making to his cause."[74] Travel agencies were also the subjects of threats and violence, as were their employees. The previously mentioned assassination of *Areíto* contributor and Antonio Maceo Brigade leader Carlos Muñíz Varela in the spring of 1979 had everything to do with his also being the cofounder of Viajes Varadero, the company facilitating the *visitas* for Cuban exiles in Puerto Rico.

For every critic, though, there was a José Raúl Rodríguez, also eighteen, who simply wanted to "see again the place where we lived."[75] Journalists also covered the heart-wrenching stories of Cubans abroad desperate to reunite with their aging and sick parents.[76] Moreover, some of those active in anticommunist political circles actually argued that the visits could be good for their efforts. As young commentator Carlos Alberto Montaner put it that June, "The exiles who are returning are contributing to the patriotic work of detoxifying their fellow citizens by offering them another version of the facts, another interpretation of the international reality."[77] While some critics saw the *visitas* as a crass attempt by the Cuban government to make money, others sensed an opportunity to undermine socialism through informational exchange, including by swapping memories and life stories.[78]

But even for those most supportive of the idea that exiles could, and should, visit home, the practicalities and perceived crookedness involved rubbed many the wrong way. From the beginning, the operations of local travel agencies with Havanatur contracts generated frustration. In February 1979, Miami police began investigating the company "Custom Tours" for reportedly selling false plane tickets.[79] Others reported phantom travel agencies that came and went, as well as cases of struggling agencies that, without returning money to customers, abruptly closed their doors.[80] Most bothersome was that the visits were all structured as package tours, costing at a minimum $750 for eight days, or $1,000 or more for certain departure cities, like New York. After Havanatur centralized its Miami link in one subcontracted agency in March, and later, managed to open its own offices in Miami and New York, the package tours they were selling to exiles were also longer and more costly than those available to average U.S. residents legally allowed to travel to the island at the same time.[81] Adding salt to the wound, all packages included a mandatory stay in a hotel, even if a traveler's intention was to stay with relatives, or spend time in rural towns far away from the hotel where they had been assigned. Such requirements only further raised suspicion that the Cuban government was interested not in a reconciliation with the exile community but rather in profiting off exiles' desires to see loved ones. Many travelers recall visiting the hotel only to eat or shop, as certain meals were included and they could pay for family members to join.[82]

Likewise, travelers smarted at the nomenclature that became the de facto way of characterizing them. On the one hand, the term "comunidad" in *visitas de la comunidad*—short for *comunidad cubana en el exterior* (Cuban community abroad)—represented a clear improvement over previous epithets. On the other, "comunidad" was a euphemism. For if the notion of "exile" was not just a neutral label but an identity category, the anodyne descriptor "the community" implicitly silenced memory narratives of "forced departure" to which the former notion was linked. The

Figure 6.1. Advertisement for package tours for Cuban exile visitors. "Cuba Awaits You, Havanatur Takes You," *El Miami Herald*, November 18, 1979, 18.

idea of a "comunidad" also skirted the real impossibility for most of returning to the island prior to that point, as well as continuing prohibitions on exiles still closely involved in anti-Castro activities from entering the country. Some island citizens also found the rhetorical shift strange, surprised at the ease with which "la comunidad" supplanted a prior lexicon of slurs.[83]

Nevertheless, the biggest controversy on both sides of the Florida Straits had little to do with the high cost of tickets, or exiles' transformation from *gusanos* to *comunitarios*. Even more shocking were the material items exiles were taking home. Landing in Havana and other points on the island through just the first three months of 1979, 22,000 exile visitors had arrived loaded down with all manner of gifts from the capitalist world: consumer durables, jeans, toiletries, even small appliances.[84] Jokes about travelers secretly carrying packs of coffee in their bras or wearing multiple, sweaty layers of clothes were legion, as everyone sought to save as much space in their luggage as they could.[85] A degree of excess characterized this charity to be sure, as some visitors sought to not only demonstrate devotion to their families but also show off the accoutrements (sometimes exaggerated, as in cases of rented jewelry) of expatriate success.[86] In such magnanimity, some Miami voices only saw more potential for the Cuban government to cash in. If official coffers did not benefit directly at first, commentators alleged that the flow of goods was helping the government ameliorate domestic shortages.[87]

The Cuban government's reaction, however, suggested that officials were spooked rather than pleased. Fidel Castro felt compelled to address the issue in his February speech to members of the Cuban Communist Party. True revolutionaries, he argued, "could not live in pure asepsis." They must embrace the "ideological battle" that interaction with "bacteria, microbes," and other forms of "temptation" implied. Behind closed doors, Castro thus deployed epidemiological metaphors for exiles that contrasted with his more neutral public rhetoric of opening to "the community." He also attempted to reassure the rank and file that the Revolution would emerge "morally, politically, and ideologically" stronger as a result of greater contact with Cuban expatriates.[88] Several weeks later, however, authorities moved to restrict some of the material exchanges that such contacts facilitated. On May 1, the Cuban government issued an updated customs law that strictly limited the weight of luggage and the amount of "noncommercial imports" that exile visitors—or any traveler—could bring into the country.[89] Yet the goal appears to have been not to cut off the material flow entirely but to direct exile visitors to channel their purchases in particular ways. Travelers recall hotel gift shops and special stores normally reserved for diplomats selling imported goods at inflated prices. If bringing in products was no longer affordable or an option, by opening such establishments to exile guests, officials guaranteed that they would buy their family gifts on the ground instead. Those funds then, in theory, could support the universal programs of the socialist state, offsetting the effect on families who did not have relatives visiting. On offer, in one traveler's memory, were Korean record players, Libby's canned fruit cocktail, and clothes produced by Panamanian subsidiaries of U.S. companies—like Gloria Vanderbilt jeans.[90]

Either way, the reaction to the new customs law in Miami was immediate. Lines faded in front of offices selling airfares to the island, and some who had already purchased tickets demanded their money back.[91] Some 4,000 fewer exiles visited the island in May than had visited in previous months.[92] As an image from the exile newspaper *Réplica* parodied, the appearance of the average traveler changed overnight—from a woman saddled down with ridiculous amounts of luggage, to a man dressed to the nines but who carried little more than a small duffle bag to his seat.[93] Nonetheless, if the new luggage restrictions decreased demand at first, by late summer, as many as 12,000 exiles per month were once again boarding planes.[94] Even state-owned Cubana Airlines sent the first passenger jet from the island to Miami in years to service one of the flights.[95] And when *El Miami Herald* reporter Helga Silva spent fifteen days in Havana in July, Cuban children she met all eagerly asked, "What did you bring?"[96]

Reunions Joyous and Fraught

Beyond the arena of material exchanges, though, the *visitas de la comunidad* played out with greater, if less documented, drama on the field of sentiment. Gifts or no gifts, reunions among family and friends could be happy, awkward, or both. The visits compelled Cubans to revisit difficult chapters in histories of interfamily and national political divides. In sharing stories of their lives across Cuba's Cold War fissures, Cubans from the island and abroad likewise confronted competing ideas and narratives about life and history on the other side. Yet interviews suggest that the power of the exchanges was also just as often their ability to decenter capital-R-revolutionary and capital-E-exile historical memory narratives to begin with. When personal and familial stories took precedence over competing public versions of the national epic, the resulting memory encounters had deeply meaningful, though sometimes unsettling and uncertain results.

It is a shame that more demographic information is not available about the exiles who did go to Cuba in 1979. Such statistics would be invaluable, because the degree of firsthand memory about what life under the Revolution was like, or had become, would necessarily have varied among exile travelers based on their date of emigration. We might surmise, for example, that exiles who left Cuba between 1959 and 1962 would have been more disoriented by the differences they found compared to someone who had departed on a Freedom Flight in 1970. Yet it is possible that members of the earliest exile waves—based on class profile—were most unlikely to have significant family members still on the island and take part in the *visitas de la comunidad* in the first place. This, in part, is what Silva recalls. In her memory, more recent exiles—from the late 1960s and 1970s—were generally the ones to go back first.[97]

Oral histories, though, do not reveal a clear pattern in terms of which cohort of exiles traveled to the island, or their age. A representative sample would be hard to conceptualize given how little we know about who went; the interviews referenced here, for reasons having to do with the numbers of years that have passed, skew toward the stories of those who returned in their twenties or thirties, having left when they were young. (The experiences and memory encounters of their elders, who often also returned to the island on the same trips, are thus accessed indirectly.) Still, even if Silva is correct that later exiles led the way, conversations suggest that those taking advantage of the *visitas de la comunidad* ultimately included those who had left at the Revolution's start as well as those who had emigrated up through the early 1970s. Other Cubans in the United States who seized on the opening were members and descendants of the smaller Cuban community that had existed in places like New York, Tampa, and Miami well before the Revolution had come about, but who had similarly been impeded from returning if they elected to continue residing in the United States after 1960.

Across the board, interview subjects tend to insist that their families never let the Revolution come completely between them. Whatever the divisions of Cuban politics, or the taboos about contact with "the other side," family was family. Many interviewees remembered sending and receiving letters over the years to stay in touch. Perhaps this was a characteristic of those who elected to travel to the island. Those who cut off all contact as a matter of political principle may have been less likely to go. Yet even for this possibly self-selecting group, interviews belie the simplicity of these claims. Whatever the emotional draw of family reunions, the intersection of family history and national saga had left charged legacies, legacies that visitors and their relatives would now be compelled to confront.

Consider the case of cousins Dora Amador and Luis Miguel Valdés.

Amador and Valdés hailed from a large middle-class family in the western province of Pinar del Río. Having grown up among handfuls of aunts and uncles, and surrounded by more than twenty-two cousins, they recalled a charmed childhood punctuated by large family gatherings and pitchers of lemonade made fresh from their grandmother's lemon tree. But their family was also divided politically. Amador's father had been a soldier of Batista in his youth, and, after divorcing her mother, he became a successful owner of car dealerships in 1950s Havana. He would leave the island on a yacht right away in 1959. Valdés's stepfather, meanwhile, was a pro-Batista soldier who had been executed for alleged complicity in the repression of anti-Batista activists immediately after the Revolution came to power. Another uncle had married a woman who became a member of the Cuban Communist Party. In this context, it is not surprising that emigration split the family apart. While Amador left alone at the age of twelve to join her father in 1962 (her mother would eventually follow in 1963 and take custody), Valdés, his mother, and his birth father (a man of the left) would remain.

For all of these reasons, Amador's decision to travel to the island alone in her late twenties involved more than just honoring her mother's request that she visit the grave of her now deceased grandmother, whose funeral neither had been able to attend. Her 1979 visit also necessarily brought out—sometimes even without anyone saying so directly—memories of the ideological fissures and experiences that had separated her family along political lines. On the one hand, Amador remembers the embrace of family members waiting for her at the Havana airport as effusive and joyous. On the other, she recalls how unsettled she felt when, after arriving at the family home in Pinar del Río, the head of the neighborhood Committee for the Defense of the Revolution knocked on the door at one in the morning to inquire what the loud conversation was all about. In retrospect Amador credits such experiences with opening her eyes to what "the system"—communism, that is—was truly like. Among family members, though, she also felt the presence of historical ghosts that no one dared to openly discuss. One aunt, she found, still brazenly kept a portrait of her deceased husband wearing a Batista-era police uniform hanging prominently in her living room. And the aunt who was a member of the Communist Party showed Dora her party membership card to make a political point.

As important to the visit was the time Amador spent in Havana with her favorite childhood cousin, Luis Miguel, who had grown up "integrated" to the Revolution and now worked in the capital as a painter and up-and-coming print designer. Here, too, the fault lines of personal memory surfaced—that is, of lives lived apart but that could have easily intersected had different choices been made. The two cousins remember their time and conversations together in different ways. By both accounts, Luis Miguel treated his cousin to a wonderful tour of Cuba's capital, including visits to museums, the old quarter, and even the famed La Bodeguita del Medio restaurant. As someone who had been educated on left-leaning university campuses in Puerto Rico, Dora confesses to arriving in Cuba initially with somewhat of an open mind and a passionate desire to reconnect with the country she left behind. But a book she says Luis Miguel gave her as a gift carried a dedication that seemed to associate her visit with an off-putting and familiar imperative of historical contrition: "Everything I give is but a small sacrifice if I can recover you for the Revolution." By contrast, Luis Miguel remembers that he was the skeptical one. When Dora allegedly shared with him a budding wish to move back to Cuba permanently, he claims to have replied: "Girl, the day that your Maybelline runs out, your enthusiasm about coming back here will go away, because this here isn't easy"—a sarcastic, if gendered, reference to Cuba's abiding material wants.[98]

In other instances, returnees encountered family members who appeared to not have moved on from the past at all. Such was the case of Emilio Cueto, who first returned to the island in 1977 but would repeat a visit under the auspices of the *visitas de la comunidad* in January 1979. It was that first visit, however, that resulted in the most vivid form of what we might think of as memory shock. After almost not being allowed into the country at customs (there were no standard procedures for cases like his at the time), he arrived at his widowed mother's Havana home to find it a veritable museum. The furniture and appliances were exactly as he had left them in 1961, but everything was falling apart. In the closet of his childhood bedroom still hung the uniforms and medals from Emilio's days at the prestigious Colegio de Belén, a private Catholic school nationalized and closed eighteen years before. Seeking to break with the past and rebuild his relationship with his mother on a clean slate, Cueto collected some keepsakes to take with him. But he threw everything else out, including dozens of letters he had sent to his mother since departing.[99]

Other memories proved too painful to revisit at all. In addition to seeing his mother, Cueto relates that he sought out a series of old acquaintances: a former schoolmate who had served a prison sentence for counterrevolutionary activities in the 1960s, as well as another who had become a Communist Party member of high rank. Most important, however, was seeing Raquel, a vivacious, captivating family friend who had practically been a second parental figure during Cueto's childhood after his father's untimely death pushed his mother into a life of solemnity. Cueto called and made an appointment to stop by, but Raquel phoned on the morning of their scheduled date to tell him not to come. "I don't ever want to see you again," she said. "You have made me remember who I was.... The Raquel that you know no longer exists." Apparently, given all that Cubans had been through, some memory lines were better left uncrossed.[100]

For other returnees, visits home permitted less time to wax nostalgic about times past or the family life that had been. In the case of Helida Pérez de Cerejido and her daughter Elizabeth, then nine years old, visiting Cuba in 1979 was all about trying to recover an even more intimate set of memories of which they had been deprived. Born in Havana in the summer of 1969, Elizabeth had been whisked away from the island in early 1970 as an infant in her mother's care. Somehow not allowed to be "claimed" by his wife's relatives already in the United States, her father, José, was ineligible for a spot on a Freedom Flight and forced to stay behind. This was intended to be temporary, however, as neither Helida nor José came from particularly "revolutionary" families. After moving in with relatives in Miami's Little Havana, Helida, a seamstress who had once sewed the uniforms for employees of Cubana Airlines, set about rededicating herself to her craft at a local factory. Her husband, a gas station attendant before and after the Revolution, planned to bide his time until the next opportunity to leave.

Circumstances and bad luck got in the way. After the Freedom Flights closed in 1973, José spent several years trying to secure Cuban government permission to emigrate and find an alternate way out of the country, possibly through Spain. But when those efforts failed, long, wistful letters in which he lamented to his wife that his daughter was growing up without him turned more accusatory. José began demanding that his wife and daughter move back—never mind that doing so was impossible at the time. Yet such wishes soon became a moot point. In 1977, José Melitón Cerejido Alonso was caught up in a police raid on black market activities in which his brother was involved and sentenced to three years in jail.

Helida and Elizabeth's visit to Cuba in 1979 thus had a singular purpose: securing José's release. Failing that, Helida at least wanted to see him, perhaps to revisit the marriage they had really only just started before they became split apart, or at least to introduce her daughter to the father that she had never really known. From the time they landed in Havana in March, therefore, the pleasantries and challenges of family reunions were overshadowed by the pressing need to secure permission to enter the prison at Havana's La Cabaña fortress, where José was being held. Most of all, Elizabeth vividly recalls walking up the colonial-era steps to the fortress's entrance, entering a large, empty waiting room, and then being greeted ever so fleetingly by her handcuffed father before being shuttled away so he and Helida could quietly talk. There was hardly enough time for "reconciliation," and even if there had been, the personal stakes of such conversations, not national politics, surely mattered most.[101]

Other travelers arrived with no less emotional anticipation but as bearers of less traumatic legacies. Such was the case of Mary Lynn Conejo, born in New York to Cuban parents who had immigrated to the United States separately in search of greater economic opportunity in the 1940s and then married. As a child growing up in a small apartment in Chelsea, Mary Lynn's home was punctuated by the frequent visits of Havana relatives. But though her immediate family was thoroughly established in the United States by the time the Revolution came about, Mary Lynn rejects the idea that Fidel Castro's rise did not impact her life. She recalls traveling to Cuba in 1960 to attend her grandmother's funeral and picking up the slogan, "Cuba sí, yanqui no!" during the visit. ("Little girl, don't be an idiot," her mother joked. "You are a Yankee!") Most grave of all was the breaking of diplomatic relations between Cuba and the United States in 1961. While her parents had not felt particularly strong about the Revolution, bilateral conflict portended the breaking of the family link.

Visiting a number of her family members who had elected to stay in Cuba was thus an opportunity for Mary Lynn and her parents to fill a personal void more than heal a political wound. The fact that they were part of the community of Cubans and Cuban Americans in the United States *before* 1959 also set their case apart. Mary Lynn's parents had never "betrayed the Revolution" per se, nor like some other exiles had they personally experienced its transformations on the ground. Her relatives on the island were also familiar with life in the United States; her closest aunt had lived in New York too in the 1950s before electing to travel back to the island to take care of her mother in the early 1960s. She and her husband had integrated themselves into the Revolution, doing what was necessary and expected as professionals in the state education system and porcine industry, respectively. But no one was a member of the Communist Party. Mary Lynn thus remembers running up the stairs to her aunt's second-floor Centro Habana home without trepidation and both launching into an unqualified, "awesome" embrace.

Still, even in her case the visit brought fraught political dynamics and legacies to the fore. For starters, Mary Lynn's presence threatened to contradict the stories younger members of her family raised entirely in Cuba had been told about life in the United States vis-à-vis common refrains about Cuba's socialist achievements. "Whatever the kids ask you

Figure 6.2. Mary Lynn Conejo (*center*), of New York, NY, with her cousins in Havana, all sporting new t-shirts from the United States. Central Havana, April 1979; courtesy of Mary Lynn Conejo.

[about life in the United States]," she remembers her aunt instructing her, "I want you to tell them the truth. But I don't want you praising the United States just for the hell of it." Mary Lynn was happy to respect that wish. Yet the size of the hotel buffets when she brought them to eat—larger than any spread of food her cousins had ever seen—probably did more to highlight the historical shortcomings (and inequities) of the socialism her young relatives had been taught to venerate than anything she could have said about her life in New York. So did Mary Lynn's attire. "Mary Lynn, where did you get those pants," she remembers her nine-year-old cousin whispering to her, in reference to her new jeans. He was incredulous that she had secured them not on "the black market" but rather in a store.[102]

Again and again interviewees—both those exiles who traveled at the time and those who lived on the island—circle back in their recollections to the impact of gifts, or to the meals and experiences that exiles were able to provide for family and friends. But what was at stake in such transfers was not just material wants satisfied or generated but also an implicit challenge to some of the ingrained narratives Cubans had long heard about socialist accomplishments and the Revolution as history fulfilled. The story of Mabel Suárez's reencounter with her aunt is instructive in this regard. Unlike in other cases, Mabel's visiting relative from abroad did not arrive with stories of success since arriving in Miami in 1965. Mabel's father *in Cuba*—drawing on earnings from a black market carpentry and pig-raising business in San José de las Lajas, a town on the outskirts of Havana—had to circuitously cover the $1,000 or more dollars his sister-in-law needed to take the trip. Still, Mabel remembers her aunt arriving in their town not only with gifts of chewing gum (which she had never seen before) and new clothes but also the even greater treasure of an instant camera that took photos in color. The only color photographs Mabel had ever laid eyes on were those arriving periodically in envelopes from Miami. Metaphorically and literally, she says, the *visitas de la comunidad* allowed her to begin seeing her own life and history "in color" for the first time.[103] She also recalls long conversations with her otherwise introverted aunt about her job working at a garment factory in Miami and about how, due to the scarcity of certain foods on the island, the culinary habits of Cubans over the past fifteen years had changed.

Carlos Abreu relates a similar set of experiences, albeit from the vantage point of a visitor. Also from a town outside of Havana—the smaller Nueva Paz—Carlos had left Cuba at age fourteen in 1968 and returned in 1979 with his parents and a half dozen other relatives. But in addition to emotional reunions with his grandmother and his father's beloved former assistant from his truck delivery business, what Carlos most remembers was an unsettling confrontation in the middle of his stay. After he carefully rationed out bottle-cap-size amounts of North American whiskey to a crowd of childhood buddies, a fistfight nearly broke out over which of them would get to keep the bottle as a souvenir. These and other experiences suggest that exile visitors' gifts compelled Cubans to reckon with the legacy of shortages in their society. To wit, when Abreu's parents brought the Nueva Paz family to Havana to eat at the Hotel Riviera and then attend the floor show at the historic Tropicana night club (all part of their package tour), Carlos remembers proud relatives—including an aunt who was a member of the Communist Party—mortifyingly stuffing leftovers into their purses.[104]

The *visitas de la comunidad* thus provoked history and memory encounters in multiple, at times contradictory, ways. On the one hand, thousands of reunited families and friends repeated the ritual of what one interviewee poetically called "velorios al revés," or "wakes in reverse."[105] When returning exiles first arrived, hugs and tears were often followed by hours of conversation late into the night as émigrés figuratively brought themselves back from the dead. Visitors also sometimes brought messages on cassette tape from other exiles who had not been able, or willing, to make the trip.¹⁰⁶ Yet the conspicuous material flows that also came with the visitors, and that Cuban authorities seemed to a point willing to facilitate, opened space for reevaluating Cuban state discourses that constantly painted the Revolution's achievements as the highest form of modern life. Allowing exiles previously synonymous with national perfidy to visit was a political and memory reversal in itself. But, as the joke put it, the *gusanos* (worms) now had become *mariposas* (butterflies), and they had cash to burn. For Cubans who had family who visited and for those who did not, the resulting exchanges could exacerbate doubts about the track record of nearly twenty years of socialist policies.

On the other hand, visitors did not necessarily walk away from the experience gloating about their capitalist achievements either. Few visitors became socialist converts. But despite witnessing material wants they could also discover a society whose history since 1959, or since their own departure dates, was more than a dystopia. As Luis Miguel Valdés surmises, perhaps convincing exiles that "aquello no era un infierno ni un calvario"—that Cuba was neither a "hell nor a prison"—was one of the primary reasons the Cuban government authorized the visits to begin with.¹⁰⁷ Besides, the very material inefficiencies that their suitcases attempted to fulfill might have raised other historical qualms. Namely, if the Revolution was so dysfunctional that many Cubans on the island were desperate for gifts, why had it been able to last so long?

Finally, as happy as the many reunions were, they could also generate retrospective bitterness. "You left, and now you're back showing off a watch and four pairs of jeans," was how Luis Miguel Valdés characterized the feelings of some, independent of whether one considered oneself "revolutionary."¹⁰⁸ Likewise, Mary Lynn Conejo remembers the resentment of one of her aunts toward certain "Cubans who left to go live with comforts in the United States" after 1959—less for betraying "the Revolution" than because she felt, rightly or wrongly, that they had turned their backs on their country.¹⁰⁹ Whether out of conviction or obligation, Cubans had sacrificed much in the name of the Revolution's historic promise, and they had personally navigated its internal conflicts and results. This made the return of exiles without the same memories or lived experiences a possible source of tension as much as a welcome revelation or cause for joy.

Conclusion: Cause and Effect?

The *visitas de la comunidad* continued through and beyond the end of 1979, resisting legal and extralegal challenges. At one point, the U.S. government went after Havanatur, labeling the Panama-based company an "illegal agent of the Cuban government."[110] Then, in late January and early February 1980, one of the *visitas'* earliest boosters, the Reverend Manuel Espinosa, staged a bizarre public reversal, alleging in a series of press conferences that Miami companies working on the trips were filled with Cuban intelligence agents and that the companies were engaging in contraband trade in violation of U.S. sanctions.[111] Havanatur claimed that Espinosa's about-face had a narrower explanation: having profited handsomely from the exile reunification business, he now owed them $430,000.[112] But even after Havanatur's U.S. offices closed, the visits kept functioning according to an earlier model. Subcontracted Miami agencies or charter airlines simply returned to working with Cuban counterparts from a distance.[113]

The complex personal and familial reckonings with the past and present that the visits made possible thus continued. Yet, ironically, while they became a formidable memory for those who traveled, the *visitas de la comunidad* did not fundamentally alter predominant public representations of the island's history in the exile world. How could they, when public opposition to those traveling remained as strong as support, and when for the most part personal details of travelers' experiences remained out of the public eye and the pages of the press? Where the visits were covered in greater depth, a focus on material exchanges dominated news coverage. But while logical, such discourses also reinforced ingrained ways of seeing the Revolution's history as a failure. Faced with the flood of gifts from the capitalist world, some Cubans *had* begun to ask themselves if all of their years of sacrifice in the name of the Revolution's goals had been for naught. But from the point of view of the exile community, this emphasis also lent itself to a suspiciously neat public triumphalism. Even as many of those who actually went to the island returned from the experience with much more equivocal feelings, observers and commentators who did not travel grabbed on to accounts of material exchange to confirm established visions of the Revolution as a historical fraud.[114]

On the island, the durability of old forms of public retrospective discourse—about the Revolution generally, and about the exile community specifically—was even more remarkable. One might have expected state media to find and celebrate cases of those who rebuffed visitors' materialism—consistent, in a way, with Fidel Castro's closed-door call to Communist Party members to do the same. Alternately, officials could have made the fawning over foreign luxuries a subject of constant satire and critique.[115] For the most part, however, Cuban newspapers, magazines, and authorities in 1979 practically said nothing about the sojourning exiles in their midst, even as the very opening to exile visitors represented a reversal of exile "disremembering" to a point. Deeply impactful as they may have been on a personal level, the visits left virtually no public trace.

Consider, too, that one of the best-known manifestations of the Revolution's "disremembering" of exiles, the spy series *En silencio ha tenido que ser* (*In Silence It Had to Be*), debuted on Cuban TV in March 1979, as the visits were taking place. Luis Miguel Valdés even remembers a former childhood friend arriving from Miami at the time and crying upon seeing the show because actor Sergio Corrieri had been his classmate before 1959 in school.[116] How ironic an expression of sentimentality amid a virtual reunion. Here was a cultural text with a familiar retrospective message — "Those people who left have nothing to offer us here" — just as the flow of planes with gift-bearing passengers from the exile community was approaching an early peak.

And yet, as soon as a bus driver slammed through the gates of the Peruvian embassy in Havana on April 1, 1980, initiating what quickly became an occupation of 10,000 Cubans, and eventually the exodus of 125,000 via Mariel harbor over the following months, *everyone* — inside and outside of Cuba — seemed to know whom to blame. The mounting international scandal, said one young Havana resident to a visiting reporter, "is a consequence of the visits to Cuba by *la comunidad*."[117] By exposing the historical myths and present reality of the Revolution as a lie, the visits had supposedly forced the socialist levy to break. As one veteran of the Antonio Maceo Brigade recalled, a functionary from the Cuban Ministry of Foreign Relations accused her and her colleagues of opening a retrospective Pandora's box with their 1977 trip.[118] As foreshadowing, in August 1979, Humberto Ortega, a twenty-eight-year-old Cuban man from a small town in Matanzas Province, stowed away to Miami in the wheel compartment of one of the Cubana Airlines planes bringing exile visitors in.[119] Even before the Peru embassy break-in, there had been several small embassy incursions and a rise in illegal departures by boat in late 1979 and early 1980. A slogan frequently used to taunt those leaving in the 1980 boatlift — *¡Se va por un pitusa!* (He/she is leaving for a pair of jeans!) — also suggested a link to the *visitas*, as if the material temptations offered by the visitors lay underneath many Cubans' subsequent decision to flee.

Is there something to this theory? Some interviewees do see the visits as cause and the Mariel boatlift as the conspicuous effect.[120] So did some Mariel migrants at the time.[121] Perhaps Cuba's gradual, albeit partial effort over the 1970s to "re-remember" exiles had backfired spectacularly, provoking uncontainable social unrest. However, others are more circumspect, wary of echoing a simplistic and, again, exile-centric narrative that would take credit for undermining the Revolution from abroad, particularly when most exiles at the time *opposed* the visits in the first place.[122] Surely, the individual rationales leading many to leave in 1980 were more complex. Some families had been waiting for years for a renewed opportunity to emigrate. For their part, island-based scholars today blame the United States for egging on a rise in illegal departures from the island in 1979 and 1980. In their view, the ongoing U.S. open door immigration policy toward Cubans, the building up of migration pressures after the end of the Freedom Flights in 1973, and the U.S. government's stalling on commitments to allow the legal migration of Cuban political prisoners released after the 1978 dialogue were more at fault for the crisis of 1980 than the demonstration effect of the *visitas* per se.[123]

Or, maybe the exodus was less a reaction to the *things* exiles brought than what they symbolized. After all, émigrés had been able to come to their home country and then freely leave—a privilege that had been denied to Cubans on the island for more than a decade. Put another way, exiles' visits may have made island residents more aware of the ways their own freedom of movement was limited, despite all they had endured and sacrificed. Former reporter Helga Silva hypothesizes that this realization is what really lead thousands in 1980 to make a break for the United States.[124] More than chasing material convenience, maybe many Cubans saw exiles' ability to enter and leave Cuba at will as the deeper historical slap in the face.

Still, even if that were the case, one would have expected an immediate Cuban government response. If it was so obvious that the disruptions caused by the *visitas* contributed directly or indirectly to the Mariel crisis, would not the Cuban government have moved right away to shut them down? The fact is, this did not occur. The *visitas* continued at a much decreased rhythm, but they continued nonetheless through 1982. In that year, the U.S. government, now under Ronald Reagan, shut down the major remaining charter company offering flights and moved to break most direct U.S.-Cuba air links while also re-imposing the wider travel ban. Family visits routed through third countries, however, were still allowed by Cuba and the United States for the time being.[125]

All of this points to an enduring paradox about this episode: if the *visitas de la comunidad* of 1979 facilitated complex and meaningful memory encounters for Cubans individually, there is no consensus claim on the collective memory of the experience as such. Neither celebrated in museums, nor talked about in most history books, the arrival of 100,000 exiles to the island in the span of one year continues to be an experience barely discussed in Miami or Havana, or recalled in private at most. The term "visitas de la comunidad" (visits from the community) was itself a euphemism, deployed to skirt the charged memories of the Revolution's unfolding that the visits themselves brought to light. In some exile corners, even admitting that one had gone to the island was unwise, lest one be accused of supporting communism. Thus, stories of those who did go largely remained off the page, stage, or airwaves.[126] And the few times the subject was revisited in subsequent years on the island—in works of literature or film, for example—texts skewed their representation toward stereotype, as if all visitors had been arrogant and materialistic, confirmation, in the inverse, of the superiority of Cuban socialist society.[127]

Like those that preceded it, this chapter has sought to fill in, as much as historicize, the memory record—in this case, both leading to and during the visits themselves. The eagerness of interviewees to share their experiences reflects the fact that the visits of 1979 represented a significant experience for individuals who went or received travelers, precisely because it created a fresh opportunity for Cubans at home and abroad to contemplate what they, their families, and their country had been through over the past twenty years. But the real contents of those countless *velorios al revés*—like so many aspects of retrospective reflection among individual Cubans over the years—are probably lost to us for good. In that, they mark a fitting end for this book. For as long as Cubans had been publicly fighting over grand narratives of national history, many also harbored private recollections that are less accessible to us and that do not neatly fit into one or another commemorative mold.

Two decades into the revolutionary era, Cubans were still struggling to find a solution, or a salve, for their nation's memory wounds. Perhaps the visits of 1979 offered a first attempt to try. But in many ways, the Mariel boatlift of 1980 reestablished the major fault lines of retrospective conflict all over again. Cuba's memory wars carried on: the Revolution did not lose all believers, and the bulk of exiles did not suddenly embrace the origin story or permanence of the socialist state. Beneath ongoing efforts to recover or consolidate paradises lost and won, Cubans continued to accumulate multivalent lived experiences that they then refracted through evolving public modes of narrating the island's history. As the coordinates of Cuba's present further shifted, Cubans still found themselves looking back. The future that awaited would be full of fresh retrospective mobilizations and angsts.

CONCLUSION
Inconsolable Memories

Walk into Havana's Museum of the Revolution today and you are as likely to see tourists wearing Panama hats as you are to encounter Cuban teenagers on a school field trip. Never mind that the building itself—the island's original Presidential Palace—is also a monument to "the Republic" (or Republics) that the Revolution overthrew. Within its impressive halls, chronologically arranged displays tell a familiar story of Cuba's foreign subjugation and internal injustices through the 1950s, followed by an epic of guerrilla struggle and anti-imperialist resistance. Perhaps the occasional elderly visitor comes to relive the passions of youth, just as some students may walk away more intrigued by the episodes they have read about in textbooks. But wax figures of guerrilla heroes also serve as metaphors for the ways the Revolution's history, sixty years after the Rebel Army rolled into Havana from the Sierra Maestra, now seems to many Cubans to be encased in repetitive political slogans, commemorative plaques, and predictable movie scripts.

The Cuban diaspora in the United States does not have an analogous institution, at least not yet.[1] Miami's Freedom Tower, headquarters for the U.S.-government-sponsored Cuban Refugee Center in the 1960s, provides one topographical marker for narrative claims to a singular exile experience. In Little Havana, a modest monument built in 1971 to fallen soldiers from the Bay of Pigs invasion also serves as a site for political gatherings, albeit one around which more ambivalent memories of U.S. anticommunist partnership wax and wane. The closest thing to a home for the quasi-official exile memory of Cuba, then, is not a formal museum, but an annual history fair. Since 1999, "Cuba Nostalgia" has provided generations of Cubans and Cuban Americans with "a journey back in time for those who remember the island's glorious times, and for those who never experienced them."[2] For a small fee, guests wind their way through a simulacrum of Havana's mid-1950s consumer modernity recreated in a convention center and retrace their steps on an aerial photograph of the city's streets blown up on the floor. Corporate-sponsored booths marketing prerevolutionary memorabilia and food brands long absent from the island's shelves entirely avoid the conflicts that led to, or followed, the Cuban Revolution in the first place.

Visitors to both the Museum of the Revolution or Cuba Nostalgia can be forgiven for concluding that Cubans have long conceptualized their past in static, polarized terms. But as a closer examination of both sites reveals, Cuban pathways of retrospective mobilization, argument, and amnesia tend to be more circuitous than meets the eye. Outside of the Museum of the Revolution's doors, most residents in Cuba's capital today are too busy trying to make ends meet to reflect on the legacy of a socialist epic. As drivers of restored North American automobiles from the 1950s, many cater to tourists who, ironically, seek to bask in the architectural and material ruins of the same "glory days" celebrated in Cuba Nostalgia's palace of disremembering. Conversely, Miami by now is filled with more children of the Revolution than those who really remember what Cuba was like before it. Many of the collectibles for sale at Cuba Nostalgia actually come from recent migrants and current island residents who have found ways to slip prerevolutionary trinkets out of the country and cash in on a past they were taught to repudiate.[3]

In a similar fashion, this book has revealed that the "routes" of Cubans' contests over their past through the late 1970s were hardly straight, even as the "roots" of antagonistic revolutionary and exile narratives of Cuban history were set in the early 1960s.[4] Following the "triumph" of the Cuban Revolution, Cubans articulated, helped forge, and identified with powerful "emblematic frameworks" for understanding the Revolution's origins and subsequent course as the culmination of political struggles that began decades before.[5] Those frameworks proved foundational for contending claims to political legitimacy and authority under an emerging revolutionary state and, in opposition to it, the budding exile community in Miami and other points north. But said frameworks were not fixed or uncontested. Cubans of all stripes argued about their past intensely, often turning to history less as material for confident celebration than as a wellspring of existential doubts, unresolved political disputes, or even dreams deferred. Contemporary memory spaces like the Museum of the Revolution and Cuba Nostalgia thus fail not just because they tell incomplete histories. They also leave out battles over national memory and history that were and continue to be critical elements of Cuba's history itself. Both spaces privilege narrow triumphalism over deep reflection. By celebrating a one-sided tale of revolutionary achievement or a pre-1959 paradise lost, they traffic in mirror nostalgias that, as Michael Kammen put it, amount to "history without guilt."[6]

What, then, do the more nuanced counterpoints of remembrance, retrospective meditation, and selective forgetting surveyed in this book tell us about Cuba and Cuban America? What do Cubans' competing uses of their past, but also their misgivings about history's results, reveal about the forces of revolution, exile, and retrospective politics in the Cuban case? How have those forces continued to evolve? Will the Cuban memory wars ever find resolution or an end point? And does it help or hurt such a goal to recover fronts of memory conflict from the 1960s and 1970s, as this book has, that many Cubans today may not remember and in which many never took part?

For one thing, a focus on what I have termed retrospective politics shows that the divide between revolution and counterrevolution in Cuba was rarely as precise or encompassing as those terms suggest. The line between in and out was a moving rather than fixed target, especially at the Revolution's start, and despite the polarities of historical language that quickly surrounded Cubans on all sides—"the Republic" versus "the pseudo-republic," Revolution versus dictatorship. Fidel Castro said things in 1959 and 1960 that later he would have considered counterrevolutionary (and thus became necessary to forget). In exile, many "counterrevolutionaries" at first claimed to be the true revolutionaries Fidel had betrayed, only to later submerge such affiliations under a mantle of unqualified longing. Explanations of what happened and where things went right or wrong evolved over time, despite the tendency of revolutionary officials and exile partisans to speak of historical constants. Certainly for the period under study, appraisals of Cuban history's results were hotly contested and intimately felt, on and across both sides of the Florida Straits, and along complex ideological, generational, and personal lines.

Second, retrospective politics help us understand revolutionary Cuba and Cuban America as having a shared history. This is obvious in many ways. But approaching the island's past through the contrapuntal relationship between insular and diaspora affairs—that is, through their relational dynamics, not just as opposites or mirror images—continues to be more counterintuitive among scholars and other Cuba observers than one would think. Emotional, ideological, and practical barriers to travel and communication between Cuba and places like South Florida at the height of the Cold War were real. Yet the history of Cuba and its U.S. diaspora not only evolved in parallel but also involved discrete and more public junctures of contact and exchange. Through the politics of the past, we can appreciate the Florida Straits (or even the ocean dividing Havana from

Cubans in New York) as a fraught borderland of political ideas and identities, not simply a one-way escape valve for a prerevolutionary elite. Beyond a straightforward tale of anticommunist flight and socialist commitment—"beyond," in the words of critic Ricardo Ortiz, "the neatness of the two-Cuba split"—"far messier" contests over past allegiances, political legitimacy, generational identities, the historical role of the United States, and the consequences of political change and emigration cut across post-1959 Cuban life.[7]

Third, this book reveals the centrality of retrospective politics to Cuban political culture. This was not new to the post-1959 period. But even if Cuban political life had revolved around cycles of "desire and disenchantment" since 1868, retrospective mobilization and rumination acquired a new intensity in the aftermath of the Cuban Revolution's victory.[8] After 1959, the generation of sweeping narratives of national historical memory was arguably as essential to drumming up support for policies in revolutionary Cuba as the policies themselves. This strategy, however, carried risks, especially when the initiatives, ambitions, and goals of the Cuban revolutionary government did not fully pan out. For exiles, too, keeping "the cause" alive required a constant effort to rally consciences around a sense of shared responsibility as well as a common historical plight. Yet the internal fractures on both sides over just what "the cause" was (over and above taking out the Castro government in Miami's case), who had the right to lead the charge, and what cost was worth paying to achieve it, often worked to stymie those goals. While it is important to acknowledge the distinct power of the revolutionary state to provide citizens on the island with common historical languages with which they were expected to identify, that state was not a monolithic abstraction, and the basic polarizations of Cuba's memory wars after 1960 were never so defining as to silence intrarevolutionary or intraexile debates, let alone cross-pollination between both fields.

A close look at the politics of the past in the Cuban case thus reinforces a theoretical understanding of retrospective politics as a dynamic, not static enterprise. Far from reflections of engrained or strictly predetermined agendas, Cuban counterpoints of retrospective rumination and contestation evolved in dynamic dialogue with distinct presents. Battles over history and memory were inextricably intertwined, and they transpired at the intersection of political discourse, mass spectacle, the media, and private experience, whether or not the latter was appropriated to serve retrospective frameworks in public settings. Like founding origin stories of the anti-Batista struggle, written, photographic, and even fictionalized representations of subsequent revolutionary events in the 1960s structured "iconic sequences with which common citizens could relate and identify."[9] Monuments, museums, speeches, and films supplied the pieces of a recognizable national story with which many Cubans could and did link their life stories. But Cubans also fashioned their own interpretations of the historical record, interpolating themselves into contending accounts of revolutionary and exile experience in sui generis ways. Besides, for Cubans on and off the island there was an additional challenge. The changing place of the past *in the here and now*—that is, how to overcome it, or how to measure up—proved as vital a concern as anything else.

The Cuban case also unsettles our sense of what retrospective politics typically look like in Latin America, or at least the primary axes around which those politics turn. For Cubans, competing accounts of violence and repression, or the secrecy surrounding state and nonstate violence, were not the only or even the central anchors of opposed memory frameworks to the degree they were and still are in other countries. Yes, exile served as a repository for countermemories of the Revolution that emphasized the government's 1959 revolutionary tribunals and subsequent treatment of its internal opponents or nonconformist citizens. Cuban officials and those who identified with the revolutionary project, in contrast, honored victims of not only Batista-era cruelty but also covert, U.S.-backed anti-Castro actions in the 1960s and exile terrorists in the 1970s. Yet these opposing pantheons of martyrs and the mutually reinforcing silences between them were important not just intrinsically but insofar as they became pieces of evidence for the primary historical argument at stake. For Cubans after 1959, whether or not the Revolution lived out its promise of finishing Cuba's "unfinished history" was the chief front in the ongoing memory wars. For some, the Revolution did constitute the culmination of Cuban history to that point—at least for a time. For others, whether right away or as the years passed, it proved the gravest of all Cuban historical cons.

Even when Cubans did reflect upon legacies of violence, the coordinates of those debates and their intersections with other fronts of retrospective struggle were not always predictable. Plenty of early exiles, for example, remembered, the Batista regime's cruelty. Conversely, a "revolutionary" playwright could look upon the violence committed by the Brigade 2506 not to indict exile "mercenaries" but to mourn a national tragedy. These dynamics become all the more complex when we move into the Revolution's second decade and consider its impact upon a younger generation on the island and abroad. Not all Miami youth in the 1970s celebrated the early anti-Castro opposition uncritically, as we saw. On the island, meanwhile, one could sympathize with an emblematic victim of the Bay of Pigs invasion like Nemesia Rodríguez, or be horrified by some exiles' involvement in the bombing of Cubana flight 455, and still be enthralled when a returning relative from Miami in 1979 confirmed that not all who left Cuba in the 1960s were the revanchists depicted on TV.

Teasing out such complexities deepens our understanding of not just Cuban cultural history, but also Cubans' evolving senses of themselves. Yet it would be dishonest for me to assert that this book has only had narrow historicist aims. Returning to a point raised in the introduction, as a Cuban American, I am also interested in the ways this material might encourage Cubans and Cuban Americans to pull apart and question the historical narratives with which they most identify. Amid the baseline oppositions in public Cuban historical discourse that still persist, this book retraces more nested struggles over the past that have tended to be forgotten or overlooked. Uncovering these lesser-known stories, I believe, invites Cubans to productively revisit their history as unsettled terrain.

In part, that means disrupting the boundaries we construct to delimit whose histories count. As Viet Than Nguyen has argued, the politics of memory are usually oriented around the imperative of "remembering one's own."[10] Nations seek to honor "their" heroes or martyrs in a war. Governments, social groups, and cultures of all political persuasions construct boundaries of membership in imagined communities that rituals and discourses of commemoration then instantiate. This book has in part traced such processes in historical motion. But it has also shown how patterns of conflict and diaspora for Cubans made the parameters of "one's own" change. Former revolutionaries periodically became the newest exiles, and some radicalized exile children found more in common with their parents' socialist enemies. Notwithstanding the hegemonic (if always contested) foundations of retrospective discourse established on both the island and in expatriate hubs like Miami in the 1960s, Cubans articulated varied historical attachments, arguments, and insecurities that unsettle the sense that the Cuban memory wars were ever divided into just two sets of claims.

By recovering this nuance, this book thus performs its own memory work. *Cuban Memory Wars* destabilizes understandings of who "one's own" were or are for Cubans in the first place. It highlights some of the multiple "ourselves" in construction and contention for Cubans over time, proving that "exile" and "revolution" were less fixed identities or political projects than terrains on which intertwined battles over history, power, and the boundaries of political community were constantly being fought. In this way, these pages gesture toward what Nguyen has called an "ethics of recognition," inviting Cuban readers to both complicate their understanding of "one's own" and deal with multiple revolutionary and exile "others" in detail.[11] In seriously historicizing "both sides" of the Cuba memory wars, and in recapturing the raw material of retrospective conflicts that in fact buck this polarized cliché, *Cuban Memory Wars* dares the island's government, exile advocates, and all Cubans caught in between to understand a history of memory struggle as a shared inheritance to overcome.

That said, I am not so naive as to think this an easy task. "Reconciliation" may sound like an appealing goal. But in practice, it is often just the next step in a nation's memory wars—a process that in its mandate to articulate a consensus and heal wounds often requires burying, eliding, or accommodating fraught legacies in ways that can and should be picked apart.[12] Besides, Cubans' memory ghosts have continued to shape-shift and multiply since the 1970s. More recent events, controversies, and experiences have become fodder for the Cuban memory wars in their own ways. And even as Cuban retrospective politics no more conform to a simple two-sided schism today than they did fifty years ago, the foundational oppositions of revolutionary and exile memory cultures remain powerful. They have outlasted newer challenges to their terms, and memory partisans on all sides continue to find ways to incorporate newer markers—again, events, experiences, and testimonies from the 1980s to the present—into familiar "emblematic frameworks" of national remembering.[13]

In the remainder of this conclusion, therefore, I first return to the moment of the Mariel boatlift where chapter 6 ends, describing its long and unresolved shadow over Cuban national life. I then bring the story of Cuban retrospective politics synoptically up to the present day, emphasizing how the prospect of mutual recognition among Cubans on the island and abroad has at times seemed to advance since the 1990s, only to recede again amid new dislocations or the reappearance of old controversies. Nonetheless, even as I am clear-eyed about the challenges and pitfalls, I proceed with the belief that there is something to be gained by undertaking this kind of survey, for Cubans especially. Aspiring to a singular, "reconciled," or consensus view of Cuba's past may be as problematic as any singularly "revolutionary" or "exile" narrative such a synthesis might attempt to replace. Nonetheless, I repeat a central premise of this book: Cubans would do well to at least take a bird's-eye view of their memory wars and begin to incorporate them into a new plural understanding of their history—or rather their *histories*.

Mariel and the 1980s

Between the spring and fall of 1980, roughly 125,000 Cubans made their way to the United States on an improvised, chaotic flotilla departing from Mariel Harbor about thirty miles west of Havana. They included some of the 10,000 Cubans who had precipitated a national crisis when they occupied the grounds of the Peruvian embassy at the beginning of April. Soon, Fidel Castro declared that not only the original asylum seekers but any Cuban wishing to leave the country could do so through the port of Mariel if Cubans abroad came to pick them up. The resulting exodus quickly became the most concentrated wave of out-migration in the island's history. (Eighty-five percent departed in just May and June.) And yet, as disruptive an event as the Mariel boatlift was for both the island and its diaspora, it remains understudied and undermemorialized.[14] In reality, over the course of the 1980s, Mariel proved to be an event that both the Cuban state and many exiles in Miami tried their hardest to forget.

For partisans of the Revolution, Mariel represented—still represents—an inconvenient memory because it exposed a significant underbelly of dissatisfaction in Cuban socialist society. The causes and origins of the social explosion continue to be debated, as we saw in chapter 6. But there can be no doubt that after a decade of relative economic stability and socialist institutionalization, coupled with a period of expanding relations with the Cuban émigré community, the boatlift represented a shock to the system, politically and ideologically. (Indeed, for a number of members of the *Areíto* cohort we met in chapter 4, Mariel represented the beginning of their own process of slow disenchantment with the Revolution over the course of the ensuing decade.) Not even a year after former *gusanos* had been welcomed back to their country of birth as visitors, on April 19, 1980, the Cuban government rallied more than a million citizens in a "March of the Combatant People" to denounce the newest would-be migrants in even stronger terms. Participants condemned those planning to leave the country as "scum" and "lumpen," "antisocial elements" that true revolutionaries would be better off without.[15] Fidel Castro would echo this framing, referring to the migrants' lack of "revolutionary genes" in a speech at the end of the country's traditional mass march on May 1.[16]

But here we begin to see how the treatment of those leaving the country through Mariel would confound past patterns of "disremembering" the departed, even as the Cuban state tried to revive them once again. One of the few books published about the boatlift on the island later described Cuban exile vessels arriving in port to pick up their relatives as "enlightening" "windows" into the corrupt prerevolutionary past that a new round of sellouts was about to join—as if by time travel.[17] Yet in reality those heading into exile were *not* holdovers of prerevolutionary Cuba. Boats leaving Mariel were filled with hundreds of working-class "new men" and "new women," many of them Cubans of color. It was in their name, in principle, that Cuban socialism had been built. This made the exodus, the frankly classist language used to denigrate the migrants, and the hateful, at turns violent "acts of repudiation" carried out against them in neighborhoods and workplaces across the country before they left, all the more difficult to interpret, let alone celebrate as milestones in the Revolution's history.[18] And they were not. In Cuban media over the course of the 1980s, the origins, unfolding, and aftermath of the Mariel boatlift were largely buried.[19]

In the exile community, a parallel, if less absolute silence took hold as the exodus exposed the limits of expatriate solidarity. At first, the Mariel boatlift prompted an outpouring of sympathy and mobilization. Exiles from the 1960s and early 1970s not only rushed to hire boats to Cuba to pick up their relatives but also mobilized to help with migrant processing in tent cities that popped up across Miami. They interpreted the Mariel migrants' departures from the island as the next chapter in their own saga of anticommunist exodus. But as much as the so-called Marielitos' stories of what they had experienced in socialist Cuba provided new reasons to indict the Cuban government, their welcome proved conditional against the backdrop of a city in the midst of an economic downturn and suspicions that "new arrivals" were "less than" their predecessors, as had occurred on a lesser scale in the late 1960s. On the one hand, Mariel migrants would help raise consciousness in the diaspora about certain episodes in Cuba in the 1960s and 1970s that were scarcely known to that point.[20] On the other, the Cuban government's characterization of the migrants as "lumpen" and "delinquents" abetted rumors that officials on the island had used the migration to "empty" Cuban prisons and psychiatric institutions to a much larger degree than turned out to be the case.[21] The U.S. government, meanwhile, pivoted away from its more or less unconditional open-door policy for Cuban migrants in the 1960s and 1970s, detaining thousands of Mariel migrants in far-flung prisons and military facilities across the country and ultimately deeming some 2,700 ineligible for admission at all. These antecedents turned a crime wave in Miami that came in the migrants' wake into a moral panic, and it left a stigma around the Marielitos that persists to this day.[22]

For all of these reasons, Mariel became a memory scar on the Cuban body politic: easier to cover over than open the wound. As critic Iván de la Nuez has put it, the boatlift remains "an unclassifiable shore in Cuban culture [and history, I would add] that still has not been deciphered in many respects." Mariel migrants found themselves "stuck between a communist government that kicked them out of the country because they did not fit in with their utopia of a perfect future and a conservative exile community that could never completely assimilate them because they did not fit in their fantasy of a perfect past."[23] Still, it is remarkable how soon after such a seismic event life in Cuba and the diaspora began to resume old form. Today, the 1980s are remembered by many Cubans on both sides of the Florida Straits as hopeful junctures in one way or another, not as a period characterized by the Mariel boatlift's persistent ripple effects.

In Miami, for example, many Cuban Americans think of the 1980s as the decade of their political and economic ascendance in the United States. Indeed, it was in the 1980s that the identity label "Cuban American" gained most traction in South Florida, in part as a way to emphasize a memory narrative of social integration and gratitude for U.S. support now that the Reagan administration had abandoned policies of "coexistence" and détente. Yet the term also implicitly distanced older migrants, and increasingly their U.S.-born or U.S.-raised children, from the memory of those other Cubans, the Marielitos, portrayed as criminals and drug dealers to such devastating stereotypical effect in 1983's blockbuster remake of the mob classic *Scarface*. Seeking to restore the community's national reputation, civic organizations like Facts about Cuban Exiles, founded in 1982, began publishing pamphlets highlighting the contributions to U.S. society principally of those exiles who had come first.[24]

This is not to say there were no Mariel success stories. There were. But it is also true that some members of the established exile enclave discriminated against the newer migrants, especially those who did not have family connections or were persons of color.[25] The Marielitos' more challenging and, by statistical comparison, less robust path to upward mobility in the United States was not, and is still not, fully recognized within most salient memory narratives in the community that celebrate Cuban immigrant achievements.[26] Regardless, the 1980s would go down as the decade of rising Cuban American political triumphalism and a transition to ethnic (not just exile) politics, with more and more community members embracing the Republican Party and beginning to run for local, state, and national office. Even the once iconoclastic members of Agrupación Abdala found themselves abandoning their anti-imperialist historical imaginary and soliciting audiences at the Reagan White House. On their last legs (the group would peter out mid-decade), they were soon eclipsed by newer and more powerful Cuban American lobbying arms.[27]

Just as the 1980s heralded a period of Cuban American political integration despite the effects of Mariel, the same era on the island would take on some trappings of renewed socialist achievement. In retrospect, many Cubans who lived through those years refer to the 1980s as the Revolution's golden age, as state stores were even more full of Cuban- and Soviet-made goods than they had been in the 1970s. The government also experimented with small allowances for free market forces and decentralization, no doubt prompted by the discontent exposed by Mariel itself. New political ideas were floating around, too. Cubans started to read about the processes of *glasnost* and *perestroika* in Spanish-language translations of Soviet magazines, though Fidel Castro resisted their application when he launched a so-called Rectification of Errors campaign mid-decade.[28] Regardless, artists took advantage of the more dynamic political climate to deconstruct the grand epic of the state, highlighting instead the more mundane, and sometimes bewildering, memories of children raised in the 1960s.[29] Famously, the lyrics of Carlos Varela's "Guillermo Tell" (William Tell), from 1989, suggested that it was time for the eponymous European folk hero to stop making his son the guinea pig for his famous stunt: shooting an arrow through an apple perched on the child's head. Against the backdrop of political rumblings in Eastern Europe and the fall of the Berlin Wall, lines like "and now it's the father's turn to put the apple on his head" sounded like thinly veiled threats, or at least a demand that younger Cubans finally be allowed to make history of their own.[30]

But we must also consider whether the nostalgia that one can find among some Cubans today for the relative openness, abundance, or critical potential of the 1980s is more a function of what came after. No Cuban could have anticipated the calamity just around the corner, let alone the deep cracks in the Revolution's historical armor that the fall of the Soviet Union would expose. Overall, the 1980s stand out as years in which dominant paradigms of collective identity and official memory on the island continued to benefit from substantial popular buy-in—even as a spirit of questioning, new citizen activism, and political debate also characterized the age. Perhaps, then, the wistfulness for the era that one sees in an increasing array of Cuban cultural production in the present is best understood as nostalgia for equal parts stability, relative abundance, and critical anticipation—a longing less for perfection than for a sense of vague possibility that in the 1990s would quickly fade.[31]

After the Fall

Following the disintegration of the Soviet Union and the Eastern bloc, the new crisis Cubans experienced made Mariel seem a distant memory. Materially and existentially, Cubans' worlds were utterly transformed. In the vortex of an unprecedented economic collapse, dominant public renditions of collective history from the revolutionary government began to exercise less of a hold on private sentiments and identities. How could it be otherwise when, in the midst of scarcity the likes of which few Cubans had ever known, the teleology of socialist progress seemed to largely, if not completely, implode?

The signs and sites of historic dislocation were as diverse as they were traumatic. Cubans watched as 80 percent of the island's foreign trade disappeared and Cuba's gross domestic product plummeted by one-third over a span of three years. Yet while the island's citizens were forced to undertake heroic efforts to get by, Fidel Castro framed the catastrophe euphemistically as a "Special Period in Times of Peace." In the summer of 1994, when 35,000 Cubans departed for the United States in makeshift rafts at the government's invitation (echoing the events of 1980), those staying behind gathered on the shores to wish their compatriots well, not shout them down as traitors as they had fourteen years before. After that point, as migration reverted to being regulated but nonetheless continued at a brisk pace, leaving the island would no longer be so automatically treated as a sign of disloyalty so much as a shared national tragedy, especially in film, literature, and song.[32]

Symbols of a maligned capitalist past also began returning with a vengeance. To deal with the crisis, the Cuban government opened the door gingerly to foreign capital and welcomed Western tourists into joint-venture hotels from which Cubans were now barred. Authorities legalized the U.S. dollar that had already begun circulating on the black market, allowed Cubans to start a tightly limited range of small businesses, and created a parallel system of stores where Cubans could spend hard currency to purchase imported food, toiletries, and other "luxuries." Such revenues did help keep basic achievements of the socialist welfare state like universal health care and education from falling apart completely. Yet mass-market tourism, a surge in prostitution, and rising inequality—all hallmarks of the prerevolutionary era in the socialist imaginary—left disenchanting scars. The relatively classless society that the Revolution had ushered in, especially in the more prosperous 1970s and 1980s, disappeared amid sharp new differences between those with access to remittances or tourists' tips and those without. Meanwhile, due to a lack of proper maintenance and materials, Cuba's decayed early to mid-twentieth-century building stock seemed to be receding not advancing in time, with more and more buildings collapsing to the ground.

In this back to the future scenario, Cuban leaders in some ways could do little more than urge citizens to "resist" and keep the faith. Trouba-

Figure C.1. The Revolution as timeless history and eternal marketing campaign. José Ángel Toirac, "Eternity," from the series *Waiting for the Right Time*, 2019. Oil on canvas, 78.25 × 118.25 inches. Courtesy of the artist and Pan American Art Projects, Miami, FL. Based on a painting originally created for the series *Tiempos modernos*, 1995–97.

dours like Silvio Rodríguez, while acknowledging his doubts about Cuba's "destiny," encouraged his listeners to hold on to their ideals and not "repent" for the causes in which they had believed, even if the world outside of the island's confines was pointing to capitalism's inevitability.[33] Nonetheless, other Cubans began sarcastically joking about the inescapable distance between postsocialist reality and the socialist historical promise that the Cuban government insisted on defending. "Since my Cuba is 100 percent Cuban," ironized singer Pedro Luis Ferrer in 1994, "tomorrow I'll reserve the best hotel in Havana."[34] Cuba's revolutionary history itself, it now seemed to artists like José Ángel Toirac, had long been marketed to the island's citizens as just another capitalist commodity, much as it was now being sold in travel agencies around the world as a sign of "otherness" and intrigue. As foreign reporters, photographers, and writers descended on the island to capture the elegiac inspiration of its crumbling buildings, Cuba resembled a land of fetishized ruins as much as a place where the struggle for equality and social justice were still alive.[35] Ironically, a country that had once endeavored to leave its past so decisively behind increasingly reaped the financial benefits of being peddled to nostalgia- and vintage-car-seeking visitors from Canada and Europe as "frozen in time"—that is, in the 1950s. And a historical process, the Cuban Revolution, once synonymous with radical change was resisting it, trying to extend its life into eternity.

It was only natural in this context that hegemonic frameworks of national remembering and forgetting, as well as some of their components, underwent some rewriting. For starters, Cuba's government amended the island's constitution, swapping references to the Soviet Union for more mentions of José Martí and recentering the long quest for national independence as the revolutionary government's primary reason for being. Cuban writers—whether through publishers at home or abroad—also began to exorcise parts of the Revolution's history dating to the 1960s that had been silenced or unconsciously buried.[36] Still, the targets of such indictments on the island had their limits, as they often addressed legacies of censorship, political exclusion, and social repression as "errors" of the revolutionary process rather than an indictment of the process itself. Thus, Cuban authors and essayists faced criticism outside the island for tacitly partaking in a damage-control strategy, one that allowed for a partial reconciliation in the cultural sphere without revisiting other injustices that exceeded it or holding responsible parties to account.[37] "The errors of the Revolution are not the Revolution," says one of the main characters in the landmark 1993 film *Fresa y chocolate* (*Strawberry and Chocolate*), which alluded to legacies of antigay discrimination in the 1960s and 1970s in unprecedented but nonspecific ways. "But who pays the bill? Who answers for the errors?," asks the other.[38] On any number of fronts, Cubans are still waiting for a reply.

Still, the post-Soviet crisis paradoxically also granted renewed life to the Revolution's traditional anti-imperialist memory canon. As now influential Cuban American politicians urged Washington to accelerate the next communist domino's fall, the saga of Cuba's longer resistance to U.S. and Cuban exile aggression acquired renewed relevance. It is fair to say that Cubans on the whole were less than thrilled with their government, but a tightening and codification of U.S. economic sanctions in 1992 and 1996, during the depth of Cuba's economic emergency, also struck many as cruel.[39] By the early 2000s, therefore, Cuban leaders were profitably spinning socialism's survival as a memorable extension of the Revolution's historic resistance to U.S. government and Miami designs. And yet, the price of this "victory" was steep. As the writer Antonio José Ponte polemically hypothesized, the collapsed buildings of foreigners' fascinations may have actually served a politically useful purpose for the government beyond attracting tourist dollars: they made cityscapes look like war zones, inculcating in Cubans the message and memory that they lived in a nation under a decades-long siege.[40]

Exile Disappointments

In the Cuban diaspora, the Revolution's survival—albeit in adulterated form—was obviously a bitter pill to swallow. Many exiles and Cuban Americans had greeted the start of the 1990s confident that, after so many years of waiting, their moment of historic liberation had finally arrived. "Nuestro día ya viene llegando" ("Our day is coming"), belted out Cuban-born singer Willy Chirino in 1991.[41] Miami-based organizations rolled out national transition and recovery plans to follow the expected democratic spring.[42] But as the Cuban government cautiously reshaped the island's economy without ceding political control, Fidel Castro's opponents were deprived of deliverance. By the time academics launched projects to pave the way for transitional justice in a post-Castro future, road maps to promised reconciliation seemed more likely to collect dust than be put to immediate use.[43] The result was burning frustration and a sense of unfulfilled hopes. At moments of renewed tension in island-exile relations—such as the Cuban Air Force's downing of two planes from the exile rafter reconnaissance organization Brothers to the Rescue near Cuban airspace in 1996, or the 1999–2000 international custody battle over Elián González, a little boy found floating off Florida's coast—decades of built-up resentments exploded into demonstrations on Miami's streets.[44]

Ironically, while denouncing the government in Havana as an outdated relic that refused to budge, anti-Castro opponents in exile also began to resemble political mummies, at least to some observers. Despite initial predictions to the contrary, capital and not democratization reigned supreme in the post–Cold War world. By the end of the 1990s, Cuba appeared to many in the United States, and to many Cubans on the island for that matter, akin to other nations with whose authoritarian, even communist governments (e.g., China, Vietnam) Washington had found a way to profitably get along. Aging exile political leaders and younger activists saw themselves as the guardians of a memory of anticommunist exodus and struggle that they were not willing to give up. Yet average citizens on the island hankering at least for a bit more economic breathing room tended to see Miami's proembargo political class as intransigent defenders of failed sanctions who had become as trapped by history as the leaders of their own government and similarly refused to move on.

By the late 1990s, newer retrospective tensions were dividing the diaspora, too. The 1994 rafter crisis led to a diplomatic agreement facilitating more regular migration between Cuba and the United States. Thereafter, upward of 20,000 legal Cuban migrants began arriving in the United States each year, some of whom did not identify as "exiles" at all. Even more so than with the Mariel migration, these "recent arrivals'" memories were not of "the Republic" lost but of the socialism, or every-man-for-himself postsocialism, they left behind. As subsequent fluctuations in U.S. travel restrictions and Cuban law allowed, this group was also more insistent about maintaining transnational ties with Cuba by visiting and sending money to support relatives back home.[45] As a result, the face of the exile community once again began to change. In fact, the Cuba Nostalgia fair with which this conclusion began got started in 1999 not simply as an effort to revitalize the celebration of the "Cuba of yesteryear" popular since the 1960s. As Albert Laguna has argued, it also embodied "nostalgia for nostalgia"—a longing for a "simpler" time when all Cubans in Miami supposedly shared the same retrospective reference points and political beliefs, even as we know from this book that this was never completely the case.[46]

Plural Nostalgias, Plural Ourselves

Indeed, one of the more significant changes in the Cuban retrospective field during and since the 1990s is that Cuban nostalgia has taken on so many new forms, as already alluded to in the discussion of the 1980s above. Longing for an imagined past is no longer predominantly the purview of the "historic" exile community from the early 1960s (or their children), or even of exiles alone. To be sure, simplistic evocations of the prerevolutionary period in Miami persist. Newer Cuban migrants from the 1990s and onward have at times bought into or found ways to profit from their appeal.[47] But such expressions now compete with powerful, if sometimes less public and more sarcastic, expressions of wistfulness for the Russian cartoons and "Russian meat" (or *carne rusa*; think Soviet Spam) of more recent Cuban migrants' childhoods.[48] Naturally, such yearnings draw from similar currents on the island, where one can find plenty of artistic and literary evocations of a time when the Revolution commanded more genuine loyalty and guaranteed a more stable economic floor.[49] Again, this has been at the same time that a still officially "revolutionary" society eager to appeal to Western tourists has repeatedly found itself trafficking in the very idealizations of pre-1959 life so long linked to the conservative exile imaginary of a lost paradise.

Developments over the past twenty years have only intensified these dynamics. Old North American cars, vintage building facades, *and* guerrilla legends on political billboards? Cuba continues to sell itself to outsiders as, all at once, a socialist museum, a charming midcentury tropical playground, and an antihegemonic outlier resisting the global capitalist order. Internally, though, enough time has passed by now that widely circulated cultural texts published or produced on the island have also memorialized Cuba's harsh transition from the relative socialist functionality of the 1980s to the 1990s crisis, albeit in often politically correct and not frontally antigovernment terms.[50] These days, it is even possible to find Cubans nostalgic for the 1990s themselves—not for the economic deprivation, which continues to be a source of trauma, but for a sense of solidarity forged among neighbors, the solitude of long bike rides in a country without fuel, or the entertainment programs and music that provided a running distraction from daily life's penuries.[51] At the same time, greater transnationalism and internet access (especially after the creation of a national Wi-Fi infrastructure in 2015) have blurred the lines between strictly "exile" and "revolutionary" retrospective worlds. Many of the biggest stars of variety shows on Cuban state television in the 1980s and 1990s have moved to Miami, where they are fixtures of late-night Spanish-language lineups and frequently reprise generationally specific bits, characters, and other forms of cultural memory from their old shows.[52] Likewise, any third-generation Cuban American can hop on YouTube and familiarize her- or himself with a bootleg copy of an ICAIC film from the 1960s, just as a member of today's Union of Communist Youth can engage in heated argument with old classmates now abroad.

Such possibilities would seem to open more channels of communication between Cubans than ever before. Indeed, some Cubans have been searching for common narratives since the 1990s. Amid the mutual dislocations of the Special Period's catastrophe and the Revolution's inexplicable survival for the exile community, notable artistic, intellectual, and testimonial interventions—on and off the island, and in third countries— did attempt to chart the terms of possible reconciliations and or at least bridges to understanding.[53] Yet, while more recent projects have carried forth these ambitions, finding common ground is also arguably now a much more complex task.[54] While some state officials now at least elliptically acknowledge previously buried repressive episodes of the Revolution's internal history, they often minimize their severity.[55] More to the point, if part of the task that Cubans face moving forward is to practice an "ethics of recognition," as I have insisted, the "other" whose unique memories and historical understandings Cubans must confront has also become dizzyingly diverse.

In this book, "remembering the other" has meant grouping revolutionary and exile histories from the 1960s and 1970s as part of a common whole. It has meant acknowledging "revolutionaries" whose political platforms were not canonized by the revolutionary state and exiles who did not consign themselves to repeating simple anticommunist talking points. Yet, what are we to do with Cuban citizens who sincerely believed in the revolutionary project for thirty years, only to become disenchanted following the Soviet collapse? Or exiles who remained devotees of the anticommunist cause, but whose children have connected to the island recently by visiting? Can young Cubans and Cuban Americans today raised entirely after the Cold War be expected to remember "the Revolution" or the classically defined "exile experience" (if there is such a thing) if they never lived them? Certain features of the Cuban memory wars have no doubt remained the same since the 1960s, but they have also become unmoored from their origin points and assumed more varied form.

Actualizaciones, Normalization's Erasures

In recent years, though, arguably the most pressing challenges facing the Cuban memory landscape have been of a different, largely external order. The island's "time capsule" qualities have remained a recurring feature of its exotic appeal to outsiders for almost thirty years. But in the aftermath of the historic move by the United States and Cuba to begin normalizing relations in December 2014, the attractiveness of Cuba's temporal anomaly for foreign audiences became even more powerfully linked to its anticipated vanishing. "Get to Cuba now," everyone was told, "before it changes forever." "Voyeuristically," as Jennifer Lambe has written, rising numbers of travelers began to indulge "doomsday prophesy in depicting the encroachment of late industrial capitalism into a space of socialist alterity"—even more so than when the first post–Cold War tourists began visiting the island in the 1990s. But in the process, foreign fantasies about "Cuba's icons of past-in-present" actually "silenced Cuban history itself"—the revolutionary *and* the exile variety.[56] The voices, memories, and life stories of Cubans living in the island's supposed historical theme park, and its diasporic counterpart, were often overlooked.

When U.S. officials invoked Cuban history in the context of Barack Obama's normalization drive, it was as a cancer to be cured. "I know the history," the president told a rapt Havana audience when he visited the island in March 2016, referring to Cuba's tumultuous legacies of internal and Cold War conflict, "but I refuse to be trapped by it."[57] Young and old Cubans listened attentively, and with modest economic liberalization afoot since Fidel Castro retired due to illness in 2008—including a greater expansion of the private sector beginning in 2010—many were eager to agree. Yet the U.S. government had a funny way of deploying its own nostalgic totems in conjunction with its forward-looking policy. Consider the

Figure C.2. Cuba as history and memory theme park. In this satirical cartoon produced in the early months of the Obama normalization era, Cubans are reduced to promoting attractions like Porky's Cove (former Bay of Pigs) and selling Soviet souvenirs. Bruce McCall, "Life in the Cuba of Tomorrow," *New Yorker*, April 20, 2015, cover. © Condé Nast.

image of Secretary of State John Kerry at the 2015 reopening of the U.S. embassy in Havana a few months before Obama's arrival. In view behind his podium, event planners had parked vintage red, white, and blue North American cars from the 1950s so common on Cuba's streets. "This island was once ours," they seemed to metaphorically promise, "and it can be once more." Not surprisingly, the display bugged Cuban government loyalists wed to a retrospective imaginary that rejected the pretension of U.S. tutelage before 1959 as a national insult. In Kerry's diplomatic act of repossession, some regular Cubans also saw much of their history from the past fifty-plus years being displaced.[58] (Plenty of island residents, after all, still drive Russian Ladas from the 1970s and 1980s.)

In other ways, Cubans could not escape their past amid the hubbub of Obama-era détente, even if they tried. Together, external normalization and internal *actualización* (the term given to Raúl Castro's planned "update" of the socialist economy following his assumption of power from his brother) generated too many incentives to look back. If foreigners saw Cuba as a time capsule, Cubans living within its walls devised ingenious, even sarcastic ways to make a buck off the stereotype. It became fashionable, for example, for new privately owned restaurants to plaster their walls with vintage 1950s Coca-Cola signs. Cuba's first independent fashion label, Clandestina (a nod to the term, *clandestinos*, used to describe anti-Batista urban underground activists in the 1950s), produced hip T-shirts that lightly poked fun at socialist agitprop. No longer just the work of the black market, the memorabilia business on the island came out into the open. In the heart of Old Havana, a privately run consignment shop called Memorias now helps Cubans find foreign and, when possible, U.S. buyers for their prerevolutionary and revolutionary-era trinkets.

On the other hand, not all Cubans had the luxury of simply treating the Revolution as kitsch to be sold or a conflict to be forgotten. The halting process of internal economic reform with which U.S. normalization intersected dredged up too many historical ironies to ignore. For instance, when the government of Raúl Castro launched its expanded opening to private enterprise, some older Cubans logically thought of small businesses taken away during the Revolutionary Offensive of 1968. What had been the point? Intensifying economic inequalities amid the expansion of tourist spaces likewise raised fresh doubts about the future of the Cuban government's famed commitment to social equality.[59] But on a more positive note, Cuban writers, artists, and filmmakers also took advantage of these dislocations to push their own treatments of Cuban socialism's past into even more daring critical terrain. In dozens of works of theater, film, documentary, and visual art over the last ten to fifteen years, Cubans young and old—and now often operating outside government-sponsored cultural institutions thanks to digital technology—have revisited, dug up, and thoughtfully revaluated chapters of the Revolution's history still due for a proper accounting.[60]

All the same, amid these ground-up forms of contesting, or complicating, the "official" revolutionary memory canon, the Cuban government has continued to adhere to its familiar commemorative calendar and modes of mnemonic reproduction. Officials looked to the past during the Obama era to communicate the message that normalization with the United States and internal reform did not mean clearing the memory slate. At international summits, President Obama dutifully listened as Cuban government representatives with whom his government was now on better terms read him a list of U.S. and Cuban exile aggressions against the island from before he was born.[61] At home, meanwhile, old memory symbols still had their use, and familiar anniversaries continued to be celebrated. Who better to sit on the dais at the Sixth Congress of the Cuban Communist Party in 2011—where Cuban officials approved their new economic road map—than the now aging Nemesia Rodríguez, the girl with the "little white shoes" from Playa Girón, and on the Bay of Pigs invasion's fiftieth anniversary to boot? (She would also appear at the Seventh Party Congress in 2016.)[62]

Meanwhile, Cuban exiles and Cuban Americans, especially those surviving from the 1960s generation, ruefully watched as U.S. travelers donning floral shirts bypassed memory claims grounded in anti-Castro opposition. Parts of Miami felt like they were in memory crisis, as the process of normalization separated U.S.-Cuba policy from the bearers of post-1959 exilic pain. In response, diverse actors clamored to make the case that their memories still mattered. Bacardí, for example—the iconic, originally Cuban spirits company nationalized in 1960 and later rebuilt abroad—began advertising its *real* Havana Club rum brand as a truer gateway to Cuba's "golden age" of "decadence" and "freedom" than the version being hawked by the communist state. (Was there really "freedom" in Cuba in the Batista-era 1950s?)[63] Miami, though, was no longer just the home of the "real Cuba" of older exiles' nostalgic fantasies. Ongoing out-migration, but also new circular migration patterns to and from the island (made possible by new synergies between U.S. and Cuban migration laws) were dramatically reshaping the city. With so many newer Cuban émigrés now visiting home regularly, maintaining formal residency on the island, and even sending money there to support private businesses from afar, one could be forgiven for thinking that the memory wars of old were destined to fade.[64]

Figure C.3. Exile nostalgia redux. "The Golden Age Aged Well." Online advertisement from Bacardi's "The Real Havana Club" marketing campaign, 2016.

Polarization's Resurgence

And yet, the past four years have confirmed a different reality. In the wake of Donald Trump's election and Fidel Castro's death in late 2016, the Cuban memory wars have come back with force. Rhetorically, the U.S. and Cuban governments have been busy replaying some of their Cold War greatest hits. Meanwhile, the old guard in exile, their descendants, and newer Cuban migrants frustrated with the pace of change on the island, have felt empowered to advocate again for a more aggressive U.S. posture toward Cuba. Historic vindication, they insist, lies just around the corner of stronger sanctions or the next Cuban economic calamity. Some have even attempted to renew appreciation for *el exilio*'s more violent anti-Castro militants from the 1960s and 1970s.[65] The Cuban government, in turn, slowed the pace of its economic opening in 2017 and dug in its political and historical heels.[66] No matter what Washington or Miami threw at them, they insisted, the Revolution would endure.

Consequently, Cubans on the island have been treated to particularly prominent memory revivals of late. In some ways, the death of Fidel Castro in November 2016 seemed the logical bookend to an era in which old hostilities between Cuba and the United States, and perhaps between

Cubans, were dissipating. But coming just weeks after the Trump election, that event ended up fueling a revolutionary rebirth, at least symbolically. Castro's remains took several days to travel from Havana to their final resting place in the eastern city of Santiago de Cuba, retracing the *comandante*'s mythical journey to the Cuban capital at the Revolution's start. As an at turns faithful and tacitly obligated Cuban citizenry chanted, "I am Fidel!" at various stations along the funeral cortege, the cult of personality around Castro's figure appeared both understated—no statues, by the deceased's own orders—and all-consuming. Fidel himself in life frequently spoke of the Revolution as a collective project. "What is the revolutionary government without the people?," he insisted in 1961.[67] Yet in the wake of his death, and in the four-plus years since, Cuban media discourses have at times appeared to reduce the history of Cuban socialism to a montage of one man's work.[68]

Faced with tightened U.S. sanctions and intensified Miami hostility, Cuba's leaders have also turned to social media to reinforce their claims to historical legitimacy. In addition to frequently invoking the memory of Fidel, under the hashtag "#TenemosMemoria" ("#We Have Memory"), Cuban diplomats, state-sponsored information warriors, and even Cuba's first post-Castro head of state, Miguel Díaz-Canel (who assumed office in 2018), now routinely tweet reminders of Washington and exile aggressions, the costs of the U.S. embargo, social conditions on the island before the Revolution, or the Batista's regime's violence that Miami's commemorative habits studiously avoid. Ironically, for a government that still calls itself revolutionary, the Díaz-Canel administration branded itself early on as representing historical "continuity" ("#SomosContinuidad"). But "continuity" provides limited consolation as Cubans face a more proximate historical apparition. Recently, the effects of the COVID-19 epidemic on global tourism have forced the government to reconsider economic reform, but the island's economy was already reeling from a series of international stressors, including the economic collapse of close ally Venezuela and a sharp decline in U.S. visitors. This has left many average citizens feeling that they are living a new "Special Period" of privation and scarcity.[69]

Forever Memory Wars

The Cuban Revolution came to power in 1959 as a broad political front uniting Cubans of diverse backgrounds and political persuasions around an overwhelming push for change. Yet if one objective drew the population to insurgent leaders, it was the hope of breaking the cycles of "desire and disenchantment" to which Cuban history had for so long appeared condemned.[70] Sixty years later, and despite all the water under the bridge,

José Ramón Cabañas ✓
@JoseRCabanas

La traducción de la frase "to support the Cuban people" dicha en inglés desde Washington en estos días significa en español retrotraer a #Cuba a la situación anterior a 1959, borrar de la memoria los últimos 60 años. Aquí van algunas cifras de aquella época. #TenemosMemoria

65 % de los médicos estaban en la capital, aún cuando esta tenía solo el 22 % de la población.

2 026 enfermeras existían en 1959.

60 niños fallecidos por cada 1 000 nacidos vivos era la mortalidad infantil.

98 hospitales y un sistema de casas de socorro que ofrecían servicios limitados de primeros auxilios.

62 % de las camas hospitalarias se encontraban en La Habana.

58 años era la esperanza de vida al nacer.

8 % y menos de la población rural recibía atención médica gratuita. El acceso a los hospitales del Estado, siempre repletos, solo era posible mediante la recomendación de un magnate político que le exigía al desdichado su voto y el de toda su familia.

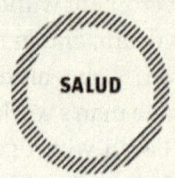
SALUD

45 % de los niños de seis a 14 años no asistían a las escuelas. En las escuelas públicas de cada 100 niños que matriculaban solo seis llegaban al sexto grado.

500 000 niños sin escuelas.

La enseñanza media y superior estaba reservada para una minoría. Habían más de medio millón de niños sin escuelas.

Decenas de miles de niños estaban obligados a trabajar para paliar el hambre en sus casas.

23,6 % de la población mayor de diez años era analfabeta y existían más de 1 000 000 de personas que no sabían leer ni escribir.

La enseñanza media llegaba solo a la mitad de la población escolar.

EDUCACIÓN

1:16 PM · May 21, 2019 · Twitter Web Client

Figure C.4. #TenemosMemoria ("#WeHaveMemory"). Samples from a prominent Cuban government Twitter slogan amid the resharpening of tensions with the United States (and the Cuban exile community), 2019. On the left, a tweet from Cuban ambassador to the United States José Ramón Cabañas, May 21, 2019, that reads, "The English phrase 'to support the Cuban people,' used in Washington these days, translates in Spanish as to send Cuba back to the [country's] situation before 1959, erasing from memory the last sixty years. Here are some statistics from that era. #WeHaveMemory." On the right, a tweet from Cuba's Ministry of Foreign Relations, May 20, 2019, that reads, "On May 20, 1902, burdened by the intervention of U.S. imperialism, the Cuban Republic was proclaimed. Only in 1959, with the triumph of the Revolution, did the Republic achieve its true independence. They would like to return us to that [prior] state of submission. #WeHaveMemory."

Cancillería de Cuba
@CubaMINREX

El #20Mayo de 1902, lastrada por la mediación del imperialismo de #EEUU se proclamó la República de #Cuba. Una república que solo en 1959, con el triunfo de la #Revolución, logró su verdadera independencia. A ese estado de sumisión desean que regresemos. Nosotros #TenemosMemoria.

CONTRA MI TIERRA, NO NOS ENTENDEMOS

CON LA #LEYGARROTE NO NOS ENTENDEMOS

HELMS BURTON

8:04 AM · May 20, 2019 · Twitter for Android

the myth of "subjunctive possibility" for many Cubans—the "now, finally" of the Cuban historical imagination—remains unfulfilled.[71] Ostensibly, both die-hard revolutionaries and disillusioned émigrés still want nothing more than to leave the past behind, whether to finally achieve socialism's utopia of equitable development and human solidarity, or to bring about the supposed panacea of the Cuban Revolution's demise. Neither seems close to fulfilling their goal.

Is there a solution? Will the Cuban people ever find retrospective peace? Can historicizing and deconstructing competing narratives of the Cuban past, as this book has, unsettle persistent polarizations enough to begin clearing the way for a new beginning? Or does recovering complicated fronts of memory struggle during the Revolution's first two decades, or since, further muddy the field when it would be better to forget and declare a clean break?[72]

The job of the historian of retrospective politics is chiefly to chart the evolution of diverse claims made in the name of memory and history, not necessarily to legitimate or undermine them.[73] This book has endeavored to adhere to that creed. Yet, in the narrative choices it has made, the erasures it has contested, and hopefully in the truths it has revealed, this study also inevitably intervenes in the Cuban retrospective field. Still, if this book is a participant in the Cuban memory wars as much as an observer of them, I especially hope it opens pathways for Cubans to incorporate their conflicts over the past as part of a new understanding of their nation's history. Again, the result may not, and probably should not, be consensus. But unless they—we—try to take a broader view, I worry Cubans will be condemned to perpetuating, or at best sublimating, old divisions eternally.

Today, though, one must admit that the possibilities of reaching anything like common ground seem remote. The Cuban retrospective field is full of paradox, overlapping nostalgias, and more thoughtful reflections than in the past. Those who experienced the beginning stages of the Cuban conflict are aging and rapidly disappearing. Yet biology provides little consolation, as memory polarizations of old are recycled in fresh public echo chambers. The contours of an "ethics of recognition" occasionally pop up in the arts or daily life, only to disappear under the trenchant antinomies of dominant political discourses on both sides of the Florida Straits. "I do not want to remember," says the main character in the novel *Memories of Underdevelopment*, which became the famous 1968 film. "I do not want to have inconsolable memories."[74] For now, and maybe for the foreseeable future, Cubans appear to have little choice.

Notes

Abbreviations

CECR
   Cruzada Educativa Cubana Records, Cuban Heritage Collection, University of Miami Libraries, Coral Gables, Fla.
El Miami Herald
   EMH
JMCP
   José Miró Cardona Papers, Cuban Heritage Collection, University of Miami Libraries, Coral Gables, Fla.
Miami Herald
   MH
Noticias de Hoy
   NH
Prensa Libre
   PL

Introduction

1. Revolution Square refers to the iconic Havana site of official mass rallies, originally envisioned in the 1950s as "Civic Square" but converted into a site of political mobilization for the revolutionary government beginning in 1959. The building known as Freedom Tower, located on Biscayne Bay in downtown Miami, was home to the U.S.-government-sponsored Cuban Refugee Program in the 1960s.

2. Steve J. Stern, *Remembering Pinochet's Chile: On the Eve of London 1998* (Durham, N.C.: Duke University Press, 2006), xxvii.

3. L. P. Hartley, *The Go-Between* (New York: New York Review Books, 2002 [1953]). Also see David Lowenthal, *The Past Is a Foreign Country* (Cambridge: Cambridge University Press, 1985).

4. Lillian Guerra, *Visions of Power in Cuba: Revolution, Redemption, and Resistance, 1959–1971* (Chapel Hill: University of North Carolina Press, 2012), 5.

5. For example, Rafael Rojas, *Tumbas sin sosiego: Revolución, disidencia y exilio del intelectual cubano* (Barcelona: Anagrama, 2006); and Rojas, *La máquina del olvido: Mito, historia y poder en Cuba* (Mexico City: Taurus, 2011).

6. Louis A. Pérez Jr., *The Structure of Cuban History: Meanings and Purpose of the Past* (Chapel Hill: University of North Carolina, 2013), 1.

7. Nicola Miller, "The Absolution of History: Uses of the Past in Castro's Cuba," *Journal of Contemporary History* 38, no. 1 (2003): 147–62; Kate Quinn, "Cuban Historiography in the 1960s: Revisionists, Revolutionaries, and the Nationalist Past," *Bulletin of Latin American Research* 26, no. 3 (2007): 378–98; Pablo Alonso González, *Cuban Cultural Heritage: A Rebel Past for a Revolutionary Nation* (Gainesville: University Press of Florida, 2018).

8. María de los Ángeles Torres, *In the Land of Mirrors: Cuban Exile Politics in the United States* (Ann Arbor: University of Michigan Press, 1999).

9. For example, Ruth Behar, ed., *Bridges to Cuba / Puentes a Cuba* (Ann Arbor: University of Michigan Press, 1995); Andrea O'Reilly Herrera, ed., *Remembering Cuba: Legacy of a Diaspora* (Austin: University of Texas Press, 2001); María de los Ángeles Torres, ed., *By Heart / De Memoria: Cuban Women's Journeys in and out of Exile* (Philadelphia: Temple University Press, 2003).

10. Anita Casavantes Bradford, *The Revolution Is for the Children: The Politics of Childhood in Havana and Miami, 1959-1962* (Chapel Hill: University of North Carolina Press, 2014); Devyn Spence Benson, "Owning the Revolution: Race, Revolution, and Politics from Havana to Miami, 1959-1963," *Journal of Transnational American Studies* 4, no. 2 (2012), https://escholarship.org/uc/item/5sb9d392; Jennifer L. Lambe, "Drug Wars: Revolution, Embargo, and the Politics of Scarcity in Cuba, 1959-1964," *Journal of Latin American Studies* 49, no. 3 (2017): 489-516; Lambe, *Madhouse: Psychiatry and Cuban History* (Chapel Hill: University of North Carolina Press, 2016); Iraida H. López, *Impossible Returns: Narratives of the Cuban Diaspora* (Gainesville: University Press of Florida, 2015).

11. Damián J. Fernández, "Cuba and lo Cubano, or the Story of Desire and Disenchantment," in *Cuba, the Elusive Nation: Interpretations of National Identity*, ed. Damián J. Fernández and Madeline Cámara Betancourt (Gainesville: University Press of Florida, 2000), 79-98.

12. The literature on Cuba's wars of independence is vast. This account draws principally from Louis A. Pérez Jr., *Cuba between Empires, 1878-1902* (Pittsburgh: University of Pittsburgh Press, 1998).

13. On the Cuban Republic through 1933, see Louis A. Pérez Jr., *Cuba under the Platt Amendment, 1902-1934* (Pittsburgh: University of Pittsburgh Press, 1991); Lillian Guerra, *The Myth of José Martí: Conflicting Nationalisms in Early Twentieth-Century Cuba* (Chapel Hill: University of North Carolina Press, 2005); and Robert Whitney, *State and Revolution in Cuba: Mass Mobilization and Political Change, 1920-1940* (Chapel Hill: University of North Carolina Press, 2001).

14. Whitney, *State and Revolution in Cuba*; Frank Argote-Freyre, *Fulgencio Batista: From Revolutionary to Strongman* (New Brunswick, N.J.: Rutgers University Press, 2006). In this book, I lowercase "communist party" in reference to the Cuban party that existed before the Revolution. Formed in the 1920s, it was known as the Communist Party of Cuba until 1944, when it changed its name to the Popular Socialist Party. I discuss the relationship of this party with Fidel Castro's 26th of July Movement and the revolutionary government that took power in 1959 further in chapter 1.

15. Charles Ameringer, *Cuba's Democratic Experience: The Auténtico Years, 1944-1952* (Gainesville: University Press of Florida, 2000); Ilan Ehrlich, *Eduardo Chibás: The Incorrigible Man of Cuban Politics* (Lanham, Md.: Rowman and Littlefield, 2015); Lillian Guerra, *Heroes, Martyrs, and Political Messiahs in Revolutionary Cuba, 1946-1958* (New Haven, Conn.: Yale University Press, 2018).

16. Guerra, *Heroes, Martyrs*, 74-121; Jonathan M. Hansen, *Young Castro: The Making of a Revolutionary* (New York: Simon and Schuster, 2019), 85-117.

17. See, for example, Jesse Horst, "Shantytown Revolution: Slum Clearance, Rent Control, and the Cuban State, 1937-1955," *Journal of Urban History* 40, no. 4 (July 2014): 699-

718; Kelly Urban, "Plagued by Politics: Cuba's National Sanatorium Project, 1936–59," *Bulletin of the History of Medicine* 91, no. 4 (2017): 772–801; and Guerra, *Heroes, Martyrs*, 92–96.

18. Louis A. Pérez Jr., *Rice in the Time of Sugar: The Political Economy of Food in Cuba* (Chapel Hill: University of North Carolina Press, 2019), 111; Pérez, *On Becoming Cuban: Identity, Nationality, and Culture* (Chapel Hill: University of North Carolina Press, 2008 [1999]), 445–68.

19. Literature on the anti-Batista struggle is expansive. In addition to Guerra, *Heroes, Martyrs*, see Thomas G. Paterson, *Contesting Castro: The United States and the Triumph of the Cuban Revolution* (New York: Oxford University Press, 1994); and Julia E. Sweig, *Inside the Cuban Revolution: Fidel Castro and the Urban Underground* (Cambridge, Mass.: Harvard University Press, 2002).

20. Pérez, *The Structure of Cuban History*, 238.

21. "Discurso pronunciado por el Comandante Fidel Castro Ruz, primer secretario del Comité Central del Partido Comunista de Cuba y Primer Ministro del Gobierno Revolucionario, en el resumen de la velada conmemorativa de los cien años de lucha, efectuada en La Demajagua, monumento nacional, Manzanillo, Oriente," October 10, 1968, http://www.cuba.cu/gobierno/discursos/1968/esp/f101068e.html.

22. Jennifer L. Lambe and Michael J. Bustamante, "Cuba's Revolution from Within: The Politics of Historical Paradigms," in *The Revolution from Within: Cuba, 1959–1980*, ed. Michael J. Bustamante and Jennifer L. Lambe (Durham, N.C.: Duke University Press, 2019), 5.

23. Rafael Rojas, "Diaspora and Memory in Cuban Literature," in *Cuba: Idea of a Nation Displaced*, ed. Andrea O'Reilly Herrera (Albany: State University of New York Press, 2003), 241.

24. Nelson Valdés, "Cuban Political Culture: Between Betrayal and Death," in *Cuba in Transition: Crisis and Transformation*, ed. Sandor Halebsky and John M. Kirk (Boulder, Colo.: Westview, 1992), 207–28.

25. Jean-Paul Sartre, *Sartre on Cuba* (New York: Ballantine, 1961), 88.

26. See Michael J. Bustamante, "'Cartearse con el Exterior': Notes toward a Lost Correspondence," *Beyond the Sugar Curtain* (blog), May 2017, https://www.brown.edu/research/projects/tracing-cuba-us-connections/news/2017/05/"cartearse-con-el-exterior".

27. On U.S.-centrism in Cuban historiography, see Lambe and Bustamante, "Cuba's Revolution from Within"; and Jennifer L. Lambe, "Whither the Empire?," in Lambe and Bustamante, *The Revolution from Within*, 306–17.

28. Román de la Campa, *Cuba on My Mind: Journeys to a Severed Nation* (New York: Verso, 2000).

29. Fernando Ortiz, *Cuban Counterpoint: Tobacco and Sugar*, trans. Harriet de Onís (Durham, N.C.: Duke University Press, 1995 [1940]).

30. Peter Burke, "History as Social Memory," in *Memory: History, Culture and the Mind*, ed. Thomas Butler (Oxford, U.K.: Blackwell, 1989), 97–113.

31. I borrow this concept from Jeffrey K. Olick, introduction to *States of Memory: Continuities, Conflicts, and Transformations in National Retrospection*, ed. Jeffrey K. Olick (Durham, N.C.: Duke University Press, 2003), 1–16.

32. José Quiroga, *Cuban Palimpsests* (Minneapolis: University of Minnesota Press, 2005), 2, emphasis added.

33. Quiroga, 2.

34. Marta Rojas, "Letra original del Himno del 26 de julio," *Radiorebelde.com*, n.d., http://www.radiorebelde.cu/26-julio-rebelde/himno26-versiones.html, emphasis added.

35. Alexandra T. Vázquez, *Listening in Detail: Performances of Cuban Music* (Durham, N.C.: Duke University Press, 2013), 79–80, emphasis added.

36. Jeffrey K. Olick, Vered Vinitzky-Seroussi, and Daniel Levy, introduction to *The Collective Memory Reader*, ed. Jeffrey K. Olick, Vered Vinitzky-Seroussi, and Daniel Levy (Oxford: Oxford University Press 2011), 2.

37. The seminal text is Maurice Halbwachs, *On Collective Memory*, trans. Lewis A. Coser (Chicago: University of Chicago Press, 1992 [1941, 1952]).

38. Olick, Vinitzky-Seroussi, and Levy, introduction, 19.

39. Stern, *Remembering Pinochet's Chile*, 1, 105.

40. Jeffrey K. Olick, "Collective Memory: The Two Cultures," *Sociological Theory* 17, no. 3 (1999): 338–48; Wulf Kansteiner, "Finding Meaning in Memory: A Methodological Critique of Collective Memory Studies," *History and Theory* 41, no. 2 (2002): 179–97.

41. Jean Franco, *The Decline and Fall of the Lettered City: Latin America in the Cold War* (Cambridge, Mass.: Harvard University Press, 2002), 253.

42. Allan Megill, *Historical Knowledge, Historical Error: A Contemporary Guide to Practice* (Chicago: University of Chicago Press, 2007), 41–62.

43. Manuel Moreno Fraginals, "La historia como arma," *Casa de las Américas* 7, no. 40 (January–February 1967): 20–28.

44. For example, Eduardo Suárez Rivas, *Los días iguales* (Miami: n.p., 1974).

45. Olick, introduction to *States of Memory*, 6.

46. Frederick C. Corney, *Telling October: Memory and the Making of the Bolshevik Revolution* (Ithaca, N.Y.: Cornell University Press, 2004), 10.

47. Jorge Macle Cruz, "Writing the Revolution's History Out of Closed Archives? Cuban Archival Laws and Access to Information," in Lambe and Bustamante, *The Revolution from Within*, 47–63.

48. On the challenges of historicizing the Cuban Revolution through oral history, see Elizabeth Dore, "Cubans' Life Stories: The Pains and Pleasures of Living in a Communist Society," *Oral History* 40, no. 1 (2012): 35–46.

49. Grethel Domenech Hernández, "*Pan fresco*: Una heterotopía para los estudios cubanos," *Hypermedia Magazine*, December 30, 2019, https://www.hypermediamagazine.com/critica/pan-fresco.

50. See Yvon Grenier et al., "¿Cuándo terminó la Revolución Cubana? Una discusión," *Cuban Studies* 47 (2019): 143–65.

51. Michael Casey, *Che's Afterlife: The Legacy of an Image* (New York: Vintage, 2009). On contested memories of the children's exodus known as Operation Pedro Pan between 1960 and 1962, see Anita Casavantes Bradford, "Remembering Pedro Pan: Childhood and Collective Memory Making in Havana and Miami, 1960–2000," *Cuban Studies* 44 (2016): 283–308. On the conflicts over the legacy of the "Struggle against Bandits," a counterinsurgency campaign against anti-Castro rebels in Cuba between 1960 and 1966, see Lillian Guerra, "Beyond Paradox: Counterrevolution and the Origins of Political Culture in the Cuban Revolution, 1959–2009," in *A Century of Revolution: Insurgent and Counterinsurgent Violence during Latin America's Long Cold War*, ed. Greg Grandin and Gilbert M. Joseph (Durham, N.C.: Duke University Press, 2010), 199–235.

52. Here I would include memory battles over the forced labor camps between 1965 and 1968 known as the Unidades Militares de Ayuda a la Producción (Military Units to Aid Production, UMAP), Cuba's military involvement in the Angolan Civil War beginning in 1975, Cuban exile terrorism and political violence in the 1970s, and the Mariel boatlift of 1980. See Abel Sierra Madero, "El trabajo os hará hombres: Masculinización nacional, trabajo forzado y control social en Cuba durante los años 60," *Cuban Studies* 44 (2016): 309-49; Marisabel Almer, "Remembering Angola: Cuban Internationalism, Transnational Spaces, and the Politics of Memories" (PhD diss., University of Michigan, 2011); Alan McPherson, "Caribbean Taliban: Cuban American Terrorism in the 1970s," *Terrorism and Political Violence* 31, no. 2 (2019): 390-409; and Abel Sierra Madero, "Here, Everyone's Got Huevos, Mister! Nationalism, Sexuality, and Collective Violence in Cuba during the Mariel Exodus," in Lambe and Bustamante, *The Revolution from Within*, 244-74.

53. Carrie Hamilton, *Sexual Revolutions in Cuba: Passion, Politics, and Memory* (Chapel Hill: University of North Carolina Press, 2014); Michelle Chase, *Revolution within the Revolution: Women and Gender Politics in Cuba, 1952-1962* (Chapel Hill: University of North Carolina Press, 2015); Rachel Hynson, *Laboring for the State: Women, Family, and Work in Revolutionary Cuba, 1959-1971* (Cambridge: Cambridge University Press, 2020); Devyn Spence Benson, *Antiracism in Cuba: The Unfinished Revolution* (Chapel Hill: University of North Carolina Press, 2016); Alejandro de la Fuente, *A Nation for All: Race, Inequality, and Politics in Twentieth-Century Cuba* (Chapel Hill: University of North Carolina Press, 2001), 219-334; Ian Lumsden, *Machos, Maricones, and Gays: Cuba and Homosexuality* (Philadelphia: Temple University Press, 1996); Susana Peña, *¡Oye Loca! From the Mariel Boatlift to Gay Cuban Miami* (Minneapolis: University of Minnesota Press, 2013).

54. See, for example, Maya J. Berry, "From 'Ritual' to 'Repertoire': Dancing to the Time of the Nation," *Afro-Hispanic Review* 29, no. 1 (2010): 55-76; Elizabeth Schwall, "The Footsteps of Nieves Fresneda: Cuban Folkloric Dance and Cultural Policy, 1959-1979," *Cuban Studies* 47 (2019): 35-56; and Spence Benson, "Owning the Revolution."

55. On the endurance of the Cuban ideology of "racelessness" under the Revolution and among Cuban exiles, see Spence Benson, *Antiracism in Cuba*, 122-52, 198-230. For an exception, see Christabelle Peters, *Cuban Identity and the Angolan Experience* (London: Palgrave, 2012), on the Cuban government's embrace of "Afro-Latinism" in the context of its military engagements on the African continent in the 1970s.

56. For example, Elizabeth Jelin, *State Repression and the Labors of Memory* (Minneapolis: University of Minnesota Press, 2003); Steve J. Stern, *Reckoning with Pinochet: The Memory Question in Democratic Chile, 1989-2006* (Durham, N.C.: Duke University Press, 2010); and Kirsten Weld, *Paper Cadavers: The Archives of Dictatorship in Guatemala* (Durham, N.C.: Duke University Press, 2014).

57. Guerra, "Beyond Paradox," 205-8.

58. Lambe and Bustamante, "Cuba's Revolution from Within," 7.

Chapter 1

1. *Album de la Revolución Cubana, 1952-1959* (Havana: Revista Cinegráfico, 1959).

2. "Postalitas," *Zig-zag*, May 9, 1959.

3. Louis A. Pérez Jr., *On Becoming Cuban: Identity, Nationality, and Culture* (Chapel Hill: University of North Carolina Press, 2008 [1999]), 483.

4. Lillian Guerra, *Visions of Power in Cuba: Revolution, Redemption, and Resistance, 1959–1971* (Chapel Hill: University of North Carolina Press, 2012), 37–74; Louis A. Pérez Jr., *The Structure of Cuban History: Meanings and Purpose of the Past* (Chapel Hill: University of North Carolina, 2013), 237–61.

5. Julia E. Sweig, *Inside the Cuban Revolution: Fidel Castro and the Urban Underground* (Cambridge, Mass.: Harvard University Press, 2002); Lillian Guerra, *Heroes, Martyrs, and Political Messiahs in Revolutionary Cuba, 1946–1958* (New Haven, Conn.: Yale University Press, 2018).

6. Fidel Castro, "Discurso pronunciado por el Comandante Fidel Castro Ruz, en el Parque Céspedes de Santiago de Cuba," January 1, 1959, http://www.cuba.cu/gobierno/discursos/1959/esp/f010159e.html.

7. Pérez, *The Structure of Cuban History*, 16.

8. Mario Llerena, title unknown, *El Mundo*, August 11, 1959, cited in Elaine Acosta González, "*El Mundo*," in *Prensa y revolución: La magia del cambio*, ed. María del Pilar Díaz Castañón (Havana: Ciencias Sociales, 2010), 30.

9. "Gibara: 17 de agosto, 1931," *PL*, August 16, 1959.

10. Pérez, *The Structure of Cuban History*, 238.

11. Nelson P. Valdés, "Cuban Political Culture: Between Betrayal and Death," in *Cuba in Transition: Crisis and Transformation*, ed. Sandor Halebsky and John M. Kirk (Boulder, Colo.: Westview, 1992), 207.

12. María del Pilar Díaz Castañón, "'We Demand, We Demand . . .' Cuba 1959: The Paradoxes of Year 1," in *The Revolution from Within: Cuba, 1959–1980*, ed. Michael J. Bustamante and Jennifer L. Lambe (Durham, N.C.: Duke University Press, 2019), 97.

13. Fidel Castro, *La historia me absolverá: Discurso pronunciado por el Dr. Fidel Castro ante el Tribunal de Urgencia de Santiago de Cuba el día 16 de octubre de 1953* (New York: Acción Cubana, ca. 1955); Antonio Rafael de la Cova, *The Moncada Attack: Birth of the Cuban Revolution* (Columbia: University of South Carolina Press, 2007).

14. Virgilio Piñera, "Nubes amenazadoras," *Revolución*, January 15, 1959.

15. Díaz Castañón, "'We Demand, We Demand,'" 98.

16. See Burt Glinn, *Cuba 1959* (New York: Reel Art, 2015); Mark Sanders, *Cuba in Revolution* (Ostfildern, Germany: Hatje Cantz, 2013); and Oswaldo Salas and Roberto Salas, *Fidel's Cuba: A Revolution in Pictures* (Hillsboro, Ore.: Beyond Words, 1998).

17. Dr. Pascual B. Marcos Vegueri, "No pasarán," *La Calle*, September 4, 1959.

18. Guerra, *Visions of Power*, 43.

19. Guerra, 42.

20. Michelle Chase, "The Trials: Violence and Justice in the Aftermath of the Cuban Revolution," in *A Century of Revolution: Insurgent and Counterinsurgent Violence during Latin America's Long Cold War*, ed. Greg Grandin and Gilbert M. Joseph (Durham, N.C.: Duke University Press, 2010), 163–98.

21. Sergio Carbó, "Cuba, ante todo," *PL*, January 17, 1959. The "March regime" refers to the date of Batista's 1952 coup: March 10.

22. "Sepultarán hoy a las víctimas del *Granma*," *PL*, February 9, 1959.

23. "El acto conmemorativo del segundo aniversario del ataque a palacio," *PL*, March 15, 1959; Sweig, *Inside the Cuban Revolution*, 18–19; Rafael Rojas, *Historia mínima de la Revolución Cubana* (Mexico City: Colegio de México, 2015), 67. Cuba's traditional communist party—even more opposed to insurgent tactics at the time of the attack, as we

will see—also called for celebrating the anniversary. See "Llama el PSP a conmemorar el 13 de marzo," *NH*, March 12, 1959.

24. Pablo Alonso González, *Cuban Cultural Heritage: A Rebel Past for a Revolutionary Nation* (Gainesville: University Press of Florida, 2018), 85.

25. Guerra, *Visions of Power*, 67-74. For film footage, see *Sexto aniversario*, directed by Julio García Espinosa (Havana: ICAIC, 1959).

26. "Tributo a los héroes del Cacahual," *La Calle*, December 9, 1959.

27. "Devolverán los restos del Dr. Antonio Guiteras," *La Calle*, December 12, 1959.

28. Carlos Rafael Rodríguez, "Contraste: Miami y Río Cristal," *NH*, June 25, 1960; "La Revolución victoriosa significará el triunfo de las esperanzas de todos," *NH*, June 25, 1960.

29. Ciro Bianchi Ross, "Aquel 20 de mayo," *Juventud Rebelde*, May 18, 2019, http://www.juventudrebelde.cu/columnas/lecturas/2019-05-18/aquel-20-de-mayo.

30. Howard N. Thompson, "El 20 de mayo, no. 1," *Bohemia*, May 17, 1959; Roberto Pérez de Acevedo, "Sentimiento de desilusión y amargura como fondo en el júbilo de la República naciente," *Bohemia*, May 22, 1959. Marial Iglesias has shown that, in fact, despite the recent U.S. military occupation and the imposition of the Platt Amendment, most Cubans did treat May 20, 1902, as a celebratory, nationalist new beginning. See Iglesias, *A Cultural History of Cuba during the U.S. Occupation, 1898-1902*, trans. Russ Davidson (Chapel Hill: University of North Carolina Press, 2011 [2003]).

31. "Veinte de mayo: Entonces y ahora," *Bohemia*, May 22, 1959.

32. Katherine Verdery, *The Political Lives of Dead Bodies: Reburial and Postsocialist Change* (New York: Columbia University Press, 1999).

33. "El gran recuento" (advertisement), *PL*, February 17, 1959; *Gesta inmortal*, directed by Eduardo Palmer (Havana: Cuban Color Films, 1959); *Surcos de libertad*, directed by Manuel de la Pedrosa (Havana: Cuban Color Films, 1959).

34. "*Historias de la Revolución*: Una película de raíz cubana," *La Calle*, January 16, 1960; "La vida comienza ahora" (advertisement), *NH*, July 31, 1960; *La vida comienza ahora*, directed by Antonio Vásquez Gallo (Havana: Cooperativa RKO de Cuba, 1960); Julio Antonio García Borrego, "*La vida comienza ahora* (1959), de Antonio Vázquez Gallo," *Cine Cubano: La Pupila Insomne* (blog), May 30, 2007, https://cinecubanolapupilainsomne.wordpress.com/2007/05/30/la-vida-comienza-ahora-1959-de-antonio-vazquez-gallo.

35. Ernesto "Che" Guevara, *Pasajes de la Guerra Revolucionaria* (Havana: Unión, 1964). These testimonies were first published as a series of articles in *Verde Olivo*, the magazine of Cuba's Revolutionary Armed Forces.

36. Jennifer Lambe, "The Medium Is the Message: The Screen Life of the Cuban Revolution, 1959-1962," *Past and Present* 246, no. 1 (February 2020): 227-67.

37. Díaz Castañón, "'We Demand, We Demand.'"

38. Guerra, *Visions of Power*, 45-47, 56-63.

39. González, *Cuban Cultural Heritage*, 106-7.

40. Iglesias, *Cultural History of Cuba*, 10-28.

41. "Niños escolares en la antigua catedral del crimen," *La Calle*, January 13, 1960; González, *Cuban Cultural Heritage*, 74-75.

42. "El Moncada transformado en centro escolar, será un gran homenaje de la Revolución a José Martí," *NH*, January 27, 1960.

43. "Ciudad Escolar '26 de Julio' inauguración 28 de enero 1960 9:00 a.m." (adver-

tisement), *NH*, January 28, 1960. Martí's poem, from the seminal *Versos sencillos* (*Simple Verses* [1891]), begins: "Cultivo una rosa blanca / en julio como en enero ..." ("I have a white rose to tend / in July as in January ...").

44. Manolo Marcer, "El pasado no volverá," *La Calle*, August 7, 1959.

45. Exact figures on the number of urban underground members remain elusive. Ronald Bonachea and Marta San Martín cite 10,000 before 1958. Lillian Guerra contends that the number was lower. Bonachea and San Martín, *The Cuban Insurrection, 1952-1959* (New Brunswick, N.J.: Transaction, 1974), 264; Guerra, *Heroes, Martyrs*, 226.

46. Robert Jackson Alexander, *A History of Organized Labor in Cuba* (Westport, Conn.: Praeger, 2002), 133-68; Sweig, *Inside the Cuban Revolution*, 120-47.

47. On the importance of the urban underground, see Sweig, *Inside the Cuban Revolution*.

48. Ilan Ehrlich, *Eduardo Chibás: The Incorrigible Man of Cuban Politics* (Lanham, Md.: Rowman and Littlefield, 2015); Guerra, *Heroes, Martyrs*, 26-122.

49. "65 jornadas heroicas," *La Calle*, July 26, 1959.

50. Sweig, *Inside the Cuban Revolution*, 29-38.

51. "Fidel Castro escribía sus artículos en nuestra redacción," *La Calle*, July 26, 1959.

52. Roberto Ardura, "El gran líder del adecentamiento político de Cuba," *La Calle*, August 16, 1959.

53. Photos appeared in *La Calle*, August 18, 1959. On the subsumed memory of Chibás after 1959, see Frank Argote-Freyre, "The Political Afterlife of Eduardo Chibás: Evolution of a Symbol, 1951-1991," *Cuban Studies* 32 (2001): 74-97.

54. Sergio Carbó, "Nuestra palabra," *PL*, January 1, 1959.

55. See, for instance, "Así combatía *Prensa Libre*," *PL*, December 29, 1959; and "Una aclaración al Comandante Guevara," *PL*, April 30, 1959.

56. Sergio Carbó, "No estorbemos a la verdadera revolución," *PL*, February 8, 1959.

57. "Las tesis hipócritas," *Combate*, March 17, 1959.

58. "Intervención en el mitin de la Sociedad de Amigos de la República, Acto del Muelle de Luz, 19 de noviembre 1955," in *Papeles del presidente: Documentos y discursos de José Antonio Echeverría Bianchi*, ed. Hilda Natalia Berdayes García (Havana: Abril, 2006), 50.

59. Fidel Castro to Ernesto "Che" Guevara, December 16, 1958, cited in Fidel Castro, *De la Sierra Maestra a Santiago de Cuba: La contraofensiva estratégica* (Havana: Publicaciones Consejo de Estado, 2010), 343-45.

60. Guerra, *Visions of Power*, 40-41.

61. See, for example, Enrique Rodríguez Loeches, "La generación del Trejo," *Combate*, October 3, 1959.

62. Felo Díaz, "Hombres de la Revolución: Eloy Gutiérrez Menoyo," *Actualidad Criolla*, n.d. (ca. January 1959), 8-11.

63. "Relato de la frustrada conspiración," *PL*, August 13, 1959; Andrés Zaldívar Diéguez and Pedro Etcheverry Vásquez, *Una fascinante historia: La conspiración trujillista* (Havana: Capitán San Luis, 2009); David Grann, "The Yankee *Comandante*: A Story of Love, Revolution, and Betrayal," *New Yorker*, May 28, 2012.

64. Robert Whitney, *State and Revolution in Cuba: Mass Mobilization and Political Change, 1920-1940* (Chapel Hill: University of North Carolina Press, 2001), 149-76.

65. Guerra, *Heroes, Martyrs*, 198-217.

66. "Batista Opens Terror Drive on Unions, CP," *Daily Worker*, August 5, 1953; "Fascist Terror Grips Cuba; Communists Ask U.S. Labor for Aid," *Daily Worker*, August 10, 1953.

67. For example, Raúl Castro attended a socialist-bloc sponsored youth conference in Vienna in 1953, after which he is reported to have traveled to Bucharest and Prague. On his return to the Americas by boat, he met Nikolai Leonov, a later influential KGB agent with whom he would retain a long relationship. Accounts vary, however, as to whether Raúl was at any point an actual member of the PSP-affiliated Socialist Youth, let alone the party as such, and for how long. One account that answers in the affirmative, though it mistakes the location of the youth conference as Prague, is Aleksandr Fursenko and Timothy Naftali, *One Hell of a Gamble: The Secret History of the Cuban Missile Crisis* (New York: W. W. Norton, 1998), 15, 37. Former PSP leader Lionel Soto echoes these claims in *De la historia y la memoria*, vol. 1 (Havana: SI-MAR SA, 2006). For a more conspiratorial account that alleges Soviet-linked forces were indirectly and directly guiding the 26th of July Movement all along, see César Reynel Aguilera, *El Soviet caribeño: La otra historia de la Revolución Cubana* (Buenos Aires: Penguin Random House, 2018).

68. On the relationship between the 26th of July Movement and the PSP, see Caridad Massón Sena, "El Partido Socialista Popular y la Revolución Cubana," in *Comunismo, socialismo y nacionalismo en Cuba (1920-1958)*, ed. Caridad Massón Sena (Havana: Instituto Cubano de Investigación Juan Marinello, 2013), 260-68; Sweig, *Inside the Cuban Revolution*, 120-35; Guerra, *Heroes, Martyrs*; and Samuel Farber, *The Origins of the Cuban Revolution Reconsidered* (Chapel Hill: University of North Carolina Press, 2006), 155-58.

69. On collaboration in the labor sector between PSP and 26th of July Movement members, see Steve Cushion, *A Hidden History of the Cuban Revolution: How the Working Class Shaped the Guerrillas' Victory* (New York: Monthly Review Press, 2016).

70. Sergio Carbó, "Sobre el camino de la patria resucitada," *PL*, January 11, 1959.

71. Guerra, *Visions of Power*, 66.

72. Andrés Valdespino, "La Revolución no necesita del comunismo," *Bohemia*, February 22, 1959.

73. Carlos Rafael Rodríguez, "La Revolución y los comunistas," *NH*, February 24, 1959.

74. Humberto Medrano, "El camarada Severo," *PL*, February 4, 1959; Guerra, *Heroes, Martyrs*, 198-213.

75. Quoted in Carlos Rafael Rodríguez, "Un necesario esclarecimiento," *NH*, April 15, 1959.

76. Argos, "Con Cien Ojos," *NH*, September 5, 1959; Euclides Vázquez Candela, "Respuesta al PSP," *Revolución*, September 10, 1959; Euclides Vázquez Candela, "Saldo de una polémica," *Revolución*, September 14, 1959.

77. Guerra, *Visions of Power*, 63-65, 100-105.

78. For example, "Víctimas de la tiranía," *NH*, February 10, 1959; "'No se puede con ellos. Estos desgraciados comunistas no hablan.' Así expresaron, desesperados, los torturadores de Octavio Basilio," *NH*, February 11, 1959.

79. Rodríguez, "Un necesario esclarecimiento," 1, 3.

80. Carlos Rafael Rodríguez, "Héroes comunistas y ataques anticomunistas," *NH*, July 13, 1959.

81. "Dignidad nacional vs. ideología imperialista: A propósito de unas declaraciones contra-revolucionarias de Gutiérrez Menoyo," *NH*, March 21, 1959.

82. Juan Marinello, "*Prensa Libre* cumple con sus amos," *NH*, January 14, 1960.

83. Argos, "Con Cien Ojos."
84. Juan Marinello, *"Prensa Libre* cumple con sus amos," 1, 4.
85. "Para que Cuba lo conozca bien," *NH*, April 11, 1959.
86. Carlos Rafael Rodríguez, "Respuesta a las calumnias," *NH*, September 11, 1959.
87. Blas Roca, "La Constitución de 1940 y las elecciones," *NH*, September 11, 1959.
88. *"El Diario de la Marina* siempre contra la Revolución," *NH*, November 24, 1959; "Nuestra opinión: *El Diario de la Marina*, ayer, hoy y mañana," *NH*, December 20, 1959.
89. "Contrabando imperialista," *Combate*, October 14, 1959.
90. "El eterno chantaje de Sergio Carbó," *Revolución*, November 17, 1959; Ernesto Vera, "Los que no fueron," *Revolución*, November 23, 1959.
91. "Carta a *Prensa Libre* del Frente Cívico de Mujeres Martianas," *PL*, November 21, 1959; "Describen cómo Sergio Carbó increpó al jefe del SIM hasta lograr que fuera puesto en libertad Raúl Castro Ruz," *PL*, November 24, 1959.
92. Marcelo Fernández, "Ni con unos ni con otros: Con Carbó," *Revolución*, November 21, 1959; "Carbó y Ernesto de la Fe, Compinches," *NH*, January 17, 1960.
93. Carlos Rafael Rodríguez, "Jupiter Desinflado," *NH*, January 16, 1960.
94. "Descuben manejos de elementos mujalistas; Denuncia el dirigente Fumero a los mujalistas de la Construcción," *NH*, August 14, 1959; "Antonio Collada, mujalista en 1958," *NH*, September 8, 1959.
95. "Refuta el ex-magistrado Elio Álvarez López cargos que le formularon hace dos días," *PL*, November 6, 1959.
96. "Emplaza Guevara a Conrado Rodríguez," *Revolución*, January 8, 1960; "Traicionaría a los mártires si no desenmascara a los malversadores, dice Rodríguez," *PL*, January 17, 1960.
97. For example, "La opinión de los colegas," *Información*, January 15, 1960.
98. Ulises Carbó, "La comparsa bermeja," *PL*, April 12, 1959.
99. Antonio Rubio, "Antesala de un ministerio," *Zig-zag*, January 31, 1959.
100. Fursenko and Naftali, *One Hell of a Gamble*, 11–12.
101. Fidel Castro, "Discurso pronunciado por el Comandante Fidel Castro Ruz, Primer Ministro del Gobierno Revolucionario, en la Universidad de Princeton, Estados Unidos," April 20, 1959, http://www.cuba.cu/gobierno/discursos/1959/esp/f200459e.html.
102. "No lograrán que nosotros suprimamos la libertad, dijo el Dr. Fidel Castro en la Shell," *PL*, February 8, 1959.
103. Fidel Castro, "Discurso pronunciado con motivo de conmemorarse el primer aniversario de la huelga del 9 de abril, en la alameda de Paula," April 9, 1959, http://www.cuba.cu/gobierno/discursos/1959/esp/f090459e.html.
104. Sergio Carbó, "De aquí y de allá," *PL*, April 10, 1959.
105. Humberto Medrano, "Los exigentes," *PL*, February 11, 1959.
106. Ursinio Rojas, "La consigna anti-comunista tiene un marcado filo contrarevolucionario," *NH*, February 20, 1959.
107. *Meet the Press*, NBC, April 19, 1959. A translated transcript of Castro's appearance appeared as "Fidel Castro ante la prensa," *PL*, April 21, 1959. Also see Sergio Carbó, "Balance favorable," *PL*, April 19, 1959.
108. "Hablará Fidel al pueblo hoy por la mañana," *NH*, April 28, 1959.
109. Guerra, *Visions of Power*, 65–66.

110. Sergio Carbó, "Una intriga rusa en el Capitolio de Washington," *PL*, July 14, 1959.
111. "'Este es el momento en que menos deseamos lo que está sucediendo,'" *Revolución*, July 18, 1959.
112. Guerra, *Visions of Power*, 68-74.
113. "'Este es el momento ...,'" 10.
114. "Carta de renuncia de Huber Matos," October 19, 1959, reproduced in Huber Matos, *Cómo llegó la noche* (Barcelona: Tusquets, 2002), 575-76.
115. Guerra, *Visions of Power*, 68-69, 84-88; "Demuestra Fidel exhaustivamente la traición de Matos," *NH*, October 24, 1959.
116. Fidel Castro, "Discurso pronunciado ante el pueblo congregado en el palacio presidencial para reafirmar su apoyo al gobierno revolucionario y como protesta contra la cobarde agresión perpetrada contra el pacífico pueblo de La Habana por aviones procedentes de territorio extranjero," October 26, 1959, www.cuba.cu/gobierno/discursos/1959/esp/f261059e.html.
117. José Pardo Llada, "Anticomunismo: Una arma política sospechosa," *La Calle*, December 1, 1959.
118. "'Si yo fuera comunista, no lo ocultaría pues para eso luchamos por la libertad de expresión,' dijo Raúl Castro en la CTC," *NH*, April 28, 1959.
119. *Proyecto de programa del Partido Socialista Popular*, pamphlet, printed March 7, 1960, text dated October 1, 1959, found among collection of *NH*, January 1960, Biblioteca Nacional José Martí, Havana; Blas Roca, "El programa del partido y la Revolución Cubana," *NH*, March 13, 1960.
120. Mirta Aguirre, "El respeto a si mismo," *NH*, July 9, 1959, emphasis added.
121. Ángel del Cerro, "Papeles son papeles," *PL*, March 9, 1960.
122. Lars Schoultz, *That Infernal Little Cuban Republic: The United States and the Cuban Revolution* (Chapel Hill: University of North Carolina Press, 2009), 103-17. Lanz long contended he had only disbursed leaflets and that the deaths on the ground were the result of misdirected Cuban antiaircraft fire.
123. Pardo Llada, "Anticomunismo," 3.
124. "Un comentario sin vergüenza," *NH*, December 8, 1959.
125. "Lea usted en SALACIONES de *Reader's Indigest*," *NH*, February 19, 1960.
126. Guerra, *Visions of Power*, 118-33.
127. Guerra, 120-21.
128. "Nuestra opinión: Libertad de prensa, para qué, para quienes?," *NH*, January 17, 1960.
129. "Los enterradores," *PL*, May 14, 1960; "Bajo el fuego," *PL*, May 15, 1960.
130. "Recibe simbólica sepultura el pasado antipatriótico de que se jactaba *Diario de la Marina*," *NH*, May 13, 1960.
131. Guerra, *Visions of Power*, 107.
132. This term, along with the related *mediated republic*, owed their origins to pre-1959 revisionist historical writing and commentary but became increasingly common in the 1960s. See Steven Palmer, José Antonio Piqueras, and Amparo Sánchez Cobos, "Introduction: Revisiting Cuba's First Republic," in *State of Ambiguity: Civic Life and Culture in Cuba's First Republic* (Durham, N.C.: Duke University Press, 2014), 5. Fidel Castro used "pseudo-republic" as early as July 1959. See Fidel Castro, "Discurso pronunciado por el

Comandante Fidel Castro Ruz, Primer Ministro del Gobierno Revolucionario, en la clausura del X Congreso Textil," July 22, 1959, http://www.cuba.cu/gobierno/discursos/1959/esp/f220759e.html.

133. To name just a few examples from the world of theater, see Virgilio Piñera, *Aire frío* (1959), José Triana, *El mayor general hablará de teogonía* (1960), and Rolando Ferrer, *Los próceres* (1960).

134. Thomas G. Paterson, *Contesting Castro: The United States and the Triumph of the Cuban Revolution* (New York: Oxford University Press, 1994).

135. "Memorandum from the Secretary of State to the President," November 5, 1959, *Foreign Relations of the United States, 1958-1960, Cuba*, vol. 6, https://history.state.gov/historicaldocuments/frus1958-60v06/d387.

136. For a useful summary of and intervention in this ongoing debate, see Farber, *The Origins of the Cuban Revolution Reconsidered*, 69-166.

137. Schoultz, *That Infernal Little Cuban Republic*, 109-17.

138. Such was the case of Eloy Gutiérrez Menoyo and William Morgan, for example. See Grann, "The Yankee *Comandante*"; and "La primera oposición cubana, 1959-1965" (dossier), *Encuentro de la Cultura Cubana* 39 (Winter 2005-6): 126-88.

139. "Respaldo al Profesor Julio Durán," *NH*, May 27, 1960.

140. Orlando González, "Lo difícil de ser revolucionario," *Combate*, May 10, 1960.

141. González, 6.

142. "Texto de juramento ante la Revolución y ante la patria," *NH*, August 15, 1960.

143. Guerra, *Visions of Power*, 145; "La declaración del yugo y la declaración de la estrella," *INRA* 9 (October 1960): 24-33.

144. For example, *Historias de la Revolución*, directed by Tomás Gutiérrez Alea (Havana: ICAIC, 1960); *El joven rebelde*, directed by Julio García Espinosa (Havana: ICAIC, 1961); *Cuba 58*, directed by José Miguel García Ascot and Jorge Fraga (Havana: ICAIC, 1962); *Crónica cubana*, directed by Ugo Ulive (Havana: ICAIC, 1963).

145. See Rainer Schultz, "The Liberal Moment of the Revolution: Cuba's Early Educational Reforms, 1959-1961," *Cuban Studies* 49 (2020): 213-35.

146. "¿Cuál es nuestro ideal?," *Combate*, December 9, 1959.

147. "Los que crean que vamos a nacionalizar las industrias," *PL*, January 8, 1959.

148. Sergio Piñeiro, "'Combatiré el comunismo con mejoras sociales' dijo Fidel Castro," *PL*, April 21, 1959.

149. Guerra, *Visions of Power*, 158-59.

150. *Maestra*, directed by Catherine Murphy (New York: Women Make Movies, 2011); Daura Olema, *Maestra voluntaria* (Havana: Casa de las Américas, 1962), later adapted into the film *En días como estos*, directed by Jorge Fraga (Havana: ICAIC, 1964).

Chapter 2

1. Viet Thanh Nguyen, *Nothing Ever Dies: Vietnam and the Memory of War* (Cambridge, Mass.: Harvard University Press, 2016), 44.

2. Considerable imprecisions and contradictions surround accounts of *Zig-zag*'s fate, with some suggesting the paper was forcibly closed by the revolutionary government in 1959, others in early 1960. However, I have seen issues from fall 1960, and scholar Amparo María Ballester López suggests the last issue was published in late December, by

which point those who would go on to found *Zig-zag Libre* had already left the island. See Ramón Fernández Larrea, "La risa en la sombra: Muerte del humor político en Cuba," *El Nuevo Herald*, May 17, 2009, http://www.elnuevoherald.com/2009/05/17/v-fullstory /449107/la-risa-en-la-sombra-muerte-del.html; Amparo María Ballester López, "Fidel en las portadas de *Zig-zag*: Diez caricaturas para la historia," *Verbiclara* (blog), August 13, 2015, https://verbiclara.wordpress.com/2015/08/13/fidel-en-las-portadas-de-zig-zag -diez-caricaturas-para-la-historia; and Enrique del Risco, "Prohías, Fidel y los bombines," *Enrisco* (blog), February 9, 2017, http://enrisco.blogspot.com/2017/02/prohias-fidel -y-los-bombines.html.

3. It is unclear in which original issue of *Zig-zag Libre* this poem appears, though there is no doubt as to its provenance. The poem appears reprinted in a commemorative issue as "El encuentro (en la puerta del Refugio)," *Zig-zag Libre*, August 10, 1972.

4. For recent examples, see Sam Verdeja and Guillermo Martínez, eds., *Cubans: An Epic Journey, the Struggle of Exiles for Truth and Freedom* (Miami: Facts about Cuban Exiles, 2011); Fernando Hernández, *The Cubans: Our Legacy in the United States: a Collective Biography* (Mountainview, Calif.: Floricanto, 2012); *Cubamerican*, directed by José Enrique Pardo, (Miami: Ño Productions, 2012); and *The Lost City*, directed by Andy García (Sherman Oaks, Calif.: CineSon, 2005). On the memory of Operation Pedro Pan, see Anita Casavantes Bradford, "Remembering Pedro Pan: Childhood and Collective Memory Making in Havana and Miami, 1960-2000," *Cuban Studies* 44 (2016): 283-308.

5. Thomas G. Paterson, *Contesting Castro: The United States and the Triumph of the Cuban Revolution* (New York: Oxford University Press, 1994), 38.

6. "Revolución quiere decir cambios fundamentales en la sociedad," *NH*, December 17, 1960.

7. María Cristina García, *Havana USA: Cuban Exiles and Cuban Americans in South Florida, 1959-1994* (Berkeley: University of California Press, 1996), 100.

8. Ernesto Montaner, "Experiencia del caso Batista," *Patria*, June 12, 1961; "Exclusivo: Habla Batista," *Patria*, January 18, 1961.

9. "Economía cubana de antes y de hoy," *Patria*, October 31, 1961.

10. Louis A. Pérez Jr., *On Becoming Cuban: Identity, Nationality, and Culture* (Chapel Hill: University of North Carolina Press, 2008 [1999]), 445-77.

11. Fulgencio Batista y Zaldívar, *Respuesta* (Mexico City: Botas, 1960), translated as *Cuba Betrayed* (New York: Vantage, 1962); Fulgencio Batista y Zaldívar, *Piedras y leyes* (Mexico City: Botas, 1961), translated as *The Growth and Decline of the Cuban Republic* (New York: Devin-Adair, 1964). Additional exculpatory literature includes E. Pizzi de Porras, *Mensaje a todos los que en el mundo se llaman Batista* (Mexico City: Botas, 1962).

12. Batista, *Piedras y leyes*, 97-112, 123-51; Lillian Guerra, *Heroes, Martyrs, and Political Messiahs in Revolutionary Cuba, 1946-1958* (New Haven, Conn.: Yale University Press, 2018), 85, 99.

13. It is possible that publication of Batista's memoirs in the 1960s received financial support from Cuban exile allies in Mexico, some of whom would found the organization Defensa Institucional Cubana, active between 1962 and 1973.

14. Antonio Rubio, no title, *Zig-zag Libre*, special supplement, July 1964.

15. "Revolución traicionada ... ¿de qué?," *Patria*, January 18, 1961.

16. "El asilo del Dr. Quevedo," *Información*, July 19, 1960. On *Bohemia*'s subsequent na-

tionalization in 1960 and conversion into a vehicle of the state press, see Richard Denis, "Una Revista al Servicio de la Nación: *Bohemia* and the Evolution of Cuban Journalism, 1908-1960" (MA thesis, University of Florida, 2016).

17. Early examples include Manuel A. de Varona, *El drama de Cuba, o La Revolución traicionada* (Buenos Aires: Marymar, 1960); and Manuel Artime, *Traición: ¡Gritan 20,000 tumbas cubanas!* (Mexico City: Jus, 1960).

18. See Esteban Fernández, "La Revolución del callo," *Baracutey Cubano* (blog), January 13, 2011, http://baracuteycubano.blogspot.com/2011/01/cuba-la-revolucion-del-callo.html.

19. U.S. Senate, Committee on the Judiciary, *The Communist Threat to the United States through the Caribbean: Hearings before the Subcommittee to Investigate the Administration of the Internal Security Act and Other Internal Security Laws of the Committee on the Judiciary of the United States Senate*, 86th Cong., 2nd sess., part 7, May 2-6, 1960 (Washington, D.C.: Government Printing Office, 1960).

20. Haynes Johnson, *The Bay of Pigs: The Leaders' Story of Brigade 2506* (New York: Norton, 1964), 23-31.

21. Richard Denis, "Propaganda Wars: *Bohemia Libre* Takes on the Soviet Union, 1960-1963," unpublished manuscript.

22. García, *Havana USA*, 122-27; María de los Ángeles Torres, *In the Land of Mirrors: Cuban Exile Politics in the United States* (Ann Arbor: University of Michigan Press, 1999), 42-61.

23. Theodore Draper, "Castro's Cuba: A Revolution Betrayed?," *New Leader*, March 27, 1961, 11.

24. Arthur M. Schlesinger Personal Papers, White House Files, Subject File, 1961-1964, "Cuba: White Paper," April 1961, AMSPP-WH06-009, John F. Kennedy Presidential Library and Museum.

25. "Aclaración al 'papel blanco' del Departamento de Estado de los Estados Unidos de América," reproduced in Batista, *Piedras y leyes*, 428-40.

26. Examples include Teresa Casuso, *Cuba and Castro* (New York: Random House, 1961); Fermín Peinado, *Beware Yankee: The Revolution in Cuba* (n.p., 1961); Humberto Medrano, *Sin patria pero sin amo* (Miami: Service Offset, 1963); Rufo López-Fresquet, *My Fourteen Months with Castro* (Cleveland: World, 1966); Andrés Suárez, *Castroism and Communism, 1959-1966* (Cambridge: MIT Press, 1967); and Mario Llerena, *The Unsuspected Revolution: The Birth and Rise of Castroism* (Ithaca, N.Y.: Cornell University Press, 1978). For film iterations, see *Historia de una traición*, directed by Eduardo Hernández "Guayo" (Havana: NotiCuba Bohemia, [1961?]); and *Castro-Cuba and Communism*, director unknown (New York: Desilu Productions, 1961).

27. Information on the life and career of José Miró Cardona culled from JMCP.

28. For example, "¡Martí contra Miró!," *Patria*, November 13, 1961.

29. See *Cuba: Satélite 13*, directed by Manuel de la Pedrosa (New York: Noticiario Panamericano, 1963).

30. J. Miró Cardona to José Ignacio Rivero, November 5, 1960, JMCP, box 22, folder 4.

31. Assorted proclamations from CRC member organizations in JMCP, box 1, folders 1-12. In particular, see "Bases del Frente Revolucionario Democrático de Cuba (FRD)," n.d., and "Manifiesto de constitución, n.d., in folder 11.

32. "A todos los trabajadores revolucionarios . . . ," n.d., JMCP, box 22, folder 2. On

Junco, see Robert Jackson Alexander, *International Trotskyism, 1929–1985: A Documented Analysis of the Movement* (Durham, N.C.: Duke University Press, 1991), 228–30.

33. R. Masferrer to J. Miró Cardona, April 23, 1961, JMCP, box 22, folder 8.

34. Ernesto Montaner, "El camarada mister Manolito," *Patria*, March 7, 1961; "Intentan imponer al camarada Ray y su fidelismo sin Fidel," *Patria*, March 22, 1963.

35. "Datos biográficos del Dr. Justo Carrillo Hernández," JMCP, box 1, folder 2; "Justo Carrillo Hernández (a) 'Justico': 'pedigree' y 'record,'" n.d., JMCP, box 6, no folder.

36. "Bases del Frente Revolucionario Democrático de Cuba" and "Manifiesto de constitución."

37. "Text of Appeal to Cubans to Revolt against Castro Regime," *New York Times*, April 9, 1961; Sam Pope Brewer, "Castro Foes Issue Call to Arms," *New York Times*, April 9, 1961.

38. Alfredo Durán, telephone interview with author, April 6, 2010; Victor Andres Triay, *Bay of Pigs: An Oral History of Brigade 2506* (Gainesville: University Press of Florida, 2001), 43, 46.

39. On faulty assumptions driving the Bay of Pigs plan, see James Blight and Peter Kornbluh, eds., *The Politics of Illusion: The Bay of Pigs Reexamined* (Boulder, Colo.: Lynne Rienner: 1998); and Jim Rasenberger, *Brilliant Disaster: JFK, Castro, and America's Doomed Invasion of the Bay of Pigs* (New York: Scribner's, 2001).

40. "Declaración del Movimiento Revolucionario del Pueblo," May 27, 1961, JMCP, box 2, folder 8.

41. J. Miró Cardona to R. Guas Inclán, May 15, 1961, JMCP, box 22, folder 10.

42. C. Bringuier to J. Miró Cardona, June 27, 1961, JMCP, box 23, folder 1.

43. Draft statement (no title), n.d. [mid-1961?], JMCP, box 13, folder 3.

44. "Discurso pronunciado por el Doctor José Miró Cardona ... en el acto obrero del 10 de octubre en el local del FORDC," October 10, 1961, JMCP, box 13, folder 3.

45. "Boletín," March 15, 1962, JMCP, box 1, folder 2.

46. "Exclúyase a ese perverso grupo," *LES MAMBI: Organización secreta para la liberación de Cuba* [Bulletin], October 25, 1961, n.p., JMCP, box 2, folder 4.

47. M. Iglesias to J. Miró Cardona, December 6, 1961, JMCP, box 22, folder 7.

48. F. Luis López to J. Miró Cardona, August 11, 1962, JMCP, box 24, folder 2.

49. José Miró Cardona, "El Castrismo: Un asesoramiento," speech delivered at the Universidad Interamericana de Puerto Rico, December 20, 1963, JMCP, box 14, folder 1.

50. J. Miró Cardona to R. Guas Inclán, May 15, 1961.

51. J. Miró Cardona to R. Guas Inclán, October 29, 1962, JMCP, box 24, folder 3; J. Miró Cardona to R. Guas Inclán, November 24, 1962, JMCP, box 24, folder 3; R. Guás Inclán to J. Miró Cardona, November 2, 1962, JMCP, box 24, folder 3; R. Guas Inclán to J. Miró Cardona, April 10, 1963, box 26, folder 4.

52. In late 1961, *Combate* fused with what was left of *La Calle* and the nationalized version of *Prensa Libre* to become *La Tarde*. *La Tarde* later merged with *Mella*, the organ of the Unión de Jóvenes Comunistas (Union of Young Communists, UJC), to become *Juventud Rebelde*. *Noticias de Hoy* and *Revolución* fused to become *Granma*, the official organ of the Cuban Communist Party, in 1965.

53. García, *Havana USA*, 35.

54. Information on Cuban Educational Crusade culled from CECR.

55. "Ciclo de descomunización, cubanización y democratización de la escuela cubana,

en la república liberada," n.d., and "Programa presentado a la Asamblea General de Cruzada Educativa Cubana," 1963, CECR, box 2, folder 22.

56. "La república democrática de Cuba, y sus niños," n.d., CECR, box 1, folder 2; "Cuba, el primero de enero de 1959, desplome de las instituciones democráticas, la crueldad y la injusticia como normas del nuevo régimen," n.d., CECR, box 13, folder 170. For another variation on this theme, see "Discurso de la Dra. María Gómez Carbonell ... pronunciado en el homenaje al magisterio cubano," September 25, 1971, CECR, box 13, folder 168. Here she refers to the Batista regime as the "last government of Sovereign Cuba."

57. Hector Maldonado, "La rehabilitación de la escuela democrática en Cuba liberada," n.d., CECR, box 4, folder 51.

58. *Cuba: Satélite 13*. The film debuted in April 1963 in eleven Spanish-language movie theaters in New York and was later screened in Miami as well.

59. *Gesta inmortal*, directed by Eduardo Palmer (Havana: Cuban Color Films, 1959). Palmer directed and de la Pedrosa was the film's producer. Palmer and de la Pedrosa worked on another film later that year, *Surcos de libertad*, cited in chapter 1.

60. For a similar case, see *La Cuba de ayer: El paraíso que el comunismo convirtió en infierno!*, directed by Manuel Alonso (New York and Miami: Noticiario Nacional, 1963), based on film the director smuggled out of Cuba. Emmanuel Vincenot, "¿Qué fue del viejo cine cubano?," in *Cine cubano: Nación, diáspora e identidad* (Benalmádena, Spain: Festival Internacional de Cortometraje y Cine Alternativo de Benalmádena, 2006), 66.

61. Lars Schoultz, *That Infernal Little Cuban Republic: The United States and the Cuban Revolution* (Chapel Hill: University of North Carolina Press, 2009), 170–87.

62. Schoultz, 187–91.

63. Jonathan C. Brown, *Cuba's Revolutionary World* (Cambridge, Mass.: Harvard University Press, 2017), 164–91.

64. See headlines of front-page articles in *Patria*, April 14, 1964, and July 30, 1964; and J. Miró Cardona to A. Rivero, March 3, 1964, JMCP, box 27, folder 7.

65. "Puntos de vista," *Boletín 2506*, June 5, 1964; "Honrar honra," *Boletín 2506*, December 10, 1964.

66. Johnson, *The Bay of Pigs*.

67. Durán, interview.

68. Mario Lazo, *A Dagger in the Heart: American Foreign Policy Failures in Cuba* (New York: Funk and Wagnalls, 1968). For a similar take, see Luis V. Manrara, *Betrayal Opened the Door to Russian Missiles in Red Cuba* (Miami: Truth about Cuba Committee, 1967).

69. Phuong Nguyen, "The People of the Fall: Refugee Nationalism in Little Saigon, 1975–2005" (PhD diss., University of Southern California, 2009).

70. See, for example, "Asunto Cuba: Aquí engavetado," *Zig-zag Libre*, August 24, 1968, cover; and Herminio Portel Vilá, "Peleando por una Cuba libre," *Bohemia Libre*, June 30, 1963.

71. Invitees included Manuel Artime, Juanita Castro (Fidel's sister, who had defected), Eloy Gutiérrez Menoyo, Carlos Prío Socarrás (former president of the Partido Auténtico), Rafael Guás Inclán (Batista's last vice president), and Manuel Ray.

72. Comité Pro-Referendum to J. Miró Cardona, October 4, 1963, JMCP, box 26, folder 3; Tom Gjelten, *Bacardí and the Long Fight for Cuba* (New York: Viking, 2008), 273–76; García, *Havana USA*, 135–37.

73. Armando García Sifredo, "Cita con la historia," *Patria*, February 4, 1966.

74. Armando García Sifredo, "Otro Gramma [sic] para Fidel: Respuesta al Dr. Prío," *Patria*, March 4, 1966. On Prío's suspiciously tardy departure from Cuba, see Reinaldo Zarate, "Carlos Prío: Un enigma," *El Mundo en el Exilio*, October 19, 1960; and "Continúa el enigma de Carlos Prío," *El Mundo en el Exilio*, December 24, 1960.

75. Ernesto Montaner, "*Bohemia* es responsable por la tragedia cubana," *Patria*, January 9, 1962.

76. I thank Richard Denis for these insights.

77. "Testamento político de Miguel Ángel Quevedo, August 12, 1959," *Contacto Magazine*, May 19, 2002, https://www.contactomagazine.com/quevedo100.htm.

78. See, for example, Guillermo de Zéndegui, *Todos somos culpables* (Miami: Universal, 1993). De Zéndegui was a prominent cultural official during the Batista regime in the 1950s.

79. R. Lorié to J. Miró Cardona, April 8, 1970, JMCP, box 30, folder 6.

80. [Unsigned] to "Mi querido amigo," April 24, 1963, JMCP, box 26, folder 1.

81. José Ignacio Rasco, "Sociología del exilio," in *Temática cubana: Primera reunión de Estudios Cubanos*, ed. María Cristina Herrera, special issue of *Exilio: Revista Trimestral* 3, no. 2-3, 4, no. 1 (Winter 1969–Spring 1970): 23; "Miami: Refugio de amigos y enemigos," *Patria*, May 24, 1961.

82. J. Miró Cardona to Ramiro Boza, January 25, 1969, JMCP, box 30, folder 3.

83. Rasco, "Sociología del exilio," 47.

84. Rasco, 47.

85. Osuna, "Maniático," *El Mundo en el Exilio*, November 2, 1960.

86. Armando García Sifredo, "Siquiátras para un exilio," *Patria*, May 14, 1965.

87. J. Miró Cardona to A. Rivero, February 25, 1964, JMCP, box 27, folder 7.

88. Billo Frómeta et al., *Así cantaba Cuba libre*, Panart Records LP-3096, [1961?].

89. For an evocative portrait of such spaces, see Susan Orlean, "The Homesick Restaurant," *New Yorker*, January 15, 1996.

90. *La Cuba de ayer*.

91. Ricardo L. Ortiz, *Cultural Erotics in Cuban America* (Minneapolis: University of Minnesota Press, 2007), 136.

92. Svetlana Boym, *The Future of Nostalgia* (New York: Basic Books, 2001), xviii.

93. Boym, 3.

94. Rasco, "Sociología del exilio," 47.

Chapter 3

1. Alfredo Durán, "Tesis del 17 de abril," *Boletín 2506*, December 10, 1964, 2.

2. William M. LeoGrande and Peter Kornbluh, *Back Channel to Cuba: The Hidden History of Negotiations between Washington and Havana* (Chapel Hill: University of North Carolina Press, 2014), 45.

3. Fidel Castro, *Speech Made by the Prime Minister of Cuba, Fidel Castro Ruz, on the 15th Anniversary of Playa Girón at Karl Marx Theater in Havana, April 19, 1976* (New York: Center for Cuban Studies, 1976), 4.

4. *El Mégano*, directed by Julio García Espinosa (Havana: Laboratorio Cinematográfico CMQ, 1955). In addition to Espinosa, future ICAIC head Alfredo Guevara took part,

along with directors Tomás Gutiérrez Alea and José Massip. See Michael Chanan, *Cuban Cinema* (Minneapolis: University of Minnesota Press, 2004), 109-10; and Julio García Espinosa, "*El Mégano*," *Revista Nuestro Tiempo* 6, no. 27 (January-February 1959): 5-6.

5. Claudia Martínez Herrera, "Protección de la naturaleza y turismo en la Revolución Cubana de 1959: El caso de la Ciénaga de Zapata," *HALAC* 1, no. 2 (March-August 2012): 193-217; Oficina Nacional de los Censos Demográfico y Electoral, *Censo de población, viviendas y electoral, enero 28 de 1953: Informe general* (Havana: P. Fernández, 1955); "El milagro de la Revolución en la Ciénaga de Zapata," *Juventud Rebelde*, December 26, 2008, http://www.juventudrebelde.cu/cuba/2008-12-26/el-milagro-de-la-revolucion-en-la-cienaga-de-zapata.

6. Lillian Guerra, *Heroes, Martyrs, and Political Messiahs in Revolutionary Cuba, 1946-1958* (New Haven, Conn.: Yale University Press, 2018), 224-78.

7. "A la Sierra con Fidel el 26: Cita histórica de la ciudad con el campo," *NH*, July 17, 1960.

8. Antonio Núñez Jiménez, *En marcha con Fidel: 1959* (Havana: Letras Cubanas, 1982), 115-26, 133-42, 159-70.

9. Martínez Herrera, "Protección de la naturaleza," 205; "Dragan la Bahía de Cochinos para recibir los equipos," *El Crisol*, April 22, 1959, cited in Martínez Herrera, "Protección de la naturaleza," 206.

10. Antonio Núñez Jiménez, "Un tesoro de la naturaleza," *Bohemia*, April 12, 1959.

11. This idea for the region in fact dated to early twentieth century. Martínez Herrera, "Protección de la naturaleza," 207; Fidel Castro, "Discurso pronunciado por el Comandante Fidel Castro Ruz, Primer Ministro del Gobierno Revolucionario, en la Universidad Central 'Marta Abreu,' de Santa Clara, Las Villas," March 15, 1959, http://www.cuba.cu/gobierno/discursos/1959/esp/f150359e.html; "Es un error confundir la generosidad con debilidad," *Revolución*, June 10, 1959; *Reclamation of Ciénaga de Zapata, Cuba* (The Hague, the Netherlands: NEDECO, 1959).

12. Quoted in Núñez Jiménez, "Un tesoro de la naturaleza."

13. See Louis A. Pérez Jr., *Rice in the Time of Sugar: The Political Economy of Food in Cuba* (Chapel Hill: University of North Carolina Press, 2019).

14. "En La Habana camiones de carbón de Ciénaga de Zapata," *NH*, November 28, 1959; "La Revolución explica su obra: Instalaciones turísticas en las zonas de la Ciénaga de Zapata," *La Calle*, February 10, 1960; Martínez Herrera, "Protección de la naturaleza," 208-14; "Cocodrilos de Zapata," *INRA* 1, no. 5 (May 1960): 32-37.

15. Fidel Castro, "Discurso pronunciado por el Comandante Fidel Castro Ruz, Primer Ministro del Gobierno Revolucionario, en la Universidad de La Habana," November 27, 1959, http://www.cuba.cu/gobierno/discursos/1959/esp/c271159e.html.

16. Antonio Núñez Jiménez, "La noche de los carboneros," *INRA* 1, no. 1 (January 1960): 47-52.

17. Hugo García, "Con los carboneros, a cenar con ellos," *Juventud Rebelde*, December 23, 2014, http://www.juventudrebelde.cu/cuba/2014-12-23/con-los-carboneros-a-cenar-con-ellos.

18. Núñez Jiménez, *En marcha con Fidel*, 289-92; Waldo Frank, *Cuba: Prophetic Island* (New York: Marzani and Munsell, 1961), 161-62; Rafael Rojas, "Nombrando el huracán," *Diario de Cuba*, March 12, 2012, http://www.diariodecuba.com/cuba/1331539208_1187.html#_ftn6.

19. "Visitó Mikoyan cooperativas agrícolas," *NH*, February 14, 1960; Jon Lee Anderson, *Che Guevara: A Revolutionary Life* (New York: Grove, 1997), 462.

20. Jean-Paul Sartre, *Sartre on Cuba* (New York: Ballantine, 1961), 135-42.

21. "La Ciénaga de Zapata," *Información*, March 29, 1960.

22. "Lo que la Revolución ha realizado en la Ciénaga de Zapata," *INRA* 2, no. 5 (January 1961): 26.

23. Carlos Marten, "En la Ciénaga de Zapata: Más ciudadanos de la Cuba nueva," *INRA* 2, no. 1 (January 1961): 58-61; Carlos Marten, "Matrimonios colectivos: De La Habana a la Ciénaga de Zapata," *INRA* 2, no. 3 (March 1961): 108-11. On "Operación Familia," see Rachel Hynson, *Laboring for the State: Women, Family, and Work in Revolutionary Cuba, 1959-1971* (Cambridge: Cambridge University Press, 2020), 91-146.

24. *Tierra olvidada*, directed by Oscar Torres (Havana: ICAIC, 1960); Elizabeth Sutherland, "Cinema of Revolution: 90 Miles from Home," *Film Weekly* 15, no. 2 (Winter 1961-62): 42-45; Chanan, *Cuban Cinema*, 130-31.

25. Martínez Herrera, "Protección de la naturaleza," 206.

26. Fidel Castro, "Discurso pronunciado por el Comandante Fidel Castro Ruz, Primer Ministro del Gobierno Revolucionario, en la clausura de los actos celebrados en Playa Girón, Peninsula de Zapata," July 27, 1961, http://www.cuba.cu/gobierno/discursos/1961/esp/f270761e.html.

27. "Lo que la Revolución ha realizado," 26.

28. Fidel Castro, "Discurso pronunciado por Fidel Castro Ruz, Presidente de la República de Cuba, en las honras fúnebres de las víctimas del bombardeo a distintos puntos de la república, efectuado en 23 y 12, frente al cementerio de Colón," April 16, 1961. http://www.cuba.cu/gobierno/discursos/1961/esp/f160461e.html.

29. See *Bohemia*, July 30, 1961.

30. Castro, "Discurso pronunciado ... en la clausura de los actos celebrados en Playa Girón."

31. See Reinaldo Funes Monzote, "Geotransformación: Geography and Revolution in Cuba from the 1950s to the 1960s," in *The Revolution from Within: Cuba, 1959-1980*, ed. Michael J. Bustamante and Jennifer L. Lambe (Durham, N.C.: Duke University Press, 2019), 117-45.

32. Fidel Castro, "Discurso de Fidel Castro tras el sepelio de las víctimas del bombardeo a La Habana," *Obra Revolucionaria* 14 (April 1961): 29.

33. *Obra Revolucionaria* 16 (May 1961): 1.

34. Fidel Castro, "Fidel Castro les habló a los trabajadores que en Cuba es hoy, como decir todo el pueblo," *Obra Revolucionaria* 16 (May 1961): 7, 8.

35. "Cayó el águila del imperialismo!," *Revolución*, May 2, 1961; *Folletos de divulgación legislativa: Leyes del Gobierno Provisional de la Revolución XXVII (1 a 31 de enero 1961)* (Havana: Lex, 1961), 311.

36. Castro, "Discurso ... tras el sepelio," 29.

37. Castro, "Fidel Castro les habló a los trabajadores," 38.

38. Castro, "Discurso ... tras el sepelio," 28.

39. Castro, "Fidel Castro les habló a los trabajadores," 38.

40. "El socialismo vence," *Bohemia*, July 23, 1961; Eugenio López, "Conquistado el espacio," *Bohemia*, April 23, 1961.

41. This slogan appears in most commemorative pieces about the invasion in the

1960s. See *Historia de una agresión: Declaraciones y documentos del juicio seguido a la brigada mercenaria organizada por los imperialistas yanquis que invadió a Cuba el 17 de abril de 1961* (Havana: Venceremos, 1962); Raúl González de Cascorro, *Gente de Playa Girón* (Havana: Casa de las Américas, 1962); *Héroes de Girón* (Havana: Comisión de Orientación Revolucionaria de la Dirección Nacional del Partido Unido de la Revolución Socialista, 1963); and Fayad Jamís, *Victoria de Playa Girón* (Havana: Empresa Consolidada de Artes Gráficas, 1964).

42. *Muerte al invasor*, directed by Santiago Álvarez and Tomás Gutiérrez Alea (Havana: ICAIC,1961); *Abril de Girón*, directed by Santiago Álvarez (Havana: ICAIC, 1961).

43. "Vencimos," *Bohemia*, April 30, 1961, special insert.

44. Viet Thanh Nguyen, *Nothing Ever Dies: Vietnam and the Memory of War* (Cambridge, Mass.: Harvard University Press, 2016), 162.

45. "La sangre numerosa," *NH*, April 18, 1961.

46. "Agresión escrito con sangre," *Bohemia*, April 23, 1961.

47. Jesús Orta Ruiz, *Al son de la historia: Poemas* (Havana: Letras Cubanas, 1986), 90–92; Hugo García, "La flor carbonera," *Juventud Rebelde*, April 20, 2011, http://www.juventudrebelde.cu/cuba/2011-04-20/la-flor-carbonera; Mayra Cue Sierra, "El Indio Naborí y al son de la historia," *Cubarte*, September 25, 2007, http://archivo.cubarte.cult.cu/periodico/columnas/tv-y-cultura/el-"indio-nabori"-y-al-son-de-la-historia/6/5509.html; Josefa Bracero Torres, *Otros rostros que se escuchan* (Havana: Letras Cubanas, 2007), 216.

48. Tom Miller, *Trading with the Enemy: A Yankee Travels through Castro's Cuba* (New York: Basic Books, 2008 [1992]), 110.

49. José Quiroga, *Cuban Palimpsests* (Minneapolis: University of Minnesota Press, 2005), 93–95.

50. Compare *Razones de una victoria*, chap. 4 (Havana: ICRT, 2011), to "La verdad de lo alejado que estuvo Fidel Castro de los escenarios bélicos de Bahía de Cochinos en abril de 1961," *Baracutey Cubano* (blog), April 17, 2010, http://baracuteycubano.blogspot.com/2010/04/cuba-giron-no-fue-solo-en-abril-la.html.

51. "Juntos criminales de guerra, ex-militares, latifundistas, mercenarios y niños bien," *Revolución*, May 5 and 6, 1961. Also see "Galería de mercenarios latifundistas," *NH*, May 3, 1961; "Galería de esbirros," *NH*, May 6, 1961.

52. "Figuran entre los presentados los hijos de Miró Cardona y de Falla," *NH*, April 21, 1961.

53. Cesar Marín, "Los hijísimos Babún vinieron a recuperar lo que es del pueblo," *Revolución*, May 10, 1961.

54. Castro, "Discurso pronunciado … en la clausura de los actos celebrados en Playa Girón."

55. *Muerte al invasor*, emphasis added.

56. Richard R. Fagen, *The Transformation of Political Culture in Cuba* (Stanford, Calif.: Stanford University Press, 1969), 47.

57. "Conozca Playa Girón en nuestra Cuba de hoy" (advertisement), *NH*, June 11, 1961.

58. "En Playa Girón: Bombardeo de lápices y libretas y 'desembarco' de alfabetizadores," *NH*, June 13, 1961.

59. For example, "Visitas a mercenarios de apellidos de M a Q," *Revolución*, May 24, 1961.

60. Leo Huberman, "Eye Witness in Havana," *Nation*, May 13, 1961, 407. My thanks to Jennifer Lambe for this source.

61. Lisandro Otero, Edmundo Desnoes, and Ambrosio Fornet, eds., *Playa Girón: Derrota del imperialismo*, vol. 4 (Havana: Revolución, 1962), 35.

62. Otero, Desnoes, and Fornet, 289-313.

63. Otero, Desnoes, and Fornet, 168-69.

64. Peter Wyden, *Bay of Pigs: The Untold Story* (New York: Simon and Schuster, 1979), 303.

65. Otero, Desnoes, and Fornet, *Playa Girón*, 494-95.

66. Huberman, "Eye Witness in Havana," 407.

67. "Cínica confesión de Kennedy sobre la intervención yanqui," *Revolución*, April 21, 1961; "Confiesa Kennedy ser el culpable de la invasión," *Revolución*, April 25, 1961.

68. "Demostrada la participación yanqui con la comparecencia de los prisioneros," *NH*, April 22, 1961; "Probada la intervención yanqui en la agresión," *NH*, April 25, 1961; Luis Báez, "Si nos dejan vivos a cinco de nosotros, matamos a los jefes que nos embarcaron," *Bohemia*, April 30, 1961.

69. Otero, Desnoes, and Fornet, *Playa Girón*, 45-46.

70. Otero, Desnoes, and Fornet, 472.

71. Otero, Desnoes, and Fornet, 191.

72. Luis González-Lalondry, *Prisioneros de guerra* (New York: Pueblo, 1976), 12.

73. Otero, Desnoes, and Fornet, *Playa Girón*, 371.

74. Castro, "Fidel Castro les habló a los trabajadores," 16.

75. Otero, Desnoes, and Fornet, *Playa Girón*, 456-58.

76. Félix Rodríguez, "El guerrero de las sombras," *El Veraz* (blog), n.d., http://elveraz.com/articulo384.htm; González-Lalondry, *Prisioneros de guerra*, 14.

77. Otero, Desnoes, and Fornet, *Playa Girón*, 459.

78. Otero, Desnoes, and Fornet, 193-224.

79. Otero, Desnoes, and Fornet, 416.

80. Otero, Desnoes, and Fornet, 404.

81. Otero, Desnoes, and Fornet, 399.

82. Otero, Desnoes, and Fornet, 404-5.

83. Castro, "Fidel Castro les habló a los trabajadores," 17.

84. González-Lalondry, *Prisioneros de guerra*, 13.

85. The Cuban press reported that the prisoners had "admitted their crimes," publishing self-impeaching written statements attributed to brigade leaders. By their own account of the trial, however, those men refused to countenance the statements as their own, or insisted that they had been written under duress. See "Aceptaron los mercenarios su gravísima culpabilidad," *NH*, March 30, 1962; "La sensacional carta de San Román a Fidel," *NH*, March 30, 1962; "Segunda vista del juicio de los mercenarios," *NH*, March 31, 1952; Haynes Johnson, *The Bay of Pigs: The Leaders' Story of Brigade 2506* (New York: Norton, 1964), 265-84; and González-Lalondry, *Prisioneros de guerra*, 54-61.

86. Dora [pseudonym?], "Páginas nuevas: Playa Girón," *Bohemia*, April 20, 1962.

87. "Castro Attends Playa Larga Festival," Radio Reloj (Havana), December 29, 1962, Foreign Broadcast Information Service, December 31, 1962, Latin American Network Information Center, http://lanic.utexas.edu/project/castro/db/1962/19621229.html.

88. See, for example, Fidel Castro, "Discurso pronunciado por el Comandante Fidel

Castro Ruz, Primer Secretario del Partido Unido de la Revolución Socialista y Primer Ministro del Gobierno Revolucionario, en el segundo aniversario de la victoria de Playa Girón," April 19, 1963, http://www.cuba.cu/gobierno/discursos/1963/esp/f190463e.html. Fidel Castro's annual anniversary speeches, most at Havana's Chaplin Theater, continued until 1971. Thereafter, speeches tended to be given every five years.

89. "Informe textual de Fidel Castro sobre las ORI," *NH*, March 27, 1962.

90. Lillian Guerra, *Visions of Power in Cuba: Revolution, Redemption, and Resistance, 1959-1971* (Chapel Hill: University of North Carolina Press, 2012), 172-181; Joanna Swanger, *Rebel Lands of Cuba: The Campesino Struggles of Oriente and Escambray, 1934-1974* (London: Lexington, 2015), 215-44; Jonathan C. Brown, *Cuba's Revolutionary World* (Cambridge, Mass.: Harvard University Press, 2017), 136-63; Lillian Guerra, "Beyond Paradox: Counterrevolution and the Origins of Political Culture in the Cuban Revolution, 1959-2009," in *A Century of Revolution: Insurgent and Counterinsurgent Violence during Latin America's Long Cold War*, ed. Greg Grandin and Gilbert M. Joseph (Durham, N.C.: Duke University Press, 2010), 199-235.

91. Ernesto "Che" Guevara, *El gran debate: Sobre la economía en Cuba* (Havana: Ocean Sur, 2005); León Rozitchner, *Moral burguesa y revolución* (Buenos Aires: Procyon, 1963).

92. Rozitchner, *Moral burguesa*, 17, 19.

93. "Dirigentes nacionales en la V Zafra del Pueblo," *El Mundo*, April 14, 1965, back page.

94. Guerra, *Visions of Power*, 293.

95. As early as July 1961, the government's planned area for drainage had already been reduced to 5,000 *caballerías* from the original 15,000. See Castro, "Discurso pronunciado ... en la clausura de los actos celebrados en Playa Girón"; Martínez Herrera, "Protección de la naturaleza," 207.

96. Guerra, *Visions of Power*, 256-316; "La UNEAC en la Zafra de los Diez Millones," *La Gaceta de Cuba* 82 (April 1970): n.p.

97. Ernesto "Che" Guevara, *El socialismo y el hombre en Cuba* (Havana: Política, 1988). Essay originally published in Uruguay under the title "Desde Argelia, para *Marcha*, la Revolución Cubana hoy," *Marcha*, March 12, 1965, n.p.

98. Guerra, *Visions of Power*, 227-55; Allen Young, *Gays under the Cuban Revolution* (San Francisco: Grey Fox, 1981); Ian Lumsden, *Machos, Maricones, and Gays: Cuba and Homosexuality* (Philadelphia: Temple University Press, 1996); Abel Sierra Madero, "El trabajo os hará hombres: Masculinización nacional, trabajo forzado y control social en Cuba durante los años 60," *Cuban Studies* 44 (Winter 2016): 309-49.

99. On the "Marquitos" case, see Miguel Barroso, *Un asunto sensible: Tres historias cubanas de crimen y traición* (Barcelona: Random House Mondadori, 2009); Newton Briones Montoto, *"Víctima" o culpable: La delación de Humboldt 7* (Panama City, Panama: Ruth Casa Editorial, 2015).

100. "Fidel en el Tribunal Supremo: Jamás la palabra de un traidor, de un delator confeso puede enfrentarse a la palabra de un revolucionario," *NH*, March 27, 1964.

101. On the *microfracción*, see Guerra, *Visions of Power*, 294-95.

102. Brown, *Cuba's Revolutionary World*, 413-50.

103. Fidel Castro, "Discurso pronunciado por el Comandante Fidel Castro Ruz, Primer Secretario del Comité Central del Partido Comunista de Cuba y Primer Ministro del Gobierno Revolucionario, en el resumen de la velada conmemorativa de los cien años de

lucha, efectuada en La Demajagua, monumento nacional, Manzanillo, Oriente," October 10, 1968, http://www.cuba.cu/gobierno/discursos/1968/esp/f101068e.html.

104. According to a secret survey conducted on Cuban Communist Party orders by University of Havana students at the time, a significant portion of Cubans concluded that Soviet actions contradicted the principle of national self-determination. See Reinaldo Escobar, "Praga, 1968: Mi primera (y tardía) decepción," *14 y medio*, August 20, 2018, https://www.14ymedio.com/blogs/desde_aqui/Praga-primera-tardia-decepcion-Primavera_de_Praga-Fidel_Castro_7_2495220454.html.

105. See Jorge I. Domínguez, *To Make a World Safe for Revolution: Cuba's Foreign Policy* (Cambridge, Mass.: Harvard University Press, 1989), 61–78; and Brown, *Cuba's Revolutionary World*, 73–101.

106. María Cristina García, *Havana USA: Cuban Exiles and Cuban Americans in South Florida, 1959–1994* (Berkeley: University of California Press, 1996), 43–44.

107. See, for example, Rafael del Pino, *Amanecer en Girón* (Havana: Dirección Política de las FAR, 1969).

108. John Mraz, "*Memories of Underdevelopment*: Bourgeois Consciousness/Revolutionary Context," in *Revisioning History: Film and the Construction of a New Past*, ed. Robert A. Rosenstone (Princeton, N.J.: Princeton University Press, 1995), 114.

109. Chanan, *Cuban Cinema*, 290.

110. *Memorias del subdesarrollo*, directed by Tomás Gutiérrez Alea (Havana: ICAIC, 1968).

111. Tomás Gutiérrez Alea, "Presentación en Karlovy Vary (1968)," in *Alea: Una retrospectiva crítica*, ed. Ambrosio Fornet (Havana: Letras Cubanas, 1998), 72–73.

112. Eduardo Heras León, *La guerra tuvo seis nombres* (Havana: UNEAC, 1968).

113. Antón Arrufat, "Los siete contra Tebas," in *Dramaturgia de la revolución*, vol. 1, ed. Omar Valiño (Havana: Alarcos, 2010), 477, 476, 479.

114. Arrufat, 467, 459.

115. One can also read a spate of earlier dramatic works in a similar way. See Abel Estorino, "Los mangos de Caín," *Casa de las Américas* 27 (December 1964): 49–64; and Juan Triana, *La noche de los asesinos* (Havana: Casa de las Américas, 1965).

116. Arrufat, "Los siete contra Tebas," 491.

117. Declaration included in the original, largely noncirculated edition: Antón Arrufat, *Los siete contra Tebas* (Havana: UNEAC, 1968), 14.

118. Jesús J. Barquet, "Antón Arrufat habla claro sobre *Los siete contra Tebas*," *Encuentro de la cultura cubana* 14 (Fall 1999): 95.

119. Mario Coyula Crowley, "¿Para qué sirve un monumento?," *Artecubano* 1, no. 1 (2007): 24; Pablo Alonso González, *Cuban Cultural Heritage: A Rebel Past for a Revolutionary Nation* (Gainesville: University Press of Florida, 2018), 114; Augusto Pérez Beato, "Monumento Playa Girón: Resultado del concurso internacional," *Arquitectura Cuba* 30, no. 331 (1964): 53–64.

120. *Girón*, directed by Manuel Herrera (Havana: ICAIC, 1972).

121. Víctor Casaus, *Girón en la memoria* (Havana: Casa de las Américas, 1970), 179–80, 247–48, 271.

122. See Eduardo Heras León, "El quinquenio gris, testimonio de una lealtad," lecture, Instituto Superior del Arte, Ciclo "La política cultural de la Revolución: Memoria y reflexión," organized by the Centro Teórico-Cultural Criterios, May 15, 2007, 11.

123. Carlos Franqui, *Family Portrait with Fidel* (New York: Random House, 1984), 125. Later in life he would semiretire to Puerto Rico.

124. The author heard this story/joke from multiple acquaintances in Havana in the spring of 2013.

125. Robin D. Moore, *Music and Revolution: Cultural Change in Socialist Cuba* (Berkeley: University of California Press, 2006), 152–53.

126. Silvio Rodríguez, "Playa Girón," *Días y flores* (LP), 1975.

Chapter 4

1. "Por qué fue a la ONU la Agrupación Abdala," *Abdala*, April 1971, 7.

2. "Editorial: El futuro será nuestro," *Abdala*, April 1971, 4.

3. Gustavo Marín Duarte, "El verdadero subdesarrollo cubano," *Abdala*, December 1972, 4.

4. "Editorial: El futuro será nuestro," 4.

5. Stuart Hall, "Cultural Identity and Diaspora," in *Identity: Community, Culture, Difference*, ed. Jonathan Rutherford (London: Lawrence and Wishart, 1990), 225.

6. Gustavo Marín Duarte, telephone interview with author, October 10, 2013; Gustavo Marín Duarte, interview with author, Miami, December 2, 2013; Gustavo Marín Duarte, email message to author, March 4, 2014.

7. Ruben G. Rumbaut, "The Agony of Exile: A Study of the Migration and Adaptation of Indochinese Refugee Adults and Children," in *Refugee Children: Theory, Research, and Services*, ed. F. L. Ahearn Jr. and J. L. Athey (Baltimore: John Hopkins University Press, 1991), 61.

8. Marín Duarte, interview, December 2, 2013; Elia Rosa Encinosa, Enrique Encinosa, Eduardo Fermoselle, José Antonio Font, Vicente Lago, Emilio Polo Núñez, Fernando Álvarez Pérez, and María de la Roza, group interview with author, Coral Gables, Fla., December 1, 2013.

9. Lisandro Pérez, "Cubans in the United States," *Annals of the American Academy of Political and Social Science* 487 (September 1986): 126–37; U.S. Department of Commerce, Bureau of the Census, *1970 Census of Population: Characteristics of the Population—General Social and Economic Characteristics* (Washington, D.C.: Government Printing Office, 1973). On the New Jersey Cuban community, see Yolanda Prieto, *The Cubans of Union City: Immigrants and Exiles in a New Jersey Community* (Philadelphia: Temple University Press, 2009).

10. "Abdala: 1968– . . . ," *Abdala*, January 1973, 2.

11. "Mail: Miami-Havana," *Zig-zag Libre*, September 14, 1968; María Gómez Carbonnel, "Páginas de historia: El primero en la frente o la moral comunista," n.d., CECR, box 13, folder 170.

12. Marín Duarte, interviews, October 10 and December 2, 2013.

13. José Antonio Font, telephone interview with author, September 25, 2013; Marín Duarte, interviews, October 10 and December 2, 2013; Encinosa et al., interview. On Abdala's ties to Rustin, see "Cuba entre los países que violan D.H.," *Abdala*, October–November 1977, 5. For economic conditions in and around New York in the 1970s, see Jonathan Mahler, *Ladies and Gentleman, the Bronx Is Burning: 1977, Baseball, Politics, and the Battle for the Soul of a City* (New York: Picador, 2005). On the YPSL and the Social-

ist Party of America, see Peter Drucker, *Max Shachtman and His Left: A Socialist's Odyssey through the "American Century"* (Amherst, N.Y.: Prometheus, 1993).

14. For an exception, see "200 cubanos arrestados en disturbios," *Abdala*, June-July 1975, 1-2.

15. Gustavo Marín Duarte, "Un yanqui llamado José," *Revista Abdala*, April 1970, 20-25.

16. Marín Duarte, interviews, October 10 and December 2, 2013.

17. Gustavo Pittaluga, *Diálogos sobre el destino* (Miami: Mnemosyne, 1969). Earlier editions by Cámara Cubana del Libro (1954) and Editorial Islas (1960), both in Havana.

18. Emilio Roig de Leuchsenring, *Cuba no debe su independencia a los Estados Unidos* (Havana: Sociedad Cubana de Estudios Históricos e Internacionales, 1950). Subsequent editions by Edición la Tertulia (Havana, 1960) and Editorial Oriente (Santiago de Cuba, 1975).

19. Marín Duarte, interview, December 2, 2013; Encinosa et al., interview; Rosario "Tati" McClain, personal communication with author, November 1, 2013.

20. Agrupación Abdala Poster Collection, Cuban Heritage Collection, University of Miami Libraries, Coral Gables, Fla.; "Recital canción protesta," *Abdala*, October-November 1975, 2; Gisela Cardonne, "The New Tourists," *Abdala*, August 1971, 8; Eric Zolov, "Expanding Our Conceptual Horizons: The Shift from an Old to a New Left in Latin America," *A Contracorriente* 5, no. 2 (Winter 2008): 47-73; Van E. Gosse, "A Movement of Movements: The Definition and Periodization of the New Left," in *A Companion to Post-1945 America*, ed. Jean-Christophe Agnew and Roy Rosenzweig (London: Blackwell, 2002), 277-302.

21. "Ideología de Abdala: Hacia una nueva sociedad, aspectos sociales," *Abdala*, May-June 1979, 7; "Pensamientos revolucionarios sobre una nueva sociedad, presentados y aprobados durante el Primer Congreso Nacional de Abdala," July 1971, http://www.abdala.info/files/76900599.pdf.

22. "Delegaciones Abdala," http://abdala.info/delegaciones.html.

23. "Editorial: Por qué somos revolucionarios," *Abdala*, May 1971, 3.

24. See Directorio Revolucionario Estudiantil en el Exilio (DRE) Records, Cuban Heritage Collection.

25. "Editorial," *Nueva Generación* 1, no. 2 (September 1965), n.p.

26. "Editorial: Por qué somos revolucionarios," 3.

27. Gustavo Marín Duarte, "Revolución," *Abdala*, September 1971, 2.

28. *Zig-zag Libre*, March 1, 1973, cover.

29. Teishan A. Latner, "Take Me to Havana! Airline Hijacking, U.S.-Cuba Relations, and Political Protest in Late Sixties' America," *Diplomatic History* 39, no. 1 (2015): 16-44; "El pueblo cubano declara y establece," *Abdala*, April 1973, 6-7.

30. "Editorial: Por qué somos revolucionarios," 3; "Editorial: Abdala, 1968-1977," *Abdala*, January 1977, 3.

31. "Editorial: El 17 de abril y la mentalidad cubana," *Abdala*, April 1973, 3.

32. "Editorial: ¿Dónde, quién, cómo y cuándo?," *Abdala*, May 1981, 3.

33. "Editorial: El 17 de abril y la mentalidad cubana," 3.

34. "Editorial: Girón, catorce años después," *Abdala*, April 1975, 3.

35. "Rechaza acusación," *Abdala*, May 1976, 1.

36. Jorge I. Domínguez, *To Make a World Safe for Revolution: Cuba's Foreign Policy* (Cambridge, Mass.: Harvard University Press, 1989), 61-78; Piero Gleijeses, "The View from Havana: Lessons from Cuba's African Journey, 1959-1976," in *In from the Cold: Latin America's New Encounter with the Cold War*, ed. Gilbert M. Joseph and Daniela Spenser (Durham, N.C.: Duke University Press, 2008), 112-34.

37. "Abdala en acción," *Abdala*, December 1974, 2. Abdala also called for the elimination of all foreign military forces on the island—whether possible Soviet submarines at Cienfuegos Bay *or* the U.S. naval station at Guantánamo Bay. The Soviets had begun construction of a nuclear submarine base in 1970. Quiet negotiations with the Nixon administration convinced Moscow to change its plans. See "Editorial," *Abdala*, December 1974, 3; and Lars Schoultz, *That Infernal Little Cuban Republic: The United States and the Cuban Revolution* (Chapel Hill: University of North Carolina Press, 2009), 251-54.

38. See "Nicaragua, un pueblo en lucha," *Abdala*, October-November 1978, 5. See positive references to the Irish Republican Army and Palestinian Liberation Organization in Calixto Sosa, "Vale la pena el terrorismo?," *Abdala*, March 1975, 1, 4; and "Discurso de Gustavo Marín en Union City," *Abdala*, March 1975, 6-7. On Puerto Rico, see "Abdala y los problemas internacionales," *Abdala*, August-September 1977, S5; and "Tratan agencias de inteligencia de Estados Unidos y Cuba de destruir la oposición anti-castrista," *Abdala*, May 1975, 7.

39. "Areíto responde," *Areíto* 1, no. 3 (October 1974): 13.

40. For example, María de los Ángeles Torres, *In the Land of Mirrors: Cuban Exile Politics in the United States* (Ann Arbor: University of Michigan Press, 1999), 89-92; María Cristina García, *Havana USA: Cuban Exiles and Cuban Americans in South Florida, 1959-1994* (Berkeley: University of California Press, 1996), 198-204; and Iraida H. López, *Impossible Returns: Narratives of the Cuban Diaspora* (Gainesville: University Press of Florida, 2015).

41. See U.S. House of Representatives, Committee of the Judiciary, *The Role of Cuba in International Terror and Subversion: Hearings before the Subcommittee on Security and Terrorism*, 97th Cong., parts 57-58 (Washington, D.C.: Government Printing Office, 1982).

42. "Falleció en Miami el médico cubano Eliseo Pérez-Stable," *Encuentro en la red*, August 19, 2005, http://arch1.cubaencuentro.com/sociedad/noticias/20050819/6f912e28 480ce208c66aae34e8cbc7ec.html; Mariana Gastón, interview with author, Brooklyn, N.Y., June 4, 2014; Román de la Campa, *Cuba on My Mind: Journeys to a Severed Nation* (New York: Verso, 2000), 24.

43. "Opinión editorial," *Abdala*, April 1978, 3.

44. Leonel Antonio de la Cuesta, "Perfil biográfico," in *Itinerario ideológico: Antología de Lourdes Casal*, ed. María Cristina Herrera and Leonel Antonio de la Cuesta (Miami: Instituto de Estudios Cubanos, 1982), 3-8; José S. Prince, "Lourdes Casal: Una vida comprometida con su verdad," in *Itinerario Ideológico*, 9-12; Gustavo Marín Duarte, interviews October 10 and December 2, 2013; Ángel Estrada, Pedro González, Miguel Socarrás, and Roberto González, group interview with author, Elizabeth, N.J., December 13, 2014.

45. Gastón, interview; Miren Uriarte, telephone interview with author, April 23, 2014.

46. Jesús Díaz, *De la patria y el exilio* (Havana: Unión, 1979), 15-16. Testimony by Albor Ruiz's brother, Elián Ruiz.

47. "Editorial," *Joven Cuba* 6 (April 1976), 2, emphasis added. For a time, Casal ap-

peared to agree. See Lourdes Casal and Rafael Prohías, *The Cuban Minority in the U.S.: Preliminary Report on Need Identification and Program Evaluation* (Boca Raton: Florida Atlantic University, 1973).

48. "Editorial," *Areíto* 1, no. 1 (April 1974): 1.

49. Rolando Feria, "Este exilio," *Abdala*, May 1971, 9.

50. "... Y lo que nunca sale (la carta enviada el pasado sept.... que nunca se publicó)," *Areíto* 1, no. 4 (1975): 32.

51. "Editorial," *Areíto* 1, no. 1 (April 1974): 1.

52. Antonio H. García-Hernández, "Lo que tus padres no te quisieron dar," *Abdala*, July 1971, 4. Gustavo Marín Duarte confirms that the scale of the exodus struck group leaders as a fundamental strategic error, a not entirely involuntarily *choice* to "self-export" an important sector of Castro's potential domestic opposition. Marín Duarte, interview, December 2, 2013.

53. Anita Casavantes Bradford, "Remembering Pedro Pan: Childhood and Collective Memory Making in Havana and Miami, 1960-2000," *Cuban Studies* 44 (2016): 283-308.

54. Grupo Areíto, *Contra viento y marea* (Havana: Casa de las Américas, 1978), 37-55; María de los Ángeles Torres, *The Lost Apple: Operation Pedro Pan, Cuban Children in the U.S., and the Promise of a Better Future* (Boston: Beacon, 2003); Casavantes Bradford, "Remembering Pedro Pan."

55. For example, "Letter to CNBC from Board of Directors of Operation Pedro Pan, Inc.," June 15, 2010, http://pedropan.org/content/letter-cnbc-board-directors-operation-pedro-pan-group-inc.

56. Luis Reina, "Mi despertar: Abdala," *Abdala*, May 1971, 2.

57. "14 de *Abdala* se encadenaron a la estatua de la libertad," *Abdala*, June 1972, 1, 4; "Marcha por la reafirmación nacional," *Abdala*, April 1974, 1.

58. Encinosa et al., interview; Marín Duarte, interview, December 2, 2013.

59. The line comes from YouTube character "Doctor Álvaro Álvarez," a fictional radio personality circa 2009 that satirized conservative Miami exile radio hosts. Videos since removed by creator.

60. "Cancelado festival castrista," *Abdala*, March 1972, 6-7.

61. "Abdala confronta a Alarcón," *Abdala*, April 1973, 1; "Abdala confronta a periodista americano," *Abdala*, April 1975, 1.

62. See, for example, the case of the Movimiento Nacionalista Cubano (Cuban Nationalist Movement, MNC), a protofascist group founded by Felipe Rivero Díaz (a former Brigade 2506 member interrogated on Cuban television, as described in chapter 3) and Guillermo and Ignacio Novo Sampoll. In 1964, members of the MNC fired a bazooka at UN headquarters when Che Guevara was delivering a speech. Alan McPherson, "Caribbean Taliban: Cuban American Terrorism in the 1970s," *Terrorism and Political Violence* 31, no. 2 (2019): 390-409. Also noteworthy is Orlando Bosch, convicted of firing a bazooka at a Polish freighter docked in Miami in 1968.

63. José Quiroga, "The Cuban Exile Wars: 1976-1981," *American Quarterly* 66, no. 3 (September 2014): 819-33.

64. García, *Havana USA*, 137-45; U.S. Senate, Committee on the Judiciary, *Terroristic Activity: Terrorism in the Miami Area: Hearing before the Subcommittee to Investigate the Administration of the Internal Security Act and Other Internal Security Laws of the Com-*

mittee on the Judiciary of United States Senate, 94th Cong., 2nd sess., 1976 (Washington, D.C.: Government Printing Office, 1976); José Luis Méndez Méndez, *Los años del terror (1974–1976): Una historia no revelada* (Havana: Ciencias Sociales, 2006).

65. "Bombing of Cuban Jetliner 40 Years Later," National Security Archive, October 6, 2016, https://nsarchive.gwu.edu/briefing-book/cuba/2016-10-06/bombing-cuban-jetliner-40-years-later.

66. "Editorial," *Areíto* 2, no. 4 (Spring 1976): 4.

67. Gastón, interview; Uriarte, interview.

68. "Confrontación con elementos castristas en Estados Unidos," *Abdala*, April 1977, 7.

69. The FLNC was responsible for bombings at Cuban embassies in Mexico, Jamaica, and Spain in 1973 and 1974. Members included not only several *abdalistas*, but also affiliates of the right-wing Movimiento Nacionalista Cubano (see note 62). In early 1976, the FLNC joined forces with Orlando Bosch to form the Coordinación de Organizaciones Revolucionarias Unidas (Coordination of United Revolutionary Organizations, CORU). CORU is widely thought responsible for the bombing of Cubana flight 455 that October. That said, Abdala's affiliation with the FLNC ended by November 1974 according to one FBI report, and Marín Duarte and other contributors to Abdala's newspaper subsequently distanced themselves from terrorism. See Michael J. Bustamante, "Anticommunist Anti-imperialism? Agrupación Abdala and the Shifting Contours of Cuban Exile Politics, 1968–1986," *Journal of American Ethnic History* 35, no. 1 (2015): 71–99.

70. Ronald Bonachea and Marta San Martín, *The Cuban Insurrection, 1952–1959* (New Brunswick, N.J.: Transaction, 1974), 73–75; Giraldo Mazola, "La noche de las cien bombas," *Bohemia*, November 8, 2017, http://bohemia.cu/historia/2017/11/la-noche-de-las-cien-bombas.

71. Blanca Bianchi, "José Antonio Echeverría," *Abdala*, March 1974, 4; "Editorial," *Areíto* 2, no. 4. Bianchi was active for Abdala in Puerto Rico.

72. Marifeli Pérez-Stable, *The Cuban Revolution: Origins, Course, Legacy*, 3rd ed. (Oxford: Oxford University Press, 2011), 121–52; Carmelo Mesa-Lago, *Cuba in the 1970s: Pragmatism and Institutionalization* (Albuquerque: University of New Mexico Press, 1978).

73. See, for example, Maurice Halperin, *The Rise and Decline of Fidel Castro* (Berkeley: University of California Press, 1972).

74. For two recent treatments of this scandal, see Jorge Fornet, *El 71: Anatomía de una crisis* (Havana: Letras Cubanas, 2013), 147–64; and Rafael Rojas, *La polis literaria: El boom, la Revolución y otras polémicas de la Guerra Fría* (Madrid: Taurus, 2018).

75. Lourdes Casal, ed., *El caso Padilla: Literatura y revolución en Cuba* (New York: Nueva Atlántida, 1971).

76. Lourdes Casal, "Dos semanas en Cuba: Entrevista con Lourdes Casal," *Areíto* 1, no. 1 (April 1974): 27.

77. "Carlos Franqui: A la búsqueda de la revolución perdida," *Abdala*, May 1978, 4, 7.

78. "El Caso Padilla," *Abdala*, May 1971, 1, 12; "Poesía," *Abdala*, October–November 1978, 6.

79. "Confrontación con elementos castristas en Estados Unidos," 7.

80. See, for example, *"Areíto* responde," 13.

81. Albor Ruiz, "Canción frustrada para Juanin Pereira," *Areíto* 1, no. 1 (April 1974): 19.

82. "Entrevista con Uxmal Livio Díaz," *Areíto* 3, no. 2–3 (April 1977): 30–35.

83. Marifeli Pérez-Stable, "Hacia dónde va la clase obrera cubana," *Areíto* 2, no. 2-3 (September-December 1975): 4-13; Max Azicri, "Las estrategias de gobierno y la descentralización del poder en Cuba," *Areíto* 3, no. 1 (Summer 1976): 4-11.

84. José R. Villalón, "Cuarta reunión de estudios cubanos," *Areíto* 2, no. 4 (Spring 1976): 35.

85. "Editorial," *Abdala*, February-March 1977, 3.

86. "Statement of Needs," Luis Santeiro Papers, box 3, folder 17, Cuban Heritage Collection.

87. Yeidy Rivero, "Interpreting Cubanness, Americanness, and the Sitcom: WPBT-PBS's *¿Qué pasa, U.S.A.?* (1975-1980)," in *Global Television Formats: Understanding Television across Borders*, ed. Tasha Oren and Sharon Shahaf (New York: Routledge, 2012), 90-108.

88. Apolinar Alzaga, Liliana Blanco, Mayra Guajardo, Eliseo J. Pérez-Stable, "Juventud búsqueda," *Areíto* 1, no. 2 (July 1974): 32.

89. Agrupación Abdala Vertical File, Cuban Heritage Collection.

90. "All PBS Stations That Carried *¿Qué pasa, U.S.A.?*," Luis Santeiro Papers, box 3, folder 15.

91. Robert Sklar, "PBS Americanizes a Cuban Family," *Chronicle of Higher Education*, April 30, 1979, R-19.

92. "The Boat Ride," January 1977, Luis Santeiro Papers, box 3, folder 8.

93. Memorandum: José R. Bahamonde, P.D., to Luis Santeiro, S.E., February 12, 1977, Luis Santeiro Papers, box 3, folder 8.

94. Episode 15: "Citizenship," *¿Qué pasa, U.S.A.? La Completa Collection*, DVD (Miami: WPBT-2, 2004).

95. Daniel T. Rodgers, *Age of Fracture* (Cambridge, Mass.: Belknap, 2012), 3.

96. Román de la Campa, "Revista *Areíto*: Herejía de una nación improbable," *Encuentro de la Cultura Cubana* 40 (Spring 2006): 137.

97. Alexandra Vázquez, "Learning to Live in Miami," *American Quarterly* 66, no. 3 (September 2014): 858.

Chapter 5

1. "Testimonios sobre el Che," *Revolución y Cultura* 7 (1972): 43-52; "Suplemento: 55 aniversario de la Revolución de Octubre," *Revolución y Cultura* 7 (1972): n.p.; "El pasado 28 de enero," *Revolución y Cultura* 8 (1973): 2; Ulf Keyn, "El legado vital de Brecht," *Revolución y Cultura* 9 (February 1973): 3.

2. *La Gaceta de Cuba* 119 (January 1974); 120 (February 1974); 122 (April 1974); 126 (August 1974), respectively.

3. For example, Haydée Santamaría, "El Moncada es la vida: Grandeza de los que cayeron y de los que quedaron," *Revolución y Cultura* 12 (July 1973): 26-40; Marta Rojas, *La generación del centenario en el juicio del Moncada*, 3rd ed. (Havana: Ciencias Sociales, 1973).

4. "Nombres de los años en Cuba desde el triunfo de la Revolución Cubana (1959-2008)," *Radio Rebelde*, n.d., http://www.radiorebelde.com.cu/50-revolucion/nombre-anos.html.

5. Pablo Alonso González, *Cuban Cultural Heritage: A Rebel Past for a Revolutionary Nation* (Gainesville: University of Press of Florida, 2018), 60-121.

6. On the 1971 National Congress of Education and Culture, see Jorge Fornet, *El 71: Anatomía de una crisis* (Havana: Letras Cubanas, 2013), 165–86. On the term *quinquenio gris*, see Ambrosio Fornet, "Quinquenio gris: Revisitando el término," *Casa de las Américas* 246 (January–March 2007): 3–16.

7. Fidel Castro, "A convertir el revés en victoria," *Con la Guardia en Alto* 9, no. 6 (1970): 18–20.

8. Carmelo Mesa-Lago, *Cuba in the 1970s: Pragmatism and Institutionalization* (Albuquerque: University of New Mexico Press, 1978), 56–58.

9. Susan Eckstein, *Back from the Future: Cuba under Castro*, 2nd ed. (New York: Routledge, 2003), 51.

10. María Antonia Cabrera Arús, "The Material Promise of Socialist Modernity: Fashion and Domestic Space in the 1970s," in *The Revolution from Within: Cuba, 1959–1980*, ed. Michael J. Bustamante and Jennifer L. Lambe (Durham, N.C.: Duke University Press, 2019), 189–217.

11. Steve J. Stern, *Remembering Pinochet's Chile: On the Eve of London 1998* (Durham, N.C.: Duke University Press, 2006), 1.

12. See Duanel Díaz Infante, "¿Humor y contrarrevolución?," *Cubaencuentro.com*, November 12, 2009, http://www.cubaencuentro.com/cultura/articulos/humor-y-contrarrevolucion-222603.

13. Heberto Padilla, "En tiempos difíciles," in *Fuera del juego* (Miami: Universal, 1998 [1968]), 13.

14. "Declaración de la UNEAC acerca de los premios otorgados a Heberto Padilla en poesía y Antón Arrufat en teatro, La Habana, 15 de noviembre de 1968," reproduced at http://rialta-ed.com/declaracion-de-la-uneac.

15. "Declaración del Primer Congreso Nacional de Educación y Cultura," *Casa de las Américas* 65–66 (March–June 1971): 18.

16. "Cuba: La institucionalización histórica," *Cuba internacional*, 1977, supplement.

17. For a visual account of the visit, see *Amistad*, directed by Jorge Fraga (Havana: ICAIC, 1975).

18. Alejo Carpentier, "Impromptu para un gran aniversario," *Revolución y Cultura* 77 (January 1979): 2. Carpentier first gained literary notoriety in the 1930s and 1940s. Between 1966 and his death in 1980, he served as cultural attaché at Cuba's embassy in Paris.

19. Fidel Castro, "Discurso pronunciado por el Comandante en Jefe Fidel Castro Ruz, Primer Secretario del Comité Central del Partido Comunista de Cuba y Primer Ministro del Gobierno Revolucionario, en el acto central en conmemoración del XXII aniversario del ataque al Cuartel Moncada, efectuado en la ciudad de Santa Clara, Las Villas," July 26, 1975, http://www.cuba.cu/gobierno/discursos/1975/esp/f260775e.html.

20. On Soviet influence in Cuban life, see "Cuba en la era soviética y post-soviética," panel discussion, Thirty-Third International Congress of the Latin American Studies Association, May 29, 2015, San Juan, Puerto Rico; and Jacqueline Loss, *Dreaming in Russian: The Cuban Soviet Imaginary* (Austin: University of Texas Press, 2013).

21. Raúl Rivero, "Por este tiempo," in *Poesía sobre la tierra* (Havana: UNEAC, 1973), 51–52.

22. Raúl Rivero, "Historia viva," *La Gaceta de Cuba* 108 (January 1973): 6.

23. *Morir por la patria es vivir*, directed by Santiago Álvarez (Havana: ICAIC, 1976); "Steven Kinzer on Cuba in the 1970s and 80s," *Beyond the Sugar Curtain* (blog), Decem-

ber 2016, https://www.brown.edu/research/projects/tracing-cuba-us-connections/news/2016/12/stephen-kinzer-cuba-1970s-and-80s.

24. See Piero Gleijeses, *Conflicting Missions: Havana, Washington, and Africa, 1959–1976* (Chapel Hill: University of North Carolina Press, 2002).

25. For example, see *Moncada: Epopeya Heroica* (Havana: Instituto Cubano del Libro, 1973); and Silvio Rodríguez, Noel Nicola, and Pablo Milanés, *Cuba canta a XX años de Moncada*, Disco Libre, DL-009 (LP), 1973.

26. Dariela Aquique, "Los octubres de Cuba," *Diario de Cuba*, October 27, 2014, http://www.diariodecuba.com/cuba/1414347485_10981.html.

27. Guevara was first reported captured and "dead of his wounds" following a battle with Bolivian military forces on October 8. For this reason, the day of his last battle and, for years, presumed death was christened thereafter in Cuba as "The Day of the Heroic Guerrilla." On the twentieth anniversary of his death, Fidel Castro acknowledged publicly that Che was actually executed on October 9. Jon Lee Anderson, *Che Guevara: A Revolutionary Life* (New York: Grove, 1997), 740.

28. Lillian Guerra, *Visions of Power in Cuba: Revolution, Redemption, and Resistance, 1959–1971* (Chapel Hill: University of North Carolina Press, 2012), 88–90; "Una flor para Camilo: Hermosa tradición revolucionaria," *Granma*, October 29, 1970.

29. Fidel Castro, "Discurso pronunciado por el Comandante Fidel Castro Ruz, Primer Secretario del Comité Central del Partido Comunista de Cuba y Primer Ministro del Gobierno Revolucionario, en la concentración conmemorativa del XVII Aniversario del Asalto al Cuartel Moncada, efectuada en la Plaza de la Revolución," July 26, 1970, http://www.cuba.cu/gobierno/discursos/1970/esp/f260770e.html; Fidel Castro, "Las manos del Che," *Bohemia*, July 31, 1970; Bertrand de la Grange, "El insólito viaje de las manos del Che," *El País*, October 14, 2007, http://elpais.com/diario/2007/10/14/internacional/1192312809_850215.html.

30. González, *Cuban Cultural Heritage*, 92–97.

31. "Museo de la Revolución festejará su cumpleaños 49," *Juventud Rebelde*, December 10, 2008, http://www.juventudrebelde.cu/cuba/2008-12-10/museo-de-la-revolucion-festejara-su-cumpleanos-49; "Museo de la Revolución" [advertisement], *Revolución*, May 20, 1961.

32. Ramiro Valdés, "Discurso pronunciado en el acto de inauguración del Memorial Granma, en La Habana, el día 1 de diciembre 1976," *Granma*, December 2, 1976.

33. González, *Cuban Cultural Heritage*, 97.

34. Hector Hernández Pardo, "En la casa natal de José Antonio Echevarría: Inauguran hoy, en Cárdenas, Museo Regional de Historia," *Granma*, October 10, 1973.

35. Conchita Pedroso, "Visitan escolares la Casa-Museo donde vivió Abel Santamaría y depositan ante la tarja la primera ofrenda floral," *Granma*, May 28, 1973; "Abren al público como museo, desde mañana, el apartamento de Abel Santamaría en 25 y O, Vedado," *Granma*, June 8, 1973.

36. "Museo Abel Santamaría Cuadrado," Consejo Nacional de Patrimonio Cultural, http://www.cnpc.cult.cu/institucion/526; René Camacho Albert, "Seleccionan monumento a Abel Santamaría que erigirán en el parque que lleva su nombre, en Santiago de Cuba," *Granma*, June 27, 1973.

37. Ricardo Bernal Mora, "Inauguran exposición en el antiguo Presidio Modelo de Isla de Pinos," *Granma*, July 30, 1973; Orlando Gómez, "Un museo para la posteridad: El an-

tiguo Presidio Modelo," *Granma*, July 25, 1974; Nora Gámez Torres, "Presidio político de Cuba en Isla de Pinos: dinamita bajo los pies," *El Nuevo Herald*, September 13, 2014, http://www.elnuevoherald.com/noticias/mundo/america-latina/cuba-es/article2102569.html; Centro de Estudio de Historia Militar, Fuerzas Armadas Revolucionarias, *Moncada: La acción*, vol. 2 (Havana: Política, 1981), 422.

38. González, *Cuban Cultural Heritage*, 133.

39. González, 135.

40. González, 135-42. Left-wing Cuban activists and writers had used the term "neocolonial" to describe U.S.-Cuban relations before 1959. However, particularly under the influence of more orthodox Marxist interpretations of the Cuban past in the 1970s, it became the standard, institutionalized shorthand, including in academic texts. See, for example, Ramón de Armas, *La revolución pospuesta: Destino de la revolución martiana de 1895* (Havana: Instituto Cubano del Libro, 1972); and Juan Pérez de la Riva et al., *La República neocolonial: Anuario de estudios cubanos*, Vols. 1-2 (Havana: Instituto Cubano del Libro, 1975-79).

41. Information culled from the Directorio de Museos, Consejo Nacional de Patrimonio Cultural, http://www.cnpc.cult.cu/directorio-museos.

42. González, *Cuban Cultural Heritage*, 132.

43. "Museo Municipal de Playa Girón," *Ecured*, n.d., http://www.ecured.cu/index.php/ Museo_Municipal_de_Playa_Girón.

44. "Ley No. 2: Ley de los Monumentos Nacionales y Locales," August 4, 1977, http://www.cnpc.cult.cu/sites/default/files/LEY%20No.%202.pdf; Directorio de Monumentos Nacionales, Consejo Nacional de Patrimonio Cultural, http://www.cnpc.cult.cu/monumentos-nacionales.

45. González, *Cuban Cultural Heritage*, 159.

46. *Girón*, directed by Manuel Herrera (Havana: ICAIC, 1972).

47. John Hess, "Bay of Pigs: Event into Concept," *Jump Cut* 4 (November-December 1974): 7.

48. Raúl Macías Pascual, *Girón: Historia verdadera de la Brigada 2506* (Havana: Casa de las Américas, 1976). Winner of a Casa de las Américas prize in 1971, the play was adapted for stage and television toward the end of that year. See Katherine Ford, "Sounds and Silences of the Habanero Stage: Theater and the Cuban 'Quinquenio Gris,'" *Colorado Review of Hispanic Studies* 8-9 (Fall 2010-2011): 364-66; and Magaly Muguercia, "Un teatro popular masivo y partidario," *Revolución y Cultura* 32 (April 1975): 72-73.

49. *¡Viva la República!*, directed by Pastor Vega (Havana: ICAIC, 1972).

50. Alison Landsberg, *Prosthetic Memory: The Transformation of American Remembrance in the Age of Mass Culture* (New York: Columbia University Press, 2004), 3.

51. González, *Cuban Cultural Heritage*, 128.

52. See Fidel Castro's reflections on youth and *rezagos* of the past in Fidel Castro, "Discurso pronunciado por Fidel Castro Ruz, Presidente de la República de Cuba, en el acto de clausura del Primer Congreso de los CDR en el XVII aniversario de su fundación, en la Plaza de la Revolución, ciudad de La Habana, el 28 de septiembre de 1977, año de la institucionalización," http://www.cuba.cu/gobierno/discursos/1977/esp/f280977e.html.

53. Pierre Nora, *Realms of Memory: The Construction of the French Past*, vol. 1, *Conflicts and Divisions*, ed. Lawrence D. Kritzman, trans. Arthur Goldhammer (New York: Columbia University Press, 1996), 1.

54. Cabrera Arús, "The Material Promise of Socialist Modernity"; *Los bolos en Cuba y una eterna amistad*, directed by Enrique Colina (Paris: RFO/Canal Overseas Productions, 2011).

55. *No tenemos derecho a esperar*, directed by Rogelio París (Havana: ICAIC, 1972).

56. "Terminan obreros industriales los dos primeros edificios construidos en Alamar con plus trabajo," *Granma*, November 2, 1971; Lídice Valenzuela, "El moderno pueblo que los constructores del regional Escambray terminaron en La Yaya, en homenaje al Che Guevara," *Granma*, October 11, 1971.

57. Cabrera Arús, "The Material Promise of Socialist Modernity."

58. Noel Nicola, Pablo Milanés, and Silvio Rodríguez, "¡Cuba va!," on *Grupo de Experimentación Sonora ICAIC 4*, Areíto Records LD-3482 (LP), 1976; Susan Buck-Morss, *Dreamworld and Catastrophe: The Passing of Mass Utopia in East and West* (Cambridge, Mass.: MIT Press, 2000), as cited in Loss, *Dreaming in Russian*, 6.

59. Lisandro Otero, "Cibernética ¿Segunda revolución industrial?," *Revolución y Cultura* 1, no. 11 (1968): 3; Jorge Pérez-López, *The Economics of Cuban Sugar* (Pittsburgh: University of Pittsburgh Press, 1991), 69; Juan Varela Pérez, "Millonarios todos los operadores de combinadas KTP-1 que cortan para los centrales de La Habana," *Granma*, June 5, 1978.

60. For example, see Miguel Cossío Woodward, *Sacchario* (Havana: Casa de las Américas, 1970).

61. *La nueva escuela*, directed by Jorge Fraga (Havana: ICAIC, 1974).

62. Magali García Moré, "Comenzarán a construir la primera central electronuclear en nuestro país en los años 1977-78," *Granma*, February 27, 1975; Jonathan Benjamin-Alvarado, "Cuba's Nuclear Power Program and Post-Cold War Pressures," *Non Proliferation Review* (Winter 1994): 18-26.

63. Arqueles Morales, "Trabajo voluntario," *Casa de las Amércias* 60 (May-June 1970): 100-103; "¡Un cubano en el cosmos!," *Granma*, September 19, 1980; Marta Denis Valle, "La gran noticia hace 30 años ¡Un cubano en el cosmos!," *Cubadebate*, September 19, 2010, http://www.cubadebate.cu/noticias/2010/09/19/la-gran-noticia-hace-30-anos-¡un-cubano-en-el-cosmos/#.VWEyxouyjwI.

64. Víctor Casaus, "Introducción a la historia de Cuba," *La Gaceta de Cuba* 146 (June 1976): 25.

65. Fidel Castro, "Discurso pronunciado por el Comandante en Jefe Fidel Castro Ruz, Primer Secretario del Comité Central del Partido Comunista de Cuba y Primer Ministro del Gobierno Revolucionario, en la clausura del II Congreso de la Unión de Jóvenes Comunistas, efectuada en el teatro de la CTC-Revolucionaria," April 4, 1972, http://www.cuba.cu/gobierno/discursos/1972/esp/f040472e.html.

66. Castro, "Discurso pronunciado ... en el acto central en conmemoración del XXII Aniversario del Ataque al Cuartel Moncada."

67. Silvio Rodríguez, "La era está pariendo un corazón," on *Cuando digo futuro*, Areíto and Fonomusic Records, 89.2070/8 (LP), reissue 1984 [1977].

68. Guerra, *Visions of Power*, 65.

69. Aníbal Escalante, "Del grito de Yara a la Declaración de La Habana," *Cuba Socialista* 1, no. 2 (1961): 1-9; Blas Roca, "Nueva etapa de la Revolución Cubana," *Cuba Socialista* 2, no. 5 (1962): 38-53; Rafael Rojas, "Tres relatos sobre el origen del comunismo en Cuba," *Libros del Crepúsculo* (blog), November 21, 2014, http://www.librosdelcrepusculo.net/2014/11/tres-relatos-sobre-el-origen-del.html. For later expressions of this interpre-

tation, see Carlos Rafael Rodríguez, *Cuba en el tránsito al socialismo, 1959-1963* (Havana: Política, 1979); and Antonio Núñez Jiménez, *En marcha con Fidel*, vols. 1-4 (Havana: Letras Cubanas, 1982).

70. "Derrota imperialista en Chile: Triunfa Allende en las elecciones presidenciales," *Granma*, September 5, 1970; "¡Viva Chile! Primer Aniversario del Gobierno de la Unidad Popular, Presidido por Salvador Allende," *Granma*, November 4, 1971; Rafael Pedemonte, "The Meeting of Revolutionary Roads: Chilean-Cuban Interactions, 1959-1970," *Hispanic American Historical Review* 99, no. 2 (2019): 275-302.

71. "Fidel en la Universidad de Concepción," *Granma*, November 19, 1971.

72. "Fidel en la CUT de Chile," *Granma*, November 23, 1971. For treatments of Fidel's Chile visit, see *El diálogo de América*, directed by Álvaro Covacevich (Santiago: Chile Films, 1971); and *De América soy hijo . . . y a ella me debo*, directed by Santiago Álvarez (Havana: ICAIC, 1972).

73. Fidel Castro, "Discurso pronunciado por el Comandante Fidel Castro Ruz, Primer Secretario del Comité Central del Partido Comunista de Cuba y Primer Ministro del Gobierno Revolucionario, en el acto clausura de la Primera Conferencia de Solidaridad de Los Pueblos de Asia, Africa y América Latina (Tricontinental), en el Teatro Chaplin, La Habana," January 15, 1966, http://www.cuba.cu/gobierno/discursos/1966/esp/f150166e.html.

74. Fidel Castro, "Discurso pronunciado por el Comandante en Jefe Fidel Castro Ruz, Primer Secretario del Comité Central del Partido Comunista de Cuba y primer Ministro del Gobierno Revolucionario, en el acto central en conmemoración del XX aniversario del ataque al Cuartel Moncada, efectuado en el antiguo cuartel convertido hoy en escuela," July 26, 1973, http://www.cuba.cu/gobierno/discursos/1973/esp/f260773e.html.

75. Castro, "Discurso pronunciado . . . en el acto central en conmemoración del XXII aniversario del ataque al Cuartel Moncada," emphasis added.

76. Fidel Castro, "Editorial: Cuba socialista," *Cuba socialista* 1, no. 1 (1961): 3.

77. "Discurso pronunciado . . . en el acto central en conmemoración del XXII aniversario del ataque al Cuartel Moncada."

78. "Documentos del Primer Congreso del Partido Comunista de Cuba, del Informe Central del PCC al Primer Congreso, presentado por el Compañero Fidel Castro Ruz, Primer Secretario del PCC," *Casa de las Américas* 95 (March-April 1976): 13-14.

79. "La estrategia de Moncada," *Casa de las Américas* 109 (July-August 1978): 31.

80. See Jonathan M. Hansen, *Young Castro: The Making of a Revolutionary* (New York: Simon and Schuster, 2019).

81. "Documentos del Primer Congreso," 18; Karl Marx, *The 18th Brumaire of Louis Bonaparte* (Rockville, Md.: Wildside, 2008 [1852]), 15.

82. "I Congreso del Partido: Tesis y resoluciones, sobre la plataforma programática del Partido," http://congresopcc.cip.cu/wp-content/uploads/2011/03/I-Congreso-PCC.-Tesis-y-Resoluciones-sobre-la-Plataforma-Programática-del-Partido.pdf.

83. *El primer delegado*, directed by Santiago Álvarez (Havana: ICAIC, 1975).

84. That other documentary, *La guerra necesaria* (Havana: ICAIC), would not debut until 1980. Santiago Juan Navarro, "Historia, mito y propaganda: Fidel Castro en el cine histórico de Santiago Álvarez," *Revista Hispano-Cubana* 43 (October 2012): 119-38.

85. *Mi hermano Fidel*, directed by Santiago Álvarez (Havana: ICAIC, 1977).

86. Michael Chanan, *Cuban Cinema* (Minneapolis: University of Minnesota Press, 2004), 359.

87. *El hombre de Maisinicú*, directed by Manuel Pérez (Havana: ICAIC, 1973); Chanan, *Cuban Cinema*, 359.

88. "Conversando con nuestros cineastas: Manuel Pérez, joven director de *El hombre de Maisinicú y Río negro*," *El Caimán Barbudo* 141 (September 1979): 16-18.

89. *Patty-candela*, directed by Rogelio París (Havana: ICAIC, 1976).

90. *El brigadista*, directed by Octavio Cortázar (Havana: ICAIC, 1977).

91. John Ramírez, "El Brigadista: Style and Politics in a Cuban Film," *Jump Cut* 35 (April 1990): 2.

92. *Río negro*, directed by Manuel Pérez (Havana: ICAIC, 1977).

93. *Guardafronteras*, directed by Octavio Cortázar (Havana: ICAIC, 1980); *Leyenda*, directed by Rogelio París (Havana: ICAIC, 1981).

94. Chanan, *Cuban Cinema*, 395.

95. Seymour Menton, "La novela de la Revolución Cubana, fase cinco, 1975-1987," *Revista Iberoamericana* 56, no. 152-53 (1990): 913-32; Fornet, *El 71*, 93-103; Duanel Díaz Infante, "Hasta sus últimas consecuencias: Dialécticas de la Revolución Cubana" (PhD diss., Princeton University, 2012), 197-263; Stephen Wilkinson, *Detective Fiction in Cuban Society and Culture* (Bern, Switzerland: Peter Lang International Academic, 2006), 109-58.

96. Luis Rogelio Nogueras, *Y si muero mañana* (Havana: Unión, 1978). The book won a UNEAC prize in 1977 and was later turned into a radio novel for Radio Progreso in 1980.

97. Enrique Álvarez Jané, *Algo que debes hacer* (Havana: UNEAC, 1977); "Algo que debe ser un homenaje," *Verde Olivo*, November 4, 1979.

98. *En silencio ha tenido que ser*, directed by Jesús Cabrera (Havana: Instituto Cubano de Radio y Televisión, Ministerio del Interior, 1979).

99. Victor Martín Borrego, "*En silencio ha tenido que ser*: Ejemplo de buena calidad," *El Caimán Barbudo* 138 (June 1979): 24.

100. *Julito el pescador*, directed by Jesús Cabrera (Havana: Instituto Cubano de Radio y Televisión, Ministerio del Interior, 1980).

101. Carlos Puebla y Sus Tradicionales, "Y en eso llegó Fidel," on *Canciones revolucionarias*, Areíto Records EPA-10008 (LP), 1965.

102. Michael Kackman, *Citizen Spy: Television, Espionage, and Cold War Culture* (Minneapolis: University of Minnesota Press, 2005), 3, 5.

103. John Corner, *Television Form and Public Address* (New York: St. Martin's, 1995), quoted in Kackman, *Citizen Spy*, 5. In addition to Corrieri, other recurring male leads in this era include Mario Balmaseda and Patricio Wood. For an example of their socialist celebrity, see "Mario, protagonista de Balmaseda," *Verde Olivo*, June 3, 1979.

104. *Un día de noviembre*, directed by Humberto Solás (Havana: ICAIC, 1972).

105. Fornet, *El 71*, 131.

106. Roberto José, "Un film de archivo," *El Caimán Barbudo* 134 (February 1979): 22-23.

107. See the textbook currently used in Cuban high schools, which devotes scarce pages to the 1970s compared to the 1960s: José C. Cantón Navarro and Arnaldo Silva León, *Historia de Cuba, 1959-1999: Liberación nacional y socialismo* (Havana: Pueblo y Educación, 2009). For a recent exception, see Emily J. Kirk, Anna Clayfield, and Isabel M.

Story, eds., *Cuba's Forgotten Decade: How the 1970s Shaped the Revolution* (London: Lexington, 2018).

108. Andrew Robinson, "Alan Badiou: The Event," *Ceasefire*, December 15, 2014, https://ceasefiremagazine.co.uk/alain-badiou-event.

109. Outside of Cuba, exceptions requiring further research might include, again, Cuba's military intervention in the Angolan Civil War, beginning in 1975, as well as the 1979 rise to power of the Sandinistas in Nicaragua.

110. See, for example, "Los desesperantes," *Detrás de la fachada*, director unknown (Havana: Instituto Cubano de Radio y Televisión, [1977?]), which includes sketches satirizing the culture of waiting in line to acquire rationed goods. *Detrás de la fachada*, a comedy about relationships between neighbors in a nondescript Havana apartment building, first aired on Cuban television in 1957. After all Cuban television stations were nationalized, the show continued airing with an evolving cast of actors through 1987.

111. Lillian Guerra, "'Somos Felices Aquí': The Revolutionary Theater State and the Mariel Crisis, 1971–1980," unpublished manuscript, 2015.

Chapter 6

1. Raúl Castro, "El diversionismo ideológico: Arma sutil que esgrimen los enemigos contra la Revolución," *Verde Olivo*, June 6, 1972.

2. Steve J. Stern, *Remembering Pinochet's Chile: On the Eve of London 1998* (Durham, N.C.: Duke University Press, 2006), 1.

3. See María de los Ángeles Torres, "El Exilio: National Security Interests and the Origins of the Cuban Enclave," in *Latino/a Thought: Culture, Politics, and Society*, ed. Francisco H. Vázquez (Lanham, Md.: Rowman and Littlefield, 2009), 313; and Duanel Díaz, "¿Gusanos?," *Cubaencuentro*, February 3, 2006, http://www.cubaencuentro.com/opinion/articulos/gusanos-11649.

4. Fidel Castro, "Discurso pronunciado por el Comandante Fidel Castro Ruz, Primer Ministro del Gobierno Revolucionario de Cuba, resumiendo los actos para festejar el tercer aniversario de la revolución socialista de Cuba, en la Plaza de la Revolución," January 2, 1962, http://www.cuba.cu/gobierno/discursos/1962/esp/f020162e.html.

5. Viet Thanh Nguyen, *Nothing Ever Dies: Vietnam and the Memory of War* (Cambridge, Mass.: Harvard University Press, 2016), 63.

6. Vincent Brown, *The Reaper's Garden: Death and Power in the World of Atlantic Slavery* (Cambridge, Mass.: Harvard University Press, 2008), 4. I thank Ada Ferrer for suggesting the parallel to Brown's work.

7. Michael J. Bustamante, "'Cartearse con el Exterior': Notes toward a Lost Correspondence," *Beyond the Sugar Curtain* (blog), May 2017, https://www.brown.edu/research/projects/tracing-cuba-us-connections/news/2017/05/%E2%80%9Ccartearse-con-el-exterior%E2%80%9D; Michael J. Bustamante, "Cold War *Paquetería*: Snail Mail Services across (and around) Cuba's Sugar Curtain," paper presented at the 36th International Congress of the Latin American Studies Association, Barcelona, May 2018.

8. Mirta Ojito, *Finding Mañana: A Memoir of a Cuban Exodus* (New York: Penguin, 2005), 18–22.

9. Ley núm. 2 de 9 de enero 1959 and Ley núm. 18 de 20 de enero 1959, in *Proclamas y leyes del Gobierno Provisional de la Revolución*, vol. 1, *1 al 31 de enero 1959* (Havana: Lex, 1959), 20, 52.

10. Ley Decreto 1463, June 10, 1954, required that all issued passports carry a "certificate of validity" from the then Ministry of State and allowed said ministry to limit the amount of time Cuban citizens were allowed to remain abroad or block travel entirely. The author's paternal grandfather's passport issued in 1958 carries such a stamp.

11. Resolución No. 454 de 29 de septiembre de 1961 del Ministro del Interior, *Gaceta Oficial de la República de Cuba*, No. 196, October 9, 1961, 19310; Ley núm. 989 de 5 de diciembre de 1961, in *Leyes del Gobierno Revolucionario*, vol. 39, *1 a 31 de diciembre de 1961* (Havana: Imprenta Nacional de Cuba, 1962), 5–9; Manuel Zayas, "La isla del nunca jamás," *Diario de Cuba*, January 17, 2012, http://www.diariodecuba.com/derechos-humanos/1326787765_626.html; Ahmed Correa Álvarez, "Cuba, migración y derecho: Reflexión preliminar sobre la no pertinencia," *Cuba Posible*, May 5, 2017, https://cubaposible.com/cuba-migracion-derecho. I am also grateful to Jennifer Lambe for her insights on this topic.

12. Julia Miranda, *Diario para Uchiram: Cuba 1962–1969* (Madrid: Verbum, 2008), 232–38.

13. See Article 32 of Cuba's 1976 Constitution: https://archivos.juridicas.unam.mx/www/bjv/libros/6/2525/51.pdf.

14. Fidel Castro, "Discurso pronunciado por el Comandante Fidel Castro Ruz, Primer Ministro del Gobierno Revolucionario, en la clausura del Congreso Nacional de Alfabetización, en el Teatro 'Chaplin,'" September 5, 1961, http://www.cuba.cu/gobierno/discursos/1961/esp/f050961e.html.

15. Castro, "Discurso . . . resumiendo los actos para festejar el tercer aniversario de la revolución socialista de Cuba."

16. See Teishan A. Latner, *Cuban Revolution in America: Havana and the Making of a United States Left, 1968–1992* (Chapel Hill: University of North Carolina Press, 2018), 27–74; and Ian Lekus, "Queer Harvests: Homosexuality, the U.S. New Left, and the Venceremos Brigades to Cuba," *Radical History Review* 89 (2004): 57–91.

17. Norberto Fuentes, "Ganar hermanos: Entrevista a Lourdes Casal," *Revolución y Cultura* 77 (January 1979): 73.

18. Lourdes Casal, "Opinión," *Nueva Generación* 22–23 (June–September 1971): n.p.

19. "Dos semanas en Cuba: Entrevista con Lourdes Casal," *Areíto* 1, no. 1 (April 1974): 21–28; Lourdes Casal, "Fragmentos de un diario de viaje," *Nueva Generación* 27 (June 1974): 1–11.

20. Mariana Gastón, interview with author, Brooklyn, N.Y., June 4, 2014; Miren Uriarte, telephone interview with author, April 23, 2014.

21. See Marta A. González, *Bajo palabra* (Havana: Venceremos, 1965).

22. Edith Reinoso Hernández, *Testimonio de una emigrada* (Havana: Ciencias Sociales, 1974); Napoleón Lizardo, on comment board below Arencibia Cardoso, "Un título equivocado: Vicente Méndez, leyenda sin acción," *Baracutey Cubano* (blog), May 4, 2011, http://baracuteycubano.blogspot.com/2011/05/cuba-un-titulo-equivocado-vicente.html.

23. "Me gradué de agente cuando mataron al Che," *Cubainformación*, July 13, 2010, http://www.cubainformacion.tv/index.php/cuba/sociedad/28722-me-gradue-de-agente-cuando-mataron-al-che; Pastor Guzmán, "Remembranzas de un oficial de inteligencia," *Escambray*, October 28, 2015, http://www.escambray.cu/2015/remembranzas-de-un-oficial-de-inteligencia.

24. Reinoso Hernández, *Testimonio de una emigrada*, 4.

25. Reinoso Hernández, 4.

26. Reinoso Hernández, x.

27. Gastón, interview; Uriarte, interview. For accounts of other early trips, see "Una vez más en Cuba: Entrevista con Mariana Gastón y Regina Casal," *Areíto* 1, no. 3 (1974): 2–10; and "Testimonios," *Areíto* 2, no. 2–3 (1975): 18–47.

28. Emilio Cueto, interview with author, September 5, 2018, Miami. Former *El Miami Herald* reporter Helga Silva also recalls the case of a friend who was able to visit in the mid-1970s thanks to a humanitarian exception to see her father in prison. Helga Silva, interview with author, December 20, 2018, Miramar, Fla.

29. Espinosa also took part in a second trip later that same year. Carlos Licea, "Espinosa vuelve a Cuba, busca familiares, diálogo," *Miami News en Español*, July 31, 1975; Zita Arocha, phone interview with author, November 2, 2018.

30. Brzezinski to President, "Cuba: Travel Restrictions, Visitation Rights, and Sugar Smut Disease," [February–early March 1977], folder "Cuba, 1-4/77," box 13, National Security Affairs, Records of the Office of the National Security Adviser, Country File, Jimmy Carter Library, Atlanta, Ga., as cited in Lars Schoultz, *That Infernal Little Cuban Republic: The United States and the Cuban Revolution* (Chapel Hill: University of North Carolina Press, 2009), 660. I am indebted to Jennifer Lambe for bringing this source to my attention. Jesús Arboleya, email communication to author, June 22, 2019.

31. "Revela el compañero Carlos Rivero Collado que la CIA y el FBI utilizan a elementos contrarrevolucionarios en las agresiones contra Cuba y que ambos órganos represivos los protegen," *Granma*, April 30, 1976; Carlos Rivero Collado, *Los sobrinos del Tío Sam* (Havana: Ciencias Sociales, 1976).

32. Carlos Rivero Collado, *Comparecencia del compañero Carlos Rivero Collado ante las cámaras de la televisión cubana, 29 abril 1976* (Havana: Ciencias Sociales, 1976), 7; Emilio Comas Paret, "Entrevista a Carlos Rivero Collado, colaborador de Kaos en la Red," *Kaos en la Red*, January 26, 2010, link broken, preserved at http://www.latinamericanstudies.org/espionage/collado.htm; Lillian Guerra, "Political Rehabilitation, Ideological Diversionists, and the Struggle for Hegemony in the Cuban Revolution, 1965–1971," paper presented at the 128th Annual Meeting of the American Historical Association, Washington, D.C., January 4, 2014.

33. Reinoso Hernández, *Testimonio de una emigrada*, 55.

34. See, for example, the reference to the Antonio Maceo Brigade in "Palabras del Presidente Cubano Miguel Díaz-Canel en el encuentro con los cubanos que viven en Estados Unidos," *Dominio Cuba*, September 28, 2018, https://medium.com/dominio-cuba/contamos-con-ustedes-somos-cuba-a091416d6b64.

35. "Editorial," *Areíto* 4, no. 3–4 (Spring 1978): 2–3.

36. Schoultz, *That Infernal Little Cuban Republic*, 291–304.

37. Jesús Arboleya, interview with author, April 23, 2015, Havana, Cuba. Arboleya was a Cuban diplomat posted at the United Nations at the time and became the chief contact with the Cuban government for *Areíto* and the early Antonio Maceo Brigade organizers.

38. José León, interview with author, Jamaica Plain, Mass., June 8, 2014.

39. Fidel Castro, "Discurso pronunciado … en la clausura del Congreso Nacional de Alfabetización."

40. Miren Uriarte, email communication to author, September 4, 2014.

41. *55 Hermanos*, directed by Jesús Díaz (Havana: ICAIC, 1978).

42. Román de la Campa, "Itinerario de la Brigada Antonio Maceo," *Areíto* 4, no. 3-4 (Spring 1978): 14.

43. See James Dietz, "Puerto Rico in the 1970s and 1980s: Crisis of the Development Model," *Journal of Economic Issues* 16, no. 2 (June 1982): 497-506.

44. Maritza Giberga, "En Ariguanabo esta vez como constructora," *Areíto* 4, no. 3-4 (Spring 1978): 23.

45. Gastón, interview.

46. Enrique Rodríguez Bocanegra, "Regreso," *Areíto* 5, no. 17 (1978): 11.

47. See *Areíto* 5, no. 19-20, número extraordinario (1979), published in the aftermath of his death. Also see *Recordando a Carlos Muñiz Varela*, directed by Juan Carlos García (San Juan: n.d.), http://vimeo.com/28193236. On the second contingent of the Antonio Maceo Brigade, see José Quiroga, "Unpacking My Files: My Life as a Queer Brigadista," *Social Text* 32, no. 4 (Winter 2014): 149-59.

48. Emilio Bejel, "Quo vadis," *Areíto* 2, no. 1 (Summer 1975): 46.

49. Lourdes Casal, "Descarga no. 2," *Areíto* 2, no. 2-3 (1975): 22.

50. In Grupo Areíto, *Contra viento y marea* (Havana: Casa de las Américas, 1978), group leaders also framed their own collective memory as exiles in the same terms.

51. Gastón, interview.

52. León, interview.

53. Cueto, interview.

54. See Piero Gleijses, *Visions of Freedom: Havana, Washington, Pretoria, and the Struggle for Southern Africa, 1976-1991* (Chapel Hill: University of North Carolina Press, 2013).

55. William M. LeoGrande and Peter Kornbluh, *Back Channel to Cuba: The Hidden History of Negotiations between Washington and Havana* (Chapel Hill: University of North Carolina Press, 2014), 155-78.

56. Augustin Alles, "Sale el Reverendo Espinosa para Cuba con otro grupo," *Réplica*, February 16, 1978; Bonnie Anderson, "Persiste enigma sobre labor del reverendo Espinosa," *EMH*, November 20, 1978.

57. Arocha, interview. Arocha's invitation, however, was withdrawn at the last minute, for reasons she never determined.

58. "Texto completo de la conferencia de prensa del Presidente del Consejo de Estado de Cuba Dr. Fidel Castro, con periodistas extranjeros y cubanos en el exterior," *Areíto* 5, no. 17 (1978), special supplement.

59. See Robert M. Levine, *Secret Missions to Cuba: Fidel Castro, Bernardo Benes, and Cuban Miami* (New York: Palgrave MacMillan, 2001).

60. "Acta final de los diálogos celebrados entre el gobierno de la República de Cuba y personalidades representativas de la comunidad cubana en el exterior, los días 20 y 21 de noviembre, y 8 de diciembre, de 1978," http://www.latinamericanstudies.org/dialogue/Dialogo-firmantes.pdf. According to Raúl Álzaga Manresa, member of the Antonio Maceo Brigade and cofounder of Viajes Varadero in Puerto Rico, the first of these trips took place December 21, 1978. See María Isabel Alfonso, "Dialogando con la emigración: ¿Cómo lograr en verdad que el país crezca?," *OnCuba*, February 15, 2020, https://oncubanews.com/opinion/dialogando-con-la-emigracion-cubana-como-lograr-que-en-verdad-el-pais-crezca.

61. LeoGrande and Kornbluh, *Back Channel to Cuba*, 188.

62. Schoultz, *That Infernal Little Cuban Republic*, 325; Elier Ramírez Cañedo, *Cuba y su emigración, 1978: Memorias del primer diálogo* (Havana: Ocean Sur, 2020).

63. "Editorial," *Abdala*, October–November 1978, 2; Silva, interview; Schoultz, *That Infernal Little Cuban Republic*, 304–61; LeoGrande and Kornbluh, *Back Channel to Cuba*, 155–224. Wayne S. Smith, long-time State Department Cuban hand and first chief of the U.S. Interests Section in Havana, was the first to reveal the extent of back channel negotiations in his memoir *The Closest of Enemies: A Personal and Diplomatic History of the Castro Years* (New York: W. W. Norton, 1988). Critical responses to these revelations among dialogue participants include Adriana Méndez, "Metamorfosis de una mariposa," *Encuentro de la Cultura Cubana* 8/9 (Spring–Summer 1998): 172–84; Roberto González Echevarría, *Cuban Fiestas* (New Haven, Conn.: Yale University Press, 2010), 112–20; and María de los Ángeles Torres, *In the Land of Mirrors: Cuban Exile Politics in the United States* (Ann Arbor: University of Michigan Press, 1999), 95–96.

64. Carmelo Mesa-Lago, "The Economy: Caution, Frugality, and Resilient Ideology," in *Cuba: Internal and International Affairs*, ed. Jorge I. Domínguez (Thousand Oaks, Calif.: Sage, 1982), 113–67; Mark S. Hamm, *The Abandoned Ones: The Imprisonment and Uprising of the Mariel Boat People* (Boston: Northeastern University Press, 1995), 45–47.

65. "Problemas objetivos de nuestra Revolución: Lo que el pueblo debe saber—Humberto Pérez entrevistado por Marta Harnecker," *Verde Olivo*, February 25, 1979; Fidel Castro, "Que se acabe la blandenguería, el compradrismo, la tolerancia, ¡que se acabe!," *Verde Olivo*, July 8, 1979.

66. Charles Romeo, "El desesperado intento de 'meter la cuchara' por algunos intelectuales," *Segunda Cita* (blog), August 13, 2018, http://segundacita.blogspot.com/2018/08/el-desesperado-intento-de-meter-la.html.

67. Abel Rosendo Castro Figueroa, *El país de la Ciguaraya* (Bloomington, Ind.: Palibrio, 2011), 136–37; Abel Castro Figueroa, email message to author, June 19, 2015; Carlos Cabrera Pérez, "Timba Diáz-Canel cayó en la trampa," *CiberCuba*, August 22, 2018, https://www.cibercuba.com/noticias/2017-08-22-u191143-e42839-timba-diaz-canel-cayo-trampa. The actual speech appears to be Fidel Castro, "Discurso del Comandante en Jefe, Fidel Castro Ruz, reunión de información a cuadros y militantes del Partido, Teatro Karl Marx," February 8, 1979, Versiones Taquigráficas del Consejo de Estado. Long passages are quoted in Ramírez Cañedo, *Cuba y su emigración*, as the author has had access to the nonpublic transcripts in the archives of the Council of State. I thank him for sharing these passages with me. Jesús Arboleya also references the speech in "El Mariel: 30 años después," *Temas* 68 (October–December 2011): 83.

68. Elizabeth Cerejido, interview with author, June 28, 2018, Miami.

69. Zita Arocha, "Cuba planea recibir 110,000 exiliados," *EMH*, January 14, 1979.

70. Zita Arocha, "Pide Espinosa $90,000 para construir iglesia," *EMH*, June 12, 1979.

71. Zita Arocha, "Agotan 're-entry' ansiosos por ir a Cuba," *EMH*, January 20, 1979.

72. Diana González, "Ticket to Havana" (Five-Part Series), WTVJ News (Miami), November 19–23, 1979, Wolfson Florida Moving Image Archives, Miami-Dade College, Miami, Fla.

73. Dora Amador, interview with author, June 26, 2018, Miami; Emilio Cueto, interview; Mary Lynn Conejo, phone interview with author, July 10, 2018; Iraida R. López, Iraida H. López, María C. López, interview with author, July 18, 2018, Miami; Zita Arocha, "Abren vía a Cuba por Mérida para exiliados turistas," *EMH*, February 8, 1979.

74. Dr. Roger Hernández, "Cuando vayas a Cuba," February 1979, Bernardo Benes Papers, box 23, folder 181, Cuban Heritage Collection, University of Miami Libraries, Coral Gables, Fla.

75. Alberto Coya, "Voces de la calle," *EMH*, January 28, 1979.

76. Zita Arocha, "No quiere morir sin ver a su hija," *EMH*, February 1, 1979, 2; Zita Arocha, "Exiliada llega tarde a ver a su padre en Cuba," *EMH*, March 4, 1979, 2.

77. Carlos Alberto Montaner, "El regreso de los exiliados cubanos a la patria," *EMH*, June 18, 1979. See also "Compatriota: Si vas a Cuba ... sé útil!," *Abdala*, February/March 1979, 1, 3.

78. Frank Soler, "Fidel Castro lucre con los exiliados," *EMH*, February 25, 1979; Rodolfo Nadal-Tarafa, "Castro hacia el poder en Miami," *EMH*, May 4, 1979; Reinaldo Pico, "Los viajes a Cuba son una estafa, dice Rolando Hernández," *Réplica*, April 5, 1979; "Viajes de exiliados benefician la economía cubana," *EMH*, February 11, 1979.

79. Zita Arocha, "Policía investiga posible estafa en viajes," *EMH*, February 12, 1979.

80. Zita Arocha, "Suspenden permiso de viajes a Cuba de la 747," *EMH*, March 14; Frank Soler, "Lo extraño de los viajes a Cuba," *EMH*, March 24, 1979.

81. Zita Arocha, "Centran en una agencia viajes a Cuba," *EMH*, March 15, 1979; Zita Arocha, "Havanatur abre agencia en Miami," *EMH*, May 13, 1979; Ileana Oroza, "Pide E.U. igualdad de tarifas en viajes a Cuba," *EMH*, July 28, 1979. This would change in September 1979, after the U.S. State and Treasury Departments threatened to shut down the company's U.S. operations over charges of discrimination. See "Cuban Exiles at Airport, Wait to Leave on $450 Tours," WTVJ News (Miami), September 25, 1979, Wolfson Florida Moving Image Archives, Miami-Dade College, Miami, Fla.

82. Diana González, "Ticket to Havana"; Dora Amador, interview; Mary Lynn Conejo, interview.

83. Mabel Suárez, interview with author, October 19, 2018, Havana.

84. Helga Silva and Guy Gugliotta, "Encara el exilio una nueva realidad," *EMH*, April 8, 1979.

85. Guillermo Álvarez Guedes, "Los viajes a Cuba," *Álvarez Guedes* 9, Gema Records, LPGS-5064 (LP), 1979.

86. "Otro criterio sobre las visitas a Cuba," *EMH*, March 23, 1979.

87. "Viajes de exiliados benefician la economía cubana."

88. Fidel Castro, "Discurso del Comandante en Jefe, Fidel Castro Ruz, reunión de información a cuadros y militantes del Partido," quoted in Ramírez Cañedo, *Cuba y su emigración*.

89. Regulations now reduced allowable luggage to forty-four pounds, and within that limit, the value of goods to be left in Cuba could not exceed the equivalent of 1,000 Cuban pesos, or roughly $1,400 dollars, per the artificial exchange rate applied. One report also alleged that, because the Cuban government technically classified them as "tourists"— despite carrying Cuban passports and entry paperwork—exiles would be barred from bringing *anything* but personal effects. "Arancel de Aduanas para las importaciones sin carácter comercial," *Bohemia*, June 8, 1979; Augustín Alles, "Las nuevas regulaciones aduaneras para los viajes a Cuba," *Réplica*, May 3, 1979.

90. Mary Lynn Conejo, interview. In 1975, the United States had lifted a prior ban on subsidiaries of U.S. companies trading with Cuba. The ban would be reimposed in 1992.

91. Cheryl Brownstein, "Exiliados cancelan viajes a Cuba," *EMH*, May 2, 1979.

92. Zita Arocha, "Declinan los viajes a Cuba," *EMH*, May 27, 1979.

93. "Antes, ahora: Los viajeros que van de Miami a Cuba," *Réplica*, May 3, 1979.

94. Zita Arocha, "Expulsa E.U. a Havanatur," *EMH*, August 29, 1979.

95. Zita Arocha, "Avión de Cubana vuela a Miami," *EMH*, July 2, 1979.

96. Helga Silva, "Regreso de exiliados causa comoción en Cuba," *EMH*, August 5, 1979; Zita Arocha, "Bolsa negra va con algunas valijas a Cuba," *EMH*, August 26, 1979; Don Bohning and Helga Silva, "Impacto en Cuba por visitas," *EMH*, May 13, 1979.

97. Silva, interview.

98. Dora Amador, interview; Luis Miguel Valdés, phone interview with author, June 27, 2018.

99. Emilio Cueto, interview.

100. Emilio Cueto, interview.

101. Elizabeth Cerejido, interview.

102. Mary Lynn Conejo, interview.

103. Mabel Suárez, interview.

104. Carlos Manuel Abreu, interview with author, August 5, 2018, Miami.

105. Eliana Rivero, phone interview with author, July 23, 2018.

106. Dora Amador, interview.

107. Luis Miguel Valdés, interview.

108. Luis Miguel Valdés, interview.

109. Mary Lynn Conejo, interview.

110. Arocha, "Expulsa E.U. a Havanatur," 1.

111. Bonnie Anderson and Ileana Oroza, "Espinosa Calls for 'All Out War' against Castro," *MH*, January 31, 1980.

112. "Havanatur: Espinosa Owes $430,000," *MH*, February 10, 1980.

113. See sample ads from late 1979: "Havanatur S.A." (advertisement), *EMH*, November 18, 1979; "Un weekend en familia: Diciembre en Cuba" (advertisement), *EMH*, December 10, 1979.

114. Álvarez Guedes, "Los viajes a Cuba"; Mario Martín, "Me voy para Cuba ¡Fuaa!," 1979.

115. For an exception poking fun at a returning exile for bringing a "sample of unbelievable toilet paper," see cartoon, no title, *Verde Olivo*, November 25, 1979.

116. Luis Miguel Valdés, interview.

117. Alfonso Chardy, "Mariel: Tema obligado en el Coppelia," *EMH*, May 17, 1980.

118. Uriarte, interview.

119. "Humberto Ortega: Stowaway after Arriving on Cubana Airways Plane in Wheel Compartment," WTVJ News (Miami), August 7, 1979, Wolfson Florida Moving Image Archives, Miami-Dade College, Miami; Andy Markowitz and Nery Ynclan, "Stowaway Cuban's Journey Ends in Freedom from Life He Hated," *MH*, August 8, 1979.

120. Emilio Cueto, interview.

121. See the testimony of Zobeida Castellanos in *In Their Own Words*, directed by Jorge Ulla (Washington, D.C.: U.S. Information Agency, 1980). She links her decision to flee via Mariel to the "shock" of the visit of her relatives from the United States the previous year.

122. Elizabeth Cerejido, interview.

123. Elier Ramírez Cañedo, "A cuarenta años de la crisis migratoria del Mariel y del fin

de la administración Carter," *La Jiribilla*, 2020 (n.d.), http://www.lajiribilla.cu/articulo/a-40-anos-de-la-crisis-migratoria-del-mariel-y-del-fin-de-la-administracion-carter-i-1.

124. Silva, interview.

125. Richard J. Meislin, "Main Air Link between U.S. and Cuba Shut Down," *New York Times*, April 17, 1982; Kenneth N. Skoug Jr., *The United States and Cuba under Reagan and Shultz: A Foreign Service Officer Reports* (Westport, Conn.: Greenwood, 1996), 26; Susan Eckstein and Lorena Barberia, *Cuban-American Cuba Visits: Public Policy, Private Practices*. Report of the Mellon-MIT Inter-university Program on NGOs and Forced Migration (Cambridge: Massachusetts Institute for Technology, Center for International Studies, 2001). The Cuban government would again restrict exile visits for a time beginning in 1985, as part of its protest over the launch of U.S.-government-financed anti-Castro radio station Radio Martí.

126. For a fictional exception, see Leopoldo Hernández, "We Were Always Afraid," in *Cuban Theater in the United States: A Critical Anthology*, ed. Luis F. González-Cruz and Francecsa M. Colecchia (Tempe, Ariz.: Bilingual, 1992), 10-23. For a partly autobiographical treatment, see René R. Alomá, "A Little Something to Ease the Pain," in *Cuban American Theater*, ed. Rodolfo J. Cortina (Houston: Arte Público, 1991), 193-238.

127. Most famous is *Lejanía* (Havana: ICAIC, 1985), directed by Jesús Díaz, of *55 Hermanos* fame. From his own eventual exile in Europe in the 1990s, Díaz would rewrite the making of *Lejanía* as the novel *La piel y la máscara*, hinting at some of the ways the original may have been compromised by censorship. See Antonio Daniel Gómez, "Jesús Díaz Rewrites Cuban Exile," in *Cuba: In Transition? Pathways to Renewal, Long-Term Development and Global Reintegration*, ed. Mauricio A. Font (New York: Bildner Center for Western Hemisphere Studies-CUNY, 2006), 309-13.

Conclusion

1. Plans for a Cuban Exile History Museum are afoot, but stalled. Nicolás Gutierrez Jr., "Cuban Exile Museum Will Highlight 'a Triumph of the American Dream,'" *MH*, July 26, 2014, https://www.miamiherald.com/opinion/op-ed/article1977116.html.

2. "Who We Are," *CubaNostalgia.org*, http://www.cubanostalgia.org/english/index.html.

3. Albert Laguna, *Diversión: Play and Popular Culture in Cuban America* (New York: New York University Press, 2017), 89-122.

4. I take this distinction from James Clifford, "Diaspora," *Cultural Anthropology* 9, no. 3 (August 1994): 302-38.

5. Steve J. Stern, *Remembering Pinochet's Chile: On the Eve of London 1998* (Durham, N.C.: Duke University Press, 2006), 1.

6. Michael Kammen, *Mystic Chords of Memory* (New York: Vintage, 1991), quoted in Svetlana Boym, *The Future of Nostalgia* (New York: Basic Books, 2001), xiv.

7. Ricardo L. Ortiz, *Cultural Erotics in Cuban America* (Minneapolis: University of Minnesota Press, 2007), 6.

8. Damián J. Fernández, "Cuba and lo Cubano, or the Story of Desire and Disenchantment," in *Cuba, the Elusive Nation: Interpretations of National Identity*, ed. Damián J. Fernández and Madeline Cámara Betancourt (Gainesville: University Press of Florida, 2000), 79-98.

9. José Quiroga, *Cuban Palimpsests* (Minneapolis: University of Minnesota Press, 2005), 93-95.

10. Viet Thanh Nguyen, *Nothing Ever Dies: Vietnam and the Memory of War* (Cambridge, Mass.: Harvard University Press, 2016), 23.

11. Nguyen, 73.

12. See Greg Grandin, "The Instruction of Great Catastrophe: Truth Commissions, National History, and State Formation in Argentina, Chile, and Guatemala," *American Historical Review* 110, no. 1 (February 2005): 46-67; Steve J. Stern, *Reckoning with Pinochet: The Memory Question in Democratic Chile, 1989-2006* (Durham, N.C.: Duke University Press, 2010); and Paloma Aguilar, *Memory and Amnesia: The Role of the Spanish Civil War in the Transition to Democracy*, trans. Mark Gordon Oakley (New York: Berghahn, 2002).

13. Stern, *Remembering Pinochet's Chile*, 1.

14. See, for example, Mirta Ojito, *Finding Mañana: A Memoir of a Cuban Exodus* (New York: Penguin, 2005); David Engstrom, *Presidential Decision Making Adrift: The Carter Administration and the Mariel Boatlift* (Lanham, Md.: Rowman and Littlefield, 1997); Kate Dupes Hawk, Ron Villella, and Adolfo Leyva de Varona, *Florida and the Mariel Boatlift of 1980: The First Twenty Days* (Tuscaloosa: University of Alabama Press, 2014); *Más allá del mar*, directed by Lisandro Pérez-Rey (Miami, 2003); Julio Capó Jr., "Queering Mariel: Mediating Cold War Foreign Policy and U.S. Citizenship among Cuba's Homosexual Exile Community, 1978-1994," *Journal of American Ethnic History* 29, no. 4 (Summer 2010): 78-106; Mark S. Hamm, *The Abandoned Ones: The Imprisonment and Uprising of the Mariel Boat People* (Boston: Northeastern University Press, 1995); and "El Mariel: 30 años después," *Temas* 68 (October-December 2011): 80-93.

15. *La marcha del pueblo combatiente*, directed by Santiago Álvarez (Havana: ICAIC, 1980).

16. Fidel Castro, "Discurso pronunciado por el Comandante en Jefe Fidel Castro Ruz, Primer Secretario del Comité Central del Partido Comunista de Cuba y Presidente de los Consejos de Estado y de Ministros, en el acto conmemorativo del primero de mayo, efectuado en la Plaza de la Revolución 'José Martí,'" May 1, 1980, http://www.cuba.cu/gobierno/discursos/1980/esp/f010580e.html.

17. Fernando Dávalos, *La frontera en Mariel* (Havana: Unión, 1983), 7-8.

18. Abel Sierra Madero, "Here, Everyone's Got *Huevos*, Mister! Nationalism, Sexuality, and Collective Violence in Cuba during the Mariel Exodus," in *The Revolution from Within: Cuba, 1959-1980*, ed. Michael J. Bustamante and Jennifer L. Lambe (Durham, N.C.: Duke University Press, 2019), 244-74.

19. For an exception, see *Los marielitos*, directed by Estela Bravo (Havana and New York: Bravo Films, 1983). Though produced independently (Bravo is a U.S. expat who still lives in Havana), the film was shown on Cuban television.

20. See *Mauvaise conduite*, directed by Orlando Jiménez Leal and Néstor Almendros (Paris: Antenne 2, 1984), which introduced many exiles to forced labor camps in Cuba during the late 1960s through the testimony of Mariel migrants who had been interned in them. The film was released in the United States under the title *Improper Conduct*.

21. Some estimates suggest that upward of 25,000 of the Mariel migrants had criminal records in Cuba. But U.S. media depictions did not differentiate between migrants possibly guilty of violent crimes versus offenses like participation in the black market also punishable by Cuban law. See María Cristina García, *Havana USA: Cuban Exiles and*

Cuban Americans in South Florida, 1959-1994 (Berkeley: University of California Press, 1996), 64-65; and Hamm, *The Abandoned Ones*, 60-65, 71. As for the forced inclusion of psychiatric patients in the boatlift, enough evidence corroborates that some of this did occur, but it was also greatly exaggerated. See Jennifer L. Lambe, *Madhouse: Psychiatry and Cuban History* (Chapel Hill: University of North Carolina Press, 2016), 202.

22. García, *Havana USA*, 72-73; Monika Gosin, *The Racial Politics of Division: Interethnic Struggles for Legitimacy in Multicultural Miami* (Ithaca, N.Y.: Cornell University Press, 2019), 57-90; Gastón A. Fernández, "Race, Gender, and Class in the Persistence of the Mariel Stigma Twenty Years after the Exodus from Cuba," *International Migration Review* 41, no. 3 (2007): 602-22.

23. Iván de la Nuez, "Extremo Mariel," *Rialta*, April 2020, http://rialta-ed.com/extremo-mariel. Originally published as "Mariel en el extremo de la cultura," *Encuentro de la Cultura Cubana* 8-9 (1998): 105-9.

24. Silvia M. Unzueta and Guillermo Martínez, "Not My-Ami," in *Cubans: An Epic Journey, the Struggle of Exiles for Truth and Freedom*, ed. Sam Verdeja and Guillermo Martínez (Miami: Facts about Cuban Exiles, 2011), 170.

25. Fernández, "Race, Gender, and Class in the Persistence of the Mariel Stigma"; Gosin, *The Racial Politics of Division*.

26. On marked differences in average household income between Mariel and pre-Mariel Cuban migrants to this day, see Alejandro Portes and Aaron Puhrmann, "A Bifurcated Enclave: The Economic Evolution of the Cuban and Cuban American Population of Metropolitan Miami," *Cuban Studies* 43 (2015): 40-63. Compare to the more bullish account in Aida Levitan, "Miami Leaders Smoothly Integrated 125,000 Cuban Refugees," *MH*, April 17, 2020, https://www.miamiherald.com/opinion/op-ed/article242091826.html. For an exception to the relative invisibility of Mariel migrants' stories in the Cuban exile community during the 1980s, see *Amigos*, directed by Iván Acosta (Miami: Manicote Productions, 1985).

27. None was more influential than the Cuban American National Foundation, founded in 1981. García, *Havana USA*, 146-56; Michael J. Bustamante, "Anti-communist Anti-imperialism? Agrupación Abdala and the Shifting Contours of Cuban Exile Politics, 1968-1986," *Journal of American Ethnic History* 35, no. 1 (2015): 91-92.

28. Jorge I. Domínguez, "Cuba in the 1980s," *Foreign Affairs* 65, no. 1 (Fall 1986): 118-35; Susan Eckstein, *Back from the Future: Cuba under Castro*, 2nd ed. (London: Routledge, 2003), 59-86; Emma Álvarez-Tabío Albó, "The City in Midair," in *Havana beyond the Ruins: Cultural Mappings after 1989*, ed. Anne Birkenmaier and Esther Whitfield (Durham, N.C.: Duke University Press, 2011), 149-72.

29. On Cuban visual and performance art in the 1980s, see Rachel Weiss, *To and from Utopia in the New Cuban Art* (Minneapolis: University of Minnesota Press, 2011); and Coco Fusco, *Dangerous Moves: Performance and Politics in Cuba* (London: Tate, 2015).

30. Carlos Varela, "Guillermo Tell," *Jalisco Park*, EGREM (LP), 1989.

31. Nostalgic takes on the 1980s in Cuba include *La vaca de mármol*, directed by Enrique Colina (Havana, 2013); *El telón de azúcar*, directed by Camila Guzmán (Paris: Luz Films, 2005).

32. For example, Carlos Varela, "Foto de familia," *Como los peces*, BMG 74321 25754 2 (CD), 1994; Frank Delgado, "La otra orilla," *La Habana está de bala* (CD), 1997. There were exceptions to this improved treatment. Cubans who "defected" from official government-

backed travel abroad or otherwise departed the country illegally continued to face prohibitions on returning home, at least for a time. Some of those prohibitions remain in force today.

33. Silvio Rodríguez, "El necio," *Silvio*, EGREM LD-4733 (LP), 1992.

34. Pedro Luis Ferrer, "100% cubano," *100% cubano*, Carapacho Productions (CD), 1994.

35. Ana María Dopico, "Picturing Havana: History, Vision, and the Scramble for Cuba," *Nepantla: Views from South* 3, no. 3 (2002): 451–93.

36. Examples in this spirit include Eliseo Alberto, *Informe contra mí mismo* (Mexico City: Alfaguara, 1996) and works of fiction like Leonardo Padura, *La novela de mi vida* (Barcelona: Tusquets, 2002).

37. Ambrosio Fornet, "Quinquenio gris: Revisitando el término," *Casa de las Américas* 246 (January–March 2007): 3–16; Rafael Rojas, *Tumbas sin sosiego: Revolución, disidencia y exilio del intelectual cubano* (Barcelona: Anagrama, 2006); Rafael Rojas, *El estante vacío: Literatura y política en Cuba* (Barcelona: Anagrama, 2009).

38. *Fresa y chocolate*, directed by Tomás Gutiérrez Alea (Havana: ICAIC, 1993).

39. The relevant pieces of legislation were the Cuban Democracy Act (or Toricelli Act) of 1992 and the Cuban Liberty and Democratic Solidarity (Libertad), or Helms-Burton Act of 1996. Together, these laws codified the bulk of the U.S. embargo and removed the prerogative for lifting it completely from the executive branch.

40. *Arte nuevo de hacer ruinas*, directed by Florian Borchmeyer (Berlin: Glück auf Film, Koppfilm, Raros Media, 2006).

41. Willy Chirino, "Nuestro día (ya viene llegando)," *Oxígeno*, Sony CDZ-80600 (CD), 1991.

42. See, for example, Cuban American National Foundation, "Transition Program for a Post-Castro Cuba," 1993. The Cuban American National Foundation and later initiatives like the Cuba Transition Project at the University of Miami (founded in 2002 and funded by the U.S. Agency for International Development) published dozens of working papers and reports of a similar kind.

43. *Cuban National Reconciliation: Task Force on Memory, Truth, and Justice* (Miami: Florida International University, 2003).

44. Founded in 1991, Brothers to the Rescue was an organization of private Cuban exile pilots who patrolled the Florida Straits and called in coordinates of Cuban rafters to the U.S. Coast Guard so they could be picked up at sea. They also flew over Cuban airspace and dispersed anti-Castro leaflets on the Cuban capital, activities that the Cuban government urged Washington to stop. See *Shoot Down*, directed by Cristina Khuly (New York: Palisades Pictures, 2007). On the Elián González affair, see Lillian Guerra, "Elián González and the 'Real Cuba' of Miami: Visions of Identity, Exceptionality, and Divinity," *Cuban Studies* 38 (2007): 1–25.

45. After several ups and downs in the 1980s, the originally controversial *visitas de la comunidad* became a more regular occurrence over the 1990s. Lorena Barberia and Susan Eckstein, *Cuban-American Cuba Visits: Public Policy, Private Practices*, Report of the Mellon-MIT Inter-university Program on NGOs and Forced Migration (Cambridge: Massachusetts Institute of Technology, Center for International Studies, 2001).

46. Laguna, *Diversión*, 91.

47. For example, Café Nostalgia, the most popular nightclub on Little Havana's Calle Ocho in the 1990s, was the brainchild of a former official of the revolutionary government's film institute who arrived in South Florida in 1994. See Mirta Ojito, "A Nightclub Bottles Cuba, before the Revolution," *New York Times*, October 13, 1998.

48. Aurora Jácome, "The Muñequitos Rusos Generation," in *Caviar with Rum: Cuba-USSR and the Post-Soviet Experience*, ed. Jaqueline Loss and José Manuel Prieto (London: Palgrave, 2012), 27–36; Nora Gámez Torres, "Cubanos de Miami tienen nostalgia por productos rusos," *El Nuevo Herald*, November 14, 2014, https://www.elnuevoherald.com/noticias/mundo/america-latina/cuba-es/article3938840.html.

49. Jacqueline Loss, *Dreaming in Russian: The Cuban Soviet Imaginary* (Austin: University of Texas Press, 2014).

50. For example, *Páginas del diario de Mauricio*, directed by Manuel Pérez (Havana: ICAIC, 2006).

51. "Toy Story," *Radio Ambulante* (podcast), April 9, 2019, http://radioambulante.org/transcripcion/transcripcion-toy-story; Mónica Baró, "Lo peor siempre fue la escacez," *El Estornudo*, May 23, 2019, https://www.revistaelestornudo.com/lo-peor-siempre-fue-la-escasez.

52. Laguna, *Diversión*, 125–26.

53. For example, Ruth Behar, ed., *Bridges to Cuba / Puentes a Cuba* (Ann Arbor: University of Michigan Press, 1995); *La Gaceta de Cuba* 5 (September–October 1996); Román de la Campa, *Cuba on My Mind: Journeys to a Severed Nation* (New York: Verso, 2000); María de los Ángeles Torres, ed., *By Heart / De Memoria: Cuban Women's Journeys in and out of Exile* (Philadelphia: Temple University Press, 2003); Ambrosio Fornet, *Narrar la nación: Ensayos en blanco y negro* (Havana: Letras Cubanas, 2009). See also the results of the "Congreso de Escritores de Estocolomo," an effort to bring together Cuban writers from the island and its diaspora in 1994. René Vázquez Díaz, eds., *Bipolaridad de la cultura cubana: Ponencias del Primer Encuentro de Escritores de dentro y fuera de Cuba* (Stockholm: Olof Palme International Center, 1994).

54. Examples include the NGO Puentes Cubanos (Cuban Bridges), active in the early 2000s, and more recently the CubaOne Foundation. See Elizabeth Cerejido, "Why Cultural Exchanges with Cuba Matter," *Latin American Working Group*, n.d., https://www.lawg.org/why-cultural-exchanges-with-cuba-matter; Jordan Levin, "Forging a New Path to Cultural Exchanges with Cuba," *MH*, June 6, 2015, https://www.miamiherald.com/entertainment/ent-columns-blogs/jordan-levin/article23090049.html; and Jessica Weiss, "New Group Offers Young Cuban-Americans Free Trips to Cuba," *Miami New Times*, April 29, 2016, https://www.miaminewtimes.com/news/new-group-offers-young-cuban-americans-free-trips-to-cuba-8424000.

55. In 2010, for example, Fidel Castro indirectly admitted knowledge of and responsibility for forced labor camps targeting gays and religious minorities between 1965 and 1968. His niece (and Raúl Castro's daughter) Mariela Castro, a leader of gay rights efforts in Cuba today, has also elliptically acknowledged histories of homophobia. However, she has also repeatedly downplayed the severity of the UMAP camps to which many gay Cuban men were sent in the 1960s. See Carmen Lira Saade, "Soy el responsable de la persecución a homosexuales que hubo en Cuba: Fidel Castro," *La Jornada*, August 31, 2010, https://www.jornada.com.mx/2010/08/31/mundo/026e1mun; and Abel Sierra Madero,

"Del Hombre nuevo al travestismo de Estado," *Diario de Cuba*, January 25, 2014, https://diariodecuba.com/cuba/1390513833_6826.html.

56. Jennifer L. Lambe, "Whither the Empire?," in Bustamante and Lambe, *The Revolution from Within*, 310.

57. "Remarks by President Obama to the People of Cuba," March 22, 2016, https://obamawhitehouse.archives.gov/the-press-office/2016/03/22/remarks-president-obama-people-cuba.

58. Odette Casamayor-Cisneros, "Cuba: Una bandera, tres almendrones y el mar ... Otra vez el mar," *Literal*, September 1, 2015, http://literalmagazine.com/cuba-una-bandera-tres-almendrones-y-el-mar-otra-vez-el-mar.

59. See Luis Manuel Otero Alcántara's performance piece *Where Is Mella?*, drawing attention to the removal of a statue of Julio Antonio Mella, founder of Cuba's first communist party in the 1920s, from a space that became occupied by Cuba's first five-star hotel. "'¿Dónde está Mella?,' pregunta Luis Manuel Otero Alcántara en la Manzana de Gómez," *Diario de Cuba*, April 24, 2017, http://www.diariodecuba.com/cultura/1493050164_30606.html.

60. There are too many examples to cite. On the legacy of Mariel, see Ulises Rodríguez Febles, "Huevos," in *El concierto y otras obras*, 141–99 (Havana: Letras Cubanas, 2007). On the "Marquitos case" from 1964 (see chapter 3), see *Los amagos de Saturno*, directed by Rosario Alfonso Parodi (Havana: independent production, 2014). On forced labor camps in the 1960s, see Carolina de la Torre Molina, *Cuando morir es más sensato que esperar* (Madrid: Verbum, 2018). For a sarcastic treatment of the Cuban 1970s, see *Aché*, directed by Eduardo del Llano (Havana: Sex Machine Productions, 2010). For a bold exploration of the trauma of veterans who fought for Cuba in Angola in the 1970s and 1980s, see *Días de diciembre*, directed by Carla Valdés León (Havana: Estudio ST, 2016). For a critical examination of the legacies and traumas of migration since 1959, see Nelda Castillo, "Departures," El Ciervo Encantado, 2017. All of these works were produced by artists and creators who reside in Cuba.

61. Michael J. Bustamante, "Nadir of the Americas: Havana and the Seventh Summit," *Foreign Affairs*, April 21, 2015, https://www.foreignaffairs.com/articles/cuba/2015-04-21/nadir-americas.

62. Angélica Paredes López, "Nemesia y su revolución viven," *Radio Rebelde*, April 19, 2016, http://www.radiorebelde.cu/noticia/nemesia-su-revolucion-viven-cuba-20160419.

63. There is a long international copyright war over use of the Havana Club brand. Havana Club rum was originally produced by the Arechabala family in Cuba (not the Bacardí family), before the company was nationalized by the revolutionary government in 1960. In the 1990s, the descendants of the Arechabalas sold their claim to the copyright in the United States to Bacardí, while Cuba began producing its version of Havana Club in a joint venture with French beverage giant Pernod Ricard. See Carmen Sesin, "Cuban Rum Wars Reignited over Bacardi's 'Havana Club' Campaign," NBC News, June 3, 2016, https://www.nbcnews.com/news/latino/cuban-rum-wars-reignited-over-bacardi-havana-club-campaign-n585241.

64. In 2009, the Obama administration eliminated any restrictions on the ability of Cubans in the United States to visit the island as frequently or for as long as they wished. (The George W. Bush administration had placed limits on such travel in 2004.) Cuba's

2012 migration reform then eliminated exit permits previously needed for international travel or migration, and it extended the period that Cubans could reside abroad without losing residency at home from one to two years. Given that Cubans who arrive in the United States can petition for legal permanent residency after one year under the Cuban Adjustment Act of 1966, this opened the door to Cubans being able to become permanent residents in the United States while still maintaining residency in Cuba. Increased temporary travel to and from the island in recent years—and not only to the United States—also has substantially bolstered the creation of informal in-kind remittance supply chains. See Julia E. Sweig and Michael J. Bustamante, "Cuba after Communism: The Economic Reforms That Are Transforming the Island," *Foreign Affairs* 92, no. 4 (July 2013): 107–9; and Jennifer Cearns, "'The Mula Ring': Material Networks of Circulation through the Cuban World," *Journal of Latin American and Caribbean Anthropology* 24, no. 4 (December 2019): 864–90.

65. Arturo Arias-Polo, "'Leyendas del exilio,' con testimonios de primera mano," *El Nuevo Herald*, October 20, 2017, https://www.elnuevoherald.com/noticias/sur-de-la-florida/article179937626.html.

66. Rafael Rojas, "Reforma y contrareforma en Cuba," *La Razón*, August 27, 2017, https://www.razon.com.mx/columnas/reforma-y-contrarreforma-en-cuba; Nora Gámez Torres, "Cuba Imposes More Taxes, Controls on Private Sector and Increases Censorship on the Arts," *MH*, July 10, 2018, https://www.miamiherald.com/news/nation-world/world/americas/cuba/article214620125.html.

67. Fidel Castro, "Discurso pronunciado por el Comandante Fidel Castro Ruz, Primer Ministro del Gobierno Revolucionario, en la clausura de la reunión del Comité Ejecutivo de la Unión International de Estudiantes, efectuada en el Capitolio Nacional," June 8, 1961, http://www.cuba.cu/gobierno/discursos/1961/esp/f080661e.html.

68. Mónica Rivero Cabrera, "Fidel Castro, unipersonal," *Revista Late*, August 13, 2018, http://www.revistalate.net/fidel-castro-unipersonal.

69. Andrea Rodríguez and Michael Weissenstein, "Shortages Hit Cuba, Raising Fears of New Economic Crisis," Associated Press, April 18, 2019, https://www.apnews.com/efb7313888ca4b61824f5b293ae9cade; Mimi Whitefield, "Cuba Is Slowly Losing a Lifeline as Venezuela Collapses," *Los Angeles Times*, October 3, 2019, https://www.latimes.com/world-nation/story/2019-10-03/venezuela-meltdown-us-sanctions-batter-cuba; Juan Triana Cordoví, "Coronavirus: Sobreviviremos, pero eso no basta," *OnCuba*, March 23, 2020, https://oncubanews.com/opinion/columnas/contrapesos/coronavirus-sobreviviremos-pero-eso-no-basta; Marc Frank, "Cuba Loosens Straightjacket on Private Sector to Stimulate Economy," Reuters, July 29, 2020, https://www.reuters.com/article/us-cuba-economy/cuba-loosens-straitjacket-on-private-sector-to-stimulate-economy-idUSKCN24U2UF. The recent decision to partially redollarize the economy, after Cuba retired the U.S. dollar from circulation in 2004, has also revived particularly vivid Special Period ghosts. See Marc Frank, "In Cuba, the Old Foe's Currency Makes a Comeback," Reuters, July 20, 2020, https://www.reuters.com/article/us-cuba-economy/in-cuba-the-old-foes-currency-makes-a-comeback-idUSKCN24L2AI.

70. Fernández, "Cuba and lo Cubano."

71. María del Pilar Díaz Castañón, "'We Demand, We Demand . . . ,' Cuba 1959: The Paradoxes of Year 1," in Bustamante and Lambe, *The Revolution from Within*, 97.

72. David Rieff, *In Praise of Forgetting: Historical Memory and Its Ironies* (New Haven, Conn.: Yale University Press, 2016).

73. Jeffrey K. Olick, introduction to *States of Memory: Continuities, Conflicts, and Transformations in National Retrospection* (Durham, N.C.: Duke University Press, 2003), 7.

74. Edmundo Desnoes, *Memorias del subdesarrollo* (Madrid: Mono Azul, 2006 [1965]), 145.

Index

Page numbers appearing in italics refer to figures.

Abdala. *See* Agrupación Abdala
abdalistas. *See* Agrupación Abdala
Abreu, Carlos, 209
Actualidad Criolla, 41–42
actualización, 234
Africa, Cuban involvement in, 160, 193, 195
agrarian reform, 34, 36, 52, 54, 99, 114, 118
Agrupación Abdala: about, 128–29, 130–31, 132–35; *Areíto* and, 140, 141–43, 145–46, 147; Franqui and, 147; nostalgia and, 149, 150, 153; public demonstrations of, 128, 135, 143–44; in 1980s, 224; views of, 134, 137, *138*, 142–43, 149, 266n37; violence and, 145–46, 268n69
Aguirre, Mirta, 56–57
Aguirre, Severo, 45
ahora sí, 30, *31*, 58, 240
Album de la Revolución Cubana, 25–27, *26*, *36*, *42*
Algo que debes hacer (Álvarez), 174
Allende, Salvador, 168, 169
Álvarez, Santiago, 171–72
Álvarez Jané, Enrique, 174
Álvarez López, Elio, 48
Álzaga Manresa, Raúl, 279n60
Amador, Dora, 203–5
"Ample Blood" (Guillén), 105
Angola, 160, 193, 195
anniversaries: of Bay of Pigs invasion, 116; of *Granma's* landing, 172; memory conclusions and, 235; memory fatigue and, 155–56, 160, 169; of Moncada Barracks attack, 33, 161, 169; of Presidential Palace raid, 33
annual thematic titles, 155
Añorada Cuba, 92
anti-Americanism, exile, 85–88, 94

anti-anticommunism, 54, 58, 59–60
anti-Castro movement: exiles and, 63–64; United States and, 60, 61, 66, 72–75. *See also specific events and groups of*
anticommunism: Abdala and, 132, 136–37, 145; as an historical ghost, 53–58; *Areíto* and, 139, 141, 145; Castro and, 28; exile community and, 28, 63, 65, 72–73, 88; United States and, 59, 72–73, 142
anti-imperialism, 60–62, 77, 92, 97, 122, 228, *238*
antinostalgia, 129, 135, 141, 148, 149–50
Antonio Maceo Brigade, 188–93, 194, 278n37
apátridas, term of, 179, 185
Aquique, Dariela, 160
Arboleya, Jesús, 278n37
Areíto: Abdala and, 140, 141–43, 145–46, 147; about, 22, 130–31, 138–41; Antonio Maceo Brigade and, 188–89, 190, 192; nostalgia and, 149, 150, 153; threats to, 145; views of, 141, 148–49; visiting Cuba and, 184–85, *186*
Argupación Montecristi, 76, 80
Arrufat, Antón, 123–24, 147
Artime, Manuel, 76, 86, 256n71
Así cantaba Cuba libre, 92
Authentic Party, 7, 39

Bacardí Rum, 88, 235, *236*, 288n63
Badiou, Alain, 177
Ballester López, Amparo María, 252–53n2
Barquín, Ramón, 74
Batista, Fulgencio: about, 6–8; communism and PSP and, 42–43, 45, 46, 53; exile community unity and, 83–84, 89; *La Calle* and, 39; misdeeds of, 30–32,

291

34; *Piedras y leyes*, 68, 253n11; *Respuesta*, 68; Revolution betrayal narrative and, 67–69; U.S. support of, 72–73
Bay of Pigs, The: The Leaders' Story of Brigade 2506 (Johnson), 87
Bay of Pigs invasion: about, 78, 87; commemoration of, 102–8, *106*, 116–17, 121, 125, 215, 259–60n41; films on, 107–8, 121–22, 164, 174; interrogations of prisoners of, 109–16, *111*, 118, 122; as justification for anti-imperialism, 96–98; recast memories of, 122–27; return of prisoners of, 116; Revolution betrayal narrative and, 72, 73, 74, 75, 77–78; trial of prisoners of, 116, 261n85
Bay of Pigs Veterans Association, 87, 145
Behind the Facade, 178, 276n110
Bejel, Emilio, 192
Benes, Bernardo, 194
Benson, Devyn Spence, 4
betrayal (alleged) of Cuban Revolution, 67–74; Batista and, 67–69; Cuban press and, 69–71; exile community and, 67, 68–69, 73–74, 84–85; FRD/CRC and, 76–78; in *siete contra Tebas*, 124; trouble with narrative of, 71–72; United States and, 72–74, 77–78
Bianchi, Blanca, 146, 268n71
Black River, 174
boatlift of 1980, 212–13, 214, 222–24, 282n121, 284–85nn19–21
Bohemia: agrarian reform and, 36; Batista and, 32, 89; Bay of Pigs invasion and, *106*, *111*, 116; Ciénaga de Zapata and, 99; Cuban independence and, 35; legitimacy disputes and, 44–45; Revolution betrayal (alleged) and, 69–71
Bohemia Libre, 71, 72
bombings, 87, 145, 159–60, 268n69
Border Guard, The, 174
Bosch, José "Pepín," 88
Bosch, Orlando, 145, 267n62, 268n69
Bourgeois Morality and Revolution (Rozitchner), 118
Brezhnev, Leonid, 158

Brigada Antonio Maceo, 188–93, 194, 278n37
Brigade 2506: about, 87; Cuban discourse on, 107, 108; films, plays, and books about, 87, 164; interrogations of prisoners of, 109–16, *111*, 118, 122; return of prisoners of, 116; Revolution betrayal narrative and, 77–78; trial of prisoners of, 116–17, 261n85. *See also* Bay of Pigs Invasion
brigadista, El, 174
Bringuier, Carlos J., 78–80
Brothers to the Rescue, 229, 286n44

Cabañas, José Ramón, 238
Café Nostalgia, 287n47
Caimán Barbudo, El, *173*, 177
Calle, La, 39
Calvert, Julio Rey, 80
Calviño, Ramón, 109
Campaña Nacional de Alfabetización, 62
Camp Columbia, 37
Caravan of Liberty, 30
Carbó, Sergio: anticommunism and, 54, 57; on Batista, 32–33; legitimacy disputes and, 44, 47–48; power jockeying by, 40–41
Carbó, Ulises, 48–49
carbón, 98, 100
carboneros, 98, 100, 101
Carbó Serviá, Juan Pedro, 120
Carpentier, Alejo, 158–59, 270n18
Carrillo, Justo, 76–77
Carter, Jimmy, 149, 193
cartoon cards, 25
Casa de las Américas, 166
Casal, Lourdes, 139–40, 141, 147, 184–85, 192, 266n47
Casal, Regina, 191
Casaus, Víctor, 125, 166
Casavantes Bradford, Anita, 4
Castellanos, Augustín, 88
Castro, Fidel: Abdala and, 138; anticommunism and, 49–52, 53, 54–56, 57; Antonio Maceo Brigade and, 191; back-

ground and overview of, 7; Bay of Pigs invasion and, 105-7, 124-25; Ciénaga de Zapata and, 99, 100-102; coming to power, 28-29, 30, 33, 34, 36, 37-38; counterrevolution and, 217; death of, 236-37; early Revolution disputes and, 27-28; error admittances of, 287n55; exile visits and, 181, 189, 194, 196-97; in film, 171-72; Guevara and, 160; Mariel boatlift and, 222; messianism of, 25, 26, 26, 27; Moncada Barracks and, 8-9, 30; national sovereignty and, 120-21; official holidays and anniversaries and, 103-4, 160; out-migration and, 183; Partido Ortodoxo and, 39-40; prisoner interrogations and, 109, 110-11, 112, 113, 114-15; PSP and, 43, 117, 249n6; on Revolution, 237; Revolutionary Directorate and, 41; Revolution betrayal (alleged) and, 67-69; Rodríguez trial and, 120; socialism and, 62, 96, 102, 104; "Special Period in Times of Peace" and, 226; terms for, 24, 29; transition to socialism of, 167-71; youth and, 166-67
Castro, Mariela, 287n55
Castro, Ramón, 48
Castro, Raúl: coming to power, 33, 34; commemoration and, 161; economy and, 234; exiles and, 179-80; socialism and, 43, 249n67; USSR and, 49
Castro Figueroa, Abel Rosendo, 196-97
Catholic Church, 65, 142-43
Cauce, Vicente, 83
CEC (Cruzada Educativa Cubana), 83-84
censorship, 32, 147, 156, 177, 228, 283n127
Central Intelligence Agency (CIA): Bay of Pigs and, 75, 87; exile support of, 72, 86, 101; in Miami, 66; Patty and, 174
Cerejido, Elizabeth, 206-7
Cerejido Alonso, José Melitón, 206-7
Chanan, Michael, 174
charcoal, 98, 100
Charcoal Festival, 116
Chase, Michelle, 32
Chibás, Eduardo, 7, 39-40
Chibás, Raúl, 39
Chile, 168-69
Chirino, Willy, 229
Christian Democrat Party, 48
CIA (Central Intelligence Agency). See Central Intelligence Agency (CIA)
Ciénaga de Zapata, 97-102, 110, 116, 119, 174
Cienfuegos, Camilo, 34, 160
Cinematic Graphics Review Corporation, 25, 26
citizenship, Cuban, 183, 198
Civic Revolutionary Front, 74
Clandestina, 234
CMQ Radio, 105
CMQ Television, 108
collective memory, term of, 15-16
collectivization, 118
Combate, 41, 47, 60-61, 62, 255n52
comic books, 25-27, 26
Comités de Defensa de la Revolución, 62, 182
commemoration: anniversaries (*See* anniversaries); of Bay of Pigs invasion, 102-8, *106*, 116-17, 121, 125, 215, 259-60n41; communion of people in Cuban Revolution and, 34-36; of Cuban Revolution, 160-65; exile, 215-16; memory fatigue and, 155-57, 160-65; monuments, 36-37, 163-64; museums, 161-63, 165, 215, 216, 283n1. *See also specific commemorations*
Committee of Seventy-Five, 194-95
Committees for the Defense of the Revolution, 62, 182
communication with exiles, 180, 182
communion of people in Cuban Revolution, 28-37; anti-Batista events and, 30-34; commemoration and, 34-36; overview of, 28-30, *31*; reform and, 33-37
communist party of Cuba, early, 7, 42, 43, 45, 242n14, 246-47n23. *See also* Popular Socialist Party (PSP)
Community Action Foundation, 150

"comunidad," term of, 199–201
Conejo, Mary Lynn, 207–8, *208*, 210
Confederación de Trabajadores de Cuba, 61
Conrado Benítez Brigades, 108
Consejo Nacional de Patrimonio Cultural (CNPC), 162
Consejo Revolucionario Cubano (CRC), 76–77, 78–81, 114, 135
Constitution of 1940, 7, 42, 47, 82, 114–15
Constitution of 1976, 167, 183, 198, 228
Coordinación de Organizaciones Revolucionarias Unidas (CORU), 268n69
Corrieri, Sergio, 174, 175, 212
Council of Mutual Economic Assistance, 156, 165
counterrevolution: anticommunism and, 59, 61; Bay of Pigs prisoners and, 112, 118–19, 124; divide between revolution and, 217; exiles as, 77, 113, 116; in film and literature, 172–76; Miami and, 57
CRC (Cuban Revolutionary Council), 76–77, 78–81, 114, 135
Crime of Barbados, 145, 159–60, 268n69
Crisol, El, 99
Cruz, Tomás, 113
Cruzada Educativa Cubana (CEC), 83–84
Cuba, post-1970s: in 1980s, 222–25; in 1990s, 225–31; in 2000s, 232–36
Cuba: Satélite 13, 84–85, 256n58
Cubana Airlines: exile visits and, 202, 212; flight 455 bombing of, 145, 159–60, 268n69
Cuban Adjustment Act of 1966, 289n64
Cuban Air Force, 229
Cuban Americanization, 129, 131, 149–52, 153, 224–25
Cuban American National Foundation, 285n27, 286n42
Cuban Communist Party (PCC): about, 82, 117, 255n52; exile visits and, 196–97, 201; First Congress of, 167, 169, 170; Revolution's ideological evolution and, 171–72; Sixth Congress of, 235; youth branch of, 166

Cuban Democratic Coordinating Junta, 88
Cuban Educational Crusade (CEC), 83–84
cubanidad, 110, 115
Cuban independence, 1, 6, 35, 120, 134, 171–72, 247n30
Cuban Institute for Cinematographic Art and Industry (ICAIC): about, 35, 98; *El brigadista*, 174; *El hombre de Maisinicú*, 172–74; *El primer delegado*, 171; *Guardafronteras*, 174; *55 Hermanos*, 189, 190–91, 192–93; *Historias de la Revolución*, 36; *Leyenda*, 174; *Memorias del subdesarrollo*, 121–22, 174; *Muerte al invasor*, 107–8; *Patty-candela*, 174; *Río negro*, 174; *Tierra olvidada*, 101; *Un día de noviembre*, 176–77
Cuban Institute of Friendship with the Peoples (ICAP), 184, 186
Cuban Interests Section, 198
Cuban Missile Crisis, 83, 86
Cuban Nationalist Movement (MNC), 187, 267n62, 268n69
Cuban National Liberation Front (FLNC), 146, 268n69
Cuban National Union of Artists and Writers (UNEAC), 123, 124, 155, 158, 275n96
Cubanness, 110, 115
Cuba no debe su independencia a los Estados Unidos (Roig), 134
Cuba Nostalgia, 215–16, 230
Cuban Refugee Center, 65, 71, 215
Cuban Revolution: betrayal (alleged) of (*See* betrayal [alleged] of Cuban Revolution); commemoration of, 160–65 (*See also* specific commemorations); communion of people and (*See* communion of people in Cuban Revolution); disputes in early, 27–28; "errors" of, 225, 228; evaluations of, 1, 9–10; films on, 62, 171–74, 176–77; ideological transformation of, 167–71; legitimacy disputes in, 44–49, 53; power jockeying in (*See* power jockeying in Cuban Revo-

lution); story revision of (*See* story of
Revolution revision)
Cuban Revolutionary Council (CRC),
76–77, 78–81, 114, 135
Cuban Revolutionary Junta, 86
Cuban Revolutionary Party (PRC), 171
Cuban Worker's Federation, 61
Cuba's Condensed History Soup
(Cedeño), 2
Cuba Transition Project, 286n42
Cueto, Emilio, 186, 205–6
"Cultivo una rosa blanca" (Martí), 37
Cundo, 64–65, 253n3
customs law, 201–2, 281n89
Custom Tours, 199
Czechoslovakia, 121, 122

Dagger in the Heart (Lazo), 87
Daily Worker, 43
Death to the Invader, 107–8
decentralization, 225
Decree-Law Number 17, 161
defections, 53–54, 69, 187
Defensa Institutional Cubana, 253n13
de la Campa, Román, 139, 153
de la Nuez, Iván, 223–24
de la Pedrosa, Manuel, 84, 85, 259n59
Delgado, Alberto, 172
Democratic Revolutionary Front (FRD), 76–77
Desnoes, Edmundo, 121
detective fiction, 174–75
détente of Washington-Havana, 179, 234. *See also* normalization between Unites States and Cuba
Detrás de la fachada, 178, 276n110
de Varona, Antonio, 114
de Varona, Carlos, 114
Diálogos sobre el destino (Pittaluga), 134
"dialogue, the," 194–95
Diario de la Marina, 47, 57–58, 69
Diario de la Marina (expatriate version), 75
Diario las Américas, 78
Díaz, Jesús, 189, 193, 283n127

Díaz-Canel, Miguel, 237
Díaz Castañón, María del Pilar, 30
Díaz Lanz, Pedro, 53–54, 57, 251n122
Directorio Estudiantil Universitario, 34
Directorio Revolucionario. *See* Revolutionary Directorate
Directorio Revolucionario Estudiantil en el Exilio (DRE), 135
disremembering, 181–84, 198, 212, 216, 222
dollar, U.S., 226, 289n69
Dorticós, Oswaldo, 43, 166
Draper, Theodore, 73
Durán, Alfredo, 87

Echeverría, José Antonio, 33, 41, 135, 161
Eckstein, Susan, 156
"Economic Denial Program," 85
economy, Cuban: of 1960s, 116, 117–19; of 1970s, 129, 146–47, 156, 177–78, 190, 195–96; of 1980s, 225; of 1990s, 225–26, 228–29; of 2000s, 234, 236, 237, 289n69
education reform, 62
Eisenhower, Dwight and administration, 59–60, 61, 72, 75
Ejército Rebelde. *See* Rebel Army
elections, promise of, 71, 114–15
"Elegía de los zapaticos blancos" (Orta), 105
Eleventh World Festival of Youth and Students, 194
embassy incursions, 212
emblematic frameworks, 15, 17, 157, 216, 221
Encanto, El, 103
En Silencio ha tenido que ser, 173, 175, 212
"Enter the Cuba of Yesterday" (Rubio), 93
Espinosa, Manuel, 186–87, 194, 198, 211, 278n29
"Eternity" (Toirac), 227, 227
ethics of recognition, 220–21, 231, 240
Ethiopia, 193
ethnic transition, 149–52
exile community: about, 63–67, 132–33; anti-Americanism of, 85–88, 94; Ba-

tista and, 67-69; betrayal (alleged) of Cuban Revolution and, 67, 68-69, 73-74, 84-85; communication with, 180, 182; Cuban discourse on, 179, 181, 183-84, 211-12; Cuban state memory and, 18-19; ethnic transition and, 149-52; "forced" migration of youth of, 142-43, 189, 267n52; Freedom Flight exiles and, 121; generational memory fractures and, 150, 153; "history" and "memory" and, 14-15; Mariel boatlift and, 223-24; migrants of 1990s and, 230, 287n47; permanent settlement of, 129; post-Castro hopes of, 229-30; Revolution evaluations by, 9-10, 11; Revolution responsibility and, 88-91; terrorist tactics of, 144-46, 158, 219-20, 267n62, 268n69; unity and, 78-81, 82-85, 88-89, 91, 92-95; visiting home by (*See* return visits of exile community)
exit permits, 183, 289n64

Facts about Cuban Exiles, 224
family reunions, 191, 202-10, *208*
"Fauna of the Captured Mercenaries, The," *111*
Ferrer, Pedro Luis, 227
5th Station, 37
55 Hermanos, 189, 190-91, 192-93
film industry of Cuba. *See* Cuban Institute for Cinematographic Art and Industry (ICAIC)
First Congress of the Cuban Communist Party, 167, 169, 170
"First Declaration of Havana," 61
First Delegate, The (Álvarez), 171-72
forced labor camps, 119, 148, 183, 284n20, 287n55. *See also* Military Units to Aid Production (UMAP)
foreign policy of Cuba, 120-21, 160, 168
Forgotten Land, 101
Fraga, Jorge, 166
Frank, Waldo, 101
Franqui, Carlos, 109, 114, 125-27, 147, 264n123

FRD (Democratic Revolutionary Front), 76-77
Freedom Flights, 121, 129, 132, 183, 185
Freedom Tower, 1, 215, 241n1
Frente Cívico de Mujeres Martianas, 48
Frente de Liberación Nacional Cubano (FLNC), 146, 268n69
Frente Revolucionario Democrático (FRD), 76-77
Fresa y chocolate, 228
Freyre, Mario, 110
Fuera del juego (Padilla), 157-58

Gaceta de Cuba, La, 155
Gagarin, Yuri, 102, 104
Garcia Delgado, Eduardo, 105, *106*
García Espinosa, Julio, 98
García-Hernández, Antonio, 142
García Silfredo, Armando, 89, 91
Gastón, Mariana, 139, 188, 191, 193
Gastón, Mauricio, 139, 191
generational memory fractures, 10-11, 130-31, 153
Generation of the Centenary, 10
Gesta inmortal, 85
Giberga, Maritza, 191
gifts of exile visitors, 201-2, 209, 210, 211, 281nn89-90
Girón. *See* Bay of Pigs invasion
Girón (Herrera), 164, 190
Girón: La verdadera historia de la Brigada 2506, 164, 272n48
Girón en la memoria (Casaus), 125
"Golden Age Aged Well, The," 236
Gómez Carbonell, María, 83
González, Elián, 229
González, Pablo Alonso, 4, 162
Good Neighbor Policy, 77
Government of 100 Days, 6-7, 34, 42
Granma yacht landing and memorial, 8, 33, 161, 172
Grau San Martín, Ramón, 7, 73
Guardafronteras, 174
Guas Inclán, Rafael, 78, 82
Guerra, Lillian, 3, 62

guerra tuvo seis nombres, La (León), 123
Guevara, Alfredo, 177, 190, 257–58n4
Guevara, Che: Bay of Pigs invasion and, 96; death of, 120, 160, 271n27; "New Man" and, 119; *Pasajes de la guerra revolucionaria*, 36; PSP and, 43; Rodríguez accusation about, 48
Guillén, Nicolás, 105
"Guillermo Tell," 225
Guiteras, Antonio, 34, 76
gusano, term of, 116, 181, 210
Gutiérrez Alea, Tomás, 121–22, 258n4
Gutiérrez Menoyo, Eloy, 41–42, 86, 256n71

Hall, Stuart, 131
Harnecker, Marta, 196
Hartley, L. P., 3
Havana Club rum, 235, 236, 288n63
Havanatur S.A., 196, 197–98, 199, 200, 210–11, 281n81
Heras León, Eduardo, 123, 125
Hernández, Ernesto, 198
Hernández Tomeu, José, 107
Herrera, Manuel, 164, 190
Historias de la Revolución, 36
"Historia viva" (Rivero), 159
Historical Analysis of the Cuban Revolution, 170
historical stiff neck, 91
Histories of the Revolution, 36
history, term of, 14–16
"History Will Absolve Me" speech, 30, 52
holidays, national, 35, 103–4, 156, 160
hombre de Maisinicú, El (Pérez), 172–74
homosexuals, 119, 287n55
Huberman, Leo, 109, 110
humanitarian exceptions to travel ban, 186, 278n28
Hurricane Flora, 160

ICAIC (Cuban Institute for Cinematographic Art and Industry). *See* Cuban Institute for Cinematographic Art and Industry (ICAIC)
identity of exiles, 131, 137, 141, 153, 199

If I Die Tomorrow (Nogueras), 174, 275n96
Iglesias, Manolo, 80
II Frente del Escambray, 41–42, 46, 48
immigrants. *See* exile community
immigration open door policy of United States, 213, 223
Immortal Feat, 85
independence of Cuba, 1, 6, 35, 120, 134, 171–72, 247n30
individual memory, 16, 17
Información, 48–49
INRA (Instituto Nacional de Reforma Agraria), 76, 99, 100, 101
institutionalization, 18–19, 147, 148, 158, 162–64, 167, 196
Instituto Cubano de Amistad con los Pueblos (ICAP), 184, 186
Instituto Cubano del Arte e Industria Cinematográficos (ICAIC). *See* Cuban Institute for Cinematographic Art and Industry (ICAIC)
Instituto de Estudios Cubanos, 140
Instituto Nacional de Ahorro y Viviendas, 36
Instituto Nacional de la Industria Turística, 100
Instituto Nacional de Reforma Agraria (INRA), 76, 99, 100, 101
Interests Section, 193, 198
internet access, 231
interrogations of Brigade 2506 prisoners, 109–16, *111*, 118, 122
In the Land of Mirrors (Torres), 4
"Introduction to the History of Cuba" (Casaus), 166

Jiménez, Guillermo, 109
Johnson, Haynes, 87
José, Roberto, 177
José Martí Women's Civic Front, 48
Joven Cuba, 34
Joven Cuba, 141
Julito el pescador, 175
Junco, Sandalio, 76
Junta Revolucionaria Cubana, 86

Kammen, Michael, 217
Kennedy, John F., and administration: Batista and, 73; Bay of Pigs invasion and, 78, 81, 85–86, 87, 110, 116; Cuban Missile Crisis and, 86
Kennedy, Robert, 85
"Kennedy-Khrushchev Pact," 86, 137
Kerry, John, 234
Khrushchev, Nikita, 32, 86
Kuchilán, Mario, 109, 111

labor camps. See forced labor camps
La Coubre freighter, 60, 103
Laguna, Albert, 230
Lambe, Jennifer L., 4, 232
land redistribution, 34, 99
Landsberg, Alison, 165
La vida comienza ahora, 36
Lazo, Mario, 87
Legend, 174
Lejanía (Díaz), 283n127
León, José, 193
LES Mambi, 80
Lesnik, Max, 136
Ley Decreto 1463, 277n10
Leyenda, 174
Life Begins Now, 36
limitations to this study, topical, 19–21
literacy, 62, 98, 102, 108, 174
Literary Teacher, The, 174
"Living History" (Rivero), 159
Llerena, Mario, 29
localization of national history, 162–63
Longed-for Cuba, 92
Long Live the Republic!, 164
López, Flavio Luis, 81
López, Iraida H., 4
Lorie, Ricardo, 90
Lucha contra Bandidos, 118
luggage weight, 201–2, 281n89

Maceo, Antonio, 6, 34
Machado, Gerardo, 6–7
Machado Rodríguez, José, 120
Macías, Raúl, 164, 272n48
Maine, USS, 6, 103

Man from Maisinicú, The (Pérez), 172–74
Manzo Cedeño, Alfredo, 2
Marazul, 198
"March of the Combatant People," 222
Marcos Vegueri, Pascual B., 30
Mariel boatlift, 212–13, 214, 222–24, 282n121, 284–85nn19–21
Marielitos, 223–24, 284–85nn19–21
Marín, Gustavo, Sr., 131–32
Marín Duarte, Gustavo, 128, 131–32, 134, 136, 144, 149, 267n52, 268n69
Marinello, Juan, 42–43, 46–47
Márquez-Sterling, Carlos, 89
Martí, José, 6, 37, 171–72
Marxism in Cuba, 163
material exchanges with exile visitors, 201–2, 209, 210, 211, 281nn89–90
Matos, Huber, 55, 56
May Day celebrations, 103–4, 114–15
Medrano, Humberto, 45, 53
"Meeting (at the Door of the Refugee Center), The" (Cundo), 64–65, 253n3
Meet the Press, 53
Mégano, El (García), 98, 99, 101
Memorias, 234
Memorias del subdesarrollo, 121–22, 174, 240
memory, term of, 14–16
memory fatigue, 155–78; background and overview of, 155–57; commemoration and, 160–65; conclusions on, 177–78; ideological transformation of the Revolution and, 167–71; modernization and, 165–66; Revolution story revision, 171–77; time of history and, 157–60
Mendoza, Manuel, 150
mercenaries, Brigade 2506 as, 110, *111*, 112, 118
methodological challenges of this study, 17–19
Miami, Fla., 63, 132
Miami Herald, El, 197, 200
migration, circular, 235, 288–89n64
migration, Cuban. See out-migration of Cuba
Mi hermano Fidel (Álvarez), 172

Mikoyan, Anastas, 57, 101
Milián, Emilio, 145
Milicias Nacionales Revolucionarias, 62
military service, obligatory, 119
Military Units to Aid Production (UMAP), 119, 148, 183, 284n20, 287n55
Miller, Nicole, 3-4
Ministerio de las Fuerzas Armadas Revolucionarias (MINFAR), 161
Ministry of Culture, 162, 163
Ministry of Interior, 174, 175
Miró Cardona, José, 74-82; background and overview of, 74-75; Bay of Pigs invasion and, 78; betrayal narrative and, 75-82; CRC resignation of, 81-82; exile unity and, 78-81, 91; "true" Revolution and, 75-76, 77; United States and, 86
modernization of Cuba, 165-66
Moncada Barracks, 8, 30, 37, 43, 155, 160, 170
Montaner, Carlos Alberto, 199
Montaner, Ernesto, 89
Montecristi Group, 76, 80
monuments, 36-37, 163-64. See also specific monuments
Monument to the *Maine*, 103
Moral burguesa y revolución (Rozitchner), 118
Mora Morales, Cándido, 111-12
Mora Morales, Menelao, 112
Moreno Fraginals, Manuel, 16
Morgan, William, 42
Movimiento de Recuperación Revolucionaria (MRR), 76, 86
Movimiento Nacionalista Cubano (MNC), 187, 267n62, 268n69
Movimiento Revolucionario del Pueblo (MRP), 76
Movimiento 26 de Julio. See 26th of July Movement
Mraz, John, 122
Muerte al invasor, 107-8
Muñiz Varela, Carlos, 190, 192, 198
Museo Casa de Abel Santamaría, 161
Museo Casa Natal de José Antonio Echeverría, 161

Museum of the Revolution, 161, 215, 216
museums, 161-63, 165, 215, 216, 283n1. *See also specific museums*
My Brother Fidel (Álvarez), 172

Nasser, Gamal Abdel, 113
Nation, 109
National Congress of Education and Culture, 156, 158
National Council of Cultural Heritage (CNPC), 162
National Institute of Agrarian Reform (INRA), 76, 99, 100, 101
National Institute of the Tourist Industry, 100
nationalism: of Cuban exiles, 65, 88; Rivero Díaz and, 113-14
nationalization of businesses and properties, 18, 54, 59, 81
National Literacy Campaign, 62
National Revolutionary Militias, 62
National Savings and Housing Institute, 36
national sovereignty, 61, 120-21
neocolonial republic, term of, 163, 272n40
New Leader, 73
"New Man," 119, 148
New School, The (Fraga), 166
New York, exile community in, 132
New Yorker, The, 233
New York Herald Tribune, 73
New York Times, 77
Nguyen, Phuong, 88
Nguyen, Viet Thanh, 181-82, 220-21
Nieves, Luciano, 145
Nogueras, Luis Rogelio, 174, 275n96
Non-aligned Movement, 195
Nora, Pierre, 165
normalization between United States and Cuba, 149, 193, 195, 232-35, 233
nostalgia: Agrupación Abdala and, 128-29, 134-35; *Areíto* and, 138, 148, 153; Batista supporters and, 68; betrayal narrative and, 79, 80-81, 84-85; Brigada Antonio Maceo and, 190-92; Cuban socialism in the 1970s and, 158-59,

171–75; for Cuban socialism in the 1980s, 225, 230; normalization between United States and Cuba and, 232–35; *¿Qué pasa, U.S.A.?* and, 151–52; for the "Special Period," 231; tourism and, 216, 227–28, 230, 232; as a unifier in exile community, 92–95, *93*; "visitas de la comunidad" and, 204–5
nostalgias, plural, 230–31
No tenemos derecho a esperar, 165
Noticias de Hoy: anti-imperialism and, 60; Bay of Pigs invasion and, 105; Ciénaga de Zapata and, 100; on communism, 57; legitimacy disputes and, 46–47, 48
"now, finally," 30, *31*, 58, 240
nueva escuela, La (Fraga), 166
Nueva Generación, 135–36
Núñez Jiménez, Antonio, 99

Obama, Barack, 232, 235
official history of Cuba, 161–65
One Day in November (Solás), 176–77
one's own, remembering, 220–21
open door immigration policy of Unites States, 213, 223
Operación Familia, 101
Operation Candela, 174
Operation Mongoose, 85–86
Operation Pedro Pan, 65, 142–43
Operation Truth, 32–33, 75
oral history, 17–18, 203
Order of Playa Girón, 102
Organizaciones Revolucionarias Integradas (ORI), 82, 117
Orta Ruiz, Jesús, 105
Ortega, Gregorio, 114
Ortega, Humberto, 212
Orthodox Party, 7, 39–40, 136
Ortiz, Fernando, 12–13
Ortiz, Richard L., 94, 218
out-migration of Cuba: disremembering and, 182–84; "forced" youth, 142–43, 189, 267n52; Freedom Flights, 121, 129, 132, 183, 185; Mariel boatlift and, 212–13, 214, 222–24, 282n121, 284–85nn19–21; of 1960s, 63, 83; of 1990s, 226, 229–30, 285–86n32; of 2000s, 235, 288–89n64
Out of the Game (Padilla), 157–58

package tours, 199, *200*, 281n81
Pact of Caracas, 74
Padilla, Heberto, 147, 157–58, 184
Palmer, Eduardo, 84, 85, 259n59
Panart Records, 92
Pardo Llada, José, 56
Partido Auténtico, 7, 39
Partido Comunista de Cuba (PCC). *See* Cuban Communist Party (PCC)
Partido Demócrata Cristiano, 48
Partido Ortodoxo, 7, 39–40, 136
Partido Revolucionario Cubano (PRC), 171
Partido Socialista Popular (PSP). *See* Popular Socialist Party (PSP)
Partido Unido de la Revolución Socialista de Cuba, 82
Pasajes de la guerra revolucionaria (Guevara), 36
passport authorization, 183, 277n10
Patria, 67–68, 88–89, 91
Patty-candela, 174
PCC (Cuban Communist Party). *See* Cuban Communist Party (PCC)
Peña, Lázaro, 49
People's Stores, 100
Pérez, Louis A., Jr., 3, 8–9, 30
Pérez, Manuel, 172–74
Pérez de Cerejido, Helida, 206–7
Pérez García, Manuel, 111
Pérez-Stable, Marifeli, 139, 188
Periquera museum, La, 162
Peruvian embassy incursion, 212, 222
Piedras y leyes (Batista), 68, 253n11
piel y la máscara, La (Díaz), 283n127
Piñera, Virgilio, 30
Piñera Llera, Humberto, 140
Pinochet, Augusto, 169
Pittaluga, Gustavo, 134
"Plan of Covert Action against the Castro Regime," 61, 75

Platt Amendment, 6, 35, 77, 137
Playa Girón. *See* Bay of Pigs invasion; Ciénaga de Zapata
Playa Girón, 126-27
Playa Girón museum, 163
Poesía sobre la tierra (Rivero), 159
polarization resurgence of 2016, 236-37, *238-39*
Ponte, Antonio José, 228-29
Popular Socialist Party (PSP): about, 42, 242n14; anti-Batista insurrection and, 42-47; anticommunism and, 42, 49, 53, 55-58, 59-60; factionalism and, 43-44, 117, 120; legitimacy disputes and, 44-48; ORI and, 82; power jockeying and, 42-44; revised story of, 169-70
Posada Carriles, Luis, 145
power jockeying in Cuban Revolution, 37-44; organizations and, 37-38, 41-44; press and, 38-42
Prague Spring, 121
Prensa Libre: about, 109, 255n52; anticommunism and, 57, 58; on Batista, 32; legitimacy disputes and, 45, 47-48; power jockeying by, 40-41; on the Revolution, 29
Presidential Palace: museum at, 161, 215; raid of, 33, 112, 120, 246-47n23
Presidio Modelo, 161-62
press, Cuban: betrayal (alleged) of Cuban Revolution and, 69-71; jockeying for power by, 38-42; legitimacy disputes in, 44-49; nationalization of, 59. *See also specific magazines and newspapers*
press, exile community, 67-68. *See also specific magazines and newspapers*
primer delegado, El (Álvarez), 171-72
Prío Socarrás, Carlos, 7, 73, 89, 256n71
prisoner releases, 116, 194-95
prisoners of Bay of Pigs invasion: interrogations of, 109-16, *111*, 118, 122; return to United States of, 116; trial of, 116, 261n85
prosthetic memory, 164-65
"pseudo-republic," 1, 59, 84, 119, 217, 251n132

PSP (Popular Socialist Party). *See* Popular Socialist Party (PSP)
public narrative versus private sentiment, 16, 17
Puebla, Carlos, 175
Puerto Rico, 190

¿Qué pasa, U.S.A.?, 150-52, 153, 154
Quevedo, Miguel Ángel, 32, 69-71, 89-90
Quinn, Kate, 3-4
Quiroga, José, 14, 105, 145

Radio Rebelde, 39, 125
Rasco, José Ignacio, 48, 90-91, 94
rationing, 117
Ray, Manuel, 76, 78, 86, 101, 256n71
Reagan, Ronald and administration, 213, 224
Rebel Army: about, 38, 248n45; Batista regime trials and, 32; Partido Ortodoxo and, 40; PSP and, 46, 55
reconverts, revolutionary, 184, 185-88
Rectification of Errors campaign, 225, 228
reentry permits, 198
reform, revolutionary, 33-37; agrarian, 34, 36, 52, 54, 99, 114, 118; education, 62
refugees. *See* exile community
Reina, Luis, 143
Reinoso Hernández, Edith, 185-86
relations, U.S.-Cuban: normalization and, 149, 193-95, 232-35, *233*; polarization resurgence of 2016, 236-37, *238-39*
remembering the other, 231-32
Reminiscences of the Revolutionary War (Guevara), 36
Réplica, 136, 202
Representación Cubana en el Exilio (RECE), 88
Respuesta (Batista), 68
retrospective politics: conclusions on, 217-19, 221, 240; methodological challenges and, 17-19, 21; social contexts and, 15-16; term of, 14, 16
return visits of exile community, 179-214; Antonio Maceo Brigade and, 188-93,

278n37; background and overview of, 179–81; Cuban discourse on, 181, 183–84, 211–12; "select," 184–88. See also *visitas de la comunidad*
revision of Cuban Revolution story, 167–78; in fiction, 174–75; in film, 171–74, 176–77; ideological transformation and, 167–71; in television, 174–75, 275n103
Revista Cinegráfico S.A., 25, 26
Revolución: anticommunism and, 57–58; Bay of Pigs invasion and, 107, 109, 114; legitimacy disputes and, 45–46, 47–48; 1959 rally organized by, 33–34
Revolución y Cultura, 155
"Revolution, the," term of, 24
Revolutionary Directorate: Abdala and, 135; *Combate*, 41, 47, 60–61, 62, 255n52; commemoration of, 33; factionalism and, 117, 120; jockeying for power and legitimacy, 40–41, 44, 47; ORI and, 82; Presidential Palace raid and, 33, 112, 120, 246–47n23; violence and, 146
Revolutionary Integrated Organizations (ORI), 82, 117
Revolutionary Offensive, 119, 234
revolutionary reconverts, 184, 185–88
Revolution in Cuba. *See* Cuban Revolution
Revolution Square, 34, 159, 161, 164, 241n1
rice initiative, 99–100, 119
Río Negro, 174
Rivero, Raúl, 159
Rivero Collado, Carlos, 187–88
Rivero Díaz, Felipe, 113–14, 267n62
RKO of Cuba, 35, 36
Rodgers, Daniel, 153
Rodríguez, Carlos Rafael: legitimacy disputes and, 45, 46, 48; power jockeying and, 42–43; prisoner interrogations and, 109, 111
Rodríguez, Conrado, 48
Rodríguez, José Raúl, 198
Rodríguez, Luis Orlando, 39, 47
Rodríguez, Marcos, 120
Rodríguez, Silvio, 126–27, 167, 227
Rodríguez Bocanegra, Enrique, 192

Rodríguez Montano, Nemesia, 105, 125, 235
Rodríguez Pérez, Fructuoso, 120
Roig de Leuchsenring, Emilio, 134
Rojas, Rafael, 3
Rojas, Ursinio, 53
Romeo, Charles, 196
Rozitchner, León, 118, 122
Rubio, Antonio, *50–51, 70, 93*
Ruiz, Albor, 140–41, 148
Ruiz, Elián, 190
Rustin, Bayard, 133

Sánchez, Celia, 161
"sangre numerosa, La" (Guillén), 105
Santamaría, Abel, 161
Santiesteban, José, 48
Santovenia, Emeterio, 88
Sartre, Jean-Paul, 10, 101
Saturn's Law, 120
Scarface, 224
Schlesinger, Arthur, Jr., 73
schools, revolutionary transition of, 37
Second Front of the Escambray, 41–42, 46, 48
segregation, 113
Selecciones de Reader's Digest, 57
self-determination, 121, 263n104
Sergeants' Revolt, 42, 47
Seven against Thebes (Arrufat), 123–24
747 Travel Agency, 197–98
Seventh Congress of Comintern, 43
shared history of Cuba and Cuban America, 217–18
shortages of goods, 119, 190, 209
Sierra Maestra insurrection, 1, 36, 99, 161, 164
siete contra Tebas, Los (Arrufat), 123–24
Silva, Helga, 202, 203, 213
Sixth Congress of the Cuban Communist Party, 235
socialism, Cuban Revolution transition to, 167–71
Socialist Party of America, 133
social transformation in Cuba, 119–20
Solás, Humberto, 176–77

Something You Should Do (Álvarez), 174
So Sang Free Cuba, 92
Sovietization of Cuba, 147, 158–59, 163, 165–66, 167
Soviet Union: collapse of, 225; Cuban Missile Crisis and, 86; Cuban ties of, 43, 45, 59–60, 84, 129; Cuban trade with, 57, 147, 177, 225; friction between Cuba and, 138; self-determination and, 121, 263n104; space flight of, 102
space flight, Soviet, 102
Spain, 6
"Special Period in Times of Peace": in Cuba, 225–29, 231, 237, 289n69; exile community response to, 229–30
Standard Oil in Cuba, 81
Stern, Steve J., 15
story of Revolution revision, 167–71
Strawberry and Chocolate, 228
Struggle against Bandits, 118
Student Revolutionary Directorate in Exile (DRE), 135
Suárez, Mabel, 208–9
subjunctive possibility, 30, 240
sugar: Ciénaga de Zapata and, 98; exports of, 8, 119, 195; harvesting of, 110–11, 129, 146, 166; U.S. interest in, 6
sugar curtain, 11

Tamayo Méndez, Arnaldo, 166
"#TenemosMemoria," 237
terminology, 14–16, 24. *See also specific terms*
terrorism, 130, 144–46, 158, 219–20, 267n62, 268n69. *See also specific acts of*
Testimonio de una emigrada (Reinoso), 185–86
"Third Way," 113
Tierra olvidada, 101
Toirac, José Ángel, 227, 227
Tomeu Hidalgo, Enrique, 107
Torres, María de los Ángeles, 4
"tortícolis histórica," 91
tourism, Cuban: initiative for Ciénaga de Zapata, 99, 100, 101; nostalgia and, 216, 227–28, 230, 232; post-Soviet collapse and, 226–27; *visitas de la comunidad* and, 196, 197–202, 200, 210–11
travel agencies, 196, 197–98, 199, 200, 210–11, 281n81
travel restrictions to/from Cuba, 180, 183, 186, 189, 193, 194, 213, 277n10
Trejo, Rafael, 34
trials: of Batista regime, 32–33, 75; of Bay of Pigs invasion prisoners, 116–17, 261n85; of Marcos Rodríguez, 120
triumphalism, 157, 216, 224
"true Revolution," 48–49, 73, 74, 75–76, 81
True Story of the Brigade of 2506, The, 164, 272n48
tweets of Cuban government, 238–39
Twenty-First Congress of the Communist Party of Soviet Union, 45
26th of July Movement: about, 8, 15, 37–38; action and sabotage operations of, 146; Civic Revolutionary Front and, 74; factionalism and, 117; *Granma* yacht landing and, 33; legitimacy disputes and, 44, 45–46; ORI and, 82; Partido Ortodoxo and, 39; PSP and, 43–44, 49–50, 59–60; Revolutionary Direcorate and, 33; socialism and, 169–70

Un día de noviembre (Solás), 176–77
unfinished histories of Cuba, 7–11, 219
Unidades Militares de Ayuda a la Producción (UMAP), 119, 148, 183, 284n20, 287n55
Unión Nacional de Escritores y Artistas de Cuba (UNEAC), 123, 124, 155, 158, 275n96
United Nations demonstration of Agrupación Abdala, 128, 135
United Party of the Cuban Socialist Revolution, 82
United States: Abdala and, 137–38; aggression against Cuba of, 103 (*See also* Bay of Pigs invasion); anticommunism and, 53–54, 56, 57, 59–60; anti-imperialism and, 61; Batista support of, 8; betrayal (alleged) of Cuban Revolution and, 72–74, 77–78; Cuban independence

and, 6, 35; exile anti-Americanism and, 85–88, 94; Cuban immigration open door policy of, 213, 223; relations with Cuba (*See* relations, U.S.-Cuban); sanctions on Cuba by, 117, 119, 228, 237, 281n90; travel restrictions to Cuba of, 180, 186, 189
University of Florida, 140
University Student Directorate, 34
urban underground, 8, 38, 42, 146, 248n45
Urrutia Lleó, Manuel, 33, 54
U.S. Department of Health, Education, and Welfare, 150
U.S. Interests Section, 193, 198

Valdés, Luis Miguel, 203–5, 210, 212
Valdés, Nelson P., 30
Valdespino, Andrés, 44–45, 140
Valdés Vivó, Raul, 109
Varela, Carlos, 225
Vázquez Candela, Euclides, 46, 57
Vega, Pastor, 164
Venceremos Brigades, 140, 184
Viajes Varadero, 197–98, 279n60
Villalón, José, 148
Villanueva University, 107, 131
violence: Abdala's position on, 145–46; of Batista regime, 20, 68, 237; Batista regime trials and, 32; of exile community, 144–46, 158, 219–20, 267n62, 268n69; exile memories of, 63; relationship to Cuban retrospective politics, 20, 219

visitas de la comunidad: background and overview of, 193–97, 279n60; conclusions on, 210–14; logistic, financial, and moral conflicts of, 197–202; restrictions on, 283n125; reunions of, 202–10, *208*; of 1990s, 230, 286n45; term of, 214
¡Viva la República!, 164

Waiting for the Right Time, 227
War Had Six Names, The (León), 123
We Don't Have the Right to Wait, 165
Westbrook Rosales, Joe, 120
"Words of Fidel, The" column, 28, 69

Young Cuba, 34
Young People's Socialist League (YPSL), 133
youth, exile: "forced" migration of, 142–43, 189, 267n52; generation memory fractures and, 150, 153. *See also* Agrupación Abdala; *Areíto*
youth of Cuba, 165, 166–67
Y si muero mañana (Nogueras), 174, 275n96

Zapata Swamp, 97–102, 110, 116, 119, 174
Zig-zag: ahora sí and, *31*; cartoon cards and, 25; Revolution betrayal (alleged) and, 64, 72, 252–53n2; "Waiting Room at a Ministry," 49, *50–51*
Zig-zag Libre: "Enter the Cuba of Yesterday," 93; Revolution betrayal (alleged) and, 64–65, 69, *70*, 71–72, 253n3

ENVISIONING CUBA

Michael J. Bustamante, *Cuban Memory Wars: Retrospective Politics in Revolution and Exile* (2021).

Daniel A. Rodríguez, *The Right to Live in Health: Medical Politics in Postindependence Havana* (2020).

Tiffany A. Sippial, *Celia Sánchez Manduley: The Life and Legacy of a Cuban Revolutionary* (2020).

Ariel Mae Lambe, *No Barrier Can Contain It: Cuban Antifascism and the Spanish Civil War* (2019).

Henry B. Lovejoy, *Prieto: Yorùbá Kingship in Colonial Cuba during the Age of Revolutions* (2018).

A. Javier Treviño, *C. Wright Mills and the Cuban Revolution: An Exercise in the Art of Sociological Imagination* (2017).

Antonia Dalia Muller, *Cuban Émigrés and Independence in the Nineteenth-Century Gulf World* (2017).

Jennifer L. Lambe, *Madhouse: Psychiatry and Politics in Cuban History* (2017).

Devyn Spence Benson, *Antiracism in Cuba: The Unfinished Revolution* (2016).

Michelle Chase, *Revolution within the Revolution: Women and Gender Politics in Cuba, 1952-1962* (2015).

Aisha K. Finch, *Rethinking Slave Rebellion in Cuba: La Escalera and the Insurgencies of 1841-1844* (2015).

Christina D. Abreu, *Rhythms of Race: Cuban Musicians and the Making of Latino New York City and Miami, 1940-1960* (2015).

Anita Casavantes Bradford, *The Revolution Is for the Children: The Politics of Childhood in Havana and Miami, 1959-1962* (2014).

Tiffany A. Sippial, *Prostitution, Modernity, and the Making of the Cuban Republic, 1840-1920* (2013).

Kathleen López, *Chinese Cubans: A Transnational History* (2013).

Lillian Guerra, *Visions of Power in Cuba: Revolution, Redemption, and Resistance, 1959-1971* (2012).

Carrie Hamilton, *Sexual Revolutions in Cuba: Passion, Politics, and Memory* (2012).

Sherry Johnson, *Climate and Catastrophe in Cuba and the Atlantic World during the Age of Revolution* (2011).

Melina Pappademos, *Black Political Activism and the Cuban Republic* (2011).

Frank Andre Guridy, *Forging Diaspora: Afro-Cubans and African Americans in a World of Empire and Jim Crow* (2010).

Ann Marie Stock, *On Location in Cuba: Street Filmmaking during Times of Transition* (2009).

Alejandro de la Fuente, *Havana and the Atlantic in the Sixteenth Century* (2008).

Reinaldo Funes Monzote, *From Rainforest to Cane Field in Cuba: An Environmental History since 1492* (2008).

Matt D. Childs, *The 1812 Aponte Rebellion in Cuba and the Struggle against Atlantic Slavery* (2006).

Eduardo González, *Cuba and the Tempest: Literature and Cinema in the Time of Diaspora* (2006).

John Lawrence Tone, *War and Genocide in Cuba, 1895-1898* (2006).

Samuel Farber, *The Origins of the Cuban Revolution Reconsidered* (2006).

Lillian Guerra, *The Myth of José Martí: Conflicting Nationalisms in Early Twentieth-Century Cuba* (2005).

Rodrigo Lazo, *Writing to Cuba: Filibustering and Cuban Exiles in the United States* (2005).

Alejandra Bronfman, *Measures of Equality: Social Science, Citizenship, and Race in Cuba, 1902-1940* (2004).

Edna M. Rodríguez-Mangual, *Lydia Cabrera and the Construction of an Afro-Cuban Cultural Identity* (2004).

Gabino La Rosa Corzo, *Runaway Slave Settlements in Cuba: Resistance and Repression* (2003).

Piero Gleijeses, *Conflicting Missions: Havana, Washington, and Africa, 1959-1976* (2002).

Robert Whitney, *State and Revolution in Cuba: Mass Mobilization and Political Change, 1920-1940* (2001).

Alejandro de la Fuente, *A Nation for All: Race, Inequality, and Politics in Twentieth-Century Cuba* (2001).

www.ingramcontent.com/pod-product-compliance
Lightning Source LLC
Chambersburg PA
CBHW021649230426
43668CB00008B/571